PRO TOOLS 101:

Pro Tools Fundamentals I

For Pro Tools 12.8 Software

Frank D. Cook

Avid Learning Partner Program

PRO TOOLS **12**

Copyright

Trademarks

Acknowledgements

Avid Worldwide Training would like to thank all Avid Certified Instructors for their ongoing suggestions and comments, based on their experience in the classroom and their professional expertise, which have resulted in the continued improvement of Avid courseware.

PT101, Version 12.8

PN: 9320-65297-01 Rev B

ISBN-13: 978-1-943446-47-6

pd 9.28.17 *PT101v12_8-Book_revB.doc*

Acknowledgments

The author would like to extend special thanks to the following individuals who have provided support, feedback, technical information, and editorial input for this version of the book.

Avid Staff. Andy Cook, Bryan Castle, Andy Hagerman, Tim Mynett, Michael Flores, and Connor Sexton

Others. Eric Kuehnl and Mark Garvey

About the Author

This book and associated coursework has been developed by **Frank D. Cook**, as the first in a series of courses designed to prepare students for Pro Tools Certification under the Avid Learning Partner program.

Frank is a bass guitarist, educator, and longtime Pro Tools user. The owner of Insource Writing Solutions and President of NextPoint Training, Inc., Frank has worked in the technical publications and education industries for more than 20 years. As a writer, editor, technical publications manager, and business owner, Frank has authored, edited, and contributed to hundreds of guides, manuals, reports, textbooks, and other publications for clients in a wide variety of industries.

Frank has been a consultant for Digidesign/Avid for over twelve years. During this time he has helped define Avid's training strategy and has developed extensive curriculum for Avid's official training and certification programs. Frank also teaches Pro Tools courses as an adjunct professor at Sacramento City College and American River College in Sacramento, California, and is an Avid Master Instructor.

Other course books by Frank D. Cook include

- *Audio Production Basics with Pro Tools | First*, with co-author Eric Kuehnl
- *Pro Tools 110: Pro Tools Fundamentals II*
- *Pro Tools 201: Pro Tools Production I*
- *Pro Tools 210M: Pro Tools Production II (Music Production)*
- *Pro Tools 310M: Advanced Music Production Techniques*

About NextPoint Training

NextPoint Training, Inc. provides advanced training, software tools, and learning resources for educators and students studying Pro Tools and other media applications. Our products include audio textbooks (such as *Audio Production Basics with Pro Tools | First*) and the Elements|ED online learning platform (ElementsED.com). On the Elements|ED platform, students and instructors can find material to supplement this and other textbooks.

Contents

Introduction

Congratulations on beginning work under the Avid Learning Partner program. Avid's award-winning Pro Tools technology is embraced by recording artists and audio production professionals around the world. This is your opportunity to join their ranks, unleashing the power and productivity of your own Pro Tools system.

This book represents the first step on a journey toward mastering Pro Tools software. The information, exercises, and projects you will find here are written for Pro Tools systems running version 12.8 software. However, the vast majority of the book applies equally to early software versions, including Pro Tools 12.x, 11.x, and 10.x. Whether you are interested only in self-study or you would like to pursue formal certification through an Avid Learning Partner, this book will develop your core skills and introduce you to the awesome power of Pro Tools software and hardware.

About This Book

This book provides a course outline for the audio enthusiast with relatively little Pro Tools experience. While this course can be completed through self-study, Avid recommends obtaining hands-on experience through an instructor-led class offered by an Avid-authorized learning partner. For more information on the classes offered through the Avid Learning Partner program, go to www.avid.com/education.

Pro Tools 12.8 Edition

This edition of the Pro Tools 101 course has been updated and improved to address recent software changes up through the Pro Tools 12.8 release. The material is focused on the principles that you need to understand to complete a Pro Tools project, from initial setup to final mixdown. Whether your project involves recording audio, preparing MIDI sequences for virtual instruments, editing and mixing audio files, or editing notation and creating scores, Pro Tools 101 will teach you the steps required to succeed.

The Download Media

This book makes use of media files for the included exercises and supplemental projects. The media files can be downloaded by pointing your browser to alpp.us/PT101-128 and downloading the PT101 Download Media (v12.8) folder. Note that the above web address is *case sensitive*, so be sure to enter it exactly as written.

Files for Exercises

The first two folders included in the Download Media folder provide files required to complete the exercises included in this book. The Completed Exercises folder provides session files of each completed exercise for reference.

Files for Supplemental Projects

The Hands-On Projects folder included in the Download Media folder provides content for the two projects included in Section II of this book. The Project 1–Music Session folder includes a session template file and associated media for Project 1, and the Project 2–Post Session folder includes a session template file and associated media for Project 2.

Course Prerequisites

Most Pro Tools enthusiasts today have at least a passing familiarity with operating a computer. If you consider yourself a computer novice, however, you should review some basics before beginning this course. You will need to know how to complete such tasks as:

- Starting up the computer
- Using the mouse to navigate and select
- Using standard menus
- Using common keyboard commands for standard operating system operations
- Locating, moving, and renaming files and folders
- Using standard cut, copy, and paste commands
- Opening, saving, and closing files

This course focuses on using Pro Tools in a digital audio recording and production environment. The work requires a basic understanding of recording techniques, processes, and equipment, such as the following:

- Miking techniques
- Mixer signal flow
- Audio monitoring equipment
- MIDI devices

If you are a beginner in the field of audio production, you can supplement this text with independently available literature or courses on audio recording tools and techniques. We recommend *Audio Production Basics with Pro Tools|First* by Frank D. Cook and Eric Kuehnl as a prerequisite for learners who have knowledge gaps in any of the above areas.

Course Organization and Sequence

This course has been designed to familiarize you with the practices and processes you will use to complete a recording, editing, and mixing project.

Section I

The first section of the book includes ten primary lessons (chapters) and ten associated short exercises. The first three lessons provide background information on Pro Tools, its history and background, and the current user interface. The subsequent lessons present specific processes and techniques that you will use to complete a project, from creating a new session, to recording and editing, and on through to mixing and completing a final bounce.

Each of the lessons in Section I is followed by a brief exercise that gives you practice applying what you have learned.

Section II

This Section II of this book includes instructions for completing the two supplemental projects included in the Download Media folder. These projects in this section can be completed at any point as you progress through the primary lessons in Section I.

Appendices

This edition of the book includes three appendices. Appendix A provides information on locating an Avid Learning Partner to enroll in the official certification program and take the course completion exam. Appendix B provides information on Avid plug-ins that are included with Pro Tools. Appendix C provides details on the AIR effects and instrument plug-ins that are included with Pro Tools.

Conventions and Symbols Used in This Book

Following are some of the conventions and symbols used in this book, and throughout the Pro Tools books in the Avid Learning Series.

- Menu choices and keyboard commands are typically capitalized.
- Hierarchy is shown using the greater than symbol (>).
- Keystroke combinations are indicated using the plus sign (+).
- Mouse-click operations are indicated by hyphenated strings, where needed.
- Brackets ([ ]) are used to indicate key presses on the numeric keypad.

Table A Examples of standard conventions used in the Avid Learning Series

Convention	Action
File > Save Session	Choose Save Session from the File menu.
Ctrl+N	Hold down the Ctrl key and press the N key.
Command-click (Mac)	Hold down the Command key and click the mouse button.
Right-click	Click with the right mouse button.
Press [1]	Press 1 on the numeric keypad.

The Avid Learning Partner Program

Pro Tools 101 has been written as a textbook for teaching and learning Pro Tools software. In addition to being an off-the-shelf guide for consumers, this book is also a required text for all levels of Avid Pro Tools professional certification. By completing the coursework in this text, you are taking an important step toward certification. And consider this: Having a certification from Avid just might help you land that next gig, find others with similar skills and interests, or even obtain your dream job in the industry.

To become certified in Pro Tools, you must enroll in a program at an Avid Learning Partner location, where you can complete additional Pro Tools coursework and take one of Avid's Certification Exams. Detailed information on current requirements is available at avid.com/education.

Curriculum and Certification Levels

Avid offers three levels of professional Pro Tools certification: Avid Certified User, Avid Certified Operator, and Avid Certified Expert. The 100-, 200-, and 300-level Pro Tools courses are designed to prepare candidates for each of these certification levels, respectively.

User Certification

The User certification program prepares individuals to operate a Pro Tools system in an independent production environment. Courses required for User certification include *Pro Tools 101: Pro Tools Fundamentals I* and either *Pro Tools 110: Pro Tools Fundamentals II* or *Pro Tools 130, Pro Tools for Game Audio*. User certification requires successful completion of two 100-level courses and their associated exams.

Figure A Training options for Avid Certified User: Pro Tools (100-level courses)

Operator Certification

The Operator certification program prepares engineers and editors to competently operate a Pro Tools system in a professional production environment. Candidates can specialize in either Music Production or Post-Production (or both).

User certification is a prerequisite for the Operator certification program. Courses required for Operator certification include *Pro Tools 201: Pro Tools Production I* and either *Pro Tools 210M: Pro Tools Production II (Music Production)* or *Pro Tools 210P: Pro Tools Production II (Post Production)*. Operator certification requires successful completion of two 100-level courses and two 200-level courses and all associated exams.

Figure B Training options for Avid Certified Operator: Pro Tools (200-level courses)

Expert Certification

The Expert curriculum offers professionals the highest level of proficiency with individual or networked Pro Tools systems operating in a professional, fast-paced environment. Candidates can specialize in Music Production, Post-Production, and/or Advanced Mixing.

User and Operator certification are prerequisites for the Expert certification program. Courses options associated with Expert certification include *Pro Tools 310M, Advanced Music Production Techniques, Pro Tools 310P, Advanced Post Production Techniques*, and *Pro Tools 310|S6, Advanced Pro Tools|S6 Mixing Workflows*. Expert certification requires successful completion of two 100-level courses, two 200-level courses, one 300-level course, and all associated exams. An additional hands-on practical exam is required at the 300-level.

Figure C Training options for Avid Certified Expert: Pro Tools (300-level courses)

Courses Offered in the Pro Tools Training Program

Avid Learning Partners offer three levels of coursework to help you become proficient using Pro Tools: 100-level, 200-level, and 300-level.

- 100-level Pro Tools courses provide the foundational skills needed to learn and function within the Pro Tools environment at a proficient level. The goal of the courses at this level is to help individuals start working effectively on their own projects in Pro Tools.
- 200-level courses build the production skills needed to competently and efficiently operate a Pro Tools | HD system in a professional environment. Pro Tools coursework at this level involves a study of general audio production essentials and specific music production and/or audio for video post-production techniques.
- 300-level courses focus on advanced operation of Pro Tools systems for music production, post-production, or hands-on mixing workflows. Coursework involves working in real-world scenarios through example exercises from advanced music production projects (Music Production track), TV and film production projects (Post-Production track), or direct hands-on control surface techniques (Advanced Mixing track).

Avid Course Configuration

Avid uses a version–specific approach to course design, enabling authorized training partners to teach classes based on products and software versions that meet their particular needs and training environments.

Audio Curriculum

Avid's audio coursework includes programs supporting certification in dedicated focus areas, including Pro Tools, Sibelius, and Live Sound. The primary Pro Tools certification paths are described above. Course components are designed to be completed individually and in sequence. However, individual training partners may offer the same content through slightly different class configurations.

Detailed descriptions of each of the courses offered through the Avid Learning Partner program are available on the Avid website. (Go to www.avid.com/education.)

Avid Certified User: Pro Tools

Pro Tools 101 is the first course of study in the training curriculum targeting User Certification. The User Certification training materials (100-level coursework) prepare students to operate a Pro Tools system in an independent production environment. Following completion of the User Certification coursework and certification exam, students can proceed to the 200-level courses to pursue Operator Certification.

Avid Certified. Real Skills, Proven.

Avid certification helps professionals attain and demonstrate the skills and credentials they need to increase their value, competency, and efficiency in the highly competitive media industry.

Avid certification programs cover the broad range of Avid products, as well as other professional roles, including Avid Certified Instructor, Avid Certified Support Representative, and Avid Certified Administrator.

How Can I Learn More?

Various additional resources are available to help you explore the topics covered in this book, review key points in each chapter, and test your knowledge of the material. Some suggested options include:

- **Pro Tools 12 Essential Training: 101**—This video series on Lynda.com covers the concepts of this course through screen-capture videos and challenge activities. The material is presented using the same organization and order as in this book. (Available at https://www.lynda.com/Pro-Tools-tutorials/Pro-Tools-12-Essential-Training-101/533108-2.html.)
- **PT101 Study Guide module**—This online module allows learners to review key concepts and information from this course and to assess their learning using practice quizzes. This module is particularly useful to help students prepare for the Avid course completion exam. (Available through the Elements|ED online learning platform at ElementsED.com.)

Information on locating an Avid Learning Partner school is provided in Appendix A of this book.

If you want to learn more about Avid training, you can check out Avid's official online resource by going to www.avid.com/education. There you will find information about Avid Learning Partners, details on the various certification options available, and course descriptions for each course offered through Avid's programs.

SECTION I

Concepts and Exercises

OVERVIEW

This part of the book provides the ten primary lessons (chapters), which familiarize you with the history of Pro Tools, digital audio concepts, the Pro Tools user interface, and operations for recording, importing, and working with audio, MIDI, and video files. Each lesson is followed by an exercise that you can use to practice what you have learned.

Lessons 1, 2, and 3 introduce Pro Tools software and the basic user interface. This part of the book covers Pro Tools' capabilities in audio, MIDI, mixing, and video post-production and reviews the evolution of Pro Tools technology. These lessons also introduce parameters used in analog-to-digital conversion and their effect on audio quality.

Lessons 4 through 7 focus on processes for creating and configuring sessions, creating audio and MIDI recordings, importing media files, using virtual instrument plug-ins, and keeping session files organized.

Lessons 8, 9, and 10 discuss selection, navigation, editing, and mixing techniques for working with audio and MIDI recordings, as well as various edit commands, moving and trimming operations, and automation techniques. This section ends with a discussion of mixdown and bouncing operations.

LESSON 1

Background Information

This lesson introduces you to Pro Tools' capabilities and uses for audio production, MIDI workflows, mixing, and video post-production. You will learn about the evolution of Pro Tools technology and get an introduction to the characteristics of analog and digital audio. You will also get an overview of the latest developments in Pro Tools 12 software and learn about the different Pro Tools configurations available today.

Duration: 75 Minutes

GOALS

- Identify common industry uses for Pro Tools software
- Recognize the contributions of historical developments in sampling and sound editing, MIDI technology, computer I/O, and recording technology to today's digital audio workstation
- Understand the relationship between sample rate and frequency response in digital audio
- Understand the relationship between bit depth and dynamic range in digital audio
- Recognize components and features of various Pro Tools systems

Key topics from this lesson are included in the *Pro Tools 12 Essential Training: 101* course on Lynda.com.

The Pro Tools Digital Audio Workstation

Pro Tools is one of the most widely used applications for music and post-production (sound for film, video, and multimedia) in the world today, integrating capabilities in audio and MIDI recording, composition, editing, and mixing, as well as support for desktop video. As such, Pro Tools software empowers both music and post-production professionals to easily achieve all of their production tasks within one easy-to-use interface.

At its core, Pro Tools is a multi-track software-based digital recording and editing system. It was the first system ever manufactured that combined the power of the personal computer with hard-disk audio recording and playback, creating the category known today as the digital audio workstation, or DAW.

Today's Pro Tools systems provide audio recording, graphical audio editing, MIDI sequencing, digital signal processing, and mixing through a single, integrated system. With the ability to incorporate QuickTime and Avid video files, Pro Tools has also established itself as an industry choice for video post-production workflows and mixing to picture.

Audio Processing

Pro Tools works with audio that is stored electronically in digital format. The software records audio performances and stores them as files on a hard drive or server. Like a digital camera that stores a photograph as a collection of discrete pixels, Pro Tools stores recorded audio as a collection of discrete *samples*. Pro Tools supports audio formats with resolutions up to 32-bit floating point and sample rates up to 192 kHz.

Just as you can use an image editor to modify, enhance, and otherwise alter your digital photographs in creative ways, you use Pro Tools to edit your digital audio. Working in the digital realm makes it easy to copy, paste, move, delete, modify, and otherwise manipulate parts of your recordings. Pro Tools lets you trim waveforms, reprocess sections of audio, correct a compromised performance, replace drum sounds, rearrange song sections, and much, much more.

MIDI Production

Pro Tools' built-in sequencing technology enables you to record and edit MIDI data along with your audio recordings. MIDI recordings differ from their digital audio counterparts in that they capture performance event data rather than sound samples. You can record MIDI signals from a keyboard (or other device) through a MIDI interface or USB port and then edit the data using Pro Tools' track displays or MIDI Editor windows.

Pro Tools' MIDI features include MIDI and Instrument tracks, MIDI Time Stamping, grid and groove quantize functions, velocity editing, tick-based and sample-based timelines, and more. Pro Tools also comes bundled with several great-sounding virtual instrument plug-ins from AIR Music Technology.

Notation and Scores

Pro Tools supports standard music notation display for MIDI notes. MIDI Editor windows provide a Notation view, in which each MIDI and Instrument track is represented on a separate staff. Additionally, Pro Tools includes a dedicated Score Editor window, allowing you to view, edit, arrange, and print MIDI data in notation form as sheet music.

The notation options in Pro Tools provide productivity and workflow enhancements for composers, songwriters, and others. The Notation view (in MIDI Editor windows) and the page layout in the Score Editor window provide additional ways to display and work with MIDI compositions, utilizing Sibelius-quality music notation and printing capabilities.

Mixing and Automation

Beyond recording, editing, and arranging, Pro Tools offers a software-based mixing environment that provides control over signal routing, effects processing, signal levels, panning, and more. The mixing operations in Pro Tools can be automated and stored with your session, enabling you to recall, edit, and refine your mixes over time. When you save a session, all routing, automation, mixing, and effects settings remain exactly as you've left them.

Additionally, Pro Tools software can be combined with hardware from Avid and third-party manufacturers in various configurations to provide multiple channels of simultaneous input and output for your Pro Tools sessions. Massive sessions including up to 768 simultaneous Audio tracks can be managed without audio degradation. Pro Tools systems can range from very simple to extremely advanced and powerful.

Audio for Video Post-Production

Pro Tools also provides a powerful audio platform for video post-production tasks. You can import QuickTime movies or Avid video files and use the Pro Tools Video window for quick visual reference or full-screen display as you "sweeten" the audio with sound effects, music, Foley, and dialog.

With support for a wide range of Avid standard- and high-definition MXF video formats, you can perform all your post-production audio tasks quickly and easily. When completed, your finished movie file can be exported with the final audio mix embedded.

Pro Tools History and Evolution

The art of manipulating digital audio has evolved with, and been dramatically influenced by, the evolution of Pro Tools. Introduced in 1991 by Digidesign, Pro Tools helped pioneer the concept of multi-track digital audio recording and is recognized for having revolutionized the audio recording industry. This technology traces its roots to humble beginnings and the experimental work of Digidesign's founders, Peter Gotcher and Evan Brooks.

Roots in Digidrums

In the early 1980s, college band-mates Peter Gotcher and Evan Brooks devised a process for recording drum and percussion sounds onto computer EPROM chips. The two began offering their chip sets for retail sale, including titles for Rock Drums, Electronic Drums, Latin Percussion, Sound Effects, and more.

This led them to launch a company called Digidrums in 1984, which grew to sell drum chips by the tens of thousands. Digidrums went on to develop additional audio-related software and hardware products.

Figure 1.1 Early drum-sound chip sets

Among their software projects was a product named Sound Designer, which allowed users to edit sounds captured by a sampling keyboard. Sound Designer was the first commercial product to combine waveform editing with a graphical display.

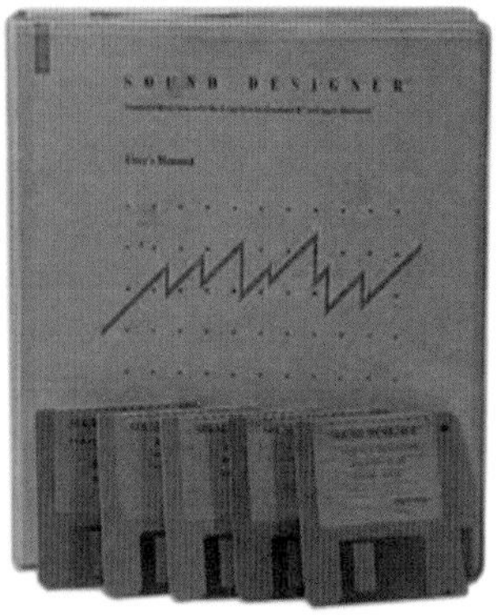

Figure 1.2 The original Sound Designer package

Digidrums Becomes Digidesign

In 1985, the company changed its name to Digidesign. Over the next few years, Digidesign began developing products for working with MIDI and synthesis on Macintosh computers.

By 1988, Digidesign began selling computer cards for playing back digital audio. The product, known as Sound Accelerator, was a CD-quality two-channel output card for the Mac II. This proved to be the first step toward enabling computer systems to provide professional-quality audio output.

Digidesign continued to develop software products for sampling and synthesis. At the same time, the company began work on products designed for digital recording.

Origins of Pro Tools

In 1989, Digidesign released Sound Tools, a two-track hard-disk recorder. Billed as the world's first "tapeless recording studio," Sound Tools consisted of Sound Designer II software, a Sound Accelerator card, and a hardware box called the AD-In that provided two analog-to-digital converters.

Figure 1.3 Components of the Sound Tools system

The first-generation Pro Tools system was released in 1991, supporting just four tracks of audio. Eventually, using additional cards and interfaces, these Pro Tools systems expanded to support up to 16 tracks of simultaneous recording and playback.

Figure 1.4 Early Pro Tools system

In 1992, Session 8 was released as the first Windows-based version of Pro Tools. Two years later, Digidesign introduced Pro Tools TDM, opening the door for real-time effects plug-ins as we now know them.

Pro Tools TDM

The Pro Tools TDM system utilized Time Division Multiplexing (TDM) technology to reliably route multiple streams of digital audio data between system components. TDM technology paved the way for rapid expansion among third-party applications and plug-in developers.

Digidesign Merges with Avid Technology

In 1995, Digidesign merged with its biggest customer, Avid Technology. Two years later, Pro Tools|24 was released, offering 24-bit audio capabilities. These systems offered an increased number of inputs and outputs and higher track counts than ever before.

In 1999, Pro Tools LE was introduced, providing *host-based* audio processing. Host-based processing is also commonly called *native* processing—this is processing done on the computer's CPU, without the need for additional DSP cards.

Control Surfaces Introduced

As Pro Tools systems evolved, so did the need for hands-on, tactile mixing control. Operating as a division of Avid, Digidesign soon began offering a line of dedicated control surfaces for Pro Tools, including ProControl and Control|24. These consoles were the first to provide touch-sensitive control of mixing, automation, and plug-in parameters.

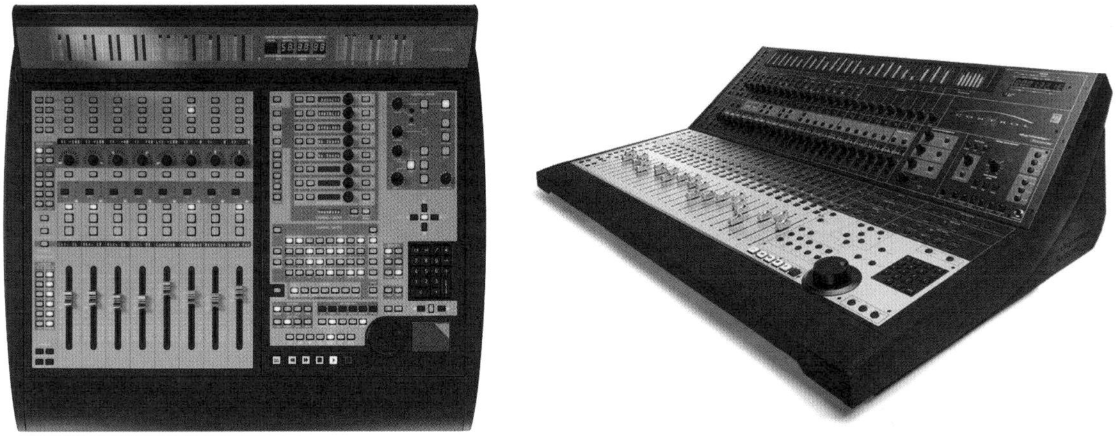

Figure 1.5 ProControl and Control|24 integrated control surfaces for Pro Tools

Pro Tools|HD Hardware Systems Take Shape

In 2002, Pro Tools|HD hardware systems were unveiled as successors to Pro Tools TDM and Pro Tools|24. These systems provided support for higher sample rates and very large mixing topologies, addressing the needs of high-end music and post-production studios.

Pro Tools Becomes a Studio in a Box

On the opposite side of the spectrum, the first Mbox was introduced as a portable "studio in a box" for the hobbyist and small project studio markets. The Digi 002 and Digi 002 Rack audio interface options followed, extending the capabilities of host-based Pro Tools LE systems.

Sibelius Joins Avid Audio

In 2006, Sibelius Software Ltd. joined the Avid Audio family. Under Avid, the Sibelius product line continues, including the well-known professional music notation package of the same name. Today, Pro Tools incorporates notation capabilities directly and can export MIDI data as a score for use in Sibelius software.

Pro Tools in This Decade

In April 2010, Avid acquired Euphonix, a company known for its high-end digital audio consoles and EUCON control surface technology. Avid's current lineup of control surfaces includes the Artist Series controllers (Artist Control, Artist Mix, Artist Transport), Pro Tools | S3, and the large-format Pro Tools | S6.

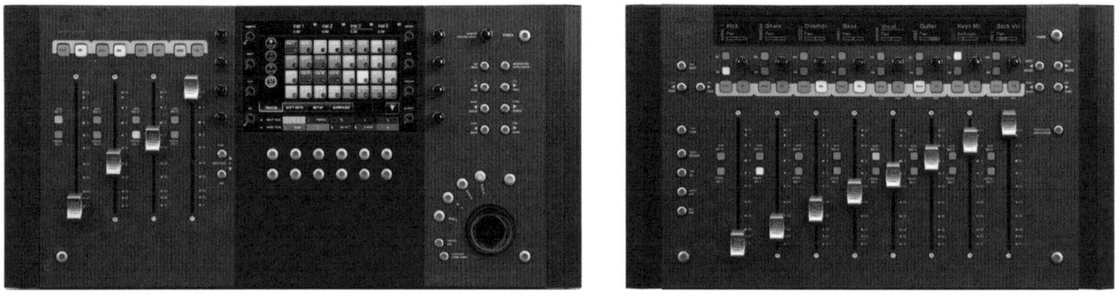

Figure 1.6 Artist Series controllers: Artist Control (left) and Artist Mix (right)

Figure 1.7 Avid Pro Tools | S6 control surface

Also in 2010, Avid released the third-generation Pro Tools Mbox family of audio interfaces, new HD-series interfaces, and the HD-Native platform.

When Pro Tools 10 was released in 2012, it introducing a new file format designed for modern 64-bit operating systems. Pro Tools 10 also introduced the new AAX plug-in format, which remains in use to this day.

In 2013, the Pro Tools 11 release completed the transition to a 64-bit native application, allowing the software to take advantage of more processors, run more plug-ins, and access more RAM. This release also incorporated the new and improved Avid Audio Engine, a new Avid Video Engine, and the long-awaited offline bounce feature, for faster-than-real-time mixdown.

The initial Pro Tools 12 release, in 2015, introduced the ability to subscribe to Pro Tools software. With a Pro Tools subscription, users have perpetual access to the latest updates, upgrades, and support. When updates are available, subscribers get them delivered automatically. This release also introduced important changes to I/O setup, improving session interchange and I/O mapping between systems.

Updates to Pro Tools 12

Over the past two-plus years, Avid has continued to release regular, incremental updates to Pro Tools 12. Some of the important features and changes in each release include the following:

- Pro Tools 12.1—New features for standard Pro Tools systems (formerly Pro Tools HD only), including track-based input monitoring and AFL/PFL solo modes, and an increase in the number of supported tracks in standard Pro Tools (128 Audio tracks and 512 Instrument tracks).
- Pro Tools 12.2—Additional improvements for standard Pro Tools, including VCA Master tracks, the Disk Cache feature, advanced metering options, and gain reduction metering.
- Pro Tools 12.3—New Track Commit and Track Bounce functions, clip transparency while editing, and improved batch fades.
- Pro Tools 12.4—New Track Freeze functionality, letting users quickly lock in all processing on one or more tracks and free up system resources.
- Pro Tools 12.5—Ability to save work as *projects* on Avid's Cloud servers and to share projects with collaborators.

A project is a Pro Tools session that can be stored in the Cloud (with a local cache on your system). Pro Tools cloud-enabled projects can be accessed through your Avid account from any system with an internet connection.

- Pro Tools 12.6—Clip Effects for Pro Tools HD software (EQ and dynamics processing), layered editing option, new playlist workflows, editing improvements, real-time fade manipulation, Workspace search enhancements, and status icon enhancements.
- Pro Tools 12.7—Soundbase browsers and a fully tagged 2 GB sample pack from Loopmasters, project Revision History (for cloud-based project documents), "save as" workflow for cloud-based projects.
- Pro Tools 12.8—Support for Dolby Atmos multichannel formats (Pro Tools HD), offline option for projects, and support for Avid NEXIS storage systems.

Other Recent Releases

In addition to the recent updates to Pro Tools software, Avid has recently released an update for Pro Tools | First software that brings cloud collaboration features, Soundbase, and other current Pro Tools functionality to the product.

Pro Tools | First is a free version of the software for users who are new to Pro Tools. It features up to 16 audio tracks, along with MIDI and Instrument tracks (up to 16 of each), Aux Input tracks, and Master Faders. Pro Tools | First stores projects in the user's Avid cloud-based storage account.

Although Pro Tools | First has some significant limitations compared to paid Pro Tools 12 software, it is remarkably full-featured and provides an excellent learning platform for users who are not yet ready for a paid version of Pro Tools 12.

For more information on Pro Tools | First and to sign up for the free software download, point your browser to http://apps.avid.com/protoolsfirst.

Getting the Most from Your System

To make the most of your experience with Pro Tools 12 and to optimize your results using the platform, it is helpful to understand some audio basics and to familiarize yourself with the software and hardware options available with Pro Tools. The remainder of this lesson focuses on these topics.

Audio Basics: Waveform, Frequency, and Amplitude

To work effectively with sound, it is helpful to understand a bit about what sound is and what gives a sound its character. When we hear a sound, what we actually experience is a variation in the air pressure around us. This variation results from vibrations in material objects—whether a knock on a tabletop, a running car engine, or a plucked guitar string. When a vibrating object moves through a back-and-forth motion, the variation in air pressure that it produces becomes an auditory event. If the object is vibrating at a frequency that falls within the range of human hearing, we perceive the varying air pressure as a sound.

The nature of the sound we hear is determined by the waveform, frequency, and amplitude of the vibration.

Waveform

The waveform of the sound pressure variations that reaches our ears creates our perception of the sound's source, be it a tabletop, a car engine, or a guitar string. The waveform is the "shape" of the sound—or, more accurately, the shape of the vibration that produced the sound. As a vibrating object moves through its back-and-forth motions, its path is not smooth and continuous. Instead, the cycles of vibration are typically complex and jagged, creating a sound that is influenced by the physical material that the object is composed of and the resonance induced by the object's surroundings. Each object vibrates differently; the waveform of the vibration gives the sound its unique character and tone.

Frequency

The frequency of the sound pressure variations that reaches our ears creates our perception of the pitch of the sound. We measure this frequency in *cycles per second* (CPS), also commonly denoted as *Hertz* (Hz). These two terms are synonymous—15,000 CPS is the same as 15,000 Hz. Multiples of 1,000 Hz are often denoted as kilohertz (kHz). Therefore, 15,000 Hz is also written as 15 kHz.

As the frequency of vibration increases, the pitch of the sound goes up—numerically higher frequencies produce higher pitches, while numerically lower frequencies produce lower pitches. Each time the frequency doubles, the pitch raises by one octave.

By way of example, the open **A** string on a guitar vibrates at 110 Hz in standard tuning. Playing the **A** note on the 12th fret produces vibrations at 220 Hz (one octave higher).

The range of human hearing is between 20 and 20,000 cycles per second, or stated another way, from 20 Hz to 20 kHz.

Amplitude

The intensity or amplitude of the sound pressure variations that reaches our ears creates our perception of the loudness of the sound. We measure amplitude in *decibels* (dB). The decibel is a logarithmic unit that is used to describe a ratio of sound pressure; as such, it does not have a linear relation to our perception of loudness.

As the amplitude of pressure variations increases, the sound becomes louder. Doubling the intensity of sound-pressure variations creates a gain of 3 dB; however, we do not perceive this change as doubling the sound's loudness. An increase of approximately 10 dB is required to produce a perceived doubling of loudness. By way of example, the amplitude of ordinary conversation is around 60 dB. Increasing the amplitude to 70 dB would essentially double the loudness; increasing amplitude to 80 dB would double it again, quadrupling the original loudness.

Recording and Playing Back Analog Audio

The task of a recording microphone is to respond to changes in air pressure—the waveforms, frequencies, and amplitudes that make up a sound—and translate them into an electronic output that can be captured or recorded. A microphone functions as a *transducer*, converting acoustic energy into an electrical current.

The continuous electrical signal produced by a microphone is an alternating current with a waveform, frequency, and amplitude that directly corresponds to, or is analogous to, the original acoustic information. This electrical signal is thus considered to represent *analog audio*.

If this continuous analog signal is captured on traditional recording media, such as magnetic tape, it can be played back by directly translating the electrical waveform, frequency, and amplitude back into analogous variations in air pressure through the means of an amplifier and a loudspeaker.

Converting Audio to Digital Format

Before you can record or edit with Pro Tools, the analog audio (electrical signal) relayed by a microphone, guitar pickup, or other device must be translated into digital numeric information (binary data). This conversion is necessary so that the signal can be stored, read, and subsequently manipulated by a computer.

The process of translating electrical signals to binary data is referred to as *analog-to-digital conversion*, commonly abbreviated as *A/D conversion*. Two essential factors affect the A/D conversion process: *sample rate* and *bit depth*.

The Importance of Sample Rate

Sampling is the process of taking discrete measurements of an electrical signal at various moments in time. Each measurement, or sample, is a digital representation of the signal voltage at that instant. Played back in succession, these samples approximate the original signal, much like a series of photographs played back in succession approximates movement in a film or video.

The sample rate is the frequency with which these digital measurements are collected.

Nyquist Theorem

The sample rate required for digital audio is driven by a fundamental law of analog-to-digital conversion, referred to as the *Sampling Theorem* or the *Nyquist Theorem*.

The Nyquist Theorem states that in order to produce an accurate representation of a given frequency of sound, each cycle of the sound's vibration must be sampled a minimum of two times. If the sample rate is any lower, the system will read the incoming frequencies inaccurately and produce the wrong tones. (In concept, this is much like the effect seen in early motion pictures, where a wagon wheel will appear to rotate backward due to the low frame rates being used.) In digital audio, the false tones produced by this type of frequency distortion are known as *alias tones*.

Minimum Sample Rate

Because the range of human hearing is generally accepted to be 20 Hz to 20 kHz, the Nyquist Theorem tells us that a sampling rate of at least 40 kHz (twice the upper range of human hearing) is required to capture full-frequency audio.

Most professional digital recording devices today offer sample rates of at least 44.1 kHz (often as much as 96 kHz or higher). The digital information on an audio CD is stored at a standard sample rate of 44.1 kHz.

The Importance of Bit Depth

Computers use binary digits called *bits* (0s or 1s) to represent each sample measurement that is collected. The number of bits used for each sample is referred to as the *binary word length*, or bit depth.

The more binary digits included in the bit depth, the greater the accuracy of each sample measurement. The relative amplitude (or loudness) of each sample is *quantized*, or rounded to the closest available whole-number value within the word length.

The range of numeric values available for each sample at a given bit depth is equal to 2 to the *n*th power (2^n), where *n* is the number of bits in the binary word.

By way of example, consider a 4-bit binary word. This word length can represent only 16 different amplitude levels (2^4). As such, this 4-bit binary word would record audio using 16 discrete amplitude levels. By contrast, a 16-bit digital word could represent 65,536 discrete amplitude levels (2^{16}), creating a much more continuous dynamic response. A 24-bit digital word could define more than 16 million discrete amplitude levels (2^{24}).

Larger binary words are able to quantify variations in amplitude with much greater accuracy. Therefore, a 24-bit audio file will always more accurately reflect the dynamic range of the original sound than its 16-bit counterpart.

Thirty-two-bit floating-point files represent discrete amplitude levels in the same way as 24-bit files. The 8 additional bits provide exponent biasing and allow for headroom above full-scale 24-bit audio.

Calculating Dynamic Range

A very general rule of thumb can be used to calculate the dynamic range capability of an A/D system. By multiplying the word size by six, you can estimate the useful dynamic range of a fixed-point system. For example, a system with an **8-bit** binary word would produce a dynamic range of about 48 dB (8 × 6), while a **16-bit** system would accommodate a 96-dB dynamic range (16 × 6). A **24-bit** system would have a theoretical dynamic range of 144 dB (24 × 6).

In theoretical terms, the dynamic range (or signal-to-quantization noise ratio) increases by approximately 6 dB for each bit added to the binary word length.

Minimum Bit Depth

The useful dynamic range of speech and music is generally considered to be from 40 to 105 dB. To capture this range, an A/D converter must be able to accurately represent differences in amplitude of at least 65 dB; stated another way, it must have a minimum 65-dB dynamic range. This would require at least 11 bits in the binary word.

To provide an adequate dynamic range to minimize the impact of the noise floor at the low end of the spectrum, and to allow a healthy amount of headroom at the high end, Pro Tools uses a minimum word length of 16 bits. Greater bit depths can be used to increase precision and accommodate a wider dynamic range.

Sample Rate, Bit Depth, and File Size

A consequence of files with higher sample rates and greater bit depths is the higher storage capacity required to record them. Each minute of 16-bit/44.1-kHz mono audio occupies about 5 MB of storage space. Higher sample rates increase the storage requirement. At 96-kHz, each minute of 16-bit mono audio requires about 11 MB of storage space.

Increasing the bit depth has the same effect. For example, one minute of 24-bit/44.1-kHz mono audio occupies about 7.5 MB of hard-drive storage space, while the same audio in a 32-bit float file (at 44.1 kHz) will require about 10 MB of hard-drive space per minute.

Stereo files require twice as much storage space as mono files, since each file includes two channels of audio (left and right).

Recording in Digital Format

When you are recording into Pro Tools using audio that is already in a digital form (from DAT or CD, for example), you don't need to translate the audio before bringing it into the system. The process of converting from digital to analog and back to digital can introduce distortion and degrade the original signal.

Digital Transfers

To prevent audio degradation, unnecessary conversions should be avoided. By keeping audio information in the digital domain while transferring between machines or devices, it will retain its sonic integrity with no discernible signal degradation.

Digital Audio Connections

On the rear panel of many Pro Tools audio interfaces are connections for accomplishing digital transfers. Common digital connections include *S/PDIF*, which uses RCA jacks (sometimes called *coaxial jacks*), and *AES/EBU*, which uses XLR-type connectors. S/PDIF is the *Sony/Philips Digital Interface* standard, a consumer format, and AES/EBU is the *Audio Engineering Society/European Broadcast Union* digital interface standard, a professional format.

Although the formats are nearly identical in audio quality, if given the choice, you should use the AES/EBU format over S/PDIF. As a professional format, AES/EBU is technically more stable, and it filters out any copy protection encoded in the digital audio stream.

Pro Tools System Configurations

The requirements for your digital audio recording projects will determine the type of Pro Tools system that you will need to use. Pro Tools 12 is available in three options: Pro Tools|First, standard Pro Tools software, and Pro Tools|HD.

Software Options

Pro Tools|First is a free version of Pro Tools, with limited track count and limited I/O capabilities. This option provides 1 GB of free cloud-based storage and does not allow projects to be saved locally.

Standard Pro Tools software provides full-featured stereo audio production capabilities for music and video post-production work. This book focuses on standard Pro Tools software features.

Pro Tools | HD software is available for use as stand-alone software or for use with Pro Tools | HD Native or Pro Tools | HDX hardware. Pro Tools | HD software provides advanced automation, video editing, and surround mixing capabilities.

All current Pro Tools systems include 1 GB of cloud storage for backup and collaboration and are eligible for cloud storage upgrades of up to 80 GB for a monthly fee. All Pro Tools options are available for both Mac and Windows operating systems.

Pro Tools vs. Pro Tools | HD

Throughout this book, we use the term **Pro Tools** to refer generically to all available software configurations and the term **standard Pro Tools** to refer specifically to non-HD software. The term **Pro Tools | HD** is used to refer specifically to Pro Tools | HD software with any supported configuration.

Host-Based Systems Versus DSP-Accelerated Systems

Pro Tools systems can either be host-based, meaning they rely solely on the processing power of the host computer for routing, mixing, and processing of audio signals, or DSP-accelerated systems, meaning that the computer's processor is supplemented by additional processor chips dedicated to digital signal processing (DSP) for mixing and real-time processing.

Host-based system configurations include Pro Tools | First, standard Pro Tools, and Pro Tools | HD software systems, as well as Pro Tools | HD Native hardware systems with one or more connected HD-series audio interfaces.

DSP-accelerated systems include Pro Tools | HDX systems with one or more connected HD-series audio interfaces.

All systems share the same file format, with full cross-compatibility between Macs and PCs, providing seamless interchange between Pro Tools systems.

Audio Interface Options

An audio interface provides the analog-to-digital conversion required for recording to Pro Tools, as well as the digital-to-analog conversion required for playback from Pro Tools to your analog speakers or headphones. Pro Tools 12 can be run without an audio interface, using your computer's built-in speakers or headphone jack for playback; however, recording options may be limited or unavailable.

Avid Audio Interfaces (Non-HD)

Avid audio interfaces that are available for Pro Tools | First and standard Pro Tools software include the following:

- **Pro Tools | Fast Track family** (Figure 1.8): includes the Fast Track Solo and the Fast Track Duo; both products feature powered USB connectivity.
- **Pro Tools | Mbox family** (Figure 1.9): includes the Pro Tools | Mbox and the high-definition Pro Tools | Mbox Pro; the Pro Tools | Mbox features powered USB connectivity and sample rates up to 96 kHz; the Pro Tools | Mbox Pro is a FireWire-powered interface, featuring sample rates up to 192 kHz.
- **Pro Tools | Eleven Rack** (Figure 1.10): a guitar recording and effects processing system designed to serve as an audio interface for Pro Tools as well as a standalone amp tone and effects signal processor; Eleven Rack provides up to eight simultaneous channels of recording at sample rates up to 96 kHz via a USB 2.0 connection.

- **Pro Tools | Duet and Quartet** (Figure 1.11): Apogee audio interfaces that integrate directly with Pro Tools through Pro Tools IO Control software; both options provide sample rates up to 192 kHz.

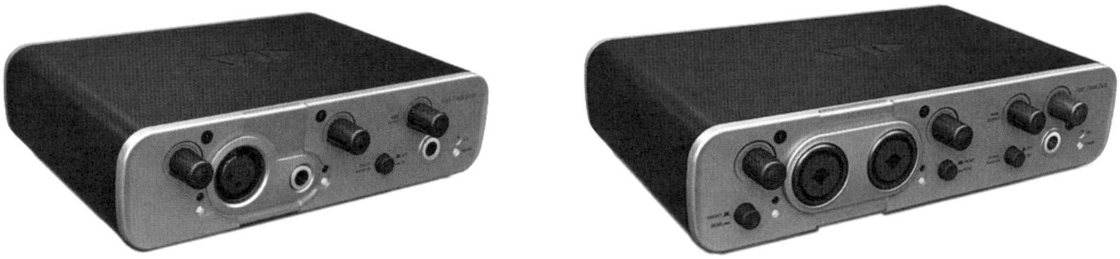

Figure 1.8 Fast Track Solo (left) and Fast Track Duo (right)

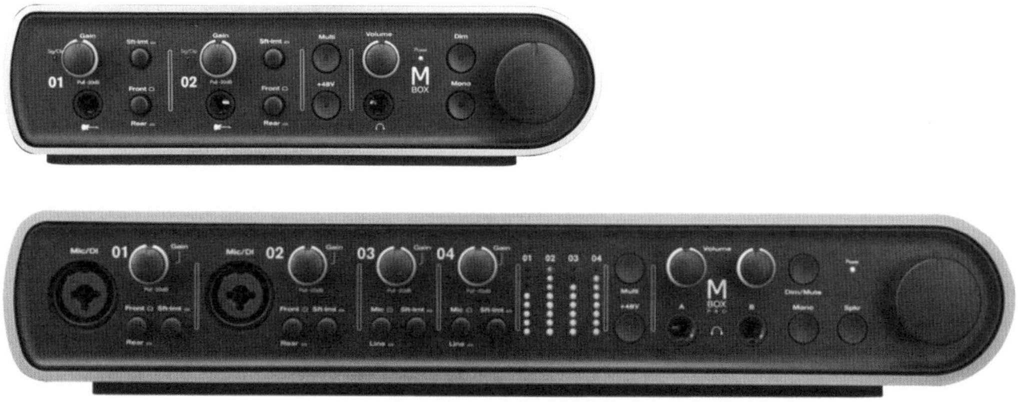

Figure 1.9 Pro Tools Mbox (top) and Mbox Pro (bottom)

Figure 1.10 Pro Tools | Eleven Rack audio interface

Figure 1.11 Pro Tools | Duet audio interface (left) and Pro Tools | Quartet audio interface (right)

Third-Party Audio Interfaces (Non-HD)

Pro Tools software is compatible with any third-party audio interface that includes a supported Core Audio (Mac) or ASIO (Windows) driver. A variety of third-party peripherals are available, providing a multitude of interface options, for up to 32 channels of I/O to the system. Many of these peripherals can be powered by the computer's FireWire or USB bus, enabling portability for laptop systems.

Pro Tools | HD-Series Audio Interfaces

Pro Tools | HD Native and Pro Tools | HDX hardware systems require at least one HD-series audio interface to be connected in order to run. Current Pro Tools | HD-series interfaces include the following:

- **HD OMNI** (Figure 1.12): provides two microphone inputs with built-in preamps, four line inputs, and eight line outputs in a single space rack-mountable chassis.
- **HD I/O** (Figure 1.13), available in three configurations: the 8×8×8 configuration provides eight analog inputs, eight analog outputs, and eight channels of AES/EBU digital I/O; the 16×16 analog configuration provides 16 channels of analog input along with 16 channels of analog output; the 16×16 digital configuration provides 16 channels of digital input and 16 channels of digital output.
- **HD MADI** (Figure 1.14): provides 64-channels of digital communication via coaxial and optical connectors, for sending and receiving digital audio streams between Pro Tools and other MADI devices.

Figure 1.12 Avid HD OMNI audio interface

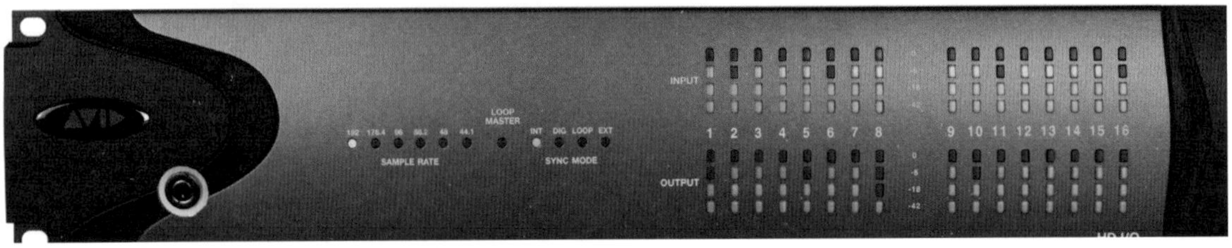

Figure 1.13 Avid HD I/O audio interface

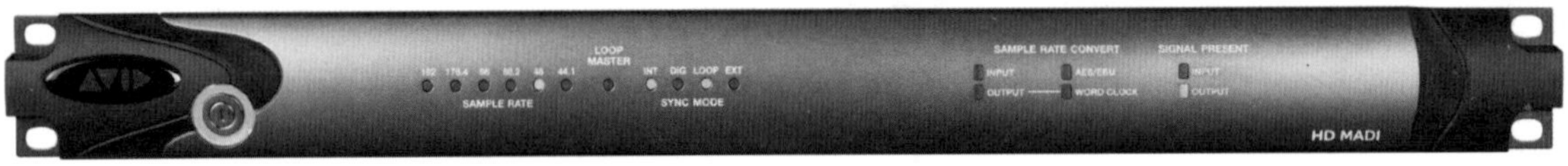

Figure 1.14 Avid HD MADI audio interface

Cross-Platform Issues

Pro Tools configurations are available for both Mac and Windows systems. Most Pro Tools controls, tools, procedures, and menus are similar on both systems. There are, however, some differences in keyboard commands and file-naming conventions that can impact your work when moving between different platforms.

Keyboard Commands

Many keyboard commands in Pro Tools use *modifier keys*, which are keys pressed in combination with other keys or with a mouse action. Modifiers and other equivalent keys can have different names on each platform. Table 1.1 below summarizes equivalent keys on Mac and Windows.

Table 1.1 Modifier Key Equivalents

Mac	Windows
Command key	Ctrl (Control) key
Option key	Alt key
Control key	Start (Win) key
Return key	Enter key on main (not numeric) keypad
Delete key	Backspace key

File-Naming Conventions

A few differences exist in the way files are named and recognized by Mac and Windows.

File Name Extensions

For cross-platform compatibility, all Pro Tools files in a session must have a three-letter file extension added to the file name. Pro Tools 10 through 12 session files use the *.ptx* extension. Pro Tools 7 through 9 session files use the extension *.ptf.* Sessions created in versions of Pro Tools older than 7 may use the extension *.pts* or *.pt5.* WAV files have the *.wav* file extension, and AIFF files have the *.aif* file extension.

Incompatible ASCII Characters

Pro Tools file names cannot use ASCII characters that are incompatible with a supported operating system. The following characters should be avoided in order to maintain cross-platform compatibility:

/ (slash)

\ (backslash)

: (colon)

* (asterisk)

? (question mark)

" (quotation marks)

' (apostrophe)

< (less-than symbol)

> (greater-than symbol)

| (vertical line or pipe)

You should also avoid any character typed with the Command key on the Macintosh.

Review/Discussion Questions

1. Name and describe five types of production tasks that Pro Tools can be used for. (See "The Pro Tools Digital Audio Workstation" beginning on page 4.)

2. What is the frequency range of human hearing? (See "Audio Basics: Waveform, Frequency, and Amplitude" beginning on page 10.)

3. What does the frequency of a sound wave affect in terms of how we perceive the sound? How is frequency measured? (See "Audio Basics: Waveform, Frequency, and Amplitude" beginning on page 10.)

4. What does the amplitude of the sound wave affect? How is amplitude measured? (See "Audio Basics: Waveform, Frequency, and Amplitude" beginning on page 10.)

5. How does the sample rate of a system relate to the frequency of audio it can capture? What is the name of the law that specifies the relationship between sample rate and audio frequency? (See "The Importance of Sample Rate" beginning on page 11.)

6. How does the bit depth of a system relate to the dynamic range of audio it can capture? How can you estimate the dynamic range of a system? (See "The Importance of Bit Depth" beginning on page 12.)

7. What are some common digital connections available on Pro Tools audio interfaces? What type of connector jack does each use? (See "Recording in Digital Format" on page 13.)

8. Name some audio interfaces that are compatible with standard Pro Tools software. (See "Audio Interface Options" beginning on page 14.)

9. Name some audio interfaces that are compatible with Pro Tools HD software. (See "Pro Tools | HD-Series Audio Interfaces" beginning on page 16.)

To review additional material from this chapter, see the PT101 Study Guide module available through the ElementsIED online learning platform at ElementsED.com.

EXERCISE 1

Audio Interface Options

In this exercise worksheet, you will identify various Pro Tools audio interfaces and the software platform that is compatible with each. The information referenced in these questions is covered in Lesson 1.

Duration: 10 Minutes **Media: None Required**

Refer to Figures 1.15 through 1.18 when answering the questions below. See the section on "Pro Tools System Configurations" in Lesson 1 for assistance.

Questions 1 and 2 refer to Figure 1.15.

1. The audio interface shown in Figure 1.15 is called the ________________________________.
2. This interface is compatible with (select all that apply):

   ❑ Pro Tools | First software

   ❑ Standard Pro Tools software

   ❑ Pro Tools|HD Native hardware

   ❑ Pro Tools|HDX hardware

Figure 1.15 A Pro Tools audio interface

Questions 3 and 4 refer to Figure 1.16.

3. The audio interface shown in Figure 1.16 is called the ________________________________.
4. This interface is compatible with (select all that apply):

   ❑ Pro Tools | First software

   ❑ Standard Pro Tools software

   ❑ Pro Tools|HD Native hardware

   ❑ Pro Tools|HDX hardware

Figure 1.16 An audio interface for guitar

Questions 5 and 6 refer to Figure 1.17.

5. The audio interface shown in Figure 1.17 is called the _____________________________________.

6. This interface is compatible with (select all that apply):

   - ❑ Pro Tools | First software
   - ❑ Standard Pro Tools software
   - ❑ Pro Tools|HD Native hardware
   - ❑ Pro Tools|HDX hardware

Figure 1.17 A single-space rack-mountable audio interface for Pro Tools

Questions 7 and 8 refer to Figure 1.18.

7. The audio interface shown in Figure 1.18 is called the _____________________________________.

8. This interface is compatible with (select all that apply):

   - ❑ Pro Tools | First software
   - ❑ Standard Pro Tools software
   - ❑ Pro Tools|HD Native hardware
   - ❑ Pro Tools|HDX hardware

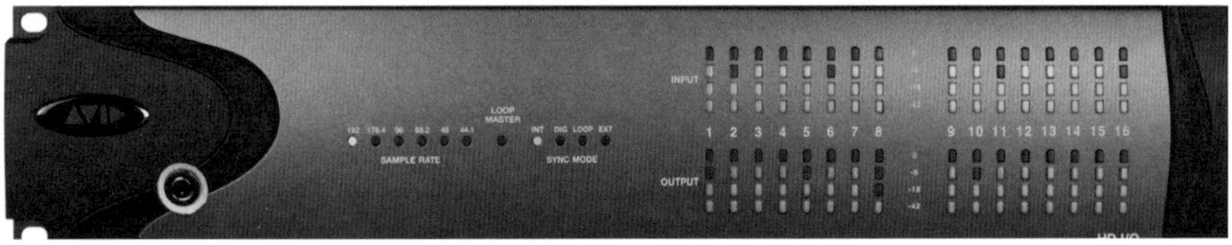

Figure 1.18 A double-space rack-mountable audio interface for Pro Tools

LESSON 2

Getting Started with Pro Tools

This lesson covers basic requirements to get up and running with Pro Tools. It reviews the Pro Tools software components and installers, as well as the file structure used for Pro Tools sessions. It also introduces the basic user interface for the software and reviews menu operations. The second half of this lesson provides an overview of the main windows in Pro Tools.

Duration: 90 Minutes

GOALS

- Understand the components included with a Pro Tools system and how to access installers
- Recognize the basic Pro Tools session file structure
- Understand basic Pro Tools software and plug-in options
- Power up a Pro Tools system
- Navigate the Pro Tools menu system to locate common commands
- Recognize and work in the main Pro Tools windows

Key topics from this lesson are included in the *Pro Tools 12 Essential Training: 101* course on Lynda.com.

This lesson presents an overview of basic Pro Tools operations and functions. You will be introduced to the filing structure that Pro Tools uses for its sessions and backups, the steps required to start up a Pro Tools system, and the primary elements of the main Pro Tools windows.

Target Systems

Although most of the concepts discussed in this book are applicable to all Pro Tools systems, the book is specifically written for Pro Tools 12.8 software. While any Pro Tools system can be used with this book, certain menus, commands, and functions may differ from one configuration to another. Additionally, Pro Tools | HD users will have access to various features that are not represented in this book.

New features introduced in a recent Pro Tools 12 update are generally identified as such in the text. All descriptions are based on the user interface and functionality in Pro Tools 12.8, unless otherwise noted.

Software Installation and Operation

All Pro Tools software options (except Pro Tools | First) use the same software installer. The Pro Tools installer also installs a variety of included software plug-ins, providing additional functionality. Supplemental plug-ins may be included as well, which require separate installation.

If you have purchased or subscribed to Pro Tools, the installers for your Pro Tools software and any additional plug-ins you have access to will be available through your Avid Master Account.

To access the installers for Pro Tools, do the following:

1. Go to Avid.com and log in to your Avid account.
2. Click on the **MY PRODUCTS AND SUBSCRIPTIONS** link under the **MY PRODUCTS** section.

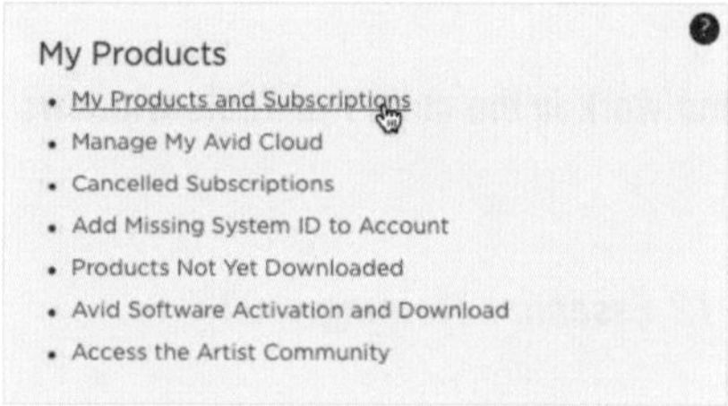

Figure 2.1 Clicking on the My Products and Subscriptions link

3. Expand the row for your Pro Tools product, if needed, and then click the **SHOW** link next to **PRODUCT DETAILS AND DOWNLOAD LINKS**.

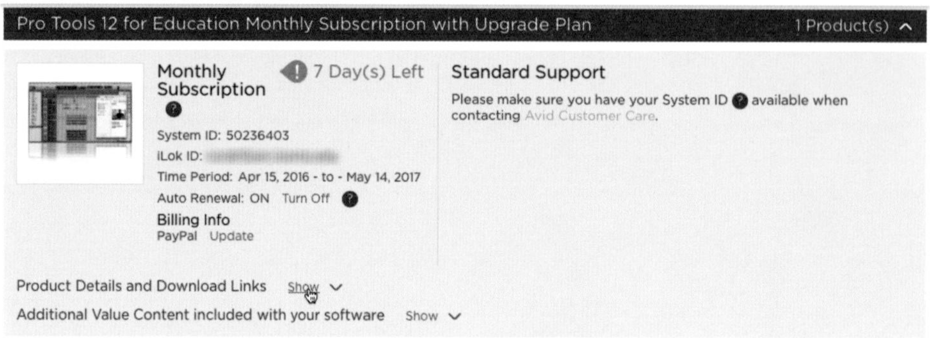

Figure 2.2 Clicking the Show link to display available installers

You will need to download and run each installer separately for each component included in your purchase or subscription.

Included Plug-Ins and Extras

Plug-ins are special-purpose software components that provide additional signal processing and other functionality within Pro Tools. Pro Tools plug-ins come in three varieties: Native plug-ins, which process audio in real time using the host computer's processing power; DSP plug-ins (Pro Tools|HDX systems only), which utilize card-based DSP chips for real-time processing; and AudioSuite plug-ins, which provide non-real-time, file-based processing.

Pro Tools | First comes with a limited set of Avid plug-ins, plus the Xpand II plug-in from the AIR Group (available via a separate installer). Standard Pro Tools and Pro Tools | HD both come with a full compliment of Avid plug-ins, as well as additional effects and instruments from the AIR Group, as described below.

Avid Audio Plug-Ins

Avid audio plug-ins include EQ, dynamics, reverb, delay, modulation and harmonic effects, and more. Over 30 separate Avid plug-ins are installed with Pro Tools, many in Native, DSP, and AudioSuite formats. The Avid audio plug-ins installed with Pro Tools are described in Appendix B, "Avid Pro Tools Plug-Ins."

Additional Avid plug-ins may be provided with your Pro Tools subscription or purchase. If so, the plug-in installers will be available through your Avid master account. Log in as described above; then click the **SHOW** link next to the **ADDITIONAL VALUE CONTENT** heading.

AIR Plug-Ins

The AIR plug-ins for Pro Tools are native (host-based) effects and instrument plug-ins. These are included with all paid Pro Tools systems. To access the AIR plug-ins, log in as described above. Under the **PRODUCT DETAILS AND DOWNLOAD LINKS**, download and run the three AIR installers for your computer platform: the AIR Effects Bundle (includes 20 AIR effects plug-ins), the AIR Instrument Bundle (includes five AIR virtual instruments), and the Xpand II installer.

A description of the included AIR plug-ins is provided in Appendix C, "AIR Effects and Instrument Plug-Ins."

Pro Tools Software Features

Pro Tools | First software will power up to 16 simultaneous mono or stereo Audio tracks, 16 Instrument tracks, and 16 MIDI tracks.

Standard Pro Tools 12 software will power up to 128 simultaneous mono or stereo Audio tracks.

Pro Tools | HD software will power up to 256 simultaneous Audio tracks without HDX hardware and up to 768 Audio tracks in an expanded HDX system. Both standard Pro Tools and Pro Tools | HD software support up to 512 Instrument tracks and 512 MIDI tracks.

Running Pro Tools | HD Software without Hardware

A Pro Tools | HD authorization enables Pro Tools | HD software functionality on any supported Mac or Windows computer, without requiring HD hardware to be present. This allows Pro Tools | HD users to run a native Pro Tools laptop system when away from the studio, for powerful on-the-go editing and mixing.

Pro Tools File Structure

With all of the software components properly installed, you will likely be anxious to launch Pro Tools and get to work. But before you create your first Pro Tools document, or *session*, it is helpful to understand how the software interacts with the various files that are related to the session. Rather than storing a session as a single file, Pro Tools stores various session components separately and maintains a roadmap to the files it uses in a session file. All of the files used for a project are grouped together in a *session folder*.

In Pro Tools 12.5 and later, you can also create your Pro Tools document as a *project* file. A project is a cloud-enabled session file that can be used for collaboration or remote access to the Pro Tools document and associated media files.

Additional information on Pro Tools projects is provided in Lesson 4.

File Organization

When you create a Pro Tools session, the system sets up a standard hierarchy for the session and its associated files by automatically creating a top-level session folder. This folder contains the session file as well as subfolders for various supplemental files used for the session. When you record, convert on import, or edit material, specific files will appear in each of these subfolders.

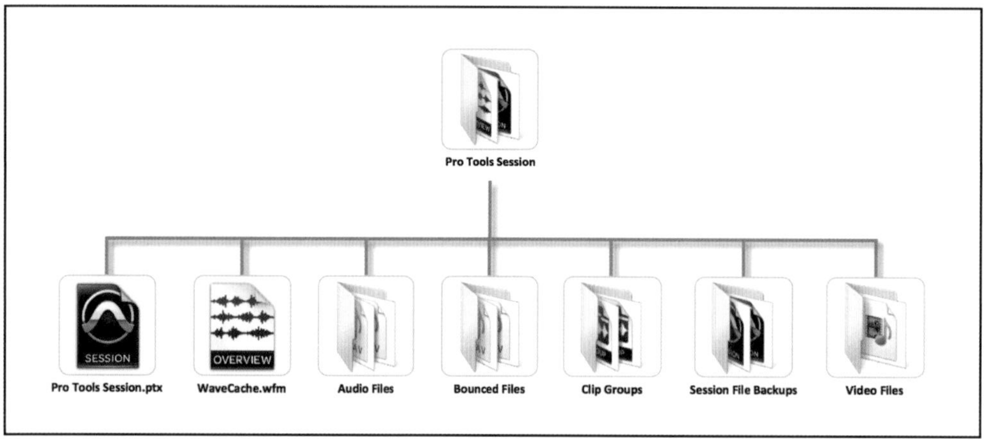

Figure 2.3 Pro Tools session file hierarchy

Pro Tools keeps related files together in this hierarchy to facilitate backups of sessions and transfers between Pro Tools systems.

Session Components

The types of files that Pro Tools generates and stores in each folder in the hierarchy are described in the following sections. Many of these files are created by Pro Tools automatically as you work on a project, although some are generated by export operations only.

Pro Tools Session File

A *session file* is the document that Pro Tools creates when you start a new project. Pro Tools creates this file (along with various subfolders) inside a session folder of the same name. Session files created in Pro Tools 10 and later are recognizable by their *.ptx* extensions. (Earlier versions of Pro Tools use the *.ptf* extension.)

The session file contains a map of all the tracks, audio files, video files, settings, and edits associated with your project. Session documents can be saved and reopened, recalling a given project with all of its edit information, input/output assignments, and links to the associated media files. You can easily copy and rename session documents, allowing you to save alternate versions of a project without changing the source audio.

WaveCache File

Each Pro Tools session you create will also have an associated *WaveCache.wfm* file created inside the session folder. This file stores all of the waveform display data for any audio in the session and enables the session to open more quickly. The WaveCache file can be included whenever a session is transferred to another Pro Tools system.

WaveCache files can be deleted without harming the session or your system. If the WaveCache is missing, Pro Tools will recalculate the session waveform data; however, the session may open more slowly.

Audio Files

When you record audio into a Pro Tools session, each recording is stored as a separate file inside the corresponding session's Audio Files folder. Pro Tools natively supports audio files in either the WAV or AIFF format. For compatibility purposes, WAV is the default file format on both Mac and Windows Pro Tools systems.

Audio that you record in Pro Tools is saved *only* in the Audio Files folder; it is not saved in the session file (.ptx). When transferring sessions between systems, be sure to copy over the entire top-level session folder in order to include all associated audio files and other material needed for the session.

MIDI Files

MIDI data is normally stored within the Pro Tools session; as such, no MIDI files will exist outside the session document. However, MIDI files can be exported from Pro Tools using the EXPORT > MIDI command. Exported MIDI files can be recognized by their *.mid* extensions.

Sibelius Files

If you work with scores inside Pro Tools (WINDOW > SCORE EDITOR), you can use either the SEND TO SIBELIUS command or the EXPORT > SIBELIUS command to generate a score file that can be opened/edited with Sibelius notation software. Exported Sibelius files can be recognized by their *.sib* extensions.

Bounced Files

The Bounced Files folder is the default directory that Pro Tools uses for files created using the Bounce to Disk function. If you do not use Bounce to Disk, this folder will remain empty and will be removed when you close the session.

Clip Groups

The Clip Groups folder is the default directory that Pro Tools uses for any clip groups you export from your Pro Tools session. If you do not export any clip groups, this folder will remain empty and will be removed when you close the session.

Rendered Files

Whenever you use rendered Elastic Audio processing, Pro Tools creates temporary files for the audio on the affected tracks. These temporary files are kept in an auto-created Rendered Files folder in the session folder. If you commit rendered Elastic Audio processing to a track, a new file is written to disk in the Audio Files folder, and the temporary rendered file is deleted from the Rendered Files folder.

If you do not use rendered Elastic Audio processing in your session, no Rendered Files folder will be created in the session folder.

Session File Backups

If you enable the Auto Backup function in Pro Tools, the Session File Backups folder will be created automatically, and auto-saved session backup files will be stored in this location.

Auto backups are enabled in Pro Tools by default. You can specify the number of backup files to maintain and the backup frequency in the OPERATION tab of the Preferences dialog box (SETUP > PREFERENCES).

Video Files

The Video Files folder is used when you copy a video from source media during certain operations in Pro Tools. However, when you import a video file (such as a QuickTime movie or an Avid video file), the session references the file in its stored location and does not copy it into your current Pro Tools session folder.

For maximum session portability, you can create a Video Files folder, if it does not already exist, and copy existing movies into it prior to importing them into your session.

Starting Pro Tools

Because Pro Tools systems are typically composed of both hardware and software, preparing your system for use might involve more than simply turning on your computer and launching the Pro Tools application. The larger the system, the more important it becomes to follow a specific startup sequence.

Powering Up Your Hardware

When starting your Pro Tools hardware, it's important to power up the system components in the proper order. Starting components out of sequence could cause a component to not be recognized, prevent the software from launching, or cause unexpected behavior.

The recommended sequence for starting a Pro Tools system is as follows:

1. Start with all your equipment (including your computer) powered off.
2. Turn on any external hard drives that require external power and wait about 10 seconds for them to spin up to speed.
3. Turn on any MIDI interfaces and MIDI devices that require external power (including any MIDI control surfaces) as well as any synchronization peripherals, if used.
4. Turn on your audio interface (if not bus powered). Wait at least 15 seconds for the audio interface to initialize.
5. Start your computer and launch Pro Tools.
6. Turn on your audio monitoring system, if applicable.

Many audio interfaces get their power from the computer (via a USB port or other connection); these interfaces do not need to be powered up in advance.

Additional steps may be required to start up a Pro Tools system with HD-series interfaces and peripherals. Consult the Getting Started guide that came with your system for details.

Using the PACE iLok System

Pro Tools software is protected with an iLok USB key, as are many other software products and plug-ins. Using an iLok key for Pro Tools enables you to use a single key for all of your plug-ins and software options.

The iLok is a USB smart key that contains licenses for your protected software products. Pro Tools 12 requires either a second- or third-generation iLok key (see Figure 2.4). A single iLok key will store hundreds of separate licenses from multiple software vendors. This design enables you to carry your software licenses with you wherever you go in a portable key. Details on iLok accounts and keys are available at www.ilok.com.

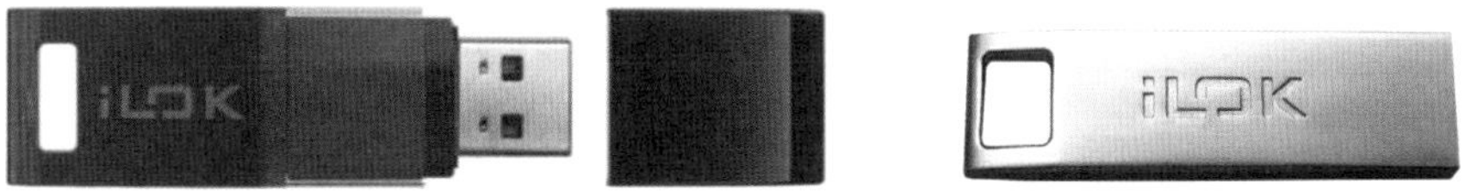

Figure 2.4 The PACE iLok key (second generation, left; third-generation, right)

Pro Tools software requires that an authorized iLok key remain present in an available USB port on your computer whenever it is running. New users will need to create an iLok account, activate the authorization in their account, and transfer the authorization to their iLok key before running Pro Tools for the first time.

Pro Tools | First software can be authorized to a specific computer and run without requiring an iLok key.

Launching Pro Tools

Pro Tools software can be launched by double-clicking on the application icon on the system's internal drive (see Figure 2.5) or by double-clicking on a shortcut to the application. In Windows systems, the Pro Tools 12 application is typically installed under C:\Program Files\Avid\Pro Tools\ProTools.exe, and a shortcut is placed on the desktop. On the Mac, Pro Tools 12 is typically placed under Applications\Pro Tools.app.

Figure 2.5 The Pro Tools application icon

On Windows systems, Pro Tools may also be available from the Start menu at the lower-left corner of the display.

Mac users might want to create a shortcut to the Pro Tools application on the Dock. To do this, simply drag the application icon onto the Dock.

When you launch Pro Tools, the application starts with no session open. From this point, you can change settings that affect the application's overall performance, depending on your needs. (Note that you will have to dismiss the Dashboard dialog box first, if not creating a session; see the "Dashboard" section in Lesson 4.)

Accessing Connected Audio Devices

When Pro Tools launches, it will generally be configured to use the currently connected audio interface or other available audio input or output device. If no supported audio interface is found, Pro Tools will launch using the built-in audio capabilities of your computer, meaning it will play back through the built-in speakers on your computer (if available) and record through the built-in microphone(s) (if available).

If your supported audio interface is connected but not recognized by Pro Tools, you may need to install or update the device drivers. Check the manufacturer's website for the latest drivers for your interface.

To configure Pro Tools to use a different audio device, such as a connected USB microphone or a separate audio interface, you will need to change the Playback Engine setting, by choosing Setup > Playback Engine.

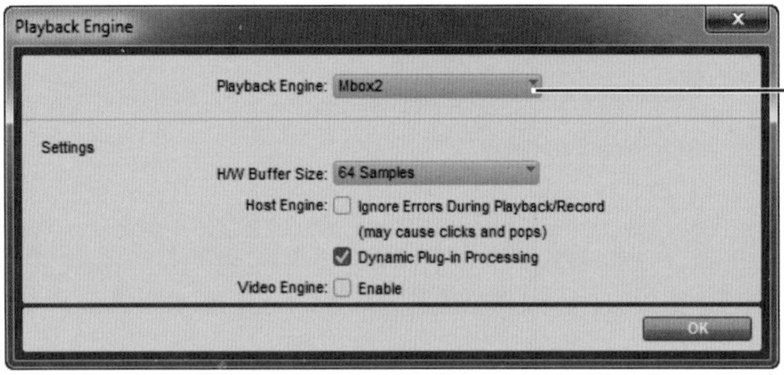

Figure 2.6 Pro Tools Playback Engine dialog box

Optimizing Host-Based Pro Tools Performance

The Playback Engine dialog box is also used to optimize the performance of standard Pro Tools software. Native Pro Tools systems utilize the computer's processing capacity (called *host-based processing*) to carry out operations such as recording, playback, mixing, and Native plug-in processing (effects and virtual instruments).

Systems with Pro Tools|HDX cards use dedicated DSP chips for accelerated audio processing; however, they can also use host-based processing for Native plug-ins.

While the default system settings are adequate for most processing tasks, Pro Tools lets you adjust a system's performance using the H/W Buffer Size and the Dynamic Plug-In Processing settings in the Playback Engine dialog box, both of which affect host-based processing tasks.

Hardware Buffer Size

The Avid Audio Engine splits plug-in processing into two domains: a low-latency domain that operates at a user-selected hardware buffer size, and a high-latency domain that operates at a fixed, high buffer size.

The H/W Buffer Size setting in the Playback Engine dialog box controls the size of the low-latency buffer. This buffer handles host-based tasks, such as Native plug-in processing, during recording or live input monitoring.

- Lower Hardware Buffer Size settings reduce monitoring latency when you are recording or monitoring live input.
- Higher Hardware Buffer Size settings provide more processing power for tracks that are recording or monitoring live input, at the cost of higher monitoring latency.

The H/W Buffer Size setting does not affect DSP processing on hardware-accelerated systems. DSP processing is available on systems with Pro Tools | HDX cards.

As a general rule, the Hardware Buffer Size should be set as low as your session will allow, in order to minimize latency when recording. Once you find the optimal setting, you can generally leave it as is, since Pro Tools 12 will automatically use the high-buffer domain for mix tracks.

Dynamic Plug-In Processing

The Dynamic Plug-In Processing option in the Playback Engine dialog box maximizes plug-in counts by dynamically reallocating host-based processing resources as needed during playback and recording.

Dynamic Plug-In Processing allows the Avid Audio Engine to take plug-ins offline under certain conditions, thereby reducing the system's overall CPU usage.

As a general rule, the Dynamic Plug-In Processing option should be enabled to ensure optimal performance.

Modifying Host-Based Processing Settings

Adjustments to the H/W Buffer Size and Dynamic Plug-In Processing settings can be made in the Playback Engine dialog box, as follows:

1. Choose SETUP > PLAYBACK ENGINE.
2. From the H/W Buffer Size pop-up menu, select the audio buffer size in samples—lower the setting to reduce latency; raise it to increase processing power for plug-ins.
3. Next to Host Engine, enable the checkbox for DYNAMIC PLUG-IN PROCESSING.
4. Click OK.

The Pro Tools Menu Structure

Before beginning to work on a session, you should have some basic familiarity with the Pro Tools software interface, including the menu structure and main windows.

Among the first things you see upon launching Pro Tools is the menu system across the top of the screen. Learning how the menus are organized will save you a lot of time when you are trying to find a specific Pro Tools function. Following is a brief description of each menu.

File Menu

File menu commands let you create and maintain Pro Tools session files and perform other file-based commands. The File menu includes options for opening, creating, and saving sessions; bouncing tracks; and importing and exporting session components.

Edit Menu

Edit menu commands allow you to edit and manipulate the media in your current selection. The Edit menu includes options for copying and pasting; duplicating, repeating, and shifting selections; trimming, separating, and healing clips; and performing similar operations.

View Menu

View menu commands affect the display within Pro Tools windows, tracks, and clips. Most View menu commands show or hide parts of the main Pro Tools windows. Selecting a command will display a component part of a window, and deselecting the command will hide it.

Though commonly confused, the View menu and the Window menu serve distinctly different functions. Commands in the View menu affect *parts* of a window or change how the elements within a window are displayed. By contrast, commands in the Window menu show or hide *entire* windows or arrange the windows on the screen.

Track Menu

Track menu commands let you set up and maintain tracks in a Pro Tools session. The Track menu includes track-based operations, such as options for creating, duplicating, grouping, deleting, and modifying tracks.

Clip Menu

Clip menu commands allow you to work with Pro Tools *clips*. Clips are essentially "pointers" to available audio or MIDI files or file segments. The Clip menu includes options for arranging, grouping, looping, warping, and otherwise modifying clips.

In Pro Tools|HD software, certain Clip menu commands are also available for working with Video clips.

Clips were known as *regions* in Pro Tools 9 and earlier.

Event Menu

The Event menu contains commands for modifying the time and tempo settings of your Pro Tools session, for working with MIDI and audio events and operations, and for adjusting various properties of MIDI recordings.

AudioSuite Menu

The AudioSuite menu allows you to access all AudioSuite plug-ins currently installed with your software. AudioSuite plug-ins apply non-real-time, file-based processing to selections in Pro Tools. AudioSuite processing applies an effect permanently, replacing a selection with a newly rendered audio file.

Options Menu

The Options menu commands let you toggle several editing, recording, monitoring, playback, and display options on/off. From this menu, you can enable loop recording, turn on pre- and post-roll, engage Dynamic Transport mode, set scrolling options, and make other similar choices.

The Options menu displays independent functions that toggle on or off. Menu items with a check mark next to them are currently on, or enabled; items without a check mark are off, or disabled. Selecting an item toggles its state on/off.

Setup Menu

The Setup menu lets you configure various Pro Tools hardware and software parameters using dialog boxes. It includes options for configuring your peripheral devices, such as audio interfaces; configuring host-based processing options; setting disk allocations; mapping I/O settings; configuring session and MIDI settings; configuring Click/Countoff behavior; and modifying your Pro Tools preferences.

All items under the Setup menu display a dialog box when selected. The choices in the Setup menu allow you to configure functions or operations that involve multiple settings.

Window Menu

Window menu commands allow you to display various Pro Tools windows. The Window menu includes commands for displaying the Edit, Mix, and Transport windows; Workspace browser windows; and the Automation window, Memory Locations window, Video window, Undo History window, and others.

Marketplace Menu

The Marketplace menu provides easy access to your Avid account, the Avid Support Center, and the plug-in marketplace, where you can rent or purchase plug-ins using an in-application web browser. Plug-ins acquired through the Marketplace are installed silently and are available for use without having to restart Pro Tools.

Help Menu

The Help menu provides links to important documentation and online resources, including the Pro Tools online help system, the Pro Tools Knowledge Base, Avid Audio Forums, the Pro Tools Reference Guide, and more.

Main Pro Tools Windows

Pro Tools software provides a host of windows you can use to perform a variety of tasks and functions. The three primary windows that you will need to be familiar with to begin working with Pro Tools are the Edit window, the Mix window, and the Transport window. Pro Tools also includes two additional window types for MIDI operations: the MIDI Editor window and the Score Editor window.

Edit Window

The Edit window provides a timeline display of audio, MIDI data, video, and mixer automation for recording, editing, and arranging tracks. It displays waveforms for the audio in your session and is the main window that you will use to work directly with audio, MIDI, and video files in Pro Tools. Each Audio, MIDI, and Instrument track in the Edit window has standard controls, such as Record Enable, Solo, and Mute buttons.

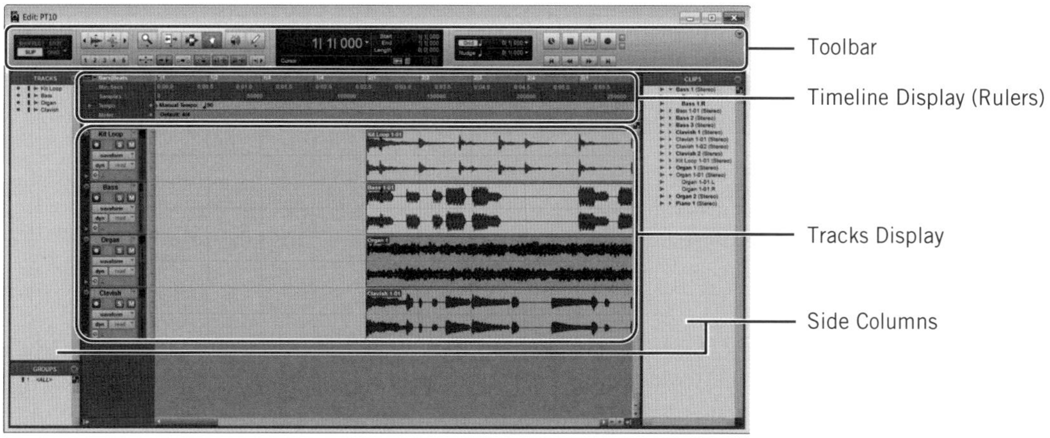

Figure 2.7 Pro Tools Edit window

Edit Window Toolbar

Pro Tools provides a variety of functions in the toolbar area at the top of the Edit window, including Edit Mode buttons, Edit tools, the Main Counter, and various optional displays.

Edit Mode Buttons. The buttons on the left side the toolbar area activate each of Pro Tools' four Edit modes. The Edit modes (Shuffle, Spot, Slip, and Grid) affect the movement and placement of audio and MIDI clips. The Edit modes also affect how commands such as Copy and Paste function and how certain Edit tools work. Additional information on Edit modes can be found in the "Edit Modes" section in Lesson 3.

Figure 2.8 Edit mode buttons, with Slip mode active

Edit Tools. The Edit tools are used to select, move, trim, and otherwise modify clips in Pro Tools. The functionality of each Edit tool is described in the "Edit Tool Functions" section in Lesson 3.

Figure 2.9 Edit tools, with the Selector tool active

Main Counter. The Main Counter is displayed to the right of the Edit tools and provides a numeric display of your current Timeline position.

Figure 2.10 Main Counter display, indicating a Timeline position at Bar 1, Beat 1

Timeline Display (Rulers)

Rulers are horizontal strips that appear in the Timeline display area of the Edit window, just above the tracks display area. Pro Tools' Rulers provide measurement indicators to help you identify specific locations in your session's Timeline. You can display or hide any of the following Rulers in the Edit window:

- **Bars|Beats.** This Ruler is useful for music editors, composers, and musicians.
- **Min:Sec.** This Ruler is useful for radio or for those who need to measure in absolute time.
- **Timecode and Timecode 2.** These Rulers are used primarily for video and film post-production.
- **Tempo.** This Ruler allows you to specify changes in tempo within the session.
- **Meter.** This Ruler allows you to specify changes in meter within the session.
- **Markers.** This Ruler allows you to create markers to identify and recall important Timeline locations.

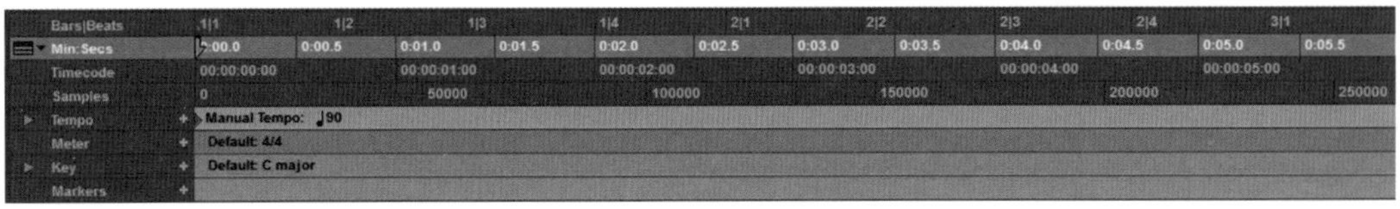

Figure 2.11 Pro Tools Ruler displays

Additional information on Rulers is provided in the "Time Scales and Rulers" section in Lesson 3.

Edit Window Side Columns

The Edit window includes columns on the left and right sides that provide additional view and display options for your session data. Along the left side is a vertical column that contains the Track List and Group List. Along the right side is a separate vertical column that contains the Clip List.

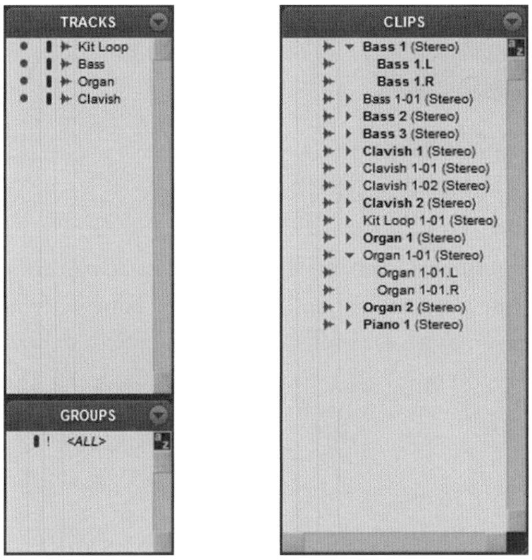

Figure 2.12 Pro Tools Edit window columns: Track List and Group List (left) and Clip List (right)

The Track List is at the top of the left column and shows a list of all the tracks in your session. Directly beneath the Track List is the Group List, where track groups are displayed. (Track groups are covered in the Pro Tools 110 course.)

The Clip List (right side column) shows a list of all the audio and MIDI files and file segments (clips) that are currently available in the session. On systems running Pro Tools HD software, the Clip List will also display Video files and clips.

Configuring the Edit Window

Pro Tools lets you customize the display of the Edit window to accommodate your needs at any given point in your project.

Customizing the Toolbar. You can customize the Edit window toolbar using the pop-up menu in the upper-right corner of the window. This menu lets you show or hide various controls and displays in the toolbar.

To show or hide a control or display, click on the Edit Window Toolbar pop-up menu (or right-click on the toolbar background) and select or deselect an item from the menu.

Figure 2.13 Using the Edit Window Toolbar pop-up menu to show or hide parts of the window

The display elements available under the Edit Window Toolbar menu include the following:

- **Zoom controls.** When selected, the Zoom controls are displayed in the Edit window toolbar.
- **Transport.** When selected, the Transport controls are displayed in the Edit window toolbar.
- **MIDI controls.** When selected, the MIDI controls are displayed in the Edit window toolbar.

Figure 2.14 Available toolbar options: Zoom controls (left), Transport controls (middle), and MIDI controls (right)

You can also move toolbar controls and arrange them according to your preferences. To move a set of controls, COMMAND-CLICK (Mac) or CTRL-CLICK (Windows) on a non-active part of the toolbar near the controls you wish to move and drag the set to a new area of the toolbar. For example, if you prefer the Zoom controls to be located to the right of the Edit tools in the toolbar, simply drag them to that location while holding the appropriate modifier.

Figure 2.15 Moving controls in the Edit window toolbar: before (left) and after (right)

Customizing the Side Columns. You can show and hide the left and right side columns independently or adjust their display widths and heights as needed. Customizing the side columns lets you control the amount of horizontal area that is available for your track display in the Edit window.

To show or hide either the left or right side column, do one of the following:

- Click the arrow icon located in the bottom corner by the column you want to show or hide. The column will slide into or out of view. Clicking the arrow icon again will return to the previous view.

  Or

- Double-click with the mouse positioned over the column separator (where the cursor changes to a double-headed arrow). The column will slide into or out of view.

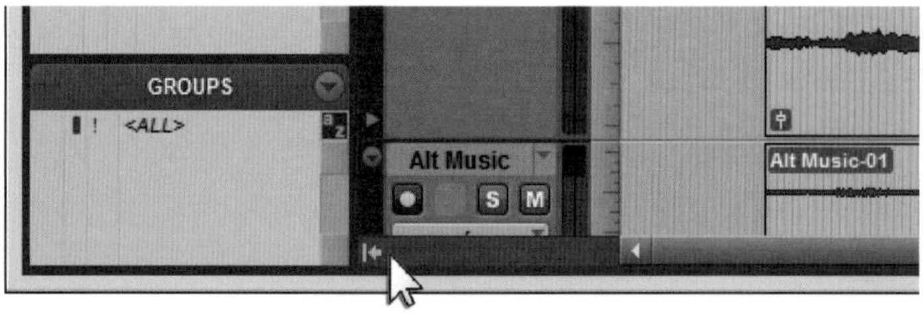

Figure 2.16 Clicking the arrow icon in the bottom corner of the Edit window to hide the left side column

To adjust column width or height, follow these steps:

1. Position the mouse over the column separator where the cursor changes into a double-headed arrow.
2. Click and drag on the column separator to adjust its position as needed.

Figure 2.17 Dragging the column separator (double-headed arrow cursor) to adjust the width of the left side column

Mix Window

The Mix window provides a mixer-like environment for working with tracks. (See Figure 2.18.) In the Mix window, tracks appear as mixer strips (also called *channel strips*). Each track displayed in the Mix window has controls for inserts, sends, input and output assignments, Automation mode selection, panning, and volume. The channel strips also provide buttons for enabling record and toggling solo and mute on and off.

Figure 2.18 Pro Tools Mix window

Signal Routing Controls

The top portion of each channel strip in the Mix window provides controls for routing signals for the track. (See Figure 2.19.) These controls include Insert selectors, Send selectors, Input selectors, and Output selectors. Insert selectors can be used to add real-time effects processing to a track using plug-ins. Send selectors can be used to route a track's signal to an available bus path or output path. The Input and Output selectors are used to route input and output signals from your audio interface for recording or playback.

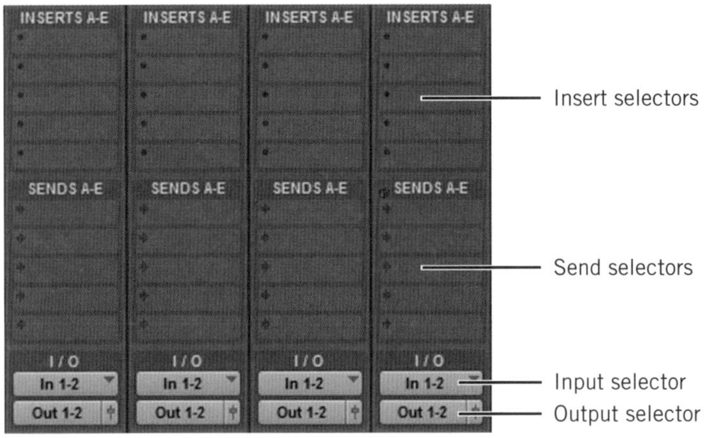

Figure 2.19 Signal routing controls

Record and Playback Controls

Immediately beneath the signal routing controls in the Mix window is a series of controls that are used to set record and playback options. (See Figure 2.20.) These include Pan controls; the TrackInput, Record Enable, Solo, and Mute buttons; and the Volume Fader for each track.

The Pan controls can be used to position the output of a track within a stereo field. The TrackInput, Record Enable, Solo, and Mute buttons can be used to activate and deactivate the respective functions for a track during record and playback. The Volume Fader can be used to adjust the playback/monitoring level of a track.

The Volume Fader in the Mix window does not affect the input gain (record level) of a signal being recorded. The signal level must be set appropriately at the source or adjusted using a preamp or gain-equipped audio interface.

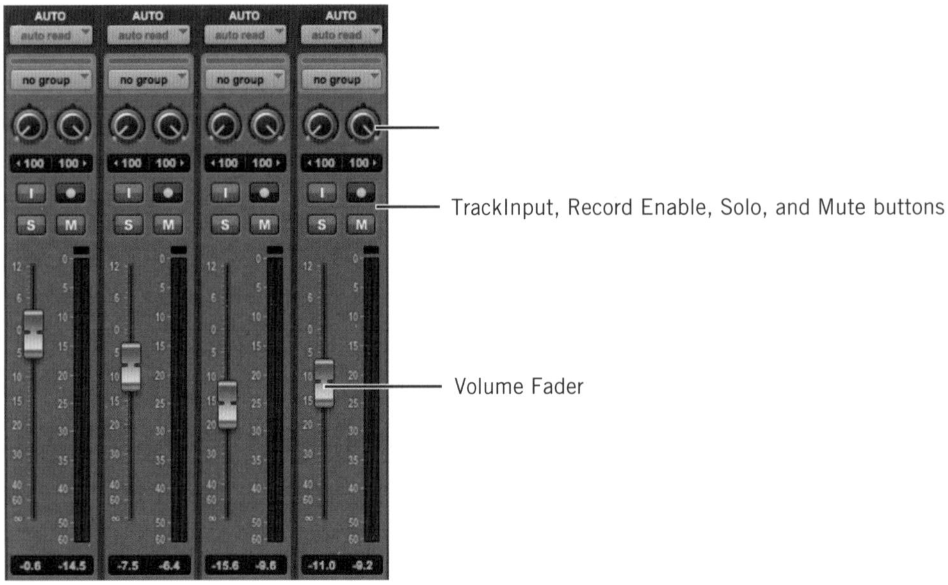

Figure 2.20 Record and playback controls

Mix Window Side Column

The Mix window includes a single column located on the left side that contains the Track List and Group List. (See Figure 2.21.) The Track List is at the top of the column and is used to display and sort tracks. Directly beneath the Track List is the Group List, where the track grouping status is displayed. (Track grouping is covered in the Pro Tools 110 course.)

As with the Edit window side columns, Pro Tools lets you customize the display of the Mix window side column as needed. You can show and hide the side column, adjust the display width, and adjust the relative height of the lists in the same manner as the columns in the Edit window.

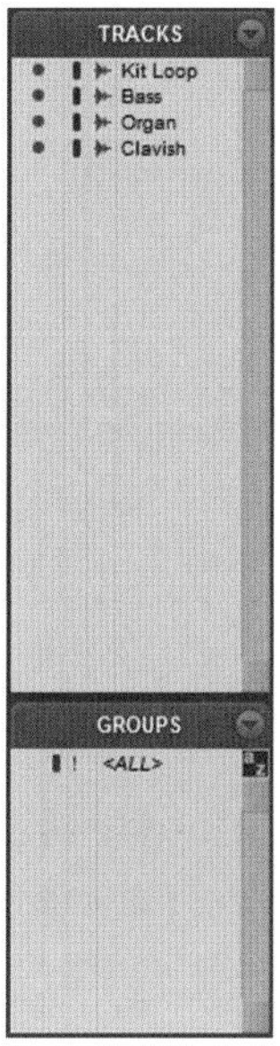

Figure 2.21 Pro Tools Mix window side column

Transport Window

The Transport window provides buttons for various transport functions, similar to the controls on a CD or DVD player. (The Transport controls can optionally be displayed in the Edit window toolbar as well.) The Transport window can also display counters (Location Indicators) and MIDI controls. The Location Indicators in the Transport window mirror the Main and Sub Counters at the top of the Edit window in normal operation.

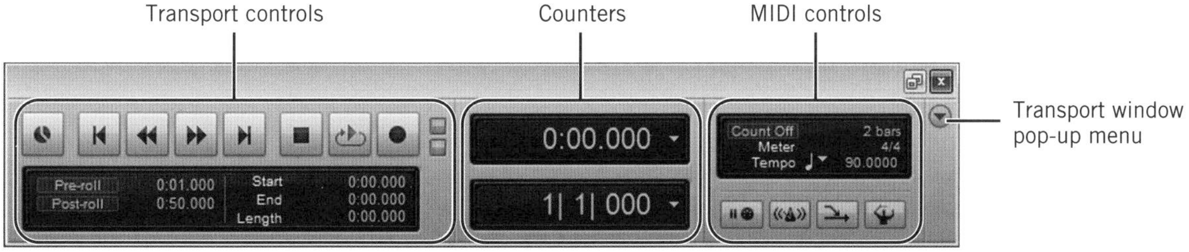

Figure 2.22 The Transport window, showing Transport controls, counters, and MIDI controls in Expanded Transport display

Controls and display elements in the Transport window can be shown/hidden using options under the main View > Transport menu or the Transport window pop-up menu.

Counters

Enabling the counters in the Transport window will display the Location Indicators to the right of the Transport controls. The counters provide information for navigating and editing via a Main Location Indicator and a Sub Location Indicator. The Main and Sub Location Indicators can be set for different Time Scale formats (such as Samples, Bars|Beats, or Minutes:Seconds).

The Main Location Indicator in the Transport window provides a convenient way to navigate to a specific time location. To navigate with the Main Location Indicator, follow these steps:

1. Click in the **MAIN LOCATION INDICATOR**.
2. Type in a location.
3. Press **ENTER** (Windows) or **RETURN** (Mac). The Timeline insertion point will automatically move to the new location.

MIDI Controls

The Transport window includes a MIDI controls section, providing options for playing back your session and recording MIDI data. The MIDI controls let you set options for triggering MIDI recording, playing metronome clicks, overdubbing MIDI, using a tempo map, and setting the tempo and meter. The functions of the MIDI controls are described in more detail in the "MIDI Control Features" section in Lesson 3.

Additional Editor Windows

Although the primary Edit window works well for general editing operations, Pro Tools provides two additional types of editor windows focused on specific editing and presentation tasks for MIDI data. These are the MIDI Editor window and the Score Editor window.

MIDI Editor Windows

Pro Tools provides MIDI Editor windows for detailed MIDI composition and editing tasks. MIDI Editor windows can show MIDI data and automation data for Auxiliary Input, Instrument, and MIDI tracks. You can open several separate MIDI Editor windows simultaneously, each providing a different view of the MIDI data in your Pro Tools session. You can also display a "docked" MIDI Editor window (also known as the *MIDI Editor view*) at the bottom of the primary Edit window.

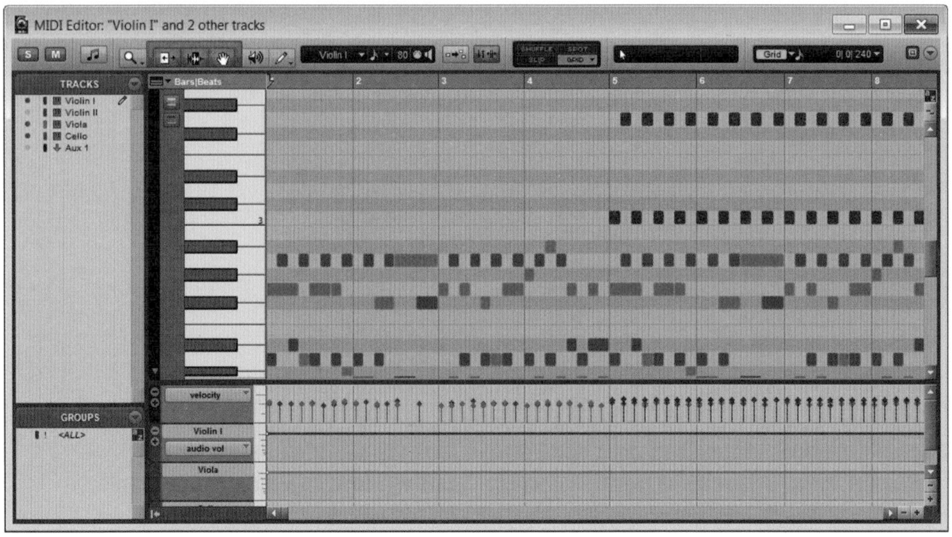

Figure 2.23 A MIDI Editor window

MIDI Editor windows let you edit MIDI data for one or more MIDI and/or Instrument tracks. When displaying multiple tracks, the MIDI Editor window superimposes the notes from each of the tracks in the MIDI Notes pane. The MIDI Editor window can also display automation and controller lanes for velocity stalks, volume automation playlists, and other continuous controller and automation data.

Score Editor Window

The Score Editor window lets you view, edit, arrange, and print MIDI data from your session as music notation. The Score Editor transcribes MIDI notes in real time and provides tools for navigating and editing in Notation view. It also provides Notation Display Track settings to specify how individual MIDI and Instrument tracks appear in the Score Editor. You can set the page layout and staff spacing and specify the title and composer for the score using the Score Setup window.

Figure 2.24 Score Editor window

Review/Discussion Questions

1. Name some of the folders and files that Pro Tools creates as part of the session hierarchy. Where is the session file (.ptx) stored? (See "Session Components" beginning on page 24.)

2. What is the WaveCache.wfm file used for? What happens if the WaveCache file gets deleted or goes missing? (See "WaveCache File" beginning on page 25.)

3. Where are audio files stored in the session hierarchy? (See "Audio Files" beginning on page 25.)

4. Where are Pro Tools' MIDI files normally stored? (See "MIDI Files" beginning on page 25.)

5. Which component should you turn on first when powering up a Pro Tools system? Which component should you turn on last? (See "Powering Up Your Hardware" beginning on page 26.)

6. What type of processing does the Hardware Buffer Size affect? What type of processing does it *not* affect? (See "Hardware Buffer Size" beginning on page 28.)

7. What kinds of commands can be found under the Pro Tools View menu? How does the View menu differ from the Window menu? (See "The Pro Tools Menu Structure" beginning on page 29.)

8. What kinds of commands can be found under the Pro Tools Options menu? How does the Options menu differ from the Setup menu? (See "The Pro Tools Menu Structure" beginning on page 29.)

9. Which main Pro Tools window displays audio waveforms and can be used to work directly with audio, MIDI, and video files on tracks? (See "Main Pro Tools Windows" beginning on page 31.)

10. Which Pro Tools window provides access to Pan controls and Volume Faders for each track? (See "Main Pro Tools Windows" beginning on page 31.)

To review additional material from this chapter, see the PT101 Study Guide module available through the ElementsIED online learning platform at ElementsED.com.

EXERCISE 2

Pro Tools Main Windows

In this exercise worksheet, you will identify the main windows in Pro Tools and their component parts. The information referenced in these questions is covered in Lesson 2.

Duration: 10 Minutes **Media: None Required**

Refer to Figures 2.25 through 2.27 when answering the questions below. Refer to the section on "The Pro Tools Software Interface" in Lesson 2 for assistance.

Questions 1 through 5 refer to Figure 2.25.

1. The window shown in Figure 2.25 is called the ______________________________ window.

2. The area labeled **A** across the top of the window is called the ___________________________________.

3. The areas labeled **B** on the sides of the window are called ____.

4. The buttons labeled **C** at the top of the window are called __________________________________.

5. The controls labeled **D** on the top-right side of the window are called ______________________________ controls.

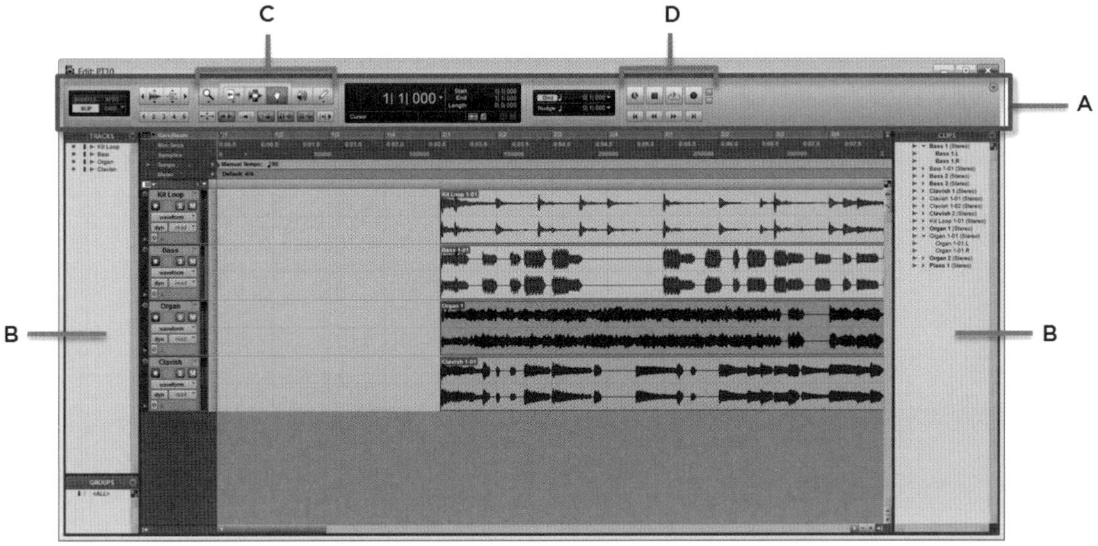

Figure 2.25 The Pro Tools window that displays audio clips

Questions 6 through 11 refer to Figure 2.26.

6. The window shown in Figure 2.26 is called the ______________________ window.

7. The signal routing controls labeled **A** at the top of the window are called ______________________.

8. The signal routing controls labeled **B** at the top of the window are called ______________________.

9. The signal routing controls labeled **C** and **D** in the I/O section are called the

   ______________________ selector and the ______________________ selector, respectively.

10. The control labeled **E** in the middle of the window is called the ______________________ selector.

11. The slider labeled **F** toward the bottom of the window is called the ______________________.

Figure 2.26 The Pro Tools window that displays channel strips

Questions 12 through 15 refer to Figure 2.27.

12. The window shown in Figure 2.27 is called the ______________________________ window.

13. The controls labeled **A** on the left side of the window are called ______________________________ controls.

14. The controls labeled **B** in the middle of the window are called ______________________________.

15. The controls labeled **C** on the right side of the window are called ______________________________ controls.

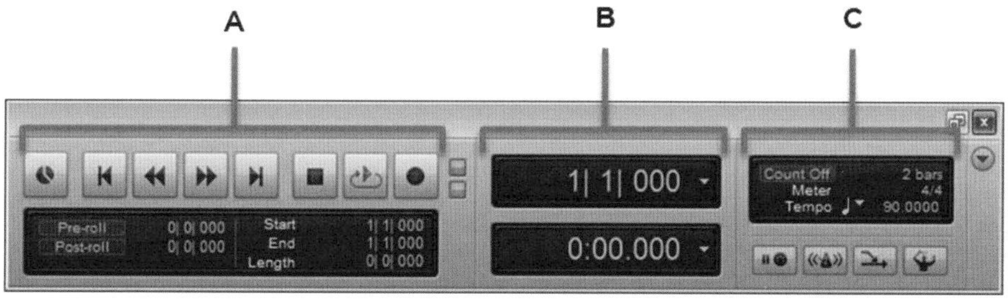

Figure 2.27 The Pro Tools window that displays playback controls

LESSON 3

Pro Tools Basic Controls

This lesson provides an overview of Pro Tools' Edit tools, Edit modes, and MIDI controls. It also discusses the Time Scales available in Pro Tools, how to set the Main and Sub Time Scales, and how to work with Rulers.

Duration: 60 Minutes

GOALS

- **Recognize the Edit tools and their functions**
- **Recognize Pro Tools' Edit modes and understand their differences**
- **Recognize displayed Time Scales and Timebase Rulers**
- **Recognize the available MIDI controls**

Key topics from this lesson are included in the *Pro Tools 12 Essential Training: 101* course on Lynda.com.

This lesson provides an overview of the controls available in the Pro Tools Edit window and Transport window. These primary controls are used day-in and day-out in Pro Tools for recording, playback, and basic editing of audio and MIDI material. Establishing some familiarity with the available tools, operational modes, and transport functions early on will help you in all aspects of the work you do in Pro Tools.

Edit Tool Functions

The Edit tools are located in a cluster on the left side of the toolbar area at the top of the Edit window. These tools provide access to various audio and MIDI editing functions, as well as basic functionality for positioning the playback or record location in a session.

From left-to-right, the Edit tools include the Zoomer tool, the Trim tool, the Selector tool, the Grabber tool, the Scrubber tool, and the Pencil tool.

Figure 3.1 Edit tool cluster in the Edit window toolbar (Selector tool active)

Zoomer Tool

You can use the Zoomer tool to zoom into and out of a particular area within a track. Zooming in is often helpful when you need to examine a clip or waveform closely.

Figure 3.2 Zoomer tool

To use the Zoomer tool, select it and click on the desired point within a track where you want to zoom in. Each click zooms all tracks in by one level, with the Edit window centered on the zoom point.

To zoom in on a particular area in the Edit window, click and drag with the Zoomer tool over the area you want to view. As you drag, a gray box will appear, indicating the range on which you will be zooming in. Release the mouse to fill the track display with the selected portion of the waveform.

> **You can also use the Zoomer tool for Marquee Zooming, allowing you to zoom in on a waveform both horizontally and vertically. To use Marquee Zooming, COMMAND-DRAG (Mac) or CTRL-DRAG (Windows) over a portion of a waveform with the Zoomer tool.**

To zoom out, hold OPTION (Mac) or ALT (Windows) while clicking with the ZOOMER tool.

> ### Reverse an Operation with the Option/Alt Key
>
> The Option/Alt modifier (Mac/Windows, respectively) provides several standard functions in Pro Tools. Among these is the Reverse Operation function. The Option/Alt modifier works with specific keyboard and Edit tool actions, causing Pro Tools to perform the reverse or opposite action. Try using this key with the Trim tool to reverse the trim direction or with the Pencil tool when editing MIDI to access the eraser.

Double-click on the ZOOMER tool to get a full track view that fills the Edit window with the longest visible track in the session.

Trim Tool

You can use the Trim tool to trim excess audio, MIDI, or video content from the beginning or end of a continuous section of program material, or *clip*. The Trim tool modifies clips nondestructively, leaving the underlying source file unchanged. This tool allows you to quickly crop a clip or adjust a clip's boundaries to hide or expose underlying material.

The first time you trim a clip, Pro Tools automatically adds a new item to the Clip List corresponding to the newly created subset clip. The subset clip is given a new name to differentiate it from the original.

Figure 3.3 Standard Trim tool

The Trim tool button also provides access to the Time Compression/Expansion (TCE) Trim tool, the Loop Trim tool, and the Scrub Trim tool (Pro Tools HD software only).

Alternate Trim tools, such as TCE Trim, Loop Trim, and Scrub Trim are covered in higher-level Pro Tools courses.

Selector Tool

The Selector tool is one of the most commonly used functions in Pro Tools. You can use the Selector tool to position the playback cursor or to select an area in a track for playback or editing.

To position the playback cursor, click with the **SELECTOR** tool at the point where you want playback to begin. To select an area for playback or editing, drag with the **SELECTOR** tool across any area on one or more tracks.

Figure 3.4 Selector tool

The Selector tool selects both horizontally and vertically, allowing you to create selections across multiple tracks in a single operation. Selected areas are represented with a dark highlight in the Edit window. The selection range is also indicated by a dark overlay in the Timeline display area (Rulers) at the top of the window. (See Figure 3.5.)

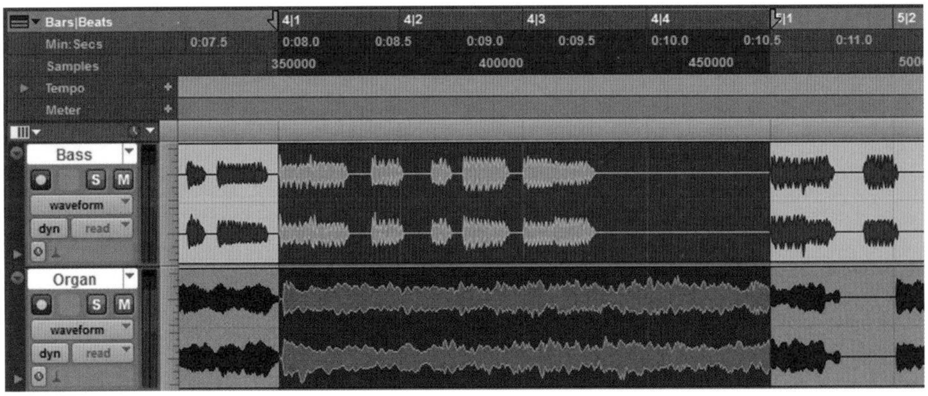

Figure 3.5 Selection across multiple tracks

You can use the Selector tool with the Shift key to quickly make a lengthy selection, as follows:

1. Click with the **SELECTOR** tool to position the playback cursor where you want the selection to start.
2. Scroll to the desired endpoint using the scroll bar at the bottom of the Edit window.
3. Shift-click at the desired endpoint to complete the selection.

Grabber Tool

The Grabber tool is commonly used for arranging clips. You can use the Grabber tool to select an entire clip with a single mouse click. You can also use the Grabber to move a clip along the Timeline, within its current track, and to move clips between tracks.

Figure 3.6 Grabber tool button

To select a clip, click anywhere on the clip in the Edit window using the **GRABBER** tool. To move a clip along the Timeline, click anywhere on the clip and drag to the left or right with the **GRABBER** tool. Dragging a clip vertically with the Grabber tool will move the clip to another track in your session.

The Grabber tool can be used to position clips in a variety of ways, depending on the Edit mode that is currently selected. An overview of the Edit modes is provided in the "Edit Modes" section later in this lesson.

The Grabber tool button also provides access to the Separation Grabber and Object Grabber tools.

Alternate Grabber tools are covered in the Pro Tools 201 course.

Scrubber Tool

The Scrubber tool can be used to "scrub" slowly across Audio tracks in the Edit window to find a particular moment or audio event. (See Figure 3.7.) Scrubbing originated in tape editing as a process of rocking the tape back and forth past the playhead to locate a precise position (usually for the sake of performing a splice). By scrubbing back and forth over an audio waveform in Pro Tools, you can listen closely and zero in on an exact edit point.

Figure 3.7 Scrubber tool

To scrub audio or MIDI in Pro Tools, click on a track in the Edit window with the SCRUBBER tool and drag left or right to begin playback in either direction. Playback results vary with zoom magnification. You'll find scrubbing to be smoother and more precise when you zoom in first to increase the magnification of the track material.

Dragging the Scrubber tool between two adjacent mono or stereo Audio tracks allows you to scrub two tracks simultaneously.

Pencil Tool

The Pencil tool is commonly used for creating and editing MIDI data. The Pencil can be used to add or draw notes of different pitches and varying durations. Different Pencil tool shapes (Freehand, Line, Triangle, Square, and Random) can also be used to edit note velocities.

Figure 3.8 Pencil tool

The Pencil tool is also particularly useful for drawing and editing different types of automation or MIDI control data—common examples include using Line for volume, Triangle for pan, or Freehand for pitch bend.

Smart Tool

The Smart Tool can be enabled to provide instant access to the Selector, Grabber, and Trim tools without switching tools. This tool is active when the Trim, Selector, and Grabber are all selected (highlighted in blue).

To activate the Smart Tool, click on the bridge area above and surrounding the Trim, Selector, and Grabber tools.

Figure 3.9 Smart Tool active in the Edit window

When the Smart Tool is active, the position of the cursor in relation to a clip or note determines how the tool functions. To use the Smart Tool as a Selector, position the tool over the middle of an audio clip, in the upper half. To use it as a Grabber, position it in the lower half. For the Trim tool, position the Smart Tool near the clip's start or end point.

The Smart Tool can also be used to create fade-ins, fade-outs, and crossfades.

The functions of the Smart Tool are covered in detail in the Pro Tools 110 course.

Edit Modes

Pro Tools has four primary Edit modes: Shuffle, Spot, Slip, and Grid. The active mode affects edit operations and clip movements on all of the tracks in your session.

The Edit mode is selected by clicking the corresponding Edit mode button on the left side of the toolbar area in the Edit window.

Figure 3.10 Edit mode buttons (Grid mode active)

You can also use function keys F1 (Shuffle), F2 (Slip), F3 (Spot), and F4 (Grid) to set the Edit mode.

The Edit mode impacts operations performed with the Selector tool, Trim tool, and Grabber tool. It also affects the results you'll get with any Edit operations that add or remove material on your tracks (audio clips, MIDI clips, and MIDI notes).

Shuffle Mode

In Shuffle mode, selections made with the Selector tool are unconstrained; however, clip movement (dragging a clip with the Grabber tool) is constrained by other clips. Additionally, any material you add or remove (with the Trim tool or an Edit menu command) will affect the placement of subsequent clips on the track.

Movements and edits made in Shuffle mode will cause timing changes for the media on affected tracks, so this mode should be used with caution when editing material that is synchronized to other tracks or aligned to a timing reference or tempo.

Moving and Placing Clips

When you move a clip in Shuffle mode, the clip will snap to the previous or next clip on the track. Clips cannot be overlapped in this mode; therefore, dragging a clip on top of another clip will cause the two clips to swap positions on the track. Any clips affected by a move operation will snap together, closing up any gap that previously existed between them.

Editing Clips

When you perform an edit (trim, cut/delete, duplicate, or paste material), all clips to the right of the edit will slide along the Timeline in train-car fashion to make space (when adding material) or to close a gap (when removing material).

You can use Shuffle mode as a way to make clips line up next to each other, without overlapping or leaving silence between them. This can be convenient when you need to shorten a line of dialog by removing a pause, cough, repeated word, or similar unwanted material.

Slip Mode

In Slip mode, you can move, trim, cut, or paste clips freely within a track without affecting the placement of other clips on the track. All selections, clip movements, and edit operations are unconstrained.

Moving and Placing Clips

In this mode, you can place a clip anywhere on a track, leaving space between it and other clips, if desired. It is also possible to move a clip so that it overlaps or completely covers another clip. In such cases, the underlying clip will be trimmed or obscured by the overlapping clip.

Editing Clips

Any edits you perform in Slip mode will not affect the timing of other clips on the track. Deleting a clip or partial clip will leave an empty gap (blank space) at the edit location. Pasted or duplicated material will overlap any other clips within the edit range.

You can use Slip mode when you want to select and edit media without any restrictions to your selections or to the clips' placement in time.

Spot Mode

In Spot mode, as in Slip mode, your selections are unconstrained and your edits do not affect the timing of other clips on the track. The difference is that Spot mode lets you move clips and trim clips using precise locations or durations specified in a dialog box. As in Slip mode, moving or editing a clip will not affect the placement of other clips on the track.

Moving and Placing Clips

When Spot mode is enabled, Pro Tools prompts you with a dialog box whenever you click on a clip with the Grabber tool. The Spot dialog box that displays allows you to specify the start, sync point, or end location for the selected clip. Clicking **OK** completes the move operation.

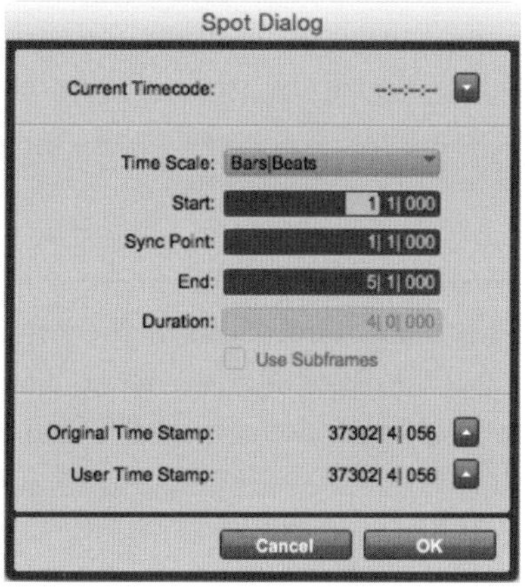

Figure 3.11 The Spot dialog box

Editing Clips

As in Slip mode, the edits you perform in Spot mode will not affect the timing of other clips on the track. Deleting a clip or partial clip will leave empty space at the edit location. Pasted or duplicated material will overlap any other clips within the edit range.

Clicking on a clip with the Trim tool will display the Spot dialog box, allowing you to specify the desired start or end location for the trimmed clip, or to specify the desired resulting clip duration. Clicking **OK** completes the trim operation.

You can use Spot mode when you want to control the placement or duration of a clip using precise numeric values or measurements.

Grid Mode

In Grid mode, selections, clip movements, and trim operations are constrained by the grid. Edit operations do not affect the timing of other clips on the track.

Moving and Placing Clips

Clips and MIDI notes that are moved in Grid mode will snap to the nearest time increment using the current Grid Value setting.

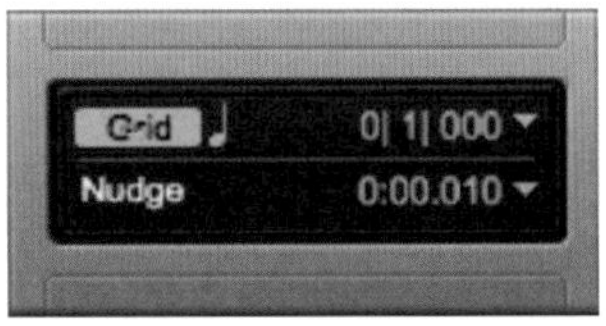

Figure 3.12 Grid Value setting in the Edit window toolbar (quarter note selected)

Clips can be placed anywhere on a track, so long as they start on a grid line. Clips can be positioned to overlap or cover other clips. As in Slip mode, any underlying clips will be trimmed or obscured by overlapping clips.

Editing Clips

As in Slip mode, editing in Grid mode will not affect the timing of other clips on the track. Deleting a clip or partial clip will leave empty space at the edit location. Pasted or duplicated material will overlap any other clips within the edit range.

Using the Trim tool on a clip will trim the start or end of the clip to the nearest grid line or increment.

You can use Grid mode for making precise edits and aligning clips and selections using precise time intervals based on the Grid Value. This is especially useful when using a Bars|Beats grid and editing musical material that is aligned to the session tempo.

Time Scales and Rulers

Every Pro Tools session uses a Main Time Scale and a Sub Time Scale. The Main Time Scale is the time format used for Transport functions; selection Start, End, and Length fields; and Grid and Nudge values. The Sub Time Scale provides additional timing reference and can optionally be displayed along with the Main Time Scale in the Counters areas of the Edit window and in the Transport window.

Figure 3.13 Counters area in the Edit window showing the Main Time Scale set to Bars|Beats

Pro Tools also provides Rulers to help you navigate along the Timeline. Rulers can be displayed for a variety of time formats, including those used for the Main Time Scale and Sub Time Scale. Rulers appear in the Timeline display area at the top of the Edit window. (See Figure 3.14.)

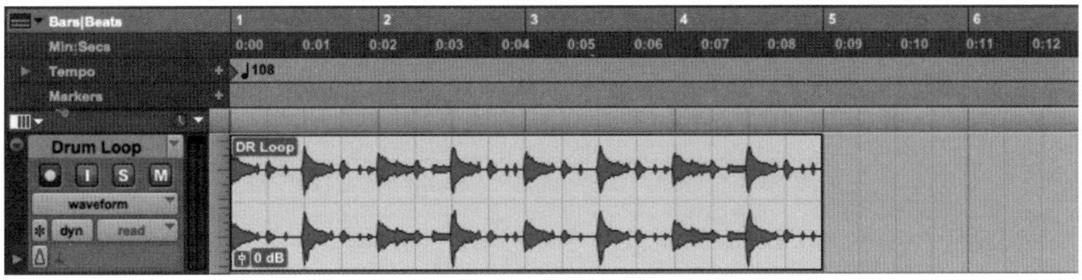

Figure 3.14 Rulers in the Timeline display area of the Edit window, above the Drum Loop track

Main Time Scale

When the Main Time Scale in a Pro Tools session is set to Min:Sec, Timeline locations are represented in minutes and seconds relative to the start point of the session. When set to Bars|Beats, Timeline locations are represented in bars, beats, and ticks relative to the start point of the session (Bar 1, Beat 1).

The Main Time Scale determines the timebase units used in Pro Tools' timing displays, including:

- The Main Counter in the Edit window
- The Main Location Indicator in the Transport window
- Selection Start, End, and Length values in either window

The Main Time Scale can be set to Bars|Beats, Minutes:Seconds, Timecode, Feet+Frames, or Samples. To set the Main Time Scale, do one of the following:

- Select the desired timebase by choosing **VIEW > MAIN COUNTER.**

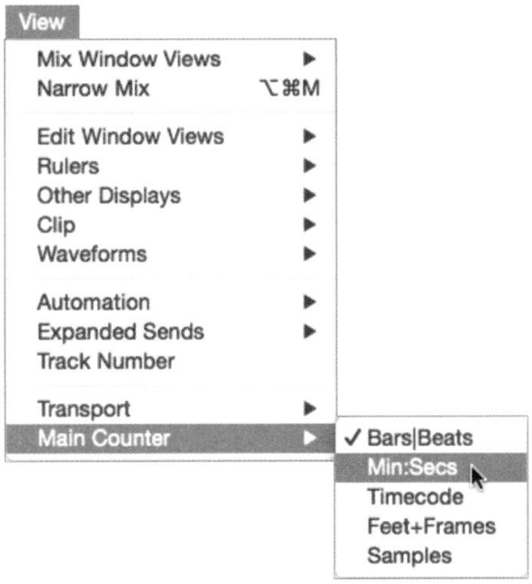

Figure 3.15 Setting the timebase from the View menu

- Select the desired timebase from the **MAIN TIME SCALE** pop-up menu (down arrow next to the Main Counter at the top of the Edit window). (See Figure 3.16.)

Figure 3.16 Setting the timebase from the Main Time Scale pop-up menu

- If a Ruler is displayed for the desired timebase, click on its name so it becomes highlighted.

Figure 3.17 Switching the Main Time Scale using Rulers

Sub Time Scale

The Sub Time Scale in a Pro Tools session is set to Samples by default, meaning that Timeline locations are represented as sample-based values, relative to the start point of the session. The Sub Time Scale provides a convenient secondary timing reference.

Like the Main Time Scale, the Sub Time Scale can be set to Bars|Beats, Min:Secs, Timecode, Feet+Frames, or Samples. To display the Sub Time Scale in the Edit menu, select **SHOW SUB COUNTER** from the bottom of the Main Time Scale pop-up menu (shown in Figure 3.16 above). To set the Sub Time Scale, select the desired timebase from the Sub Time Scale pop-up menu. (See Figure 3.18.)

Figure 3.18 Selecting a timebase from the Sub Time Scale pop-up menu

Ruler Display Options

Pro Tools provides two types of Rulers that can be displayed in the Edit window: *Timebase Rulers* and *Conductor Rulers*.

The Pro Tools Timebase Rulers measure time in various ways. The Timebase Rulers include the following:

- Bars|Beats
- Min:Secs

- Samples
- Timecode
- Timecode 2
- Feet+Frames

Timebase Rulers are commonly referred to as *Timelines* in the industry.

The Pro Tools Conductor Rulers contain events that map out locations, characteristics, and changes within a session. These include the following:

- Markers
- Tempo
- Meter
- Key
- Chords

Showing Rulers

You can customize your sessions to display any Timebase Rulers and/or Conductor Rulers that you want to work with.

To display a Ruler, do the following:

- Choose View > Rulers and select the desired Ruler from the submenu.

Selecting any unchecked Ruler from the Rulers submenu will cause that ruler to appear in the Timeline display area at the top of the Edit window

Hiding Rulers

To maximize your screen space for tracks, you can hide any Rulers that you do not need to use in a session.

To remove a Ruler from the display, do one of the following:

- Choose View > Rulers and click on a checked Ruler to deselect it.
- Option-click (Mac) or Alt-click (Windows) directly on the Ruler's name display in the Timeline display area.

Figure 3.19 Option-clicking/Alt-clicking on the Samples Ruler name display to hide the Ruler

Hide Views with the Option/Alt Key

A handy feature of the Option or Alt key (Mac or Windows, respectively) is the *Hide Views* function. By holding the Option/Alt key while clicking on the name display of a Ruler or Edit window column, you can cause Pro Tools to instantly hide that Ruler or column view.

The Ruler that corresponds to the session's Main Time Scale cannot be deselected/hidden. (The Main Time Scale Ruler is indicated by a highlight across the Ruler.)

Rearranging Rulers

You also have the option to change the display order of the Rulers, arranging them as needed to best fit your work style.

To change the display order for the Rulers, do the following:

- Click directly on the Ruler's name display and drag up or down to the desired location.

In the following example, the Min:Secs Ruler is moved below the Timecode Ruler:

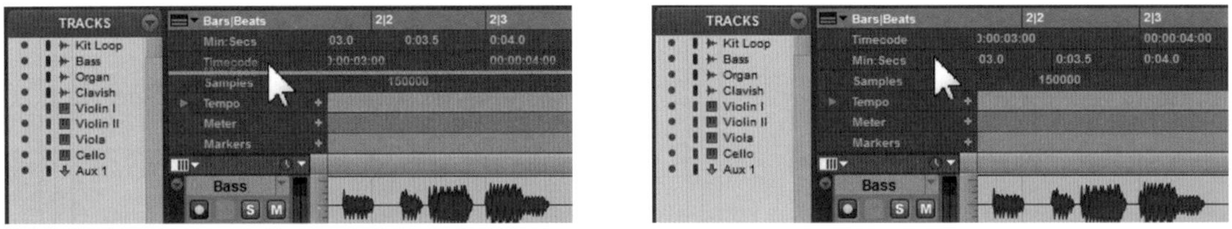

Figure 3.20 Rulers before and after moving the Min:Secs display

MIDI Control Features

The Edit and Transport windows provide access to various additional controls and options that affect playback and recording operations. These controls are grouped together in a cluster known as the MIDI Controls.

The available functions in the MIDI Controls section include Wait for Note, Metronome, MIDI Merge, Tempo Ruler Enable, Countoff, Meter, and Tempo.

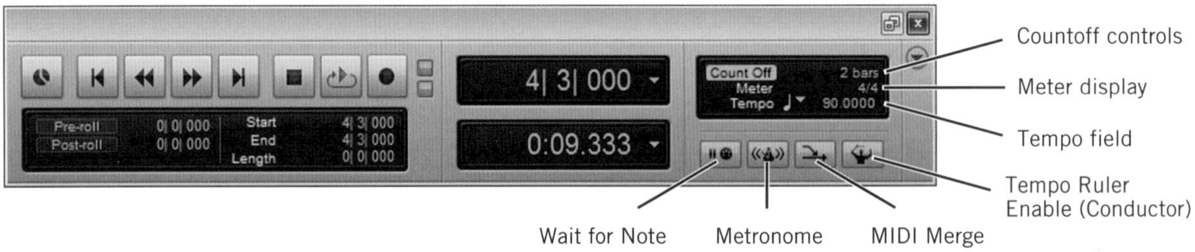

Figure 3.21 Functions in the MIDI Controls section of the Transport window

Wait for Note

This option is used primarily for MIDI recording workflows. When the Wait for Note button is engaged, recording does not begin until a MIDI event is received. This ensures that a MIDI record pass does not begin until you start to play and that the first MIDI event is recorded precisely at the beginning of the record range.

You can configure a setting in the Preferences dialog box (SETUP > PREFERENCES > MIDI) to use the F11 key to activate/deactivate Wait for Note.

Metronome

The Metronome button is used in conjunction with a click track and controls whether or not the click will be audible. When the Metronome button is selected, a metronome click will sound during playback and recording, as specified by the settings in the Click/Countoff Options dialog box (SETUP > CLICK/COUNTOFF). (Note that metronome playback requires a click track or other click source to be configured for your session.)

To modify the click settings, choose SETUP > CLICK/COUNTOFF or double-click the METRONOME button in the Transport window. Enter the desired settings in the Click/Countoff Options dialog box.

The Metronome button will have no effect if your session does not include a click track or other source to generate an audible click.

Details on creating a click track and configuring click settings are covered in Lesson 5.

Countoff Controls

The Countoff controls are used in combination with the click track and Metronome button. When the Count Off button is selected (highlighted) in the MIDI controls section, Pro Tools counts off a specified number of bars (measures) with a click before playback or recording begins. The number of bars used for Count Off is indicated in the Count Off field.

To change the Count Off settings, choose SETUP > CLICK/COUNTOFF or double-click the Count Off field in the Edit or Transport window. Enter the desired settings in the Countoff area of the Click/Countoff Options dialog box. (See Lesson 5 for details.)

MIDI Merge Mode

MIDI Merge mode is used for certain MIDI recording workflows. When the MIDI Merge button is active, the recorded MIDI performance will be merged with existing MIDI data on the track, overdubbing the track. When this button is not active (Replace mode), recorded MIDI data will replace existing track material.

To engage MIDI Merge mode, click on the MIDI Merge button in the Transport window so that it becomes highlighted in blue. Click a second time to return to Replace mode.

Tempo Ruler Enable

The Tempo Ruler Enable button is used to switch the session tempo between two states: Tempo Map mode and Manual Tempo mode. When this button is selected, Pro Tools uses the tempo map defined in the Tempo Ruler for the click tempo during playback and recording. When deselected, Pro Tools switches to Manual Tempo mode and ignores the tempo map.

In Manual Tempo mode, the tempo can be adjusted by typing a value directly into the Tempo field or clicking and dragging up or down on the Tempo field.

The session tempo also affects the spacing of the bars and beats on the Bars|Beats ruler and the display and playback speed of MIDI performances.

Meter Display

The Meter display indicates the session's current meter based on the play location. Double-click the Meter display to open the Meter Change dialog box.

The Meter determines how many beats are included in each measure on the Bars|Beats ruler. It also affects the playback of the click sound. (The click places emphasis on the first beat of every measure.)

Tempo Field

The Tempo field displays the session's current tempo based on the play location. In Manual Tempo mode (or when the session tempo has not yet been defined) you can enter a BPM value directly into this field. In addition, when the Tempo field is selected, you can tap in a tempo from a MIDI controller or from the computer keyboard using the **T** key.

Tool Tips

The Pro Tools user interface provides Tool Tips in all main windows to help you identify the various controls, tools, selectors, and functions in the software. When you hover the cursor over an unlabeled control or tool, or an abbreviated name or display, Pro Tools will display the full name of the control, function, or item.

Tool Tips settings can be changed under the Tool Tips Display options in the Preferences dialog box (**SETUP > PREFERENCES, DISPLAY** tab). Tool Tips settings provide two options: *Function* shows the basic function of the item, and *Details* shows the complete name of an abbreviated name or item.

Tool Tips can be set to display either or both of these options, or they can be turned off altogether.

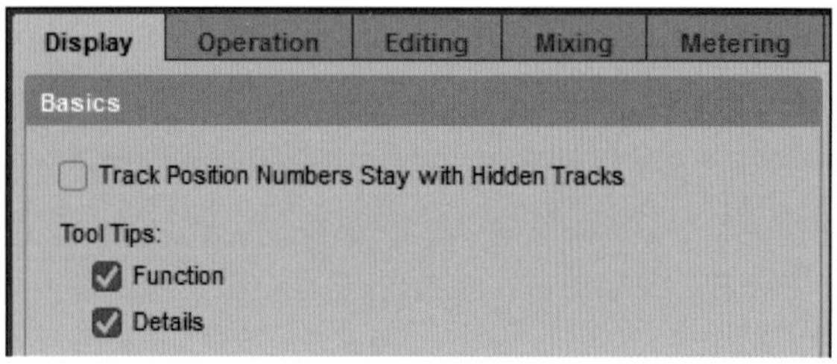

Figure 3.22 Basics section of the Display tab in Preferences, showing selected Tool Tips options

Review/Discussion Questions

1. What icon is used for the Zoomer tool in the Edit window? How can you use this tool to quickly zoom out to fill the Edit window with the longest track in the session? (See "Zoomer Tool" beginning on page 46.)

2. Which Edit tool is represented by a hand icon? What is this tool used for? (See "Grabber Tool" beginning on page 48.)

3. Which tool is active when the Trim, Selector, and Grabber icons are all selected (highlighted in blue) in the Edit window toolbar? (See "Smart Tool" beginning on page 49.)

4. What are the four Edit modes in Pro Tools? How can you switch between them? (See "Edit Modes" beginning on page 50.)

5. Why should you use caution when editing synchronized material in Shuffle mode? When is Shuffle mode useful? (See "Shuffle Mode" beginning on page 50.)

6. How does editing a clip in Slip mode affect the timing of other clips on the track? (See "Slip Mode" beginning on page 50.)

7. When is it helpful to work in Spot mode? When it is helpful to work in Grid mode? (See "Spot Mode" and "Grid Mode" beginning on page 51.)

8. What are some ways to set the Main Time Scale in Pro Tools? (See "Main Time Scale" beginning on page 53.)

9. What are the two types of Rulers available in Pro Tools? What is the difference between them? (See "Ruler Display Options" beginning on page 54.)

10. What are some ways to hide Rulers that you do not need displayed in a session? (See "Hiding Rulers" beginning on page 55.)

11. Which Pro Tools windows provide access to MIDI controls, such as Wait for Note, Metronome, and MIDI Merge? (See "MIDI Control Features" beginning on page 56.)

12. What is the purpose of the Metronome button in the MIDI Controls area? What kind of track must be added to a session for the Metronome button to work? (See "Metronome" beginning on page 57.)

13. What are the two states or modes available for controlling the current session tempo? How can you switch between these modes? (See "Tempo Ruler Enable" beginning on page 57.)

14. What is displayed by the Tempo field in the MIDI Controls area? What are some ways to set the session tempo using this field? (See "Tempo Field" beginning on page 58.)

To review additional material from this chapter, see the PT101 Study Guide module available through the ElementsIED online learning platform at ElementsED.com.

EXERCISE 3

Primary Tools and Controls

In this exercise worksheet, you will identify various Pro Tools controls within the Edit and Transport windows. The information referenced in these questions is covered in Lesson 3.

Duration: 10 Minutes **Media: None Required**

Refer to Figures 3.23 through 3.25 when answering the questions below. Refer to the sections on "Edit Tool Functions" and "MIDI Control Features" in Lesson 3 for assistance.

Questions 1 through 3 refer to Figure 3.23.

1. The button labeled **A** in Figure 3.23 is called the ________________________ tool.

2. The button labeled **B** in Figure 3.23 is called the ________________________ tool.

3. The button labeled **C** in Figure 3.23 is called the ________________________ tool.

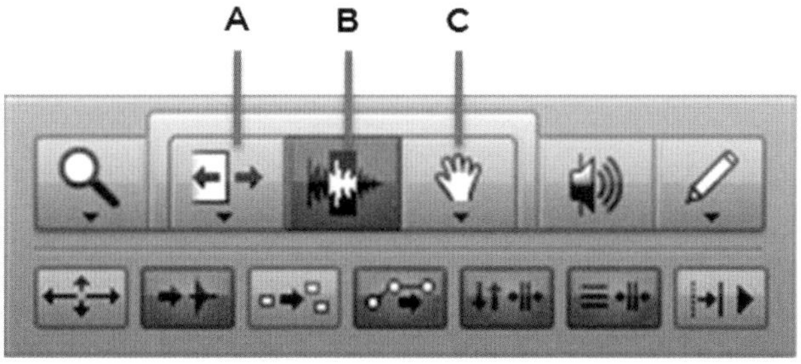

Figure 3.23 Tool cluster in the Pro Tools Edit window

Question 4 refers to Figure 3.24.

4. The combo button labeled **A** in Figure 3.24 is called the ________________________ tool.

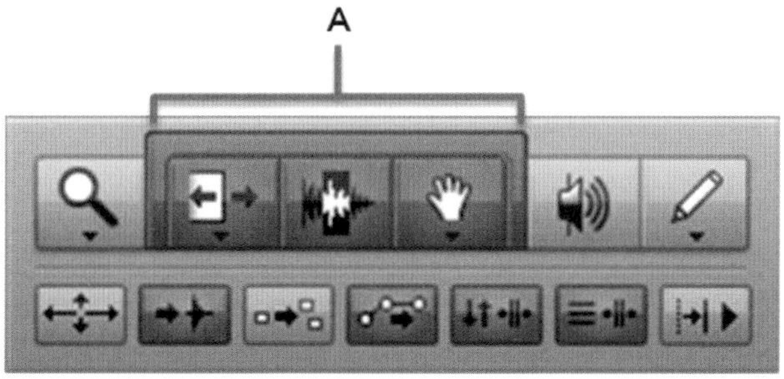

Figure 3.24 Specialized tool in the Pro Tools Edit window

Questions 5 through 8 refer to Figure 3.25.

5. The button labeled **A** in Figure 3.25 enables the ______________________________ function.

6. The button labeled **B** in Figure 3.25 enables the ______________________________ function.

7. The button labeled **C** in Figure 3.25 enables the ______________________________ function.

8. The button labeled **D** in Figure 3.25 is called the ______________________________ button.

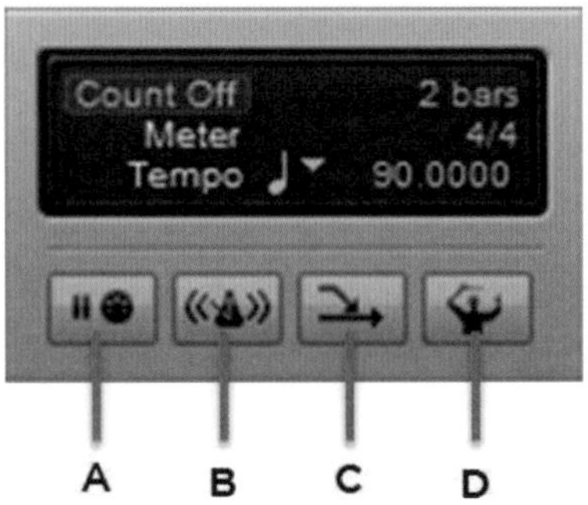

Figure 3.25 MIDI Controls in Pro Tools

LESSON 4

Creating Your First Session

This lesson covers the basics of working with Pro Tools sessions. It introduces session configuration options, playback and navigation options, and session saving and opening operations.

Duration: 90 Minutes

GOALS

- Recognize the difference between a Pro Tools session and a Pro Tools project
- Choose appropriate session parameters for a session or project
- Create and name tracks in Pro Tools
- Recognize the difference between the playback cursor and the edit cursor
- Navigate your session for playback and editing
- Save, locate, and open sessions on available storage drives

Key topics from this lesson are included in the *Pro Tools 12 Essential Training: 101* course on Lynda.com.

Before you can begin working with audio or MIDI in Pro Tools, you need to have a Pro Tools file open. This lesson covers the basics of creating a session document or Pro Tools project, adding tracks to your session or project, using basic navigation for your tracks, and saving and reopening session documents.

The Dashboard

When you first launch Pro Tools, the Dashboard is displayed, giving you quick access to options for creating or opening a session or project.

The Dashboard lets you complete any of the following actions:

- Create a new blank session on local storage.
- Create a new blank project, with or without cloud backup
- Create a new session or project from a template.
- Open a session or project from a list of recently opened Pro Tools documents.
- Open a project that you created or are a collaborator on.
- Open a session from a connected storage location on your system.

Press Command+Up Arrow or Down Arrow (Mac) or Ctrl+Up Arrow or Down Arrow (Windows) to select different tabs in the action pane on the left side of the Dashboard.

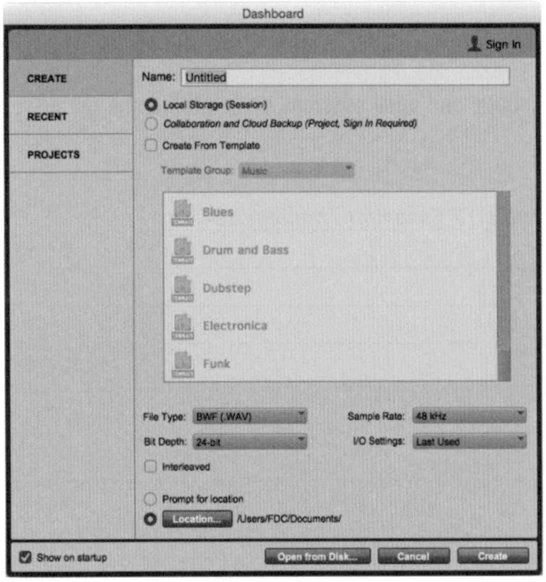

Figure 4.1 The Dashboard dialog box (Pro Tools 12.8 shown)

Creating and Configuring a Pro Tools Document

From the Dashboard, you can begin a new recording project by selecting the **Create** tab at the top left. By default, the Dashboard will be configured to create a *session* document using local storage, as described in Lesson 2. Alternatively, you can create your Pro Tools document as a cloud-enabled *project* instead.

Creating and Using Session Documents

To create a session document, leave the radio button at the top of the Dashboard set to **Local Storage (Session)**. Using this option will allow you to save your Pro Tools work to a specified folder location on your computer's internal drive or other connected storage device, such as a USB hard disk drive or solid state drive.

You'll likely find it easiest to use sessions rather than projects for this course. The exercises and examples used herein are based on local session configurations. Feel free to use cloud-based projects instead, however, if you have available cloud storage with your Avid account.

Creating and Using Project Documents

To create or open a project, you must first sign in to your Avid Master Account from within Pro Tools. To sign in, click on the **Sign In** icon in the upper right corner of the Dashboard. A sign-in dialog box will display where you can log in with the email address and password for your account. (You will need to have an active Internet connection for your initial login.)

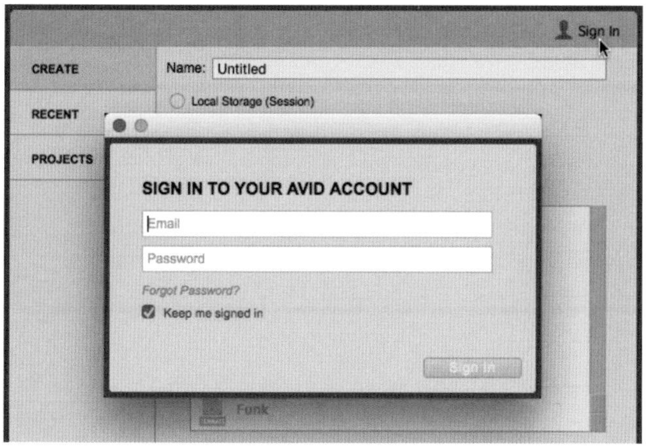

Figure 4.2 Signing in from the Dashboard

In Pro Tools 12.8 and later, you can create a project with or without cloud backup. Currently, there is no advantage to creating a project without cloud backup over creating a session using local storage.

This book focuses primarily on creating and working with sessions. However, nearly all Pro Tools operations are identical, regardless of whether you are using a session document or a project document.

The reasons you might want to use a project with cloud backup include the following:

- To protect your Pro Tools work against loss in the event of a drive failure or other computer mishap. So long as any file loss is restricted to your local system, the online cloud project will be unaffected.
- To be able to access your projects from anywhere with an Internet connection. You can create a project on a system at a school lab or commercial studio location and later access the same project from your home Pro Tools system or a project studio without having to transfer files.
- You can collaborate with other Pro Tools users anywhere in the world. You can share a cloud-based project with other users by adding them as contacts in Pro Tools and inviting them to the project.

Collaboration workflows are covered in higher-level Pro Tools courses.

If you choose to create a project for any of the above purposes, be sure to enable the **Backup to Cloud** option at the bottom of the Dashboard. This option is only available when the **Collaboration and Cloud Backup** radio button is selected at the top of the Dashboard.

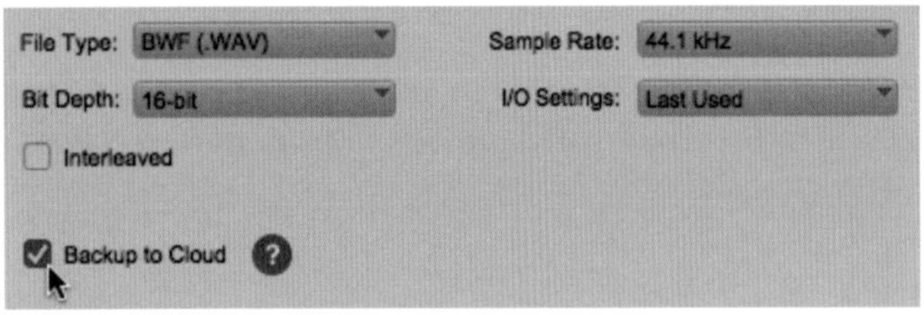

Figure 4.3 Backup to Cloud enabled in the Dashboard

Using Templates

When you create a new session or project, you can choose to either start from scratch or build your document from a template, by enabling the **Create from Template** checkbox. For the purposes of getting familiar with Pro Tools, it will be best to always start from a blank session or project.

> **Pro Tools Session Templates**
>
> The Pro Tools installer disc includes factory templates that are preconfigured with common track and mixer setups. Once you are comfortable with Pro Tools tracks, signal routing, and processing, you can use these templates to explore ideas and save time when you start a new session or project document.

Choosing Parameter Settings

The parameter settings available for sessions and projects include selections for file type, sample rate, bit depth, and I/O settings.

Audio File Type

Pro Tools stores audio as WAV or AIFF files. WAV is the default file type on all platforms. Use the default (WAV) format unless you intend to use your files for another purpose that requires the AIFF format.

Audio Sample Rate

Pro Tools supports sample rates up to 192 kHz with a compatible audio interface. To optimize the file sizes in your session, choose the lowest sample rate that meets the needs of your project.

A sample rate of 44.1 kHz is often adequate for home- and project-studio recordings. Higher sample rates can be chosen for demanding projects, to capture a greater frequency response from the source audio and to minimize sound degradation throughout the project life cycle. However, with higher sample rates come greater disk space requirements for your session. (See Table 4.1 in the "File Size Considerations" section later in this lesson.)

For more details on sample rates, see "The Importance of Sample Rate" in Lesson 1.

Audio Bit Depth

Pro Tools works with files in 16-bit, 24-bit, or 32-bit floating-point audio resolution. The 16-bit option generates smaller files and is typically adequate for basic recording projects. The 24-bit and 32-bit float options provide greater dynamic range in your recorded audio (see "The Importance of Bit Depth" in Lesson 1) and lower the noise floor. These options should be used for high-end recordings, especially those that include very quiet passages (such as a classical orchestra), recordings that require intensive processing, and recordings intended for media that support high resolution audio, such as DVD and Blu-ray disc.

For the highest quality audio, record at 24-bit or 32-bit float and properly dither down, if needed, during the final mix. Dithering is covered in the Pro Tools 110 course.

To provide maximum compatibility and interchange with older Pro Tools systems (Pro Tools 9 and earlier), use 16- or 24-bit resolution.

I/O Settings Selection

The I/O Settings selector defaults to LAST USED but also provides preset input and output configurations for stereo and surround mixing options. (Surround mixing is available with Pro Tools|HD only.) The Last Used option will load the settings from your last session, including any customizations you've made. However, it is good practice to select the Stereo Mix setting when creating a new Pro Tools document on a system you are not familiar with or whenever your I/O settings may have been inadvertently changed.

Use the Stereo Mix option to ensure that you are using the default stereo input and output paths for your current audio interface.

Interleaved File Checkbox

The Interleaved checkbox lets you specify whether recorded stereo files are stored with the left and right channels combined in a single file (interleaved) or stored using separate mono files for each channel (multi-mono). This setting affects how the files are saved on disk, but it has no impact on how Pro Tools operates or how recorded files look and behave within a session.

Interleaved files are generally more convenient, since you have fewer overall files to manage.

Save Location

When creating a session, you can choose to be prompted for a save location or to use a pre-configured save location. You can select the save option using the radio buttons at the bottom of the Dashboard.

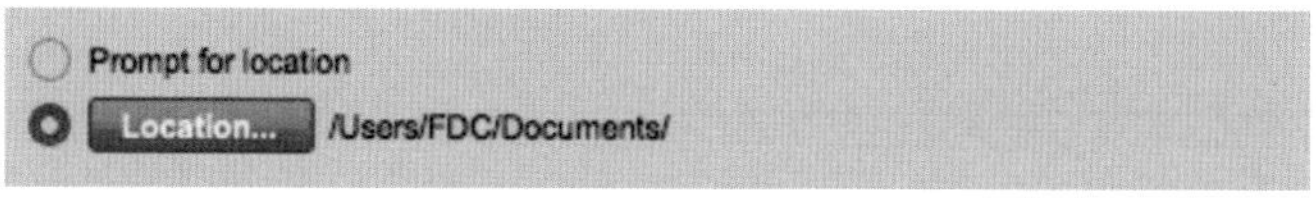

Figure 4.4 Radio buttons for save options in the Dashboard

By default, Pro Tools will be configured to save new sessions in the Documents folder for your user account. This is not necessarily the best location for your session folder and associated media files. Most professional users prefer to store their Pro Tools work on a dedicated drive or partition, isolated from their system drive and applications.

You can change the default save location by clicking on the LOCATION button in the Dashboard and navigating to the desired drive location in the resulting dialog box. The selected location will henceforth be used as the save location when you click the CREATE button in the Dashboard.

Alternatively, you can select the PROMPT FOR LOCATION option in the Dashboard. With this option selected, Pro Tools will prompt you to choose a drive location once you click the CREATE button.

File Size Considerations

A tradeoff of choosing higher sample rates and bit depths for your Pro Tools audio is an increase in the amount of disk space required to store your audio files. Table 4.1 shows the relationship between sample rate, bit depth, and disk space consumption for the standard configurations supported in Pro Tools 12.

Table 4.1 Audio Recording Storage Requirements (Approximate)

Session Sample Rate	Session Bit Depth	Megabytes/Track Minute (Mono)	Megabytes/Track Minute (Stereo)
44.1 kHz	16-bit	5 MB	10 MB
44.1 kHz	24-bit	7.5 MB	15 MB
44.1 kHz	32-bit float	10 MB	20 MB
48 kHz	16-bit	5.5 MB	11 MB
48 kHz	24-bit	8.2 MB	16.4 MB
48 kHz	32-bit float	11 MB	22 MB
88.2 kHz	16-bit	10 MB	20 MB
88.2 kHz	24-bit	15 MB	30 MB
88.2 kHz	32-bit float	20 MB	40 MB
96 kHz	16-bit	11 MB	22 MB
96 kHz	24-bit	16.5 MB	33 MB
96 kHz	32-bit float	22 MB	44 MB
176.4 kHz	16-bit	20 MB	40 MB
176.4 kHz	24-bit	30 MB	60 MB
176.4 kHz	32-bit float	40 MB	80 MB
192 kHz	16-bit	22 MB	44 MB
192 kHz	24-bit	33 MB	66 MB
192 kHz	32-bit float	44 MB	88 MB

Working with Tracks

Once you've created a new session or project, the Pro Tools document will open, with no tracks in the Edit and Mix windows. At this point, you will need to create and name new tracks.

In Pro Tools, tracks are where audio, MIDI, and automation data are recorded and edited. Audio and MIDI data can be edited into clips that are copied or repeated in different locations, to rearrange sections or entire songs, or to assemble material from multiple takes.

Adding Tracks

To add tracks to your session, choose **TRACK > NEW** to open the New Tracks dialog box (see Figure 4.5) and then choose the number of tracks and the track format, type, and timebase using the dialog box controls.

Figure 4.5 The New Tracks dialog box

Shortcuts for Creating Tracks

Numerous shortcuts are available to speed up the process of creating new tracks. All share the Command/Ctrl modifier (Mac/Windows, respectively).

Use Command+Shift+N (Mac) or Ctrl+Shift+N (Windows) to open the New Tracks dialog box. Once displayed, use the following shortcuts to modify the settings within the New Tracks dialog box:

Change track format	Command+Left/Right arrow or Ctrl+Left/Right arrow
Change track type	Command+Up/Down arrow or Ctrl+Up/Down arrow
Change track timebase	Command+Option+Up/Down arrow or Ctrl+Alt+Up/Down arrow
Add/remove rows	Command+Shift+Up/Down arrow or Ctrl+Shift+Up/Down arrow

Track Number

The New Tracks dialog box allows you to add multiple tracks to your session simultaneously. To add multiple tracks with the same format, type, and timebase, enter the number of tracks to add in the Track Total field. To add multiple tracks using different configurations, click on the Add Row button (plus sign).

You can simultaneously add as many tracks with as many different configurations as your session will allow.

Tracks will be added to your session in the order shown in the New Tracks dialog box. To rearrange the track order, click on the Move Row control and drag the row to a new position.

Figure 4.6 Arranging tracks using the Move Row control (up and down arrows)

Track Format (Mono or Stereo)

Within the New Tracks dialog box, you can choose a format for the track or tracks you are adding to your session. Available options include mono or stereo (multi-channel surround formats are available on Pro Tools|HD systems). Stereo tracks automatically link both the left and right channels for editing, mixing, and clip renaming.

Track Type

Track types supported in Pro Tools include the following:

- Audio tracks
- MIDI tracks
- Instrument tracks
- Video tracks (Pro Tools|HD required for multiple tracks)

- Auxiliary inputs
- VCA Masters
- Master Faders

Any combination of supported track types can be added using the New Tracks dialog box.

Standard Pro Tools software does not include Video tracks in the New Tracks dialog box, because only a single Video track is supported. A Video track will be created only if you import video into your session.

Audio Tracks

Audio tracks allow you to import/record and edit an audio signal as a waveform. Audio tracks can be mono, stereo, or any supported multi-channel format (Pro Tools | HD only).

Standard Pro Tools software can create up to 128 Audio tracks in a session, while Pro Tools | HD software can create up to 768 Audio tracks, with playback and record capabilities dependent on hardware. However, the session sample rate, the system hardware, and the continuity of audio all impact how many tracks can actually play back and record simultaneously.

Pro Tools software systems and Pro Tools | HD Native hardware systems use the host computer's CPU to mix and process Audio tracks. Computers with faster clock speeds and greater processor counts will support more tracks and plug-in processing than computers with slower CPUs or fewer processors.

MIDI Tracks

MIDI tracks store MIDI note and controller data. Pro Tools includes an integrated MIDI sequencer that lets you import, record, and edit MIDI data in much the same way that you can when working with audio. MIDI data appears in tracks in the Pro Tools Edit window, referencing the same Timeline as Audio tracks.

Note that you do not specify a track format (mono or stereo) for MIDI tracks, since no audio passes through the track; MIDI tracks are data-only.

Instrument Tracks

Instrument tracks combine the functions of MIDI tracks and Auxiliary Inputs (see the "Auxiliary Inputs" section below) into a single track type, making them ideal for composing with virtual instrument plug-ins, sound modules, and all your other MIDI devices.

Video Tracks

Video tracks let you add or import video to the Timeline. Standard Pro Tools software lets you add or import one Video track per session and use a single video clip on the track. Pro Tools | HD software lets you add multiple Video tracks to the Timeline and use multiple video files and video clips on each Video track. Only one Video track can be active, or *online*, at any time.

Auxiliary Inputs

Aux Input tracks function like a mixer channel in Pro Tools, allowing you to route audio through your mix without recording the audio.

An Aux Input track can be used as an effects return, a destination for a submix, an input to monitor or process live audio (such as the output of a synthesizer triggered from a MIDI source), or a control point for any other audio routing task. Auxiliary inputs can be mono, stereo, or any supported multi-channel format.

VCA Master Tracks

Like Aux Input tracks, VCA Master tracks cannot be used for recording. But unlike an Aux Input track, audio does not get routed through a VCA Master track. Instead, each VCA Master track is associated with a Mix group, and the tracks in the Mix group can then be controlled by the VCA Master.

Mix and Edit groups are covered in the Pro Tools 110 course book.

VCA Master tracks are covered in the 200-level Pro Tools courses.

Master Faders

A Master Fader is a single fader used to control hardware output levels and bus paths. Master Fader tracks control the overall level of the audio routed to the session's main output paths or busses. In Pro Tools, you can create a Master Fader track for mono, stereo, or any supported multi-channel format.

Track Timebase

The track *timebase* refers to the Time Scale that material on the track is associated with. All track types can be set to either sample-based (referencing the Samples Time Scale) or tick-based (referencing the Bars|Beats Time Scale), with different tracks set to different timebases, as needed.

Audio tracks are sample-based by default, meaning that audio clips and events have absolute locations on the Timeline, correlated to specific sample locations. Material on sample-based tracks maintains an absolute position on the track, regardless of tempo or meter changes specified in the session.

By contrast, MIDI and Instrument tracks are tick-based by default. As such, MIDI clips and events are associated with bar and beat positions, which move relative to the sample Timeline as meter and tempo changes occur.

Although Audio tracks are sample-based by default, Elastic Audio–enabled tracks can be switched to tick-based in order to automatically follow tempo changes in your session and conform to the session's tempo map.

Pro Tools | First uses Elastic Audio and tick-based timing on all Audio tracks by default.

You can select whether a track is sample-based or tick-based when you create it; however, you can also change timebases later as needed.

Sample-based editing and tick-based editing are covered in more detail in the Pro Tools 110 and 210M courses.

Naming Tracks

When you create tracks in Pro Tools, they are added to the session using generic names, such as Audio 1, Audio 2, MIDI 1, and so on. To change a track name to something more meaningful, double-click the track name within the Edit window or the Mix window. A dialog box will appear, allowing you to rename the track. (See Figure 4.7.)

You can also name a track by right-clicking on the track name and choosing RENAME from the pop-up menu.

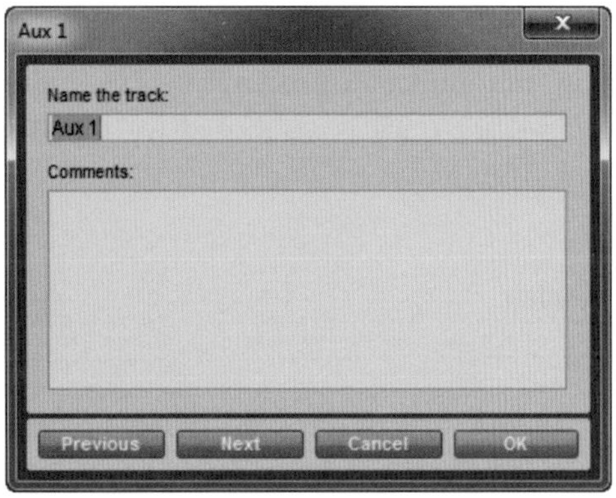

Figure 4.7 The Track Name dialog box

Using the Track Name dialog box, you can also add comments to a track and cycle through the tracks in your session, renaming and adding comments to each, using the NEXT and PREVIOUS buttons. Comments you add will be visible in the Comments area, if displayed, at the bottom of the channel strip (Mix window) or at the head of a track (Edit window).

COMMAND+LEFT/RIGHT ARROW (Mac) or CTRL+LEFT/RIGHT ARROW (Windows) in the Track Name dialog box to cycle through your tracks and rename each without leaving the keyboard.

Deleting Tracks

When you delete tracks, your audio or MIDI clip data will *remain* in the Clip List, but your arrangement of the clips on the deleted track (the track's playlist) will be lost. This is also true of video clips in Pro Tools | HD.

The Track Delete command cannot be undone.

To delete a track, follow these steps:

1. Click the track nameplate to select the track; SHIFT-CLICK or COMMAND-CLICK (Mac)/CTRL-CLICK (Windows) to select multiple tracks.
2. Choose TRACK > DELETE.
3. If all selected tracks are empty, they will be deleted immediately; if any tracks contain data, you will be prompted with a verification dialog box. Click DELETE to permanently remove the selected tracks from the session.

You can also right-click on a track name and choose DELETE from the pop-up menu to remove all selected tracks.

Adding Audio to Tracks

Once you have created one or more Audio tracks in your session, you can begin adding audio, either by recording to your track(s) or by importing existing audio files. When you record audio or import audio from a hard drive (or other volume) into tracks in your session, Pro Tools also places the audio files in the Clip List.

Audio recording is covered in Lesson 5, and audio importing is covered in Lesson 6.

Controlling Playback

The Edit window displays two different types of cursors: a *playback* cursor and an *edit* cursor. The playback cursor is a solid, non-blinking line that moves across the screen during playback and indicates where the current playback point is. The edit cursor (or edit location) is a blinking line that appears on a track playlist when you click with the Selector tool in a track.

During playback, the playback cursor's time location is reflected in the session's Main and Sub Counters (in both the Edit window and the Transport window).

Timeline Selections

When you click the Play button (or press the SPACEBAR), Pro Tools begins playback based on the timeline location (or timeline selection).

The timeline location is represented by a split blue arrow icon on either side of a blinking cursor in the Rulers area at the top of the Edit window. A timeline selection is represented by blue half-arrows (In and Out Points) on either side of a dark overlay in the Rulers area.

Figure 4.8 The timeline location at Bar 18, Beat 1 (left) and a timeline selection from Bar 18, Beat 1 to Bar 18, Beat 4 (right)

The timeline location or timeline selection determines the playback point or playback range for Pro Tools. You can position the timeline location by clicking on a ruler with any Edit tool active. Clicking and dragging in a ruler will create a timeline selection.

A timeline selection can exist with or without an edit selection.

Edit Selections

An edit selection is represented by a dark highlight across one or more tracks in the Edit window. You can create an edit selection by clicking and dragging on a track playlist with the Selector tool. By making a selection on a track, you define an area for Pro Tools to perform a desired editing task.

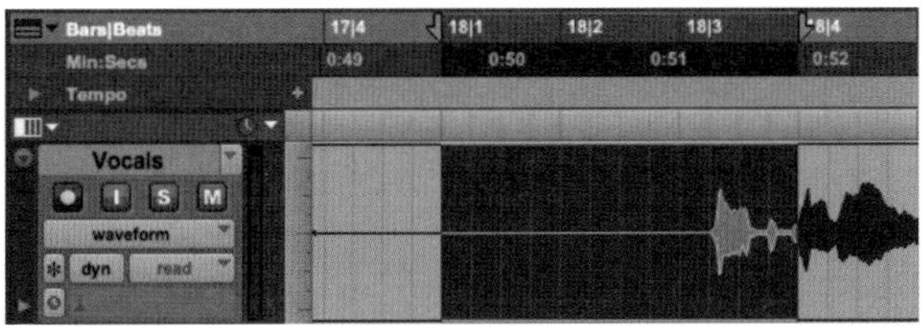

Figure 4.9 Edit selection from Bar 18, Beat 1 to Bar 18, Beat 4

Working with Linked Timeline and Edit Selections

The timeline location/selection is linked to the edit cursor location/edit selection in Pro Tools by default. This means that whenever you position the edit cursor on a track, you also position the timeline location in the rulers. Similarly, whenever you create an edit selection on a track, you create a corresponding timeline selection in the rulers. As a result, you can easily control the playback point or playback range while working on a track.

To link or unlink the timeline and edit selections, choose OPTIONS > LINK TIMELINE AND EDIT SELECTION. The option should remain enabled (linked) for this course.

With the timeline and edit selections linked, the playback point will always match the edit cursor location.

Starting and Stopping Playback

As mentioned previously, you can set the playback point using the Selector tool by clicking directly on a track.

To play back a portion of your session or project, follow these steps:

1. In the Edit window, click the SELECTOR tool. The cursor will turn into an I-beam when positioned over a track.
2. Click and release the mouse button anywhere within an existing track.
3. Press the SPACEBAR to begin playback from this point.
4. To stop playback, press the SPACEBAR again.
5. To move to a different playback point in the track, click the SELECTOR at the new position and press the SPACEBAR again.

You can also set the playback point (with any tool selected) by clicking on a Ruler in the Edit window. This allows you to set the playback point without changing tools. Clicking on a Timebase Ruler provides a common way to set the playback point regardless of whether the timeline and edit selections are linked.

Locating the Playback Cursor

At times, the playback cursor might be off screen. For example, if the No Scrolling option is selected (see "Scrolling Options," below), the playback cursor will move off screen after reaching the edge of the Edit window.

To help you locate the cursor in these situations, Pro Tools displays a Playback Cursor Locator (small blue triangle) in the Main Timebase Ruler. You can click on this icon to jump to the playback cursor location.

If the playback cursor is not visible in the Edit window, the Playback Cursor Locator will appear in the Main Timebase Ruler, as follows:

- On the left edge of the ruler if the playback cursor is located before the visible area
- On the right edge of the ruler if the playback cursor is located after the visible area

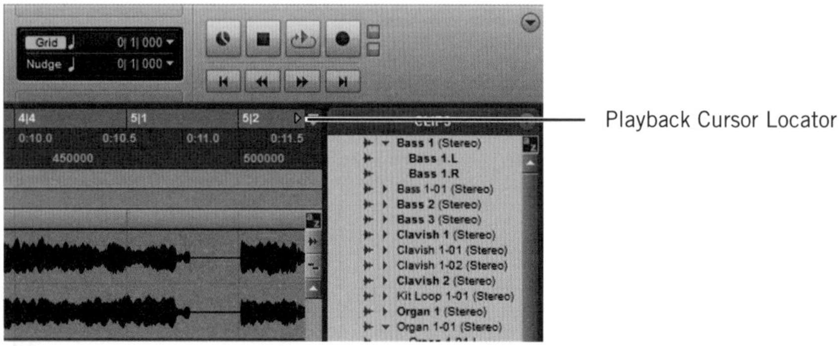

Figure 4.10 Playback Cursor Locator (blue triangle in the Main Timebase Ruler)

The Playback Cursor Locator turns red when any track is record-enabled.

To locate the playback cursor when it is off screen, click the PLAYBACK CURSOR LOCATOR in the Main Timebase Ruler. The Edit window's waveform display will jump to the playback cursor's current location.

Selecting the Scrolling Behavior

Pro Tools offers several different scrolling options that affect how the contents of the Edit window are displayed during playback and recording. The most commonly used scrolling options are No Scrolling and Page Scrolling. Additional options are discussed in Lesson 9 and in advanced Pro Tools courses.

No Scrolling

Scrolling can be turned off by choosing OPTIONS > SCROLLING > NO SCROLLING. This option prevents Pro Tools from scrolling the Edit window during playback and recording. In this mode, the playback cursor moves off screen and Pro Tools does not reposition the window when playback or recording is stopped.

Page Scrolling

To scroll the Edit window one screen (or "page") at a time as the playback cursor moves across the Timeline, enable the Page Scrolling option. To select this option, choose OPTIONS > SCROLLING > PAGE.

When Page Scrolling is enabled, the playback cursor moves across the Edit window until it reaches the right edge of the window. Each time the playback cursor reaches the right edge, the entire contents of the window are scrolled, one screen at a time, and the playback cursor continues from the left edge of the Edit window.

When the zoom magnification of the Edit window is too high, Page Scrolling may not function properly. If you experience problems, decrease the zoom magnification to enable Page Scrolling.

Saving, Locating, and Opening Pro Tools Files

As with most software applications, Pro Tools provides commands for saving and opening your files under the File menu. The following sections describe the options for saving, locating, and opening your Pro Tools documents and other files related to your Pro Tools work.

Saving a Session or Project

While working in Pro Tools, it is important to save your work often. When you save your progress using one of the commands explained below, you are saving only the Pro Tools document file, not its associated files. (The Pro Tools audio files are written directly to disk, so you don't have to save them independently.) Consequently, even very large sessions and projects can be saved quickly.

Save Command

Saving can be done manually by choosing the Save command from the File menu. This saves the changes you have made since the last time you saved and writes the session or project in its current form over the old version. You cannot undo the Save command.

Save As Command

The Save As command is useful for saving a copy of a session under a different name or in a different drive location. Because the Save As command leaves the original session unchanged and allows you to continue working on the renamed copy, it is particularly useful for experimenting and saving successive stages of your work. You can save each stage under a different name, such as Edit Session-Day 1, Edit Session-Day 2, and so on. By working this way, you can always retrace your steps if you should want to go back to an earlier stage of the project.

To use the Save As feature, follow these steps:

1. From within an open session, choose **FILE > SAVE AS**. The Save Session As dialog box will appear.
2. Type a new name for the session in the dialog box.
3. Click **SAVE**.

The renamed, newly saved session will remain open for you to continue your work.

The Save As command should not be used to transfer a session to a portable drive. Doing so will copy the session file only, without including the associated audio files.

A third Save command, Save Copy In, allows you to create a copy from your current session with different session parameters and place it, along with copies of all associated audio files, in a new location. The Save Copy In command is discussed in Lesson 10.

Save As New Version Command

This command is available only when working on project documents. Pro Tools projects are stored in the Project Media Cache location for your system, with the optional cloud back-up option. As such, you cannot make a copy of a project in a new drive location without first converting it into a session.

The process of converting a project to a session is covered in higher-level Pro Tools courses.

The Save As New Version command allows you to save a copy of a project under a different name, giving you similar benefits to the Save As command for sessions.

To use the Save As New Version feature, follow these steps:

1. From within an open project, choose **FILE > SAVE AS NEW VERSION**. The Save New Version dialog box will appear.
2. Type a new name for the project version in the dialog box.
3. Click **OK**.

The renamed version of the project will remain open for you to continue your work.

Locating and Opening a Session File

Most Pro Tools work today is still done using session files. If you know the location of a session file you want to open, you can open it directly from the File menu (choose **FILE > OPEN SESSION**). To open a recently used session, you can choose **FILE > OPEN RECENT** and select the session that you wish to open from the submenu.

If you need to work on a session has not been opened recently and you are not sure of its location, you can use a special window called a *Workspace browser* to search for the session on your system.

About Workspace Browsers

Pro Tools lets you use Workspace browsers to quickly locate, manage, and open Pro Tools sessions and related media files. Workspace browsers provide more meaningful search, navigation, file information, and audition capabilities than standard operating system–level functions.

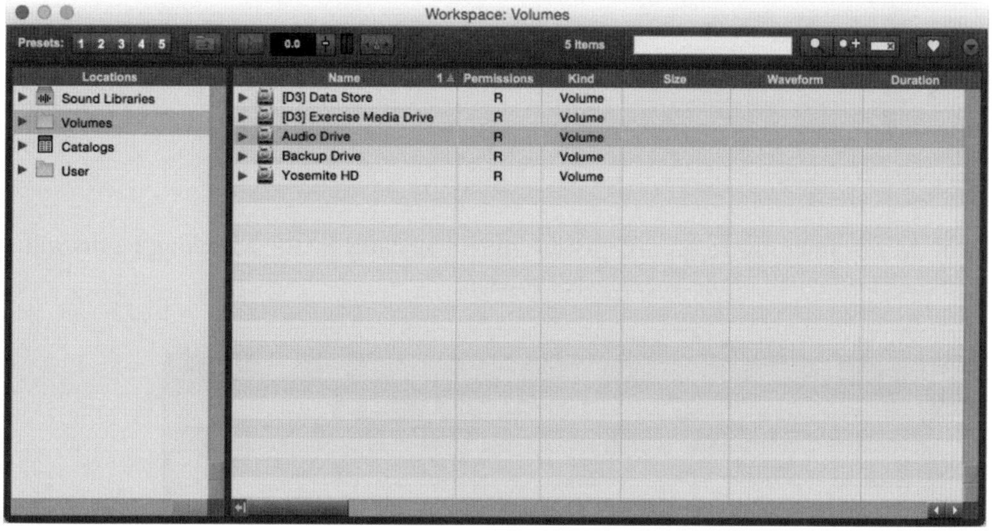

Figure 4.11 Workspace browser window

Locating a Session

Workspace browser windows use powerful search tools that let you search for Pro Tools files by type, such as session files, audio files, and video files.

To search for Pro Tools sessions in a Workspace browser, follow these steps:

1. Choose **WINDOW > NEW WORKSPACE > DEFAULT**. A Workspace browser will open as the active window.
2. In the Workspace browser window, click the **ADVANCED SEARCH** button (magnifying glass with a plus symbol) to reveal the Advanced Search filters rows and selectors. The button will be highlighted in blue when Advanced Search is active.

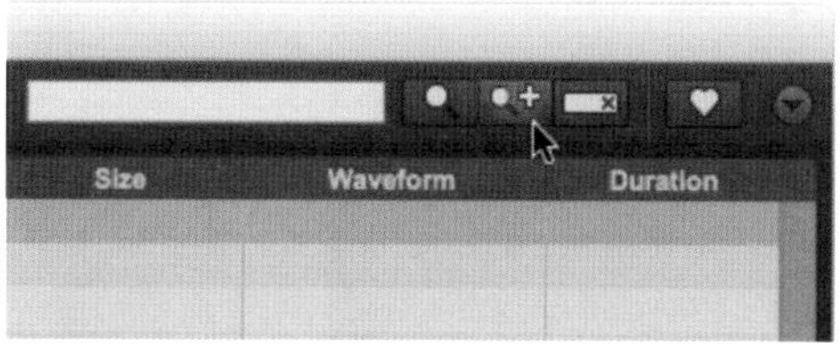

Figure 4.12 Clicking the Advanced Search button in a Workspace browser

3. Choose the volume or folder you want to search by selecting it in the Locations pane (left column). Note that you can navigate through the file system by clicking the triangle icons to expand or collapse volumes and folders.

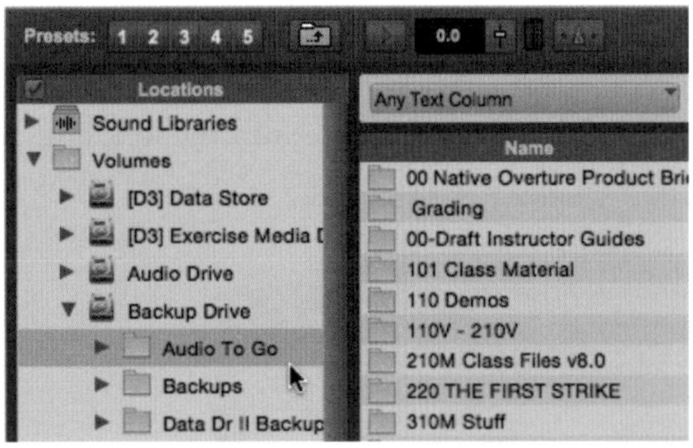

Figure 4.13 Selecting a folder to search

4. Use the selectors in the first filter row to specify **<KIND> <IS> <SESSION FILE>**. Matching results will begin appearing in the bottom half of the Workspace browser.

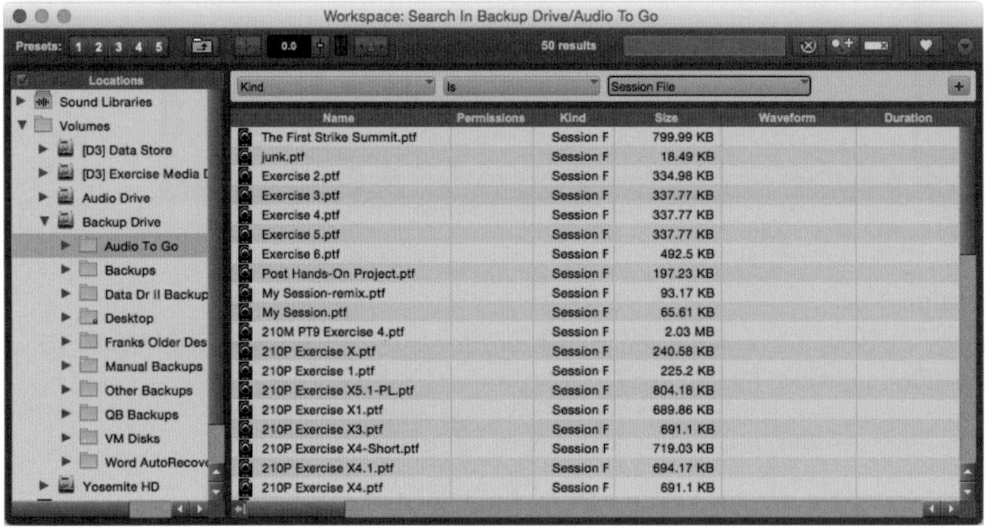

Figure 4.14 Search results shown in the Workspace browser

5. If desired, click on the **PLUS** symbol at the end of the row to add a second filter row. Use the selectors to specify **<NAME> <CONTAINS>**, and enter a search term in the displayed text field. The results in the bottom half of the browser will be filtered to match the specified text.

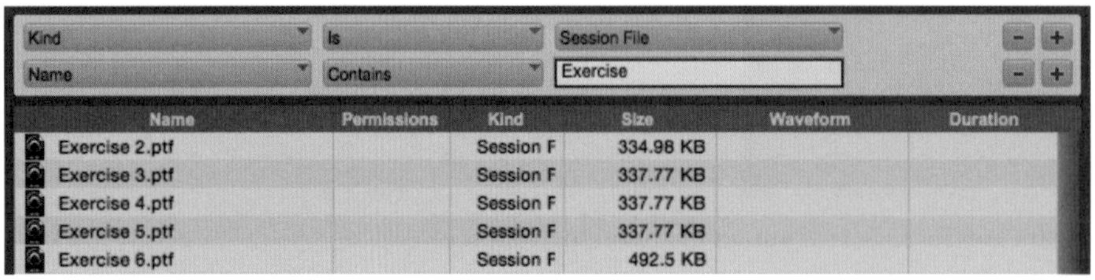

Figure 4.15 Search results filtered to contain the word "Exercise" in the session name

Opening a Session

Once you have located the session you are interested in, you can open the session directly from the Workspace browser window by double-clicking on it. (You can also open Pro Tools sessions from the computer's hard drive by double-clicking on the session file in an Explorer or Finder window.)

Pro Tools can have only one session open at a time. If you attempt to open a session while another session is open, Pro Tools will prompt you to save the current session and close it before opening the selected session.

The Pro Tools session will open with all windows and display options appearing exactly as saved. Any previously created tracks will appear in the Edit and Mix windows, and all audio and MIDI clips associated with the session will appear in the Clip List at the right of the Edit window.

If the Edit and/or Mix windows are not displayed in a session you have opened, you can display them by choosing the corresponding command in the Window menu.

Review/Discussion Questions

1. What are some actions that can be initiated from the Dashboard? (See "The Dashboard" beginning on page 64.)

2. What is the difference between a session and a project in Pro Tools? (See "Creating and Configuring a Pro Tools Document" beginning on page 64.)

3. What is required to create a project document? What are some reasons you might want to create a project instead of a session? (See "Creating and Using Project Documents" beginning on page 65.)

4. What are some available options for parameter settings in the Dashboard? (See "Choosing Parameter Settings" beginning on page 66.)

5. What audio file types are supported in Pro Tools? What is the default file type? (See "Choosing Parameter Settings" beginning on page 66.)

6. What is the maximum sample rate supported in Pro Tools? What is the maximum bit depth? (See "Choosing Parameter Settings" beginning on page 66.)

7. What menu command lets you add tracks to your session? How many tracks can you add at one time? (See "Adding Tracks" beginning on page 68.)

8. Describe some track types supported in Pro Tools. (See "Adding Tracks" beginning on page 68.)

9. Which timebase do Audio tracks use by default? Which timebase do MIDI and Instrument tracks use by default? (See "Track Timebase" beginning on page 71.)

10. What happens to the audio and MIDI data on a track when the track gets deleted from your session? Can the Track > Delete command be undone? (See "Deleting Tracks" beginning on page 72.)

11. Name the two types of cursors available in the Edit window. What is the difference between them? (See "Controlling Playback" beginning on page 73.)

12. Which tool can be used to set the playback point by clicking directly on a track? (See "Starting and Stopping Playback" beginning on page 74.)

13. What is the Playback Cursor Locator used for? Where will the Playback Cursor Locator appear (in what Ruler)? (See "Locating the Playback Cursor" beginning on page 74.)

14. What is the purpose of the Save As command? Which session will be open after completing the Save As command—the original or the renamed copy? (See "Save As Command" beginning on page 75.)

15. How can you open a session after locating it in a Workspace browser? (See "Opening a Session" beginning on page 78.)

To review additional material from this chapter, see the PT101 Study Guide module available through the ElementsIED online learning platform at ElementsED.com.

EXERCISE 4

Creating a Session

In this exercise tutorial, you will create a Pro Tools session, add four tracks to the session, name each of the tracks, and set the Main Time Scale and other display options for the session. You will then save the session for use in subsequent exercises.

Duration: 10 to 15 Minutes **Media: None Required**

> **Downloading the Media Files**
>
> To complete the exercises in this book, you will be using the **PT101 Download Media** files. If you haven't done so already, you can download the media files now. Be sure to save the files to a location that you will have ongoing access to as you complete the exercises and projects in this book.
>
> To download the media files, point your browser to http://alpp.us/PT101-128.
>
> *Note: The above URL is **case sensitive**.*

Getting Started

To get started, you will need to open Pro Tools and create a new 44.1 kHz, 24-bit session. You can do this by launching Pro Tools and configuring the Dashboard for a session. Then you will need to specify the associated parameters for the session.

Launch Pro Tools and configure it for a session:

1. Power up your computer and any connected hardware, as described in Lesson 2.
2. Do one of the following to launch Pro Tools:
   - Double-click on the PRO TOOLS shortcut icon on the desktop.
   - Click the PRO TOOLS icon in the Dock (Mac).
   - Click START > PRO TOOLS 12 (Windows).
3. In the Dashboard, select the CREATE tab at the top left, and enable the LOCAL STORAGE (SESSION) option.

> **If you have an Avid Master Account with available cloud storage, you can create a project instead, with cloud backup. Use this option if you will need to access your work later from a system in a different location. (Internet access will be required.)**

4. Make sure the CREATE FROM TEMPLATE checkbox is deselected (unchecked).
5. At the top of the Dashboard, provide an initial name for your session, such as *PT101-XXX*, where *XXX* is your initials.

Specify the session parameters:

1. At the bottom of the Dashboard, set the audio parameters as follows:
   - File Type: BWF (.WAV)
   - Bit Depth: 24 Bit
   - Sample Rate: 44.1 kHz
   - I/O Settings: Stereo Mix
2. Enable (check) the **INTERLEAVED** option, and select the **PROMPT FOR LOCATION** radio button.

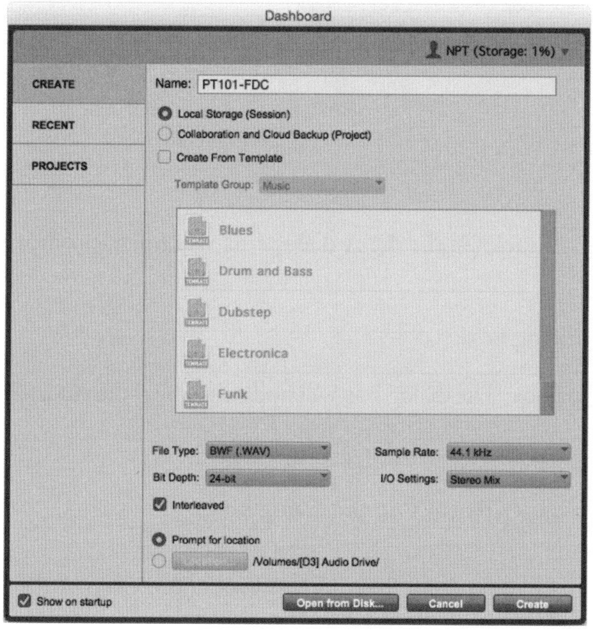

Figure 4.16 Session Parameters configured in the Dashboard

3. Once the parameters are configured, click the **CREATE** button.
4. In the resulting dialog box, navigate to an appropriate location to save your session.
5. Click **SAVE** to save the session in the selected location.

Creating and Naming Tracks

In this exercise, you will be working in the Edit window. Make sure the Edit window is displayed (**WINDOW > EDIT**), and then maximize or resize the window as needed to utilize the available space on your desktop.

In the next series of steps, you will create four new tracks for the session and then rename them with appropriate descriptive names.

Create the tracks for the session:

1. Choose **TRACK > NEW** to open the New Tracks dialog box.

Try using the keyboard shortcut for the TRACK > NEW command: COMMAND+SHIFT+N (Mac) or CTRL+SHIFT+N (Windows).

2. Leave the first row in the New Tracks dialog box configured for a single mono Audio track.
3. Click the plus sign on the right side to add a second row; configure this row for two stereo Audio tracks.
4. Click the plus sign at the end of the row to a third row; configure this row as a Stereo Master Fader.

Figure 4.17 New Tracks dialog box configured for three Audio tracks and a Master Fader

5. Click **CREATE** to create the tracks.

Name the newly created tracks:

1. Double-click on the track nameplate of the first track (Audio 1). A dialog box will open, prompting you to name the track.
2. Rename the track to VO without closing the dialog box.
3. Click the **NEXT** button at the bottom of the dialog box. The dialog box will update to show the Audio 2 track.
4. Rename the Audio 2 track to Drums and click the **NEXT** button again.
5. Rename the Audio 3 track to Guitar and then click **OK** to close the dialog box.

Setting Display Options

In this section, you will set the Main Time Scale, Sub Time Scale, and other display options for the session.

Set the Main Time Scale and Sub Time Scale:

1. Choose **VIEW > MAIN COUNTER > BARS|BEATS** to set the Main Time Scale to Bars|Beats.

   The Bars|Beats Ruler will display highlighted above the tracks in the Edit window, and the Main Counter will display its location information in Bars|Beats.

2. If the Sub Counter is not already displayed, click the down arrow next to the Main Counter and select **SHOW SUB COUNTER** from the pop-up menu. The Sub Counter will display under the Main Counter.

Figure 4.18 Selecting the option to show the Sub Counter

3. Click on the down arrow next to the Sub Counter and select **MIN:SECS** for the Sub Time Scale.
4. Verify that the Min:Secs ruler is displayed (**VIEW > RULERS > MIN:SECS**).

Display the side columns (Track List and Clip List):

1. If needed, click the arrow icons in the bottom corners of the Edit window to display the Edit window side columns. (See Figure 4.19.)

   The Track List will display in the left side column of the Edit window, and the Clip List will display in the right side column.

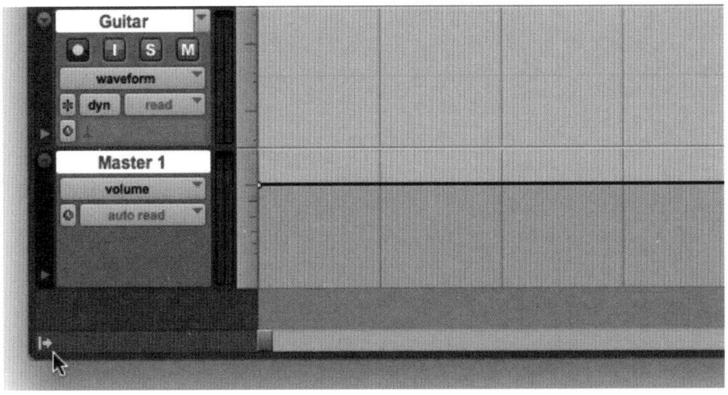

Figure 4.19 Clicking the arrow icon to display the left side column

Finishing Up

To complete this exercise tutorial, you will need to save your work under a new name and close the session. Note that you will be reusing this session in Exercise 5, so it is important to save the work you've done.

Finish your work:

1. Choose FILE > SAVE AS to create a copy of the session with a new name.

   To save a copy of a project file with a new name, choose File > Save As New Version instead.

2. In the SAVE SESSION AS dialog box, rename the session as *Exercise04-XXX* (where *XXX* is your initials), and click SAVE.

   DO NOT move the renamed session to a different save location. The exercises revisions you create in this book should all remain within the original session folder (PT101-XXX).

3. Choose FILE > CLOSE SESSION to close the session.

   You cannot close a Pro Tools session by closing the Mix and Edit windows. This common mistake leaves the session open with no active windows. Instead, you must choose CLOSE SESSION from the FILE menu.

LESSON 5

Making Your First Audio Recording

This lesson covers the steps required to begin recording audio into a Pro Tools session or project document. It also describes the types of audio clips your document will include and covers processes for keeping your clips and audio files organized.

Duration: 90 Minutes

GOALS

- Set up Pro Tools hardware and software for recording audio
- Create and configure a click track
- Record audio onto tracks in your session or project
- Recognize whole-file clips and subset clips
- Organize your clips and audio files after recording to minimize clutter and optimize your session

Key topics from this lesson are included in the *Pro Tools 12 Essential Training: 101* course on Lynda.com.

Many Pro Tools projects require extensive audio recording. After all, multi-track recording is a cornerstone of what any DAW is all about. Many of the recording controls and processes in Pro Tools are largely intuitive; nonetheless, getting the results you're after can be difficult if you are new to Pro Tools or DAWs in general.

This lesson provides the background information you'll need to get started on the right foot. Whether your audio endeavors involve a simple setup in a home studio or an elaborate system in a professional environment, this information will help you to get the audio you want onto your tracks in Pro Tools and take your first step toward creating a successful recording.

Before Recording

Before you begin recording in a session, you should ensure that your system has enough storage space for your planned work. The amount of storage space consumed by audio clips in a project will vary, depending on the bit depth and sample rate of the session. (See the "Converting Audio to Digital Format" section in Lesson 1 for a detailed discussion of bit depth and sample rate.)

Audio Storage Requirements

Pro Tools records all audio using sample rates ranging from 44.1 kHz to 192 kHz, with bit depths between 16-bit and 32-bit floating point. At a sample rate of 44.1 kHz, each track consumes approximately 5 megabytes (MB) of disk space per minute for 16-bit audio (mono), 7.5 MB per minute for 24-bit audio (mono), and 10 MB per minute for 32-bit floating-point audio. With increasing bit depth and sample rates, hard disk space consumption increases correspondingly; recording at a sample rate of 88.2 kHz, therefore, consumes twice as much space as recording at 44.1 kHz. Similarly, recording in stereo consumes twice the space of recording in mono.

Table 4.1 in Lesson 4 shows approximate storage consumption at the different data rates supported by Pro Tools.

Pro Tools audio files require a small amount of additional disk space to store associated clip metadata; this can add approximately 0.3 MB per minute to the total file size.

Calculating File Sizes

The sample rate and bit depth of a recorded audio file are directly related to the resulting file size. In fact, you can calculate file sizes using these two parameters with the following equations:

Sample Rate x Bit Depth = Bits per Second

Sample Rate x Bit Depth x 60 = Bits per Minute

In the binary world of computers, 8 bits make a byte, 1,024 bytes make a kilobyte (KB), and 1,024 KB make a megabyte (MB). Therefore, the file size equation can be restated as follows:

(Sample Rate x Bit Depth x 60) / (8 bits per byte x 1,024 bytes per kilobyte x 1,024 kilobytes per megabyte) = Megabytes (MB) per Minute

Reducing terms gives us the following:

Sample Rate x Bit Depth / 139,810 = MB per Minute

So by way of example, recording audio at a sample rate of 44,100 samples per second with a bit depth of 24 bits per sample would generate files that consume space at the following rate:

44,100 x 24 / 139,810 = 7.57 MB per Minute

Disk Usage Window

With a session running, you can monitor storage space and estimate the amount of available record time remaining on your storage media using the Disk Usage window.

To access the Disk Usage window, choose **WINDOW > DISK USAGE**.

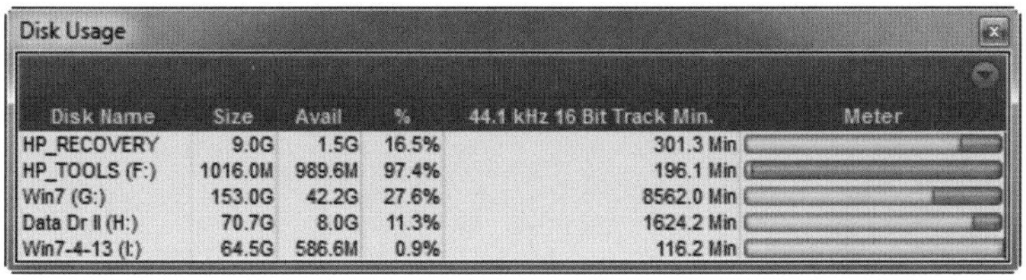

Figure 5.1 Disk Usage window

The Disk Usage window shows the number of continuous track minutes available on each mounted hard drive, using the current session's sample rate and bit depth.

Preparing to Record

Once you have created a session or project, added an Audio track (or tracks) to record onto, and verified that you have adequate disk space available, you will need to prepare your hardware and software for recording. If your session does not already include a click track, you might want to add one to use as a tempo reference while recording. Whether or not you use a click track, the general processes you will use to prepare for recording audio are as follows:

1. Check the hardware connections.
2. Record-enable the Audio track(s).
3. Set the track input path and input level.

Creating a Click Track (Optional)

When you're working with a song or other composition that is bar- and beat-based, it can help to record tracks while listening to a metronome click in Pro Tools. This ensures that recorded material, both MIDI and audio, will align with your session's bar and beat boundaries.

Aligning track material with beats allows you to take advantage of many useful editing functions in Pro Tools. It also enables you to arrange your song in sections by copying and pasting measures in Grid mode.

To set up a click track, use the **CREATE CLICK TRACK** command at the bottom of the **TRACK** menu. This command inserts the Click II plug-in on a new Aux Input track. The Click II plug-in is a mono sound module that creates an audible metronome click during session playback. You can use this click as a tempo reference when performing and recording.

The Click II plug-in receives its tempo and meter data from the Pro Tools application, enabling it to follow any changes in tempo and meter that you have made in a session. Several click sound presets are included for you to choose from.

To create a click track, do the following:

- Choose **TRACK > CREATE CLICK TRACK**. A new click track will be created in your session.

To configure the Click II plug-in, do the following:

1. Choose **OPTIONS > CLICK** to enable the Click option, if not already active (or enable the Metronome button in the Transport window).
2. From the Insert panel for the click track (Mix or Edit window), click on the **CLICK II** plug-in button. The Click II plug-in window will open.

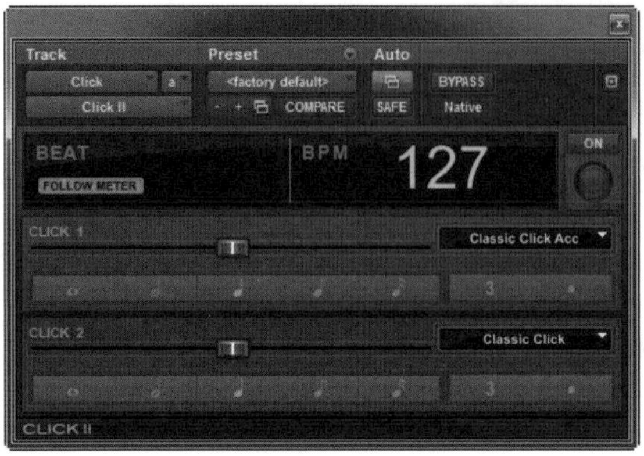

Figure 5.2 The Click II plug-in window

Additional details on plug-in inserts are presented in Lesson 10.

3. Set the click options as desired:
   - **Click 1:** Use the controls in this area to set the output level and click sound for the accented beat (Beat 1 of each bar) of the audio click.
   - **Click 2:** Use the controls in this area to set the output level and click sound for the unaccented beats of the audio click.
4. Click the **CLOSE** icon in the upper-left corner (Mac) or upper-right corner (Windows) to exit the Click II plug-in window.

To configure the click and countoff settings, do the following:

1. Choose **SETUP** > **CLICK/COUNTOFF** to open the Click/Countoff Options dialog box. (See Figure 5.3.)

You can also open the Click/Countoff Options dialog box by double-clicking the METRONOME button in the Transport window.

2. Choose when the click should sound using the radio buttons at the top of the dialog box.
3. Select whether to limit the countoff to record passes only, and specify the countoff duration at the bottom of the dialog box.

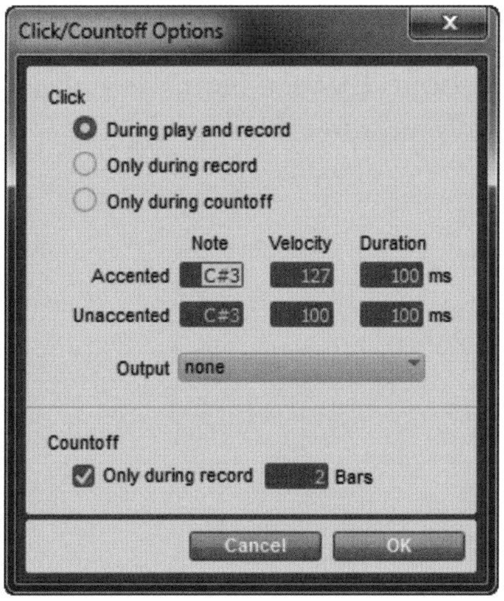

Figure 5.3 Click/Countoff Options dialog box

> **The Note, Velocity, Duration, and Output options in this dialog box are used with MIDI instrument–based clicks and do not affect the Click II plug-in.**

4. Click **OK** to close the Click/Countoff Options dialog box.
5. Use the MIDI controls in the Transport window to enable/disable the click (Metronome button) and the countoff (Countoff button) as needed.

> **With the Numeric Keypad mode set to Transport (default), you can press [7] on the numeric keypad to enable the click and [8] on the keypad to enable the countoff.**

> **To set the mode for the numeric keypad, choose SETUP > PREFERENCES > OPERATION. Select the desired mode under Numeric Keypad in the Transport section.**

When you begin playback, a click is generated according to the tempo and meter of the current session, the settings in the Click/Countoff Options dialog box, and the state of the MIDI controls in the Transport window.

Checking Hardware Connections

Recording audio involves connecting an instrument, microphone, or other sound source to your Pro Tools system. Most audio interfaces have inputs designated for different sound sources and input types. Before starting to record, you should verify that your sound source is connected to the appropriate inputs of the audio interface and that the signal is being passed through correctly. For basic recording, it is simplest to use the lowest available inputs on your audio interface that match your needs (for example, Input 1 for a mono source or Inputs 1 and 2 for a stereo pair).

If necessary, check the configuration of your audio interface and/or the Hardware Setup of your system to ensure correct routing of inputs or to change existing settings. Depending on your audio interface, you can use physical controls or switches, the controls in the Hardware Setup dialog box, or a separate control panel to define which physical inputs on the device are routed to available input paths in Pro Tools.

> **Example: The source selector switches on the front panel of an Mbox Pro let you choose which connector source (front or rear) is routed to each Pro Tools input.**

Record-Enabling Tracks

To set up a Pro Tools Audio track for recording, click the track's RECORD ENABLE button in either the Edit window or the Mix window. The button will flash red when the track is record-enabled.

Figure 5.4 Record Enable buttons: Mix window (left) and Edit window (right)

When a track has been record-enabled, the Track Fader turns red, indicating that it is now functioning as a record monitor level control.

To record-enable multiple Audio tracks, click the RECORD ENABLE buttons on additional tracks. To record-enable all tracks of a particular type in the session, OPTION-CLICK (Mac) or ALT-CLICK (Windows) on any track's RECORD ENABLE button.

Setting Input Path, Level, and Pan

With your sound source connected to the inputs of your Pro Tools interface, you are now ready to set Pro Tools to receive a signal from your source and to pass the signal through the system for recording and monitoring purposes.

Input Path

Each Audio track has an *Audio Input Path selector* in the track's I/O section. This selector allows you to route a signal from an input on your interface to the track for recording.

To set the incoming signal, do the following:

1. Locate the I/O section of the channel strip for the track you will record to in the Mix window.
2. Verify that the input displayed on the Input Path selector matches the input that your sound source is plugged into on your audio interface. (See Figure 5.5.)

Figure 5.5 The Input Path selector in the Mix window

3. If necessary, click the **INPUT PATH SELECTOR** to make changes, selecting the correct input path from the pop-up menu. (Note: Stereo tracks will have a pair of inputs routed to the track.)

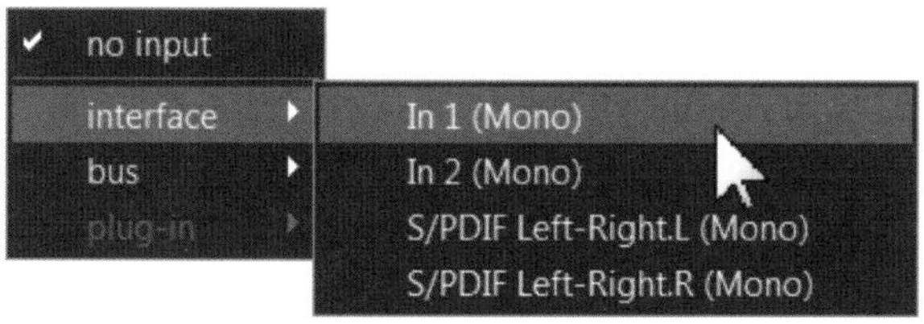

Figure 5.6 Input Path selector pop-up menu

Setting Input Paths for Recording on Multiple Tracks

When recording to multiple tracks simultaneously, each track will need to have a unique input routed to it. For example, suppose you are recording a vocalist with an acoustic guitar accompaniment on Tracks 1 and 2 of your session. You might have the vocal mike connected into Input 1 of a USB audio interface, and the guitar mike connected into Input 2.

In the Pro Tools Mix window, you would set the Input Path for your first track to **IN 1 (MONO)** (or the corresponding input path name that receives signal from Input 1 on your interface). Similarly, you would set the Input Path for your second track to **IN 2 (MONO)** (or the corresponding input path name that receives signal from Input 2 on the interface).

This setup will allow you to record and process the vocal signal on the first track separate from the guitar signal on the second track.

Input Level

As a general rule, input levels should be adjusted to obtain a strong, clean signal while avoiding clipping. Unlike when recording to tape, however, you do not need to record at the highest possible level in Pro Tools. Recording too hot can leave little room for subsequent gain-based processing (such as EQ) and can lead to digital clipping, which is always detrimental to audio quality. For best results, aim for an average peak input level around –6 dBFS or lower, keeping the track meter in the yellow range. To do this, adjust the level of your analog source while monitoring the indicator lights on your onscreen track meter.

Meters in the Pro Tools mixer measure loudness in decibels relative to full-scale audio (dBFS), with full scale represented by 0 at the top of the meter. Digital clipping occurs whenever a signal exceeds 0 dBFS at an input or output.

Adjusting the input level will typically require you to change the source volume, adjust the microphone placement, or modify the incoming signal strength using a mixer or preamplifier, because record levels cannot be adjusted within Pro Tools. Note that although a track's Volume Fader can be used to increase or decrease playback levels, the Volume Fader *does not* affect record levels.

Many audio interfaces provide preamplifier gains for their inputs. For all other I/O devices, record levels are set entirely from the source or pre-I/O signal processing.

Pan Position

Setting the pan affects the stereo placement of a signal for monitoring and playback purposes only; it has no effect on how the audio files are actually recorded.

To set the pan position of the signal, change the position of the Pan knob(s) for the track in the Mix window. The pan on a mono track is initially set to >0<, signifying the center of the stereo field. Pan settings range from <100 (hard left) to 100> (hard right).

Recording and Managing Audio

With your sound source routed to one or more tracks and the desired tracks record-enabled, you are ready to begin recording audio. Pro Tools offers a variety of recording modes that can be used in different audio recording situations. We will use the default mode (Nondestructive Record) for all work done in this course.

Other recording modes are covered in advanced courses.

To begin recording audio, do the following:

1. Display the Transport window, if it is not already showing (**WINDOW > TRANSPORT**). (Alternatively, you can use the Transport controls in the Edit window, if displayed.)
2. Optionally display the Expanded view in the Transport window (click the Maximize button in the upper-left corner [Mac] or upper-right corner [Windows]).
3. Verify that one or more tracks have been record-enabled. (See the "Record-Enabling Tracks" section earlier in this lesson.)
4. Click the **RECORD** button in the Transport window to enter Record Ready mode. The button will turn red and begin to flash.

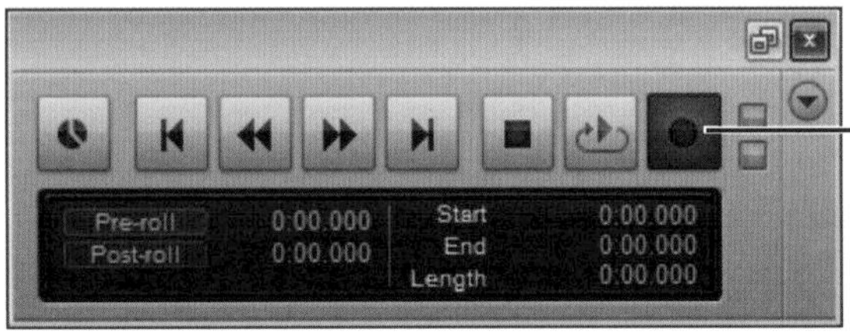

Figure 5.7 The Transport window in Record Ready mode (Expanded Transport view)

5. When you're ready, click **PLAY** in the Transport window to begin recording (or press the **SPACEBAR**).

You can also press COMMAND+SPACE BAR (Mac), CTRL+SPACE BAR (Windows), or Function key F12 to start recording immediately without first entering Record Ready mode.

Certain keyboard operations in Pro Tools conflict with system settings on Mac-based computers. To use these key combinations in Pro Tools, you will need to remap conflicting operations (such as Spotlight) in the Mac's System Preferences. Consult your course instructor or Pro Tools installation documents for suggested settings.

6. When you have finished your record take, click the STOP button in the Transport window (or press the SPACEBAR).

Organizing after Recording

Once you've completed a successful record pass, you should complete a few housekeeping steps. This will help you to stay organized and will also help prevent accidents while editing.

Return to Playback Mode

Returning record-enabled tracks to Playback mode will prevent unintended recording onto those tracks during subsequent operations in your session.

To return a track to Playback mode and adjust the playback settings, do the following:

1. Click the RECORD ENABLE button on the Audio track to take it out of Record Ready mode. The track's Volume Fader will now function as a playback level control rather than as an input-monitoring level control.
2. Click PLAY in the Transport window.
3. Adjust the playback level and panning as necessary.

If you have overloaded your audio inputs during recording and caused clipping, the topmost indicator on the level meter will stay lit. Click the indicator light to clear it.

Organize Audio Files and Clips

Each time you record audio into Pro Tools, you create a single audio file that appears both in the Clip List and in the Track Playlist (i.e., in the arrangement of clips on a track in the Edit window). An *audio file* is an entire unedited, continuous audio recording.

Audio files—or *whole-file clips*, as they are known in Pro Tools—are written and stored externally from your session file. Organizing audio files involves maintaining information both within the Pro Tools session and within the external files.

When you record audio into a Pro Tools session, the audio files are stored in the session's Audio Files folder by default.

As you begin to edit, you also create smaller pieces of the original sound file, called *subset clips*, or simply *clips*. An audio subset clip is an electronic pointer within the session document that references some portion of an audio file. Clips can range in length from one sample to many hours. Subset clips do not store audio information directly, but instead are used to display, edit, and play back audio information contained within the whole-file clip or audio file. Audio subset clips are generally internal to the Pro Tools session only.

Recognizing Audio Files and Clips

The Clip List in the Edit window shows all subset clips and whole-file clips that have been used in your session.

Pro Tools lists all whole-file clips in boldface type and all other clips in normal type. When sound files are recorded onto stereo Audio tracks, the word *stereo* is shown in parentheses at the end of the file name. Examples of these clip types are shown in Figure 5.8.

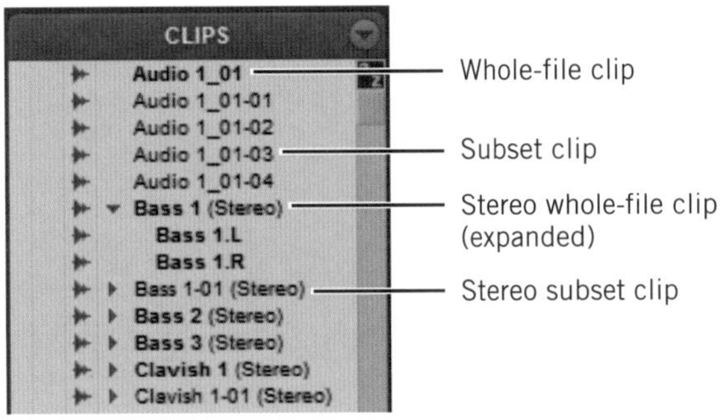

Figure 5.8 Audio clips in the Clip List

Note that clips on stereo Audio tracks can be expanded to display the left and right channels separately by clicking the disclosure triangle to the left of the clip name.

Audio clips represent pieces of audio data that can be moved or edited within Pro Tools. Clips are created during normal editing, either by the user or automatically by Pro Tools, and can refer to any type of audio, such as music, dialogue, sound effects, Foley, or automated dialogue replacement (ADR).

Clips can also appear in the Track Playlist. As shown in the following figure, each audio clip on a track is displayed using a solid rectangle to clearly delineate the clip boundaries.

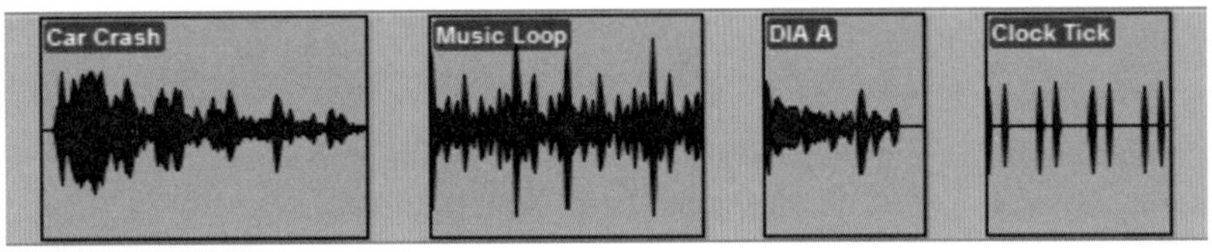

Figure 5.9 Audio clips as displayed in a Track Playlist

Naming Audio Files and Clips

During recording and editing, Pro Tools assigns default names to audio files and clips. At times, you might want to rename clips to make their names more meaningful and the clips easier to recognize.

Default Naming Conventions

When you record audio on a track, Pro Tools names the resulting file (a whole-file clip) using the name of the track as the base name. Pro Tools also appends an underscore and take ID to the clip name. (The take ID is a sequential number based on the number of times you've recorded on that track).

Following are examples of the file names Pro Tools automatically creates after recording for the first time on a mono track and on a stereo track:

Audio 1_01	Where *Audio 1* is the mono track name and *01* is the take number
Music_01 (Stereo)	Where *Music* is the stereo track name and *01* is the take number

When you edit a whole-file clip on a track, Pro Tools retains the original file and creates a new, edited subset clip, naming the file by appending a hyphen followed by the edit ID (a sequential number based on the number of edits you have created from that whole-file clip).

Following are examples of the clip names Pro Tools automatically creates for the first edit to whole-file clips on a mono track and on a stereo track:

Audio 1_02-01	Where *Audio 1_02* is a whole-file clip on a mono track and *01* is the edit number for the subset clip
Music_02-01 (Stereo)	Where *Music_02* is a whole-file clip on a stereo track and *01* is the edit number for the subset clip

Changing File and Clip Names

You can change the default name that Pro Tools assigns to a whole-file clip or subset clip at any time.

To rename a clip, do one of the following:

- Double-click the file or clip in the Edit window (with the GRABBER tool) or in the Clip List.

Double-clicking on a MIDI clip opens the MIDI Editor window by default. This behavior can be changed using the associated Preference setting (SETUP > PREFERENCES > MIDI).

- Right-click on the file or clip in the Edit window or Clip List and select RENAME from the pop-up menu.

The Name dialog box will open.

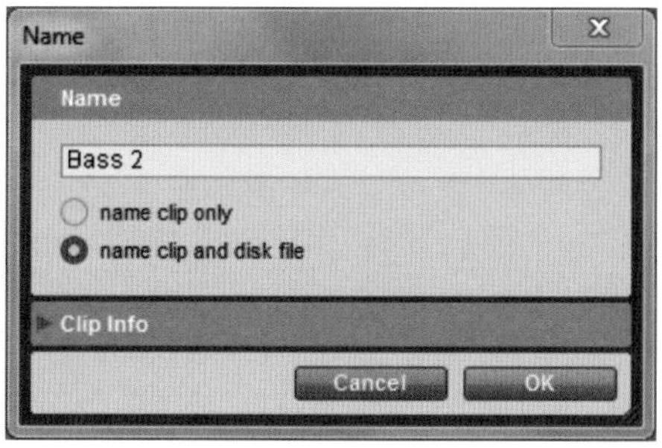

Figure 5.10 The Name dialog box

When renaming a whole-file clip, you can select from the following options in the Name dialog box:

- **Name Clip Only.** Renames the clip in Pro Tools but leaves the original file name unchanged on the hard drive.
- **Name Clip and Disk File.** Renames the clip in Pro Tools and renames the file on the hard drive as well.

Note that when you rename a stereo file or clip, both corresponding left and right channels are renamed accordingly.

Removing Audio Clips and Deleting Audio Files

Pro Tools makes an important distinction between removing clips from a session and deleting files from a hard drive:

- When you remove a clip from a session, the parent audio file remains on the hard drive and can be used in other clips elsewhere in the session or in other sessions.
- When you delete an audio file from the hard drive, all clips referring to that file are removed from the session and will be missing in any other session that references the audio file.

Removing Audio Clips

As your Clip List grows in your session, you might want to periodically remove the audio clips you no longer need, in order to reduce clutter. However, because removing audio clips does not delete the audio files, this action will have no effect on hard drive usage of the session.

To remove unwanted audio clips from the Clip List, do the following:

1. Select the clips in the Clip List that you want to remove.
    - To select multiple clips, COMMAND-CLICK (Mac) or CTRL-CLICK (Windows) on clips individually.
    - To select a continuous range, click on the first clip in the range and SHIFT-CLICK on the last clip.
2. Choose CLEAR from the Clip List pop-up menu.

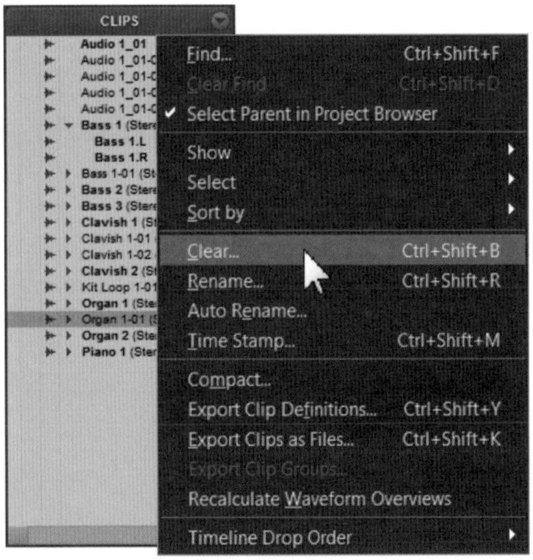

Figure 5.11 Clip List pop-up menu

3. In the resulting Clear Clips dialog box, click REMOVE to remove the clips from the session, while leaving all parent audio files on the hard drive.

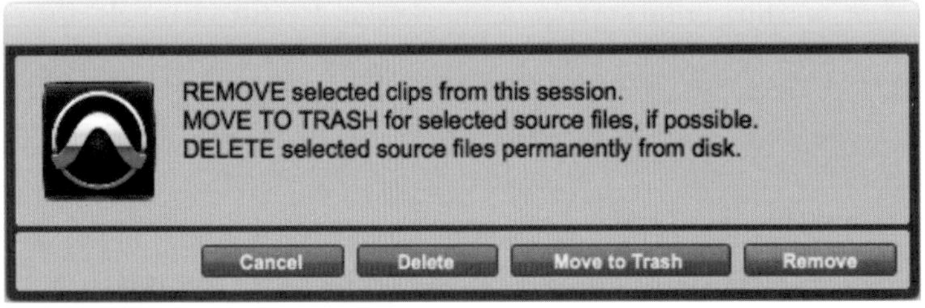

Figure 5.12 The Clear Clips dialog box

Pro Tools requires that all clips used on any Track Playlist, in the Undo queue, or on the Clipboard remain in the Clip List. If you attempt to remove a clip that is currently on a track, on the Clipboard, or in the Undo queue, the warning dialog box shown in Figure 5.13 appears.

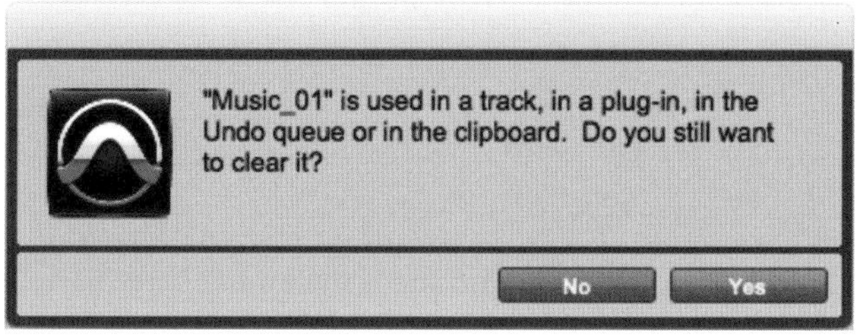

Figure 5.13 Warning dialog box when clearing clips

Choose one of the following:

- **Yes.** This option clears the clip from the Clip List and the corresponding track, Undo queue, or Clipboard.
- **No.** This option cancels the Clear command.

Moving or Deleting Audio Files

As you work on your session, you may also accumulate unwanted whole-file clips from test recordings or unusable takes. At times, you might want to delete these unneeded audio files from your hard drive.

By removing audio files from the hard drive, you can free up additional drive space and reduce the overall storage requirements of your session. In addition to utilizing hard drive space more effectively, this will also help reduce transfer time for your sessions.

To remove clips from the Clip List and remove or delete the associated audio files from the hard drive, do the following:

1. Complete Steps 1 and 2 in the "Removing Audio Clips" section earlier in this chapter.
2. In the Clear Clips dialog box, click MOVE TO TRASH or DELETE to remove the selected clips from the Clip List *and* remove or delete any selected parent audio files from your hard drive.

The Delete option permanently and irreversibly deletes audio files from your hard drive. This will affect the current session and any other sessions that reference the audio file. This operation is immediate and cannot be undone. Use this command with caution.

Just like when you are removing audio clips, if you attempt to move or delete a file that has been placed on a track, on the Clipboard, or in the Undo queue, you will receive a warning message.

- Click YES to permanently remove the file from the session and from the hard drive.
- Click NO to leave the file untouched in the session and on the hard drive.

Pro Tools will prevent you from moving or deleting an audio file that is referenced by clips within the same session. If you attempt to move or delete an audio file that is referenced by other clips in the session, the dialog box shown in Figure 5.14 will appear.

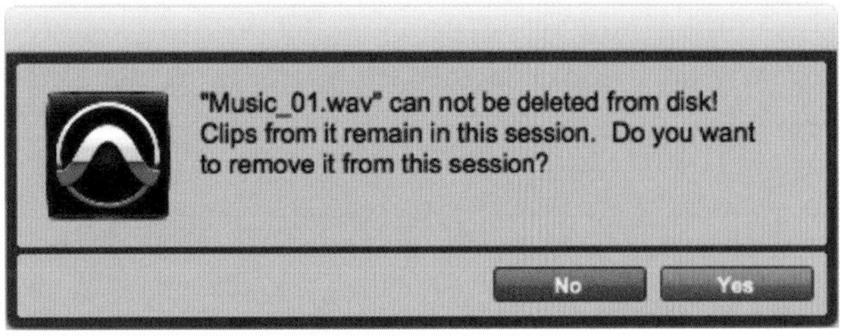

Figure 5.14 Dialog box displayed when unable to move or delete

- Click **YES** to remove the whole-file clip from the Clip List, while leaving the audio file on the hard drive.
- Click **NO** to leave the whole-file clip untouched in the Clip List and on the hard drive.

If no other confirmation dialog box appears first, Pro Tools will prompt you with the following warning before completing the Delete command:

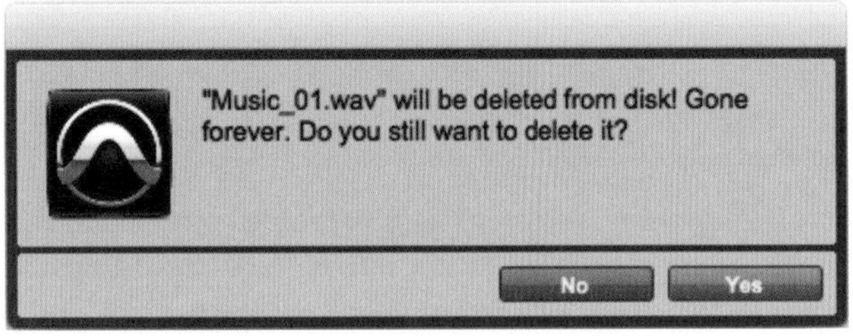

Figure 5.15 Delete warning dialog box

- Click **YES** to permanently remove the file from the session and from the hard drive.
- Click **NO** to leave the file untouched in the session and on the hard drive.

To bypass repeated warnings when you are clearing or deleting multiple files or clips, OPTION-CLICK (Mac) or ALT-CLICK (Windows) on the YES or NO button. This will prevent multiple warnings from appearing.

Review/Discussion Questions

1. How much disk space is consumed per minute by a mono track at a sample rate of 44.1 kHz and a bit depth of 16-bit? What happens to disk space consumption if the sample rate is doubled to 88.2 kHz with the same bit depth? (See "Audio Storage Requirements" beginning on page 88.)

2. How can you monitor the storage space available on your system to determine the amount of record time remaining for each mounted hard drive? (See "Disk Usage Window" beginning on page 89.)

3. How can you create a click track for a session? What kind of track is used for a click track? (See "Creating a Click Track (Optional)" beginning on page 89.)

4. What window(s) can you use to record-enable an Audio track? (See "Record-Enabling Tracks" beginning on page 92.)

5. What selector can you use to route a signal from an input on your audio interface to a track for recording? (See "Input Path" beginning on page 92.)

6. How can you adjust the input level going to a record-enabled track? Can you use the Volume Fader to achieve a strong signal going to disk? (See "Input Level" beginning on page 93.)

7. How can you place a session in Record Ready mode after record-enabling a track? What modifiers/shortcuts are available to initiate recording without first entering Record Ready mode? (See "Recording and Managing Audio" beginning on page 94.)

8. Where are recorded audio files stored for Pro Tools sessions? (See "Organize Audio Files and Clips" beginning on page 95.)

9. What term is used to describe an unedited audio file in Pro Tools? What term is used to describe the smaller, edited pieces of the original sound file? (See "Recognizing Audio Files and Clips" beginning on page 96.)

10. What types of clips are represented by boldface text in the Clip List? What type is represented by normal (plain) text? (See "Recognizing Audio Files and Clips" beginning on page 96.)

11. How do track names affect the default names of the audio files you record in Pro Tools? (See "Default Naming Conventions" beginning on page 96.)

12. Describe two ways to rename an audio file after recording into Pro Tools. (See "Changing File and Clip Names" beginning on page 97.)

13. How would you go about removing unwanted audio from the Clip List without deleting the files from disk? (See "Removing Audio Clips" beginning on page 98.)

14. How would you go about deleting unused whole-file clips to erase them from your hard drive? Can this action be undone? (See "Moving or Deleting Audio Files" beginning on page 99.)

To review additional material from this chapter, see the PT101 Study Guide module available through the ElementsIED online learning platform at ElementsED.com.

Recording Audio

In this exercise tutorial, you will be recording a voiceover (VO) for a radio advertisement you'll be creating for a surf shop. You have two options available to complete this exercise.

Option 1: Live Recording. For this option, you will first need to connect a microphone to your audio interface. If you are using Pro Tools without an audio interface, you might be able to use a microphone connected to an input on your computer or even use the computer's built-in microphone. Alternatively, you might be able to record through a USB microphone connected to an available port on your computer.

This exercise does not include instructions for routing audio from a USB microphone into Pro Tools. Refer to the section in Lesson 2 called "Accessing Connected Audio Devices" for basic setup information. Consult the documentation that came with your microphone for additional details.

Option 2: Bus Recording. If the above live input recording options are not available or are impractical, you can instead record from an existing bus in the starter session (included in the download media) by routing the bus to the input of the VO track.

Duration: 10 to 15 Minutes

Media: Exercise 5 Starter.ptx (Optional)

Media Files

To complete this exercise using Option 2, you will need to use the Recording Exercise Starter file included in the PT101 Download Media. You should have downloaded the media files in Exercise 4.

If needed, you can re-download the media files by pointing your browser to http://alpp.us/PT101-128.

Note: The above URL is ***case sensitive.***

Getting Started

You will start by opening the Pro Tools session for the option that you will use to record the voiceover for the radio ad.

Open the session and save it as Exercise 5:

1. Launch Pro Tools and choose FILE > OPEN SESSION (or choose OPEN FROM DISK from the Dashboard).
2. Navigate to the appropriate location for the option that you will be using:
   - **Option 1, Live Recording:** Open the session file that you created in Exercise 4 (Storage Drive/Folder > PT101-XXX > Exercise04-XXX.ptx).

- **Option 2, Bus Recording:** Open the *Recording Exercise Starter.ptx* file from the download media (PT101 Download Media > 01. Exercise 5 > Recording Exercise Starter.ptx).

3. Select and open the target session. The session will open displaying four tracks in the Edit window.

4. Choose FILE > SAVE AS and name the session *Exercise05-XXX*, keeping the session inside the original session folder (for Option 1) or moving the session into your PT101-XXX folder (for Option 2).

5. Toggle the display to the Mix window by choosing WINDOW > MIX or by pressing COMMAND+= (Mac) or CTRL+= (Windows).

Preparing to Record

To get started, you will need to route audio from a connected microphone to the VO track. If you have chosen Option 2 and are not recording live input, you can instead route the Scratch VO bus to the track.

If recording from a microphone, you will also need to set the input level going to the track.

Route the signal to the audio input of the VO track:

1. Locate the AUDIO INPUT PATH SELECTOR for the VO track. This will be the top selector in the I/O section.

Figure 5.16 Audio Input Path selector for the VO track in the Mix window

2. Click on the AUDIO INPUT PATH SELECTOR and do one of the following to route audio to the track:

   - Select INTERFACE > ANALOG 1 (or the corresponding input or port where your microphone is connected) for recording the voiceover as live input.
   - Select BUS > SCRATCH VO to record the voiceover from existing audio included in the session.

3. Record-enable the track by clicking on the RECORD ENABLE button so that it begins flashing red. (See Figure 5.17.)

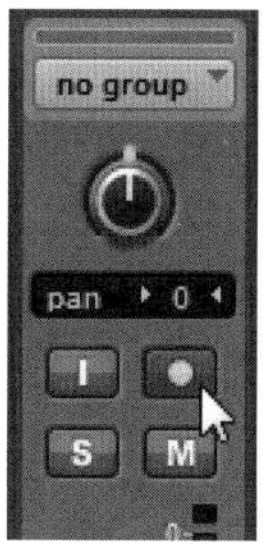

Figure 5.17 VO track after being record-enabled

Set the input level for the track (live recording only):

1. If recording from a microphone, test the input level by speaking into the microphone in the same manner that you will use when recording. (Keep the distance and volume consistent while speaking.)

   Try using the first line of the voiceover script as you set the level: "Summer's here and it's time for some fun in the sun."

2. Keep an eye on the track meter as you speak into the mike. If necessary, adjust the gain on your audio interface or make other adjustments to get a strong input signal with consistent levels around two-thirds of the way up the meter.

Be careful not to push the meter into the top half of the orange zone, as this could lead to irreversible clipping in the recorded audio file.

Recording the Voiceover

With the input routed and the level set, you will now record the voiceover for the commercial. If you are recording live from a microphone, you will want to practice the script a few times to determine proper pacing.

To practice the script (Option 1 only):

1. Review the voiceover script below.

   Summer's here and it's time for some fun in the sun. But don't hit the dunes unprepared! Spicoli's Surf Shop has the coolest beach gear so you don't get baked by the sun. Our gnarly accessories include swimming apparel, sun block, boogie boards, flip flops, and oversized beach towels with sand-free technology. So keep the sand at the beach and the waves within reach. Stop by Spicoli's Surf Shop today!

2. Toggle the display to the Edit window by choosing **WINDOW > EDIT** or by pressing **COMMAND+=** (Mac) or **CTRL+=** (Windows).

3. Press the SPACEBAR to begin playback and read the script aloud to get a sense of the proper pacing.

   Keep an eye on the Sub Counter display at the top of the Edit window as you practice. The voiceover should start around 2-3 seconds into the session and end shortly before reaching the 30-second mark (0:30.000).

This is a 30-second radio spot, so you will not have much time to complete the script. Practice keeping a brisk pace without sounding rushed.

4. Press the SPACEBAR when finished to stop playback.

5. Repeat the process as needed to refine your timing.

To record the voiceover:

1. If needed, choose WINDOW > TRANSPORT to display the Transport window.
2. With the VO track record-enabled, record-arm the Transport window. The Record button will flash red.

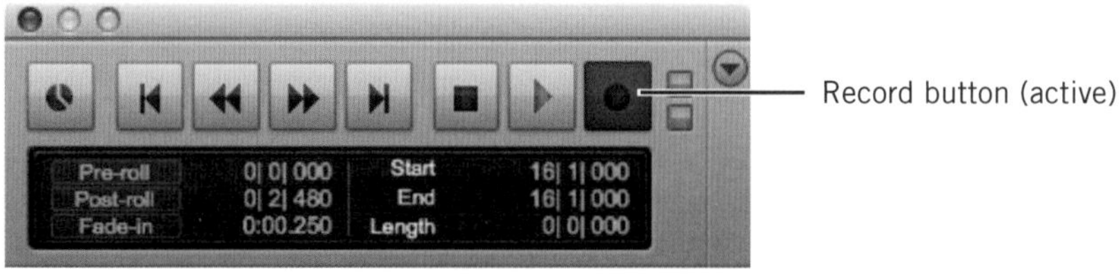

Figure 5.18 The Transport window with the session in Record Ready mode

3. Before recording toggle the display to the Edit window, if not already displayed, by pressing COMMAND+= (Mac) or CTRL+= (Windows).
4. When ready, click the PLAY button or press the SPACEBAR to begin recording.
5. Read the script (if recording live) or let the script complete (if recording from a bus).
6. When finished, click the STOP button or press the SPACEBAR a second time to stop recording.
7. If needed, repeat the above process to record additional takes until you are satisfied with the results.
8. When satisfied, click the RECORD ENABLE button on the VO track to take the track out of record mode.

Finishing Up

To complete this exercise tutorial, you will need to save your work and close the session. You will be reusing this session in Exercise 6, so it is important to save the work you've done.

You may also want to listen to your work before exiting.

Review and save your work:

1. Press ENTER or RETURN to place the cursor at the beginning of the session.
2. Press the SPACEBAR to play back the session and confirm your results.
3. Press the SPACEBAR a second time when finished.
4. Choose FILE > SAVE to save the session.
5. Choose FILE > CLOSE SESSION to close the session.

Remember that you cannot close a Pro Tools session by closing its windows. You must choose CLOSE SESSION from the FILE menu.

LESSON 6

Importing and Working with Media

This lesson introduces various processes for importing audio and video files into a Pro Tools session or project. It describes file formats and types that can be imported, explains the functions of the Import Audio dialog box and other methods of importing audio, and discusses importing video files.

Duration: 90 Minutes

GOALS

- **Determine whether an audio file's parameters are compatible with your session or project**
- **Understand how Pro Tools treats stereo files**
- **Understand the functions available in the Import Audio dialog box**
- **Import audio files to the Clip List or to Audio tracks in the Edit window**
- **Import video files to a Video track in the Edit window**

Key topics from this lesson are included in the *Pro Tools 12 Essential Training: 101* course on Lynda.com.

Many music and post-production projects require you to work with media files that have been created outside of your current session. Whether you'd like to import music loops, add tracks recorded by others, import sound effect files from a sound library, or place a video clip in your session, you will need a way to get outside media into Pro Tools. This lesson discusses how to use the import options provided in Pro Tools for these kinds of situations.

Considerations Prior to Import

Pro Tools allows you to import audio and video files that already reside on a storage drive (or other volume) and place them in your session. You can import media using one of several techniques, depending upon the type of media you are importing. Pro Tools can read some file formats directly and can convert many other audio formats on import.

Prior to importing a file, you should understand whether the file is compatible with your session and how the file will change if it needs to be converted.

File Characteristics

The types of media files that you can successfully import into a Pro Tools session will depend in part on how your session was originally configured. Some important considerations for importing an audio file include the file's sample rate and file format. The primary consideration for video files is the file format.

Audio Bit Depth and Sample Rate

The bit depth of a Pro Tools session or project will be 16-bit, 24-bit, or 32-bit floating point, and the sample rate will be anywhere from 44.1 kHz to 192 kHz. These settings are specified when the Pro Tools document is created. (See "Choosing Parameter Settings" in Lesson 4.)

Although the bit depth of the Pro Tools file can be different from the audio files it references, the sample rate must match between the session and its audio files. This means that any imported audio files must match the session sample rate, or be converted, in order to play back correctly.

Audio File Formats

The native audio file formats used in a Pro Tools session include Audio Interchange File Format (AIFF) and Waveform Audio File Format (WAV). This is another characteristic that you specify when creating the session. (See "Choosing Parameter Settings" in Lesson 4.)

To determine the bit depth, sample rate, and file format of an existing open session, choose SETUP > SESSION.

Pro Tools recognizes compatible file formats that match the sample rate of your session, allowing you to add them to the Clip List without requiring any file translation. All WAV and AIFF files can coexist in a session without requiring conversion. However, any files in another format as well as any files that have a different sample rate from the session, regardless of format, must be converted.

Pro Tools will convert files on import, if necessary. Pro Tools can import many common audio file formats, including the following:

- **Sound Designer II (SD II).** SD II is a monophonic or stereo interleaved file format supported on Macintosh systems only. This format supports sample rates up to 48 kHz and can be imported into Pro Tools with conversion.
- **Audio Interchange File Format (AIFF).** This file format is used primarily on Macintosh systems, although Pro Tools supports this file format natively on both Mac and Windows. AIFF files can be

recorded directly or imported without requiring conversion. The AIFF file format is commonly used with media programs such as Final Cut and QuickTime software.

- **Audio Interchange File Compressed (AIFC).** A variant of the AIFF audio file standard, AIFC provides audio compression for AIFF files. In Avid systems, AIFC file compression is usually turned off; as such, there is essentially no difference between the Avid AIFC format and the standard AIFF file format.
- **Waveform Audio File Format (WAV).** Pro Tools reads and plays back any standard WAV (WAVE) format files. However, it records and exports WAV files in the Broadcast WAV or BWF format. (Like other WAV files, BWF files are denoted by the *.wav* extension.) BWF files are ideal for file interchange operations due to the way they store timestamps. BWF is the default file format for all Pro Tools systems. BWF files can be recorded directly and imported (without conversion) on either platform, allowing seamless audio file exchange between Mac and Windows.
- **MP3 (MPEG-1 Layer-3).** MP3 files are supported on all common computer platforms and employ file compression of up to 10:1, while still maintaining reasonable audio quality. Because of their small size and cross-platform support, they have traditionally been popular for email messages, portable music players, and social media. MP3 files must be converted for import to a Pro Tools session.

Video File Formats

Pro Tools 11 and later can import video files in the QuickTime format as well as a wide range of Avid MXF video formats. Video file import and playback in Pro Tools requires that the Avid Video Engine be enabled, which can be done at anytime from the Playback Engine dialog box (SETUP > PLAYBACK ENGINE).

Split Stereo versus Interleaved Files

When it comes to digital audio, a stereo recording can be stored in two different ways: as split stereo files or as an interleaved stereo file. These two options have no audible difference between them. The difference is purely in how the audio is stored on disk.

- **Split stereo (multi-mono).** In split stereo files, the audio is represented in separate mono files for the left and right channels. The split stereo file format is supported on all Pro Tools systems (and Avid picture-editing systems).
- **Interleaved stereo.** In an interleaved stereo file, the stereo information is combined (interleaved) into a single file that contains both left and right channel information. Using interleaved files can simplify file management.

Either format can be imported into current Pro Tools systems without requiring conversion, although the format that Pro Tools uses for recording depends on the current session parameter configuration.

For Pro Tools sessions with the INTERLEAVED option enabled, all stereo and multi-channel audio is recorded as interleaved audio files.

Importing Audio

When you import audio from a hard drive (or other volume) into your session, Pro Tools places the audio files in the Clip List. Pro Tools provides several options for importing audio into a session.

Import Audio Dialog Box

Audio files and clips can be imported directly to the Clip List or imported to new tracks using the Import Audio dialog box. This dialog box can be used to add, copy, and/or convert audio files for use in your session.

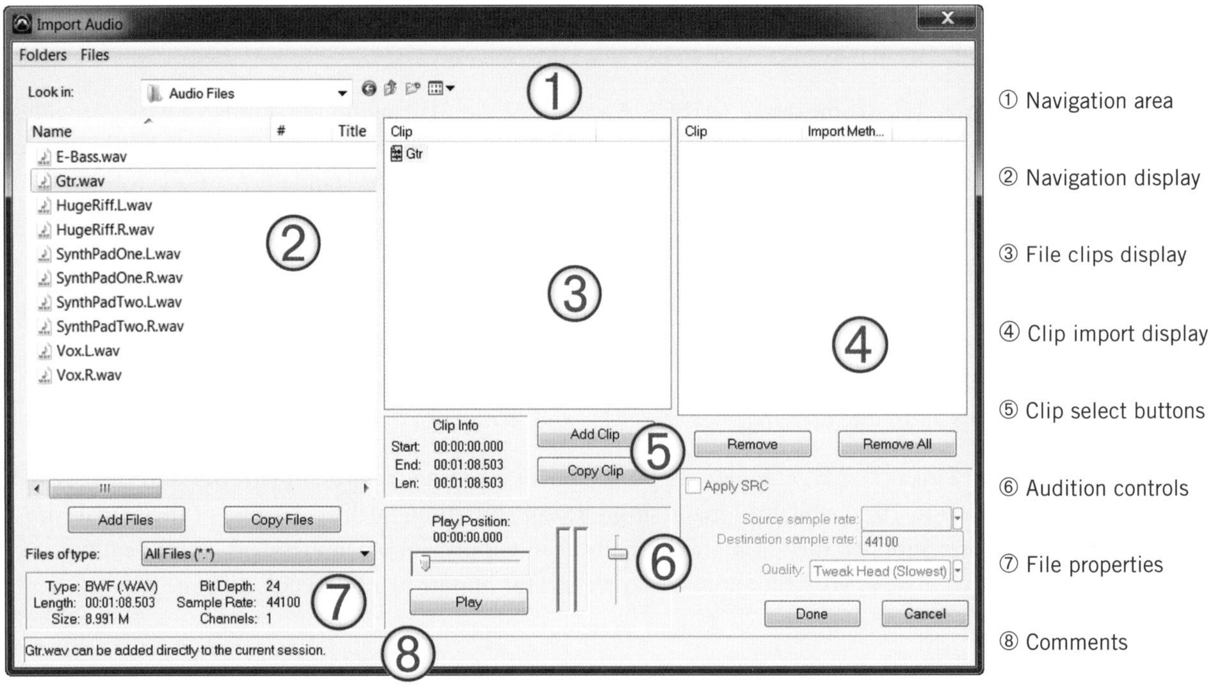

Figure 6.1 Import Audio dialog box (Windows)

Although the Import Audio dialog box is displayed somewhat differently on Mac and Windows systems, it includes the following main areas on both:

- **File navigation.** A standard navigation area at the top of the dialog box (①) combined with the navigation display (②) allows you to locate and select audio files on your system.
- **File properties.** The file properties area (⑦) lists the file type, length, size, bit depth, sample rate, and number of channels (1=mono, 2=stereo interleaved) for the selected file.
- **Comments.** The comments area (⑧) describes how the selected file can be imported into the session and provides other related information about the file.
- **File clips.** The file clips area (③) shows the currently selected file (parent file) and any subset clips included in the file. Two types of icons can appear in this area, indicating whether the item is a parent file or a subset clip.

   **Parent file.** An icon that looks like a document containing an audio waveform with the upper-left corner turned down is used to identify a parent audio file.

   **Subset clip.** An icon that looks like a selected portion of a waveform is used to identify an audio subset clip. (Subset clips can be embedded within the selected parent audio file.)
- **Clip select buttons.** The Add Clip and Convert Clip/Copy Clip buttons (⑤) are used to select audio to add or copy into your session. Clicking one of these buttons places the selected audio file or clip in the clip import area of the dialog box.
- **Audition controls.** The audition controls (⑥) allow you to start, stop, rewind, and fast-forward playback of the currently selected file or clip.
- **Clip import.** The clip import area (④) displays the audio files and clips that you have selected to import to your current session and the import method that will be used. You can remove clips from this list using the buttons beneath the display area.

Importing Audio with the Import Command

Audio files can be imported to tracks or to the Clip List, making the files available to be placed into tracks later. Compatible files or clips can be imported directly without adding them to the Audio Files folder, by referencing the existing files in their current location. Files that are not directly compatible must be converted to match; the converted files are placed in the session's Audio Files folder by default.

Files in a supported format (WAV or AIFF) that match the session sample rate are directly compatible with the session. Files that are not directly compatible must be converted to match the session parameters during import.

To import audio, follow these steps:

1. Choose FILE > IMPORT > AUDIO. The Import Audio dialog box will appear.
2. Select an audio file in the navigation window to display its properties and any clips it contains.
3. Place a file or clip in the clip import window by clicking any of the following buttons:
   - **Add/Add All.** Use these buttons to import compatible files or clips *without* copying them to the Audio Files folder. Clips that do not match the sample rate of the current session can also be added using these buttons, but they will not play back at the correct speed and pitch.

   The Add buttons reference the original audio file(s) and do not copy them into your session's Audio Files folder. If the original files are moved or if the session is transferred to a different system, the session may no longer be able to play the referenced files.

   - **Copy/Copy All.** Use these buttons to import compatible files or clips *and* force-copy them to the session's Audio Files folder. The Copy buttons change to Convert buttons when the selected audio file or clip is not directly compatible with the current session.
   - **Convert/Convert All.** Use these buttons to convert files or clips that are not directly compatible with your session. All converted files will automatically be copied to the session's Audio Files folder as new files that match the session parameters, with the correct speed, length, and pitch.
4. Click DONE to begin importing the audio to your session.

   When audio files or clips are being copied or converted, a dialog box will appear, prompting you to select a target destination for the files.
5. In the CHOOSE A DESTINATION FOLDER dialog box, select the desired folder location and choose USE CURRENT FOLDER. (The session's Audio Files folder will be selected by default.)
6. When the AUDIO IMPORT OPTIONS dialog box appears (Figure 6.2), do one of the following:
   - Select NEW TRACK and choose a start location from the drop-down list. New Audio tracks will be created for each clip you import, and each clip will be placed at the specified location on its track.
   - Select CLIP LIST to import the audio to the Clip List for later use. The imported audio will appear in the Clip List in the session but will not be added to any tracks during import.

Figure 6.2 The Audio Import Options dialog box

Importing Audio with Workspace Browsers

As discussed in Lesson 4, Pro Tools provides specialized windows called Workspace browsers that you can use to quickly locate, manage, and open Pro Tools sessions and compatible files. Workspace browsers provide powerful search, navigation, file information, and audition capabilities for Pro Tools.

You can import audio into Pro Tools by dragging files into a session from a Workspace browser window. All files imported in this manner are automatically converted to be compatible with the session parameters, if needed. If no conversion is necessary, the original files will be referenced and not copied.

Like the Import Audio dialog box, a Workspace browser can be used to import audio to the Clip List or to existing or new tracks in a session.

Importing to the Clip List

To import audio directly into the Clip List using a Workspace browser, follow these steps:

1. Choose **WINDOW > NEW WORKSPACE > DEFAULT.**
2. To conduct a search of audio files only, follow these steps:
   - In the Workspace window, click the **ADVANCED SEARCH** button on the right side of the toolbar. When Advanced Search mode is active, Advanced Search tools will display in the Browser pane.

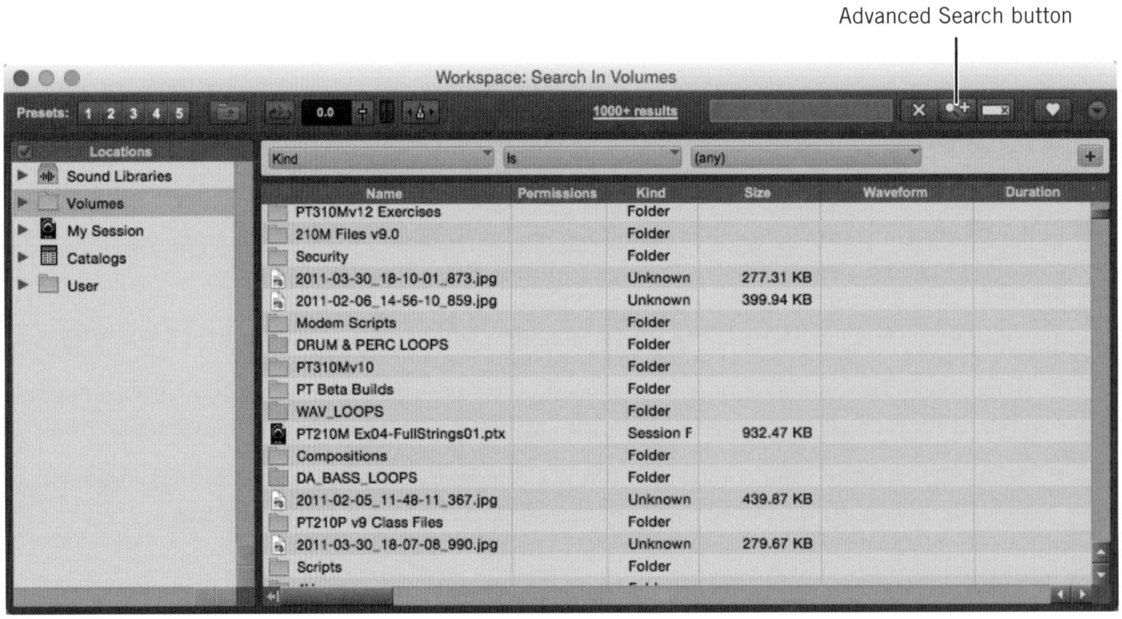

Figure 6.3 Advanced Search mode active in a Workspace browser

- Choose the volume or folder that you want to search by selecting it in the Locations pane on the right side of the window. (See Figure 6.4.) Note that you can drill down through the file system by clicking the arrow icons to expand volumes and folders.

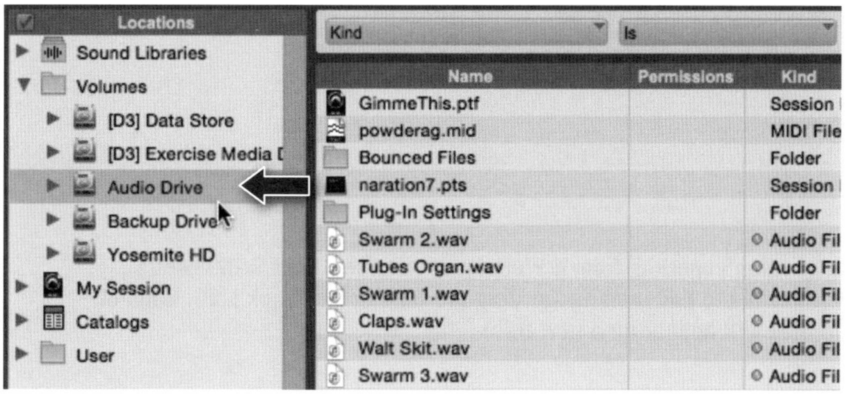

Figure 6.4 Selecting a search location

- Click on the **SEARCH COLUMN** selector in the Advanced Search tools and select **KIND**, if not already selected.
- Click on the **FILE TYPE** selector and select **AUDIO FILE**. The search results will update in the Browser pane to show only audio files.

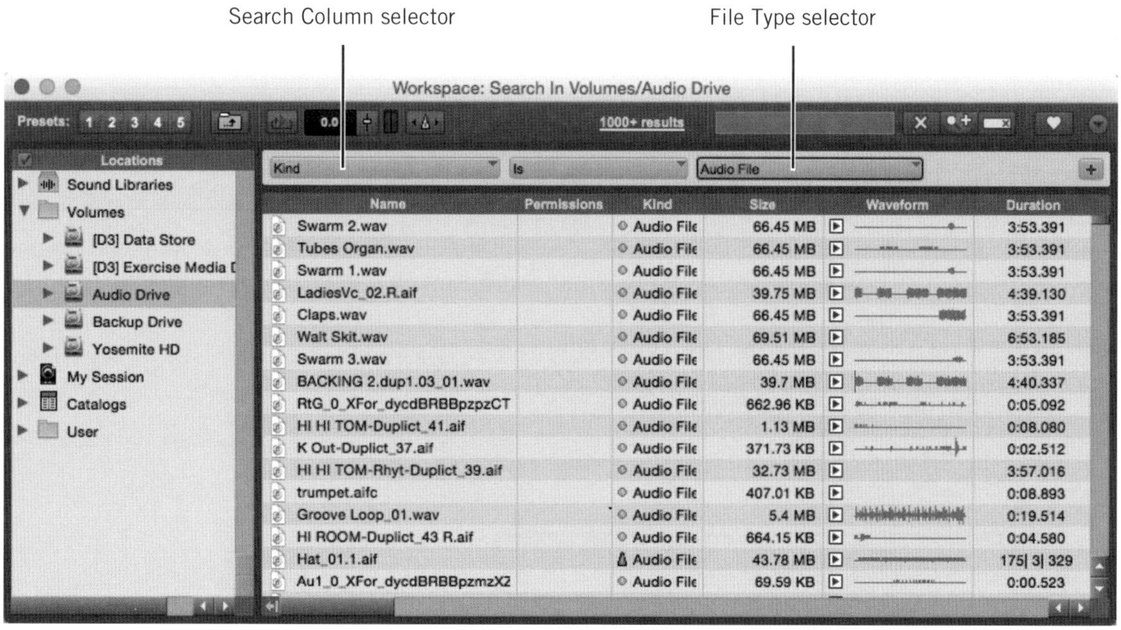

Figure 6.5 Search results displayed in a Workspace browser

3. Drag the audio files you want to import from the Workspace browser into the Clip List.

The files will automatically be converted to the file format and sample rate of the session, if necessary, and will appear in the Clip List.

Imported audio that is directly compatible with the session parameters will be referenced in its original location and not copied into the session's Audio Files folder. To force-copy a file, hold OPTION (Mac) or ALT (Windows) while dragging the file to the Clip List.

Importing to Tracks

To import audio to tracks using a Workspace browser, follow these steps:

1. Choose **WINDOW > NEW WORKSPACE > DEFAULT** and use the Workspace browser to locate the audio files you want to import. (See Step 2 in the preceding "Importing to the Clip List" section.)
2. Drag the audio files from the browser onto an existing track or tracks in the Pro Tools Edit window.

The files will automatically be converted to match the session parameters, as needed, and will appear on the selected track or tracks.

To create new tracks when importing from a Workspace browser, hold SHIFT while dragging the audio files to the Edit window (or drag the files to the Track List). Each of the imported audio files will appear on a new track.

Batch Importing Audio

You can quickly import a set of audio files from any open folder on your system. Files that have a different sample rate from the session or project will be converted on import, as will any files with a non-native file format.

To batch import files, follow these steps:

1. With a Pro Tools session open, browse the files on your system using an Explorer or Finder window.
2. Select the audio files to import and drag them onto the Pro Tools application icon or shortcut.

Each of the files will appear in the Clip List in the session.

Importing Video

To play back an imported video file in Pro Tools, you will first need to enable the Avid Video Engine. If the Video Engine is not already enabled, you will be prompted to launch it when importing video.

To enable the Avid Video Engine for Pro Tools, follow these steps:

1. Choose **SETUP > PLAYBACK ENGINE.**
2. Select the **ENABLE** checkbox next to the Video Engine option.

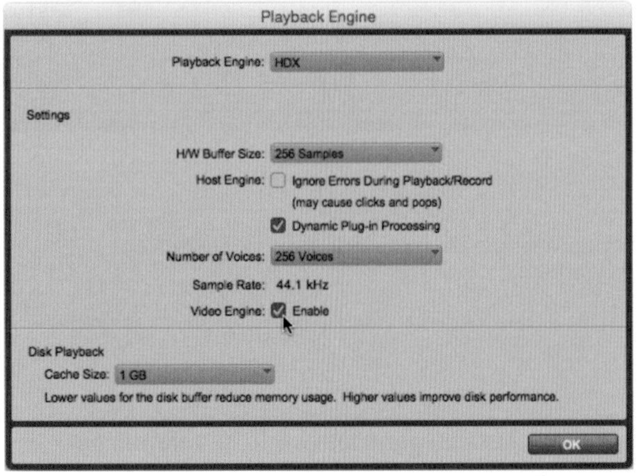

Figure 6.6 Enabling the Avid Video Engine in the Playback Engine dialog box

3. Click **OK** to close the Playback Engine dialog box.

With the Avid Video Engine enabled, you can import video using the following steps:

1. Choose **FILE > IMPORT > VIDEO**. A dialog box will open, allowing you to select the video file to import.
2. Navigate to and select the desired QuickTime movie or Avid MXF file.
3. Click **OPEN**. The Video Import Options dialog box will appear.

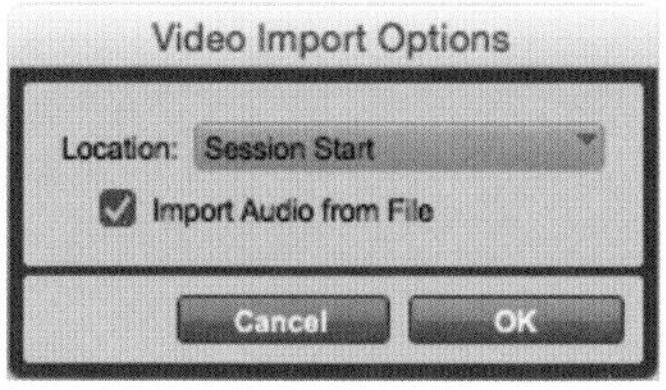

Figure 6.7 The Video Import Options dialog box

4. Select the desired import options as follows:
   - Select a start location from the **LOCATION** drop-down list.
   - If you wish to import audio embedded in a QuickTime movie, select **IMPORT AUDIO FROM FILE**.
5. Click **OK**.

Pro Tools will import the movie onto its own Video track in the Edit window and open the floating Video window. The first frame of the movie will be placed at the selected start time in your session, unless otherwise specified during import.

If you chose to import audio, you will be prompted to choose a destination folder for the audio file. After copying to the desired folder, the audio will appear in a new Audio track in the session.

Video Track Display

Depending on the setting of your Video track view, the movie will display in the Edit window as blocks or as a picture-icon (picon) "thumbnail" overview of the frames of the movie it represents. The Video track will show greater or lesser detail depending on your current zoom level in the Edit window—the closer in you zoom, the more individual frames will be displayed in the Video track; the farther out you zoom, the fewer individual frames will be displayed.

Working with Video Tracks

The Video track behaves much like a Pro Tools Audio or MIDI track in that you can move the video clip with the Grabber or other editing tools. This allows you to offset the movie to any start point.

Only one video file can be associated with a standard Pro Tools document at a time. If you want to import a different movie into a session, repeat the preceding steps. The new movie will replace the original in the session.

The Video track takes its name from the imported video file. Video tracks can subsequently be renamed, in the same manner as other tracks in your session. (See the "Naming Tracks" section in Lesson 4 for details.)

Using Frames view on the Video track may cause your computer to exhibit sluggish performance. If this happens, switch the Video track to Blocks view or hide the track.

Review/Discussion Questions

1. What audio file formats can be imported to Pro Tools without requiring conversion? (See "Audio File Formats" beginning on page 108.)

2. What condition would cause a file in one of Pro Tools' native formats to require conversion on import? (See "Audio File Formats" beginning on page 108.)

3. Name some common audio file formats that Pro Tools can convert on import. (See "Audio File Formats" beginning on page 108.)

4. What are some video file formats that can be imported by Pro Tools? (See "Video File Formats" beginning on page 109.)

5. What is the difference between split stereo and interleaved stereo? Which is/are supported for importing into Pro Tools 12? (See "Split Stereo versus Interleaved Files" beginning on page 109.)

6. What is the difference between the Add button in the Import Audio dialog box and the Copy button? Which button will force-copy the files into your session's Audio Files folder? (See "Importing Audio with the Import Command" beginning on page 111.)

7. What happens when you use the Workspace browser to import audio that is not compatible with your session's parameters (in other words, audio that requires conversion)? What happens when you import audio that does not require conversion? (See "Importing Audio with Workspace Browsers" beginning on page 112.)

8. What steps are required to conduct a search for an audio file using the Workspace browser? (See "Importing Audio with Workspace Browsers" beginning on page 112.)

9. How would you go about importing a QuickTime movie file to Pro Tools while simultaneously importing the audio embedded in the file? (See "Working with Video Tracks" beginning on page 115.)

10. How many video files can be associated with a standard Pro Tools session at once? (See "Working with Video Tracks" beginning on page 115.)

To review additional material from this chapter, see the PT101 Study Guide module available through the ElementsIED online learning platform at ElementsED.com.

Importing Audio

In this exercise tutorial, you will import audio files into the session you've been working on in earlier exercises. First, you will import audio files to the Clip List for use with existing tracks in the session; next, you will import additional audio files to new tracks.

Duration: 10 to 15 Minutes

Media: Bass_02.wav, Beach FX_01.wav, Drums_01.wav, GTR_01.wav

Media Files

To complete this exercise, you will need to use various audio files included in the PT101 Download Media. You should have downloaded the media files in Exercise 4.

If needed, you can re-download the media files by pointing your browser to http://alpp.us/PT101-128.

*Note: The above URL is **case sensitive**.*

Getting Started

You will start by opening the Pro Tools session you saved at the end of Exercise 5. If that session is not available, you can use the Exercise05 Sample file in the 03. Completed Exercises folder within the PT101 Download Media folder.

Open the session and save it as Exercise 6:

1. Open the session file that you created in Exercise 5 (Storage Drive/Folder > PT101-XXX > Exercise05-XXX.ptx).

   Alternatively, you can use the Exercise05 Sample file (PT101 Download Media > 03. Completed Projects > Exercise05 Sample.ptx).

2. Choose FILE > SAVE AS and name the session *Exercise06-XXX*, keeping the session inside the original session folder (if working from your previous session) or moving the session into your PT101-XXX folder (if working from the sample file).

The session will open with the Edit window displayed and the previously recorded clip on the VO track.

Importing Audio to the Clip List

In this part of the exercise, you will import audio files to the Clip List for use on existing tracks. You will then drag the audio onto the appropriate tracks in your session.

Import audio files to the Clip List:

1. Choose **FILE > IMPORT AUDIO** and navigate to the Exercise Media folder from your downloaded files (PT101 Download Media > 02. Exercise Media).
2. Copy the files into your session by clicking the **COPY** or **COPY FILES** button.
3. Select the following audio files by clicking on the Drums file, then **COMMAND-CLICKING** (Mac) or **CTRL-CLICKING** (Windows) on the GTR clip.
   - Drums_01.wav
   - GTR_01.wav
4. Copy the files into your session by clicking the **COPY** or **COPY FILES** button and then clicking **DONE** to import the audio. A dialog box will open, prompting you to select a save location.

Be sure you choose the button to *copy* files, not the button to *add* files.

5. Save the files in the Audio Files folder for your session (the default) by clicking **OPEN** (Mac) or **USE CURRENT FOLDER** (Windows). A progress bar will appear as the audio is copied to your session.
6. When the Audio Import Options dialog box appears, choose the option to import to the Clip List and click **OK**. The files will appear selected in the Clip List on the right side of the Edit window.

Figure 6.8 The Audio Import Options dialog box configured to import to the Clip List

Place the imported audio files on existing tracks:

1. Select the **GRABBER** tool (hand icon) in the Edit window toolbar.
2. Click in the blank space below the clips in the Clip List to deselect the clips you imported.
3. Select only the Drums_01 clip in the Clip List and drag it anywhere on the Drums track.
4. Next, select the GTR_01 clip in the Clip List and drag it anywhere on the Guitar track.

Position the clips properly on the tracks:

1. Using the Grabber tool, drag the Drums_01 clip to the very start of the Drums track.
2. Click on the **SPOT** button on the left side of the Edit window toolbar to activate Spot mode. (See Figure 6.9.)

Figure 6.9 Spot mode active

3. Click on the GTR_01 clip with the Grabber tool to display the Spot dialog box.
4. Set the Time Scale at the top of the dialog box to **MIN:SECS**.
5. Configure the Start location in the Spot dialog box to 0:01.951 and click **OK**. The clip will move to start at the specified location.

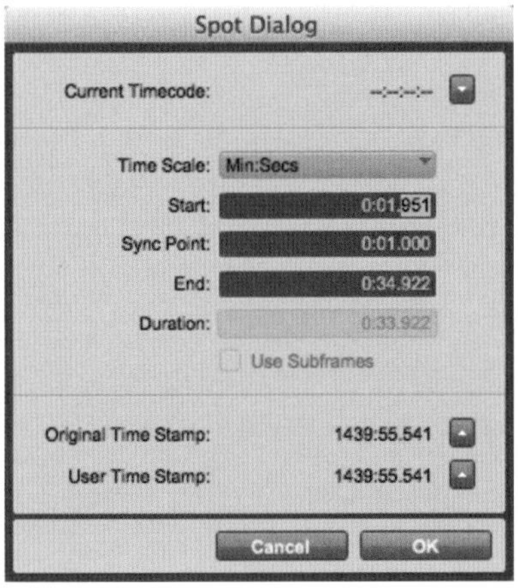

Figure 6.10 Spot dialog box configured for the GTR_01 clip

6. Click the **GRID** button (underneath the Spot button) to put the session into Grid mode.
7. Choose **FILE > SAVE** to save your work in progress.

Importing Audio to Tracks

In this part of the exercise, you will import additional audio files, placing them directly onto new Audio tracks. You will then rename the Audio tracks with descriptive names for the session.

1. With the GTR_01 clip still selected, choose **FILE > IMPORT > AUDIO** and again navigate to the 02. Exercise Media folder.
2. Copy the following files into your session (select the files and click the **COPY** or **COPY FILES** button):
   - Bass_02.wav
   - Beach FX_01.wav
   - Fire FX.wav
3. Click **DONE** to import the audio and proceed through to the prompt to choose a save location.
4. Choose the default save location (Audio Files folder), as before. A progress bar will appear as the audio is copied to your session.

   Once again, the Audio Import Options dialog box will appear.

5. This time, choose the option to import to a new track, and set the LOCATION pop-up to Selection. (See Figure 6.11.) This will cause the clips to align with the GTR_01 clip, each on its own track.

Figure 6.11 The Audio Import Options dialog box configured to import to new tracks

6. Click **OK**. Three new tracks will appear in your session, with each of the audio clips aligned to start with the GTR_01 clip.

Rename the tracks and position the Beach FX_01 clip:

1. Double-click on the track nameplate of the Bass_02 track and shorten its name to Bass; then click the NEXT button and shorten the Beach FX_01 track name to Beach FX.
2. Click **OK** when finished.
3. Using the Grabber tool, drag the Beach FX_01 clip to the very start of the Beach FX track.
4. Mute the Fire FX track for now. You will return to this track in a later exercise.
5. Double-click on the ZOOMER tool icon in the Edit window toolbar to fit the session timeline within the Edit window display.
6. Re-activate the GRABBER tool when done.

Finishing Up

To complete this exercise tutorial, you will need to save your work and close the session. You will be reusing this session in Exercise 7, so it is important to save the work you've done.

You may also want to listen to your work before exiting.

Review and save your work:

1. Press ENTER or RETURN to place the cursor at the beginning of the session.
2. Press the SPACEBAR to play back the session and confirm your results.
3. Press the SPACEBAR a second time when finished.
4. Choose FILE > SAVE to save the session.
5. Choose FILE > CLOSE SESSION to close the session.

Remember that you cannot close a Pro Tools session by closing its windows. You must choose CLOSE SESSION from the FILE menu.

LESSON 7

Making Your First MIDI Recording

This lesson covers the basics of recording and working with MIDI data in Pro Tools. It describes how to set up and record onto MIDI-compatible tracks, how to use virtual instrument plug-ins, and how to select different views for the MIDI data on your tracks.

Duration: 120 Minutes

GOALS

- Understand the basics of the MIDI protocol
- Identify the two types of MIDI-compatible tracks that Pro Tools provides
- Recognize the difference between sample-based operation and tick-based operation
- Set the Main Time Scale to Bars|Beats
- Prepare a system to record MIDI data
- Set up a virtual instrument to play MIDI data recorded on an Instrument track

Key topics from this lesson are included in the *Pro Tools 12 Essential Training: 101* course on Lynda.com.

Recording and editing MIDI data is similar to working with audio; many of the tools, modes, and menu functions work in a similar fashion. However, MIDI data is fundamentally different from audio; therefore, some of the processes and operations you use to work with this data will be different. This lesson introduces Pro Tools features that will allow you to record and edit MIDI data in ways that are specific to this protocol.

MIDI Basics

MIDI, or *Musical Instrument Digital Interface*, is a protocol for connecting electronic instruments, performance controllers, and computers so they can communicate with one another. MIDI data is different from data stored in an audio file in that MIDI data does not represent sound waves; instead, it represents information about a performance, such as the pitch, duration, and intensity of the notes in the performance.

MIDI devices transmit performance data via MIDI messages, which are composed of 8-bit numbers (or *bytes*) and include information such as *note* or *pitch number* (indicating an individual note in a scale) and *velocity* (typically affecting an individual note's volume). Up to 16 separate channels of MIDI information can be sent over a single MIDI cable, allowing a single cable path to control multiple MIDI devices or to control a single device that is capable of multi-channel (or *multi-timbral*) operation.

The Format of a MIDI Message

The most significant bit in a MIDI message byte is reserved to distinguish between status bytes and data bytes. The remaining seven bits represent the unique data of the message byte, encompassing a range of values from 0 to 127. The maximum length for a standard MIDI message is three bytes, consisting of one status byte and one or more data bytes.

Status Byte	Data Byte 1	Data Byte 2
1tttnnnn	0xxxxxxx	0xxxxxxx

Where:

t is used to specify the type of status message being sent
n is used to specify the associated MIDI Channel Number
x is used to specify the associated data value, such as a note number (pitch) or velocity value

Many other kinds of information can be conveyed via MIDI messages, such as pan and general MIDI volume information for instruments that support these, as well as program change events, or commands that tell MIDI instruments which of their available sounds, or *patches*, to use.

A *MIDI sequencer* allows you to store, edit, and play back MIDI information that can be used to control MIDI-compatible devices, such as synthesizers, sound modules, and drum machines. These devices don't have to be external hardware devices—today many synthesizers, samplers, and other sound modules are available as virtual instrument plug-ins, enabling you to add devices directly to tracks from within your DAW.

MIDI in Pro Tools

Pro Tools includes an integrated MIDI sequencer that lets you import, record, and edit MIDI in much the same way that you work with audio. MIDI data appears in tracks in the Pro Tools Edit window, referencing the same Timeline as your Audio tracks. Corresponding channel strips appear in the Pro Tools Mix window and include familiar mixer-style controls that affect MIDI data in the track. MIDI Editor windows are also available in Pro Tools for detailed MIDI composition and editing tasks.

As you learned in Lesson 4, Pro Tools provides two types of tracks for working with MIDI data: MIDI tracks and Instrument tracks.

- A *MIDI track* stores MIDI note and controller data only; no audio can pass through a MIDI track. MIDI tracks are often used in conjunction with Aux Input tracks for monitoring and playback of a synthesizer or virtual instrument that is triggered by the MIDI data.
- An *Instrument track* provides MIDI and audio capability in a single channel strip. Like MIDI tracks, Instrument tracks store note and controller data. Instrument tracks can also route audio signals generated by a virtual instrument on the track for monitoring and playback purposes. This capability simplifies the process of recording, editing, and monitoring MIDI data.

Creating MIDI-Compatible Tracks

If your session does not already contain them, you will have to create one or more MIDI-compatible tracks for your MIDI recording. The type of track you use (MIDI track or Instrument track) will depend on your preferences and the MIDI devices you use.

Some considerations for selecting a track type include whether you will be using a virtual instrument with the track (see "Using Virtual Instruments" later in this chapter) and the complexity of your setup. For basic MIDI recording with virtual instruments, you will probably find Instrument tracks to be easier to use, due to the simplified manner in which they allow you to route audio from your MIDI devices through your session.

To add MIDI-compatible tracks, do the following:

1. Chose TRACK > NEW to open the New Tracks dialog box.
2. Specify the number of desired tracks in the Track Total field.
3. Select either MIDI TRACK or INSTRUMENT TRACK in the Track Type drop-down list. The Track Timebase drop-down will default to Ticks.
4. For Instrument tracks, choose between MONO and STEREO in the Track Format drop-down list. (Additional multi-channel formats are available with Pro Tools HD software.)

Figure 7.1 Creating two stereo Instrument tracks in the New Tracks dialog box

5. Click CREATE.

When you create a track for working with MIDI data, the track timebase defaults to Ticks, indicating that the track uses tick-based timing (also known as *bar-and-beat-based timing*). MIDI operations are typically bar-and-beat-based, whereas audio operations are typically sample-based.

Sample-Based Operation versus Tick-Based Operation

The differences between sample-based operation and tick-based operation are essentially the differences between how audio data is stored and how MIDI data is stored.

Sample-Based Operation

In sample-based operation, recorded information is tied to fixed points in time relative to the beginning of the session. Audio data is stored as individual audio samples in a file. In Pro Tools, audio clips are represented on sample-based tracks by default. Audio clips that reside on a sample-based track are located at particular sample locations on the Timeline.

You can think of these sample-based locations as *absolute locations* in time, measured by the number of samples that have elapsed since the beginning of the session. Sample-based audio clips are not affected by the session tempo and will not move from their sample locations if the session tempo changes—though the audio clips' positions relative to the session's bars and beats will change.

Audio tracks can also be set to tick-based operation to perform specialized functions, such as tempo matching for Elastic Audio. For the purposes of this course, whenever we discuss recording and editing audio, we will assume sample-based operation unless otherwise stated.

Tick-Based Operation

In tick-based operation, recorded information is tied to specific Bar|Beat locations in an arrangement. When you record MIDI data, Pro Tools uses tick-based timing to determine the locations of your MIDI events.

MIDI events are recorded relative to particular bar and beat locations (such as Bar 16, Beat 1), and their locations in time adjust based on the session tempo—if the tempo increases, the MIDI data will play back faster, and individual events will occur earlier in time; if the tempo decreases, the MIDI data will play back more slowly, and the same events will occur later in time.

The Elastic Audio capabilities in Pro Tools enable the same functionality for audio on tick-based tracks, allowing audio clips to automatically speed up or slow down to conform to the session tempo.

Pro Tools subdivides the bars and beats in your session into ticks, with 960 ticks comprising a quarter note. Timing can thus be specified with a precision (or resolution) of up to 1/960th of a quarter note when measuring in bars and beats.

You can think of tick-based locations as *relative locations* in time, measured by the number of bars, beats, and ticks that have elapsed since the beginning of the session. A tick-based event maintains its rhythmic location relative to other tick-based events in the song, regardless of the session tempo—but a tempo change will cause the event to occur earlier or later in *absolute* time, thereby changing its location relative to any sample-based audio in the session.

Tick-based tracks and data coexist with sample-based tracks and data within the same Pro Tools session.

Pro Tools displays relationships between audio and MIDI accurately in the Edit window at all zoom levels, with MIDI event durations drawn in proportion to the Timeline, according to tempo.

Though MIDI tracks are typically tick-based, they can also be set to sample-based to perform specialized functions. For the purposes of this course, whenever we discuss MIDI recording and editing, we will assume tick-based operation unless otherwise stated.

Sample-based MIDI operations are discussed in advanced courses.

Time Scale and Rulers for Working with MIDI

When you are working with MIDI data in a session, you will frequently reference the Bars|Beats Time Scale. This Time Scale is represented on the Bars|Beats Ruler. You will also commonly work with the tempo and meter settings, which are displayed in the Tempo and Meter Rulers, respectively.

Setting the Timebase Ruler and Main Time Scale

For music-based MIDI recording and editing, you will find it helpful to display the Bars|Beats Timebase Ruler and to set the Main Time Scale to Bars|Beats. This will let you reference any recorded material, track selections, and edits to the bar and beat locations in the piece.

To set the Timebase Ruler and Main Time Scale, do the following:

1. Display the Bars|Beats Ruler by choosing VIEW > RULERS > BARS|BEATS.
2. Set the Main Time Scale to Bars|Beats by doing one of the following:
   - Click on BARS|BEATS in the Ruler View area of the Edit window.
   - Select VIEW > MAIN COUNTER > BARS|BEATS.
   - Click on the MAIN COUNTER SELECTOR in either the Edit window or the Transport window and select BARS|BEATS from the pop-up menu.

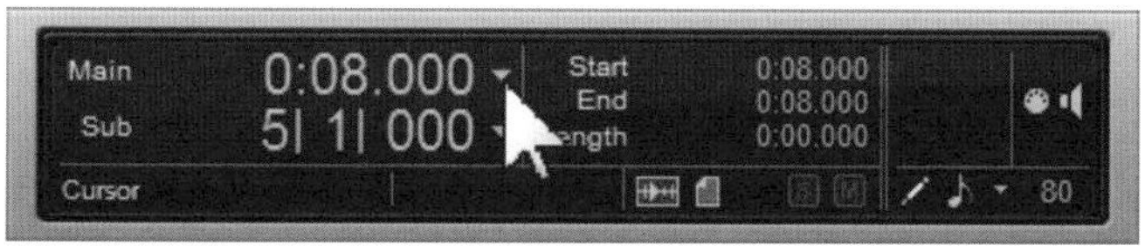

Figure 7.2 Main Counter selector in the Edit window

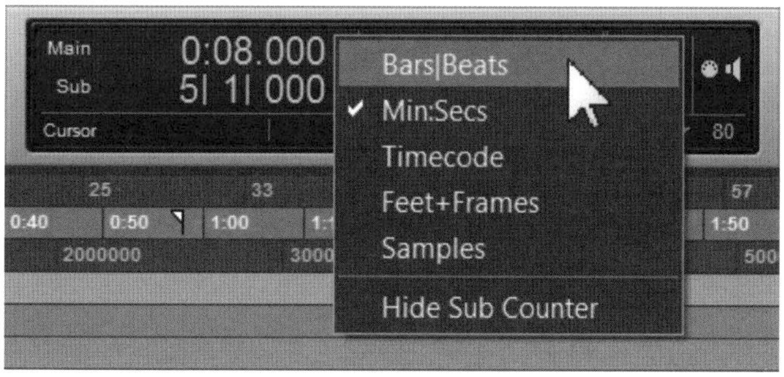

Figure 7.3 Selecting Bars|Beats from the Main Counter pop-up menu

Refer to Lesson 3 for more information on the Main Time Scale.

The Bars|Beats Time Scale displays information in the following format:

1|1|000 (Bar Number|Beat Number|Tick Number)

The first number in this format represents the bar number with respect to the zero point on the session Timeline. The second number represents the beat number within the current bar. The final number represents the tick number within the current beat, based on the division of 960 ticks per quarter note.

Displaying the Tempo and Meter Rulers

The Tempo and Meter Rulers allow you to specify the base tempo and meter for your session and to set tempo and meter changes at any point along the session Timeline. To display either of these Rulers, choose VIEW > RULERS and select TEMPO or METER from the submenu.

Setting the Base Meter and Tempo

Before you begin recording MIDI data, you should determine the required meter and tempo for the performance and make any necessary changes in Pro Tools to match. The following sections describe how to set the meter and tempo for your composition.

Setting the Base Meter

When you create a new session or project in Pro Tools, the meter defaults to 4/4. If you intend to record with the click and will be working with a different meter, you'll need to set the session meter accordingly. Meter events can occur anywhere within a Pro Tools session, and are added and displayed using the Meter Ruler.

To set the base meter for a session, do the following:

1. With the Meter Ruler displayed in the Edit window, click on the ADD METER CHANGE button. The Meter Change dialog box will open.

Figure 7.4 The Add Meter Change button on the Meter Ruler

Figure 7.5 The Meter Change dialog box

> **You can also double-click on the CURRENT METER display in the Transport window to add a meter change.**

2. Enter the meter you will use for the session and enter 1|1|000 in the LOCATION field.

3. (Optional) Choose a note value that corresponds to the desired click timing. This may be desirable for meters such as 6/8 to play a click based on something other than the default quarter-note value.
4. Click **OK** to insert the new meter event at the beginning of the session, replacing the default meter.

Setting the Base Tempo

When you open a new session in Pro Tools, the tempo defaults to 120 beats per minute (BPM). If you intend to record with the click and you are working with a different tempo, make sure to set the tempo accordingly. If you know the tempo you will use for the session, you can insert a tempo event at the beginning of the session.

Tempo events, which can occur anywhere within a Pro Tools session, are added and displayed using the Tempo Ruler.

To set the session tempo, do the following:

1. With the Tempo Ruler displayed and the Tempo Ruler Enable option selected (see "Tempo Map Mode" later in this lesson), click on the **ADD TEMPO CHANGE** button.

Figure 7.6 The Add Tempo Change button on the Tempo Ruler

2. Enter the BPM value you will use for the session and enter 1|1|000 in the **LOCATION** field.

Figure 7.7 The Tempo Change dialog box

You can also use the Tap Tempo function to set the tempo in the Tempo Change dialog box. With the BPM value selected, tap the T key on your computer keyboard at the desired tempo.

3. To base the beat on something other than the default quarter note, select the desired note value.
4. Click **OK** to insert the new tempo event at the beginning of the session, replacing the default tempo.

Tempo Map Mode

When you create a new Pro Tools session, the session is configured by default to follow the tempo events in the Tempo Ruler (also known as the session *tempo map*). The tempo map can be toggled on and off as needed. To use the tempo map, ensure that the **TEMPO RULER ENABLE** button is active in the Transport window.

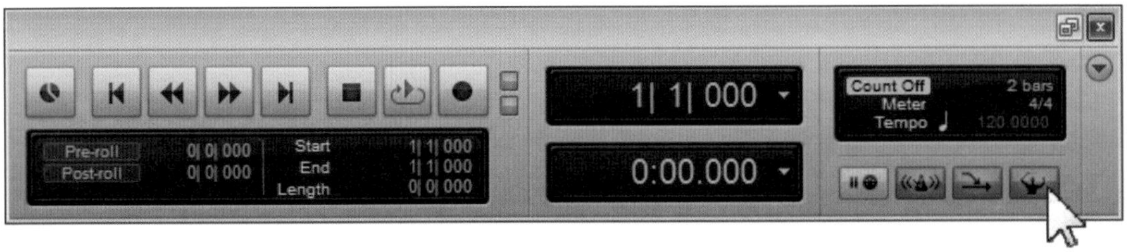

Figure 7.8 Enabling the Tempo Ruler in the Transport window

Manual Tempo Mode and Tap Tempo

In Manual Tempo mode, Pro Tools will ignore the tempo events in the Tempo Ruler. In this mode, the tempo can be adjusted by typing a value directly into the Current Tempo field in the Transport window. The tempo can also be tapped in using a MIDI controller or the **T** key on your computer. Manually adjusting the tempo during playback will momentarily interrupt playback.

To put Pro Tools into Manual Tempo mode, click to deselect the **TEMPO RULER ENABLE** button in the Transport window.

> **Setting the Session Key Signature**
>
> When you create a new session or project in Pro Tools, the key signature defaults to C major. To use the key signature functionality in Pro Tools, make sure to set the base key signature for your session correctly. Once you know the key you will use for the composition, you can insert a Key Change event at the beginning of the session to specify the proper key. The selected key signature will display in the Score Editor window and on any printed scores that you create from your Pro Tools document.
>
> Key Change events are added and displayed using the Key Signature Ruler and can be set to any major or minor key.

Preparing to Record MIDI

With MIDI-compatible tracks added to your session and the meter and tempo configured as desired, you will next need to prepare your MIDI device and software for recording. The general processes you will use to prepare for recording MIDI are as follows:

1. Connect a MIDI device.
2. Check the track inputs/outputs.
3. Record-enable the track(s).
4. Set record options.

Connecting a MIDI Device

Recording MIDI data typically involves connecting a keyboard, a drum machine, or another MIDI device as an input to your Pro Tools system. Before starting to record, you should verify that the MIDI device you will use for input (also called a *MIDI controller*) is connected to your system through an input on your MIDI interface or a USB port on your computer, if applicable. You might also need to connect a MIDI output from your interface as a return to this device or as an input to a separate MIDI device, such as a synthesizer, for monitoring and playback purposes.

Example: Using MIDI Cables

For basic recording, you can connect a MIDI cable from the MIDI Out port on the back of a keyboard to the MIDI In port on an Mbox Pro or similar interface. For monitoring and playback purposes, you can also connect the MIDI Out port of the Mbox Pro to the MIDI In port on the keyboard (assuming onboard sound capabilities) or to a separate synthesizer unit.

Connecting a MIDI device to Pro Tools with a USB cable provides both MIDI input and MIDI output for the device.

Checking MIDI Inputs/Outputs

Once your MIDI device is connected, you will need to configure the inputs and outputs of your MIDI-compatible track(s) with the appropriate settings to route the MIDI signals into and out of the tracks.

MIDI Input

The MIDI Input selector in the Edit or Mix window for a MIDI-compatible track is the functional equivalent to the Audio Input selector for an Audio track. This selector determines which incoming MIDI data gets recorded onto the track in Pro Tools.

On MIDI tracks, the MIDI Input selector is located in the I/O view (Edit window) or in the I/O section of the channel strip (Mix window), where the Audio Input Path selector would be on an Audio track. On Instrument tracks, however, the MIDI Input selector appears in the Instrument view. This view is used only for Instrument tracks and needs to be displayed separately. (See Figure 7.9.)

To display the Instrument view, do one of the following:

- Choose VIEW > MIX WINDOW > INSTRUMENTS. The Instrument MIDI controls will appear at the top of the channel strip.
- Choose VIEW > EDIT WINDOW > INSTRUMENTS. The Instrument MIDI controls will appear at the head of the track display.

The MIDI Input selectors for MIDI-compatible tracks are set to ALL by default, meaning that the MIDI signals from all connected and enabled input devices will be received for the track. If you prefer, you can use the MIDI Input selector to set the MIDI Input to a specific device (port) and channel. This allows you to more tightly control the routing of MIDI data.

Advanced MIDI routing operations are discussed in the Pro Tools 210M course.

Figure 7.9 The MIDI Input selector as it appears in a MIDI track and an Instrument track

MIDI Output

The MIDI Output selector for a MIDI-compatible track determines which device or port is used for monitoring and playing back MIDI data. Live MIDI signals can be routed to an audio sound source for monitoring purposes when MIDI Thru is enabled under the Options menu (default). Similarly, recorded MIDI signals can be routed to an audio sound source for playback purposes. You use the MIDI Output selector to configure the device or port and the MIDI channel that the signal is routed to for both of these purposes.

When using MIDI Thru, you might need to disable Local Control on your MIDI keyboard controller. Otherwise, your keyboard could receive double MIDI notes, which can lead to stuck notes.

On MIDI tracks, the MIDI Output selector is located where the Audio Output selector would be on an Audio track; on Instrument tracks, it is located in the Instrument view in the Mix window or Edit window.

To set the MIDI Output, do the following:

1. Click on the **MIDI OUTPUT SELECTOR** in the Edit or Mix window.
2. Select the instrument or port and channel you wish to route the output to for MIDI playback. (Note that this process is typically not required when using a virtual instrument on an Instrument track.)

Record-Enabling MIDI-Compatible Tracks

The process you use to enable recording on a Pro Tools MIDI track or Instrument track is the same as you use for an Audio track: Simply click the track's **RECORD ENABLE** button in either the Edit window or the Mix window. As with an Audio track, the Record Enable button flashes red when a MIDI-compatible track is record-ready.

Setting Record Options

Pro Tools provides various record options that are specific to working with MIDI data. You will need to set the MIDI controls and other options as desired prior to beginning to record onto your MIDI tracks.

MIDI Controls

As discussed in Lesson 3, the Pro Tools Transport window can be set to show MIDI controls that you can use when recording MIDI data.

To display MIDI controls in the Pro Tools Transport window, do the following:

1. Select **WINDOW > TRANSPORT** to display the Transport window, if it is not currently showing.
2. Select **VIEW > TRANSPORT > MIDI CONTROLS** to display the MIDI controls, if they are not currently showing.

> **The MIDI controls can also be displayed in the Edit window. Choose MIDI CONTROLS from the Edit Window Toolbar pop-up menu in the upper-right corner of the window.**

Before you begin recording MIDI data, you can take any of the following optional steps to set the MIDI controls:

1. Enable **WAIT FOR NOTE** and/or **COUNT OFF** in the Transport window or Edit window, if desired. Use Wait for Note to begin recording automatically when you begin playing; use Count Off in conjunction with a metronome click to count off a specified number of measures before recording begins.
2. Enable the **METRONOME**, if desired, and specify the settings in the Click/Countoff Options dialog box (**SETUP > CLICK/COUNTOFF**).

> **The simplest way to enable playback of the metronome click is to set up a click track. See the "Creating a Click Track" section in Lesson 5 for details.**

3. Disable **MIDI MERGE** for initial recording. Once you have recorded a MIDI pass that you want to keep, you can enable this control to layer additional MIDI data on top of the existing recording.

> **With the Numeric Keypad mode set to Transport (the default), you can press [9] on the numeric keypad to enable/disable MIDI Merge mode.**

4. Set the tempo for recording by doing one of the following:
   - Engage the **TEMPO RULER ENABLE** button (Conductor Track) to follow the tempo map defined in the Tempo Ruler.
   - Disengage the **TEMPO RULER ENABLE** button (Conductor Track) to set the tempo using the Tempo field in the Transport window or Edit window.

The functions of each of the MIDI controls are described in detail in the "MIDI Control Features" section in Lesson 3.

Input Quantize

The Input Quantize feature enables you to automatically align, or *quantize*, all recorded MIDI notes to a specified timing grid. This creates a style of recording similar to working with a hardware sequencer or drum machine.

Do not use the Input Quantize feature if you want to preserve the original "feel" of the performance.

To enable Input Quantize, do the following:

1. Choose **EVENT > EVENT OPERATIONS > INPUT QUANTIZE.** The Event Operations window will open with Input Quantize selected in the Operation drop-down list. (See Figure 7.10.)
2. Select the **ENABLE INPUT QUANTIZE** checkbox.

Note that Input Quantize will *remain enabled* after closing the Event Operations window. Be sure to deselect the ENABLE INPUT QUANTIZE checkbox when you are finished using it to avoid unexpected behavior during subsequent MIDI record passes.

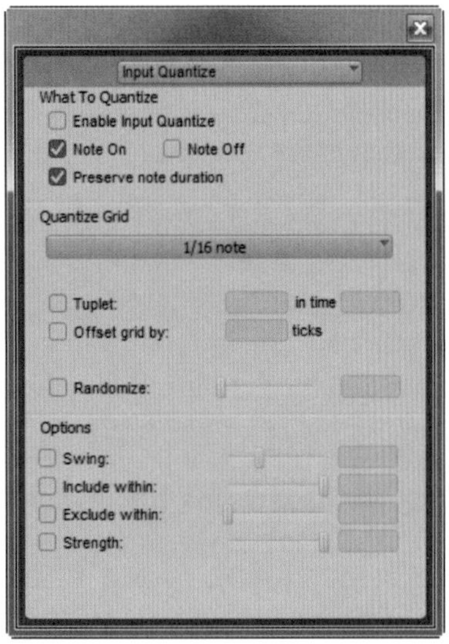

Figure 7.10 The Event Operations window

3. In the **WHAT TO QUANTIZE** section of the window, choose the MIDI note attributes to quantize:
   - **Attacks.** Aligns note start points to the nearest grid value (commonly used).
   - **Releases.** Aligns note end points to the nearest grid value (used only for specific situations).
   - **Preserve Note Duration.** Preserves the note durations of the performance by moving end points in concert with start points. If this option is not selected, note start and end points can be moved independently, changing the duration of the note.
4. Set the quantize grid to the smallest meaningful note value for the performance. All notes in the performance will be aligned to the nearest value on the specified grid.
5. In the **OPTIONS** section of the Input Quantize page, select any other desired options.

Using Virtual Instruments

Virtual instruments are the software equivalents of outboard synthesizers or sound modules. Many virtual instruments are available for Pro Tools in the form of real-time plug-ins. The Xpand!2, Boom, and Structure Free plug-ins are examples of virtual instruments that are included with Pro Tools.

Virtual instrument plug-ins can be added to Aux Input tracks or Instrument tracks and can be triggered by MIDI events routed to them.

For basic recording with a virtual instrument, you will want to create an Instrument track and connect a MIDI controller as described earlier in this chapter.

Placing a Virtual Instrument on an Instrument Track

A virtual instrument plug-in can be placed directly on an Instrument track, allowing the instrument to be triggered by the MIDI data on the track during playback or by MIDI data passing through the track for live input monitoring.

To add a virtual instrument such as Xpand!2, Boom, or Structure Free to an Instrument track in Pro Tools, do the following:

1. Display the track inserts, if not already shown, by choosing VIEW > MIX WINDOW VIEWS or VIEW > EDIT WINDOW VIEWS and selecting INSERTS A-E or INSERTS F-J.
2. Click an insert on the Instrument track, choose PLUG-IN > INSTRUMENT, and select the virtual instrument to use on the track. The track's MIDI Output will automatically be assigned to the virtual instrument plug-in, and the instrument's user interface will open.

Figure 7.11 Selecting the Xpand!2 virtual instrument plug-in

Stereo Instrument tracks provide two options for plug-ins: multichannel plug-ins and multi-mono plug-ins. Choose multichannel plug-ins for stereo virtual instruments; choose multi-mono plug-ins for mono virtual instruments.

3. Assign the appropriate hardware outputs, if not already selected, using the AUDIO OUTPUT PATH SELECTOR (for monitoring and playback purposes).
4. Set the track's VOLUME FADER to the desired output level.
5. Record-enable the track and play notes on your MIDI controller. The meters on the Instrument track will register the instrument's audio output.

The MIDI signal received on an Instrument track is displayed by the MIDI meter in the Instrument view. If the MIDI meter on an Instrument track does not register a signal, verify that the MIDI output has been assigned with the MIDI Output selector.

Using Xpand!2

Xpand!2 is an AIR virtual instrument designed to provide fast access to many high-quality sounds directly from within Pro Tools. Xpand!2 comes equipped with thousands of preset *patches* (plug-in settings) and combinable *parts* (individual sounds). The Xpand!2 sound library includes synth pads, leads, pianos, organs, strings, vocals, brass and woodwinds, mallet percussion, ethnic instruments, loops, and more.

To use Xpand!2, add the plug-in to an Instrument track as described in "Placing a Virtual Instrument on an Instrument Track" earlier in this lesson. The plug-in user interface will open, displaying selectors for each of the plug-in's four individual parts (A, B, C, and D).

Figure 7.12 The Xpand!2 virtual instrument plug-in user interface

The plug-in initially opens to the <factory default> setting, with a sound assigned for part A only. Xpand!2 includes numerous additional patches to choose from, organized into folders by type. Each patch is composed of a blend of up to four parts (individual sounds) in slots A through D.

To select a different patch setting (or plug-in preset), click the **LIBRARIAN MENU** in the plug-in window and navigate to the desired folder and patch. Each patch contains an Xpand!2 preset configuration.

Librarian menu

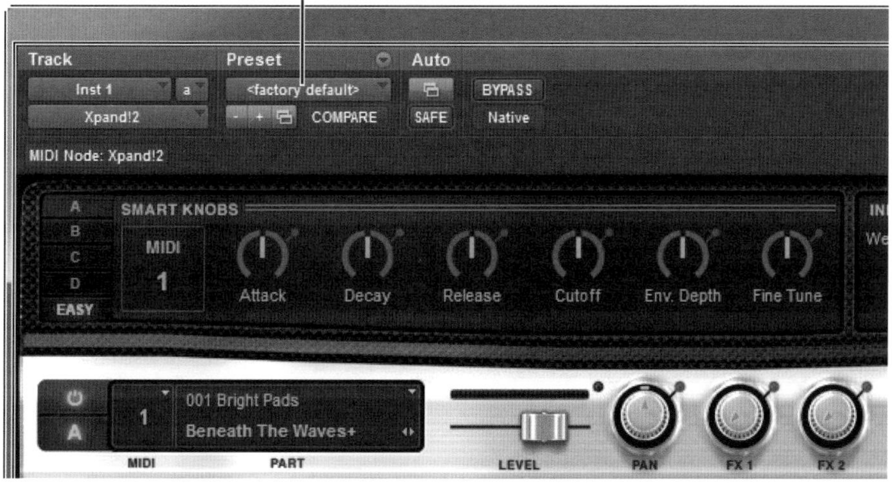

Figure 7.13 Librarian menu for selecting a different Xpand!2 patch/preset

Each of Xpand!2's sound parts can be turned on or off at any time by clicking on the On/Off power indicator above the part letter. (When toggled off, the power indicator turns a dimmed gray color.)

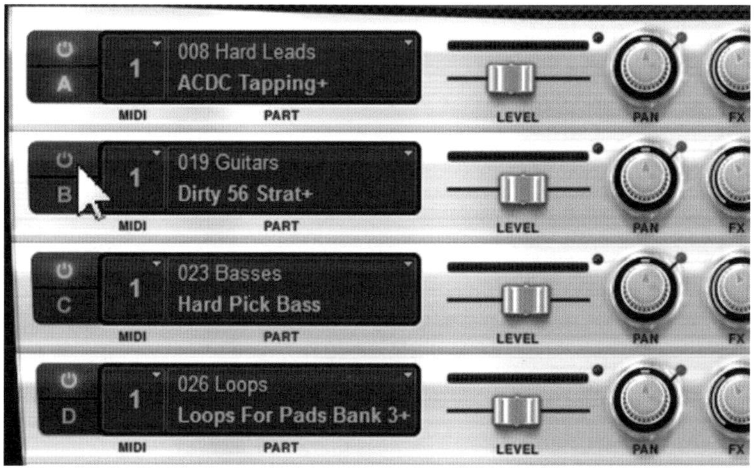

Figure 7.14 Clicking on the power indicator to turn off sound Part B

Using Boom

Boom is a virtual drum machine featuring a selection of percussion sounds. The Boom user interface provides a simple, drum-machine-style pattern sequencer. Boom comes with 10 drum kits inspired by classic electronic drum machines.

To use Boom, add the plug-in to an Instrument track as described in "Placing a Virtual Instrument on an Instrument Track" earlier in this lesson. The Boom user interface will open, displaying the pattern for the <factory default> preset.

Figure 7.15 The Boom virtual instrument plug-in user interface

The Matrix Display on the left side of the plug-in window presents a visual display of the current pattern in Boom's sequencer. The Matrix provides a way to work with patterns and to keep track of the step that Boom is playing at any given time. Each lit LED in the sequencer corresponds to the instrument that is sequenced to play at that step.

You can click each LED directly to add a note on that step. Successive clicks toggle through velocity levels (represented by different brightness levels) or toggle the note on/off.

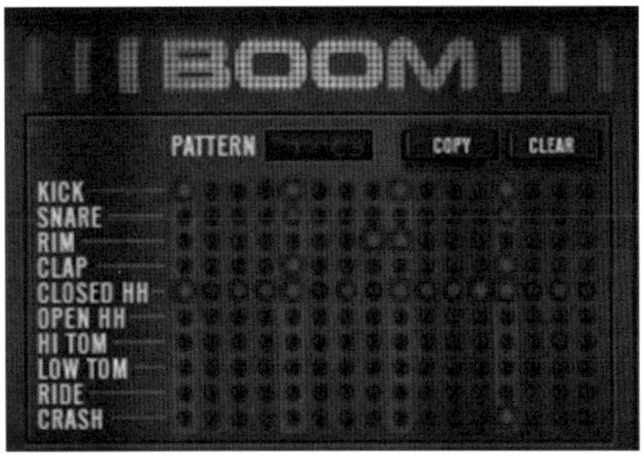

Figure 7.16 The Boom Matrix Display

The Kit Selector menu at the bottom of the plug-in window provides access to the 10 drum kits in Boom: Urban 1, Urban 2, Dance 1, Dance 2, Electro, Eight-O, Nine-O, Fat 8, Fat 9, and Retro. (See Figure 7.17.)

Figure 7.17 The Boom Kit Selector menu

You can use MIDI data on your Instrument track to control Boom playback. Boom responds to two main ranges of MIDI notes:

- From C1–D#2, Boom plays each of the instruments in the current drum kit. This allows you to use Pro Tools' MIDI sequencer to create drum tracks, rather than using Boom's built-in pattern sequencer.
- From C3–D#4, each note triggers one of the 16 patterns in the current preset, switching between them on the fly.

Using Structure Free

Structure Free is a sample playback plug-in that reads and plays all Structure libraries and factory content. To use Structure Free, add the plug-in to a stereo Instrument track as described in "Placing a Virtual Instrument on an Instrument Track" earlier in this lesson. The Structure Free user interface will open with the Sine Wave Patch loaded. (See Figure 7.18.)

Figure 7.18 The Structure Free sample player user interface

To select a different patch preset, click the **QUICK BROWSE** menu and navigate to the desired folder and patch. Structure Free comes with several preset patches, including drum kits, drum loops, bass and guitar patches, and more. Each patch calls up a preset Structure Free configuration.

Figure 7.19 Selecting a patch from the Quick Browse menu

Recording MIDI

With a MIDI controller connected to your Pro Tools system, the MIDI signal routed to a MIDI-compatible track, and the track record-enabled, you are ready to begin recording.

To record to a MIDI-compatible track, do the following:

1. Display the Transport window, if it is not already showing (**WINDOW > TRANSPORT**).
2. In the Transport window, click the **RETURN TO ZERO** button so the start and end times are cleared. This ensures that you'll start recording from the beginning of the track.
3. Verify that one or more tracks have been record-enabled. (See "Record-Enabling MIDI-Compatible Tracks" earlier in this lesson.)
4. Click the **RECORD** button in the Transport window to enter Record Ready mode. The button will turn red and begin to flash. If you are using Wait for Note, the Play button will also flash green.

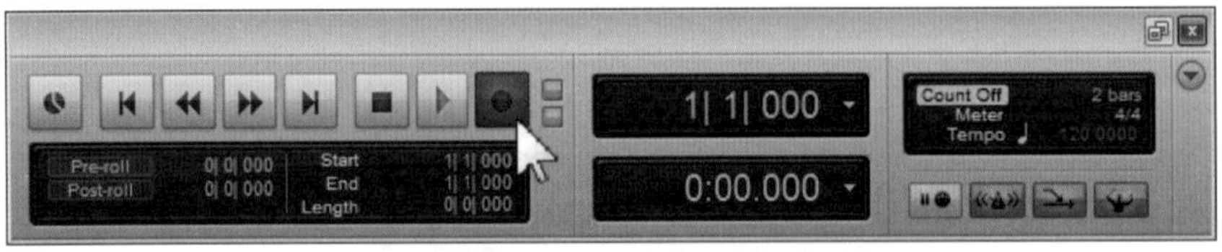

Figure 7.20 The Transport window in Record Ready mode

5. When you're ready, click **PLAY** in the Transport window, or if you're using Wait for Note, simply begin playing. Recording will begin.

> **If the Count Off button is enabled, the Record and Play buttons will flash during the countoff, after which recording will begin.**

6. When you have finished recording, click **STOP**.

To play back the track through a connected virtual instrument or outboard device, do the following:

1. Click the RECORD ENABLE button on the Instrument track to disable recording.
2. In the Transport window, click the RETURN TO ZERO button.
3. Click PLAY in the Transport window to begin playback.

Viewing MIDI Data on MIDI-Compatible Tracks

After you've completed a recording, your MIDI data will appear in the Edit window, arranged in a Track Playlist, against the same Timeline as audio. Your MIDI information can be viewed in a variety of ways in Pro Tools, allowing you to perform editing tasks that affect different attributes of the data.

The Edit window allows you to select from several view formats, including *Notes* view, *Clips* view, and *Velocity* view. Alternatively, you can view and work with your MIDI data in a MIDI Editor window, giving you access to multiple types of data at once.

You can quickly toggle between Notes and Clips views in the Edit window by pressing CONTROL+MINUS (-) (Mac) or START+MINUS (-) (Windows) whenever your edit cursor is located in a MIDI-compatible track.

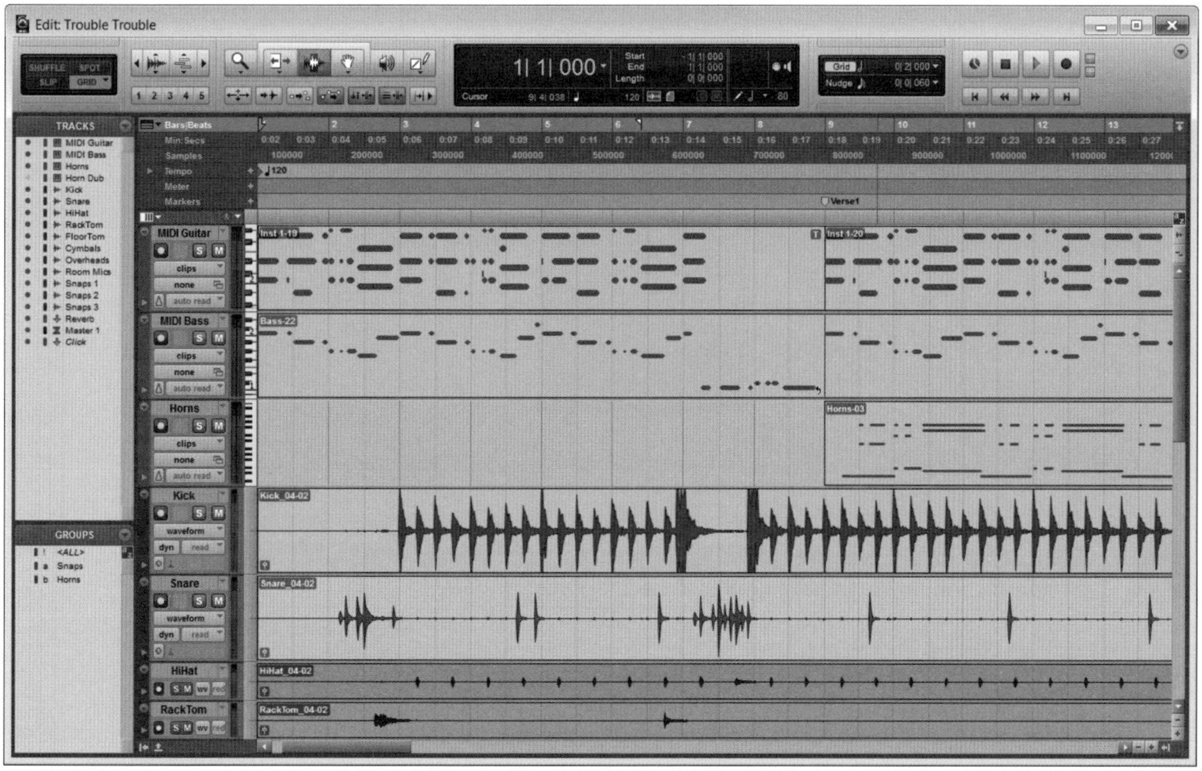

Figure 7.21 MIDI-compatible tracks and Audio tracks in the Edit window

MIDI Clips View

MIDI data is initially displayed in Clips view by default. MIDI Clips view shows MIDI notes grouped together into clips, similar to clips on Audio tracks. MIDI clips act as containers for the MIDI data within the clip boundaries. While notes are visible in Clips view, they cannot be individually edited in this view.

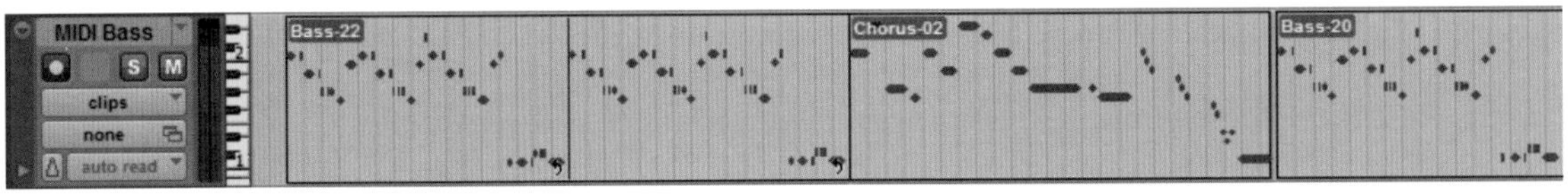

Figure 7.22 An Instrument track in Clips view

MIDI clips can be selected, copied, cut, and trimmed in the same way as audio clips, allowing you to quickly arrange song phrases or sections.

If a MIDI-compatible track has been set to a different view, you can easily change back to Clips view using the key command or the Track View selector.

To view a track in Clips view, do one of the following:

- Click anywhere in the track with the **SELECTOR** tool and press **CONTROL+MINUS (-)** (Mac) or **START+MINUS (-)** (Windows) to toggle to Clips view. Depending on the currently selected view, you might have to toggle twice.
- Click on the **TRACK VIEW SELECTOR** for the track and choose **CLIPS** from the pop-up list.

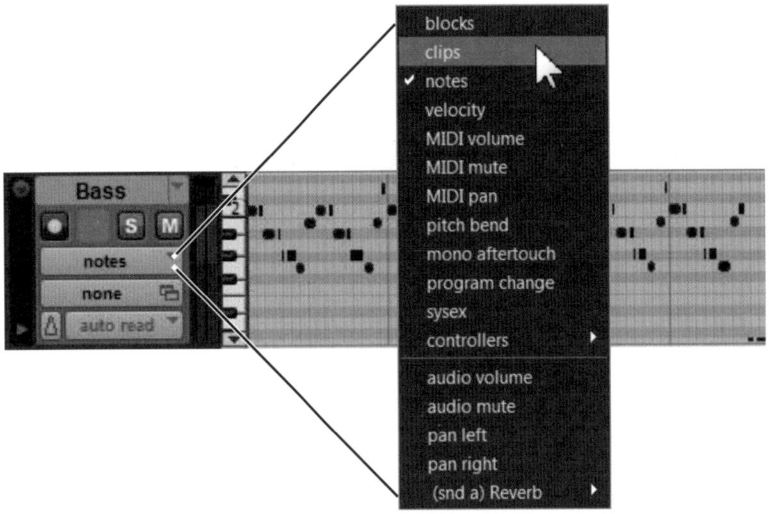

Figure 7.23 Selecting Clips view from the Track View selector pop-up menu

When Zoom Toggle is active, pressing CONTROL+MINUS (Mac) or START+MINUS (Windows) will toggle between Notes view and Velocity view.

MIDI Notes View

MIDI Notes view shows individual MIDI notes in a piano-roll format, with pitch shown on the vertical axis and duration shown on the horizontal axis. The pitch range displayed in a track will depend on the track height and the current zoom value. A mini-keyboard on the left side of the track allows you to scroll up or down to see all pitches in the track. (See Figure 7.24.)

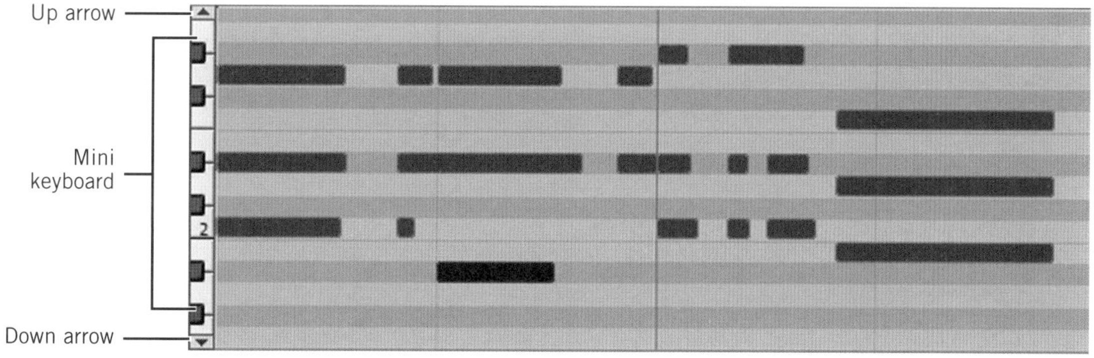

Figure 7.24 Mini-keyboard with scroll arrows

When a track's notes do not fit within the track's current height, notes above or below the viewed area are shown as single-pixel lines at the very top and bottom of the track display.

You can audition pitches on the mini-keyboard by clicking on any key in Notes view. The selected note is played through your connected virtual instrument or outboard device.

You can display a MIDI-compatible track in Notes view at any time using the key command or the Track View selector.

To switch to Notes view, do one of the following:

- Click anywhere in the track with the SELECTOR tool and press START+MINUS (-) (Windows) or CONTROL+MINUS (-) (Mac) to toggle to Notes view.
- Click on the TRACK VIEW SELECTOR for the track and choose NOTES from the pop-up list.

Velocity View

The MIDI Velocity view shows the attack velocity of each note in the MIDI track with a vertical indicator called a *velocity stalk*. Velocity stalks can be dragged up or down, individually or in groups, to change the velocities of their associated notes.

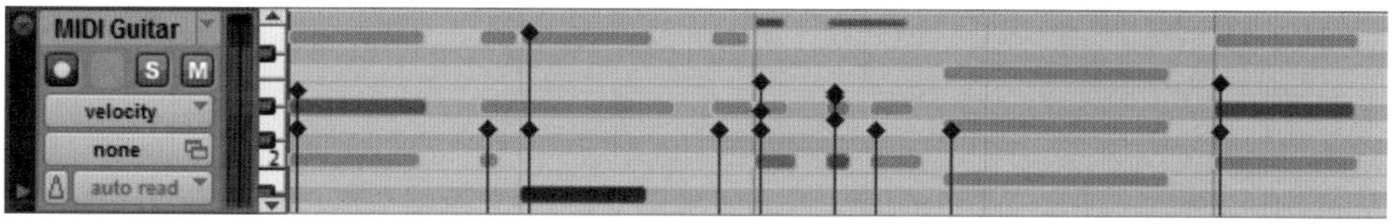

Figure 7.25 MIDI track in Velocity view

MIDI Editor Window Views

MIDI data on your tracks can also be viewed using a MIDI Editor window. MIDI Editor windows can show MIDI data and automation data simultaneously for all of your Aux Input, Instrument, and MIDI tracks.

When displaying multiple tracks, the MIDI Editor window superimposes the MIDI notes from each of the tracks in the MIDI Notes pane. The MIDI Editor window can also display automation and controller lanes at the bottom of the window for velocity stalks, volume automation playlists, and other continuous controller and automation data. (See Figure 7.26.)

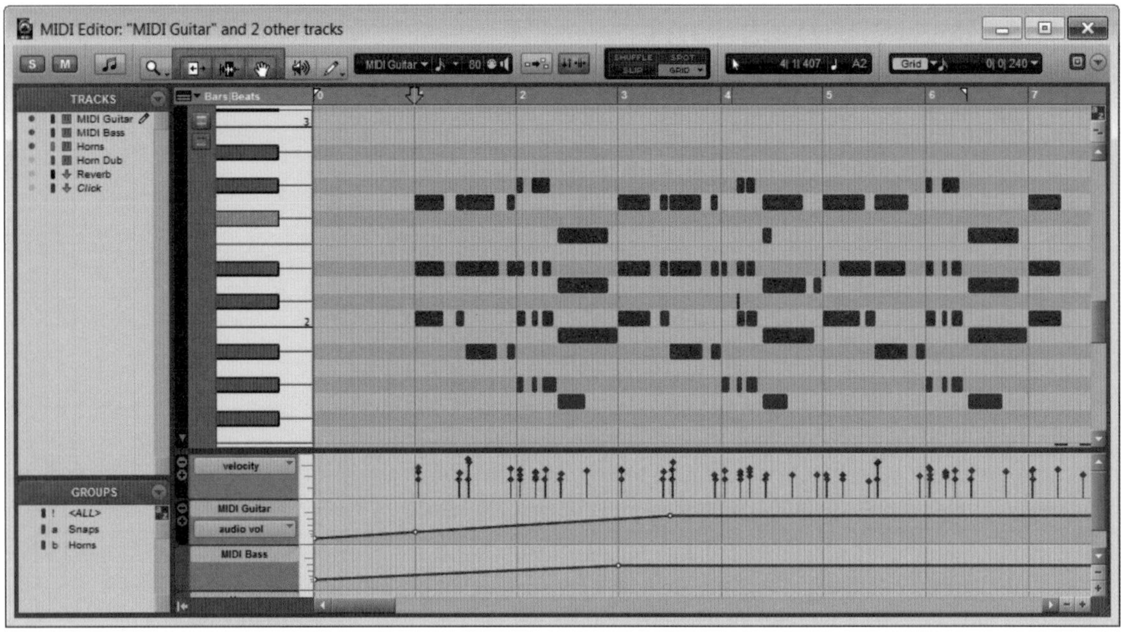

Figure 7.26 MIDI notes, velocity stalks, and volume automation displayed in a MIDI Editor window

To display MIDI data in a MIDI Editor window, do one of the following:

- Double-click on a MIDI clip in the Edit window (Clips view) with the GRABBER tool.
- Select WINDOW > MIDI EDITOR or press CONTROL+= (Mac) or START+= (Windows).

MIDI Editor windows allow you to toggle between Notes view and Notation view for the displayed MIDI and Instrument tracks. To toggle the view, click on the NOTATION DISPLAY ENABLE button on the left side of the MIDI Editor window toolbar.

Figure 7.27 Toggling to Notation view in the MIDI Editor window

Review/Discussion Questions

1. What does the term MIDI stand for? How is MIDI data different from the data stored in an audio file? (See "MIDI Basics" beginning on page 122.)

2. How many channels of MIDI information can be sent over a single MIDI cable? (See "MIDI Basics" beginning on page 122.)

3. What two types of tracks does Pro Tools provide for working with MIDI data? What is the difference between the two track types? (See "MIDI in Pro Tools" beginning on page 122.)

4. How many ticks are in a quarter note in Pro Tools? (See "Tick-Based Operation" beginning on page 124.)

5. Describe three ways to set the Main Time Scale to Bars|Beats. (See "Setting the Timebase Ruler and Main Time Scale" beginning on page 125.)

6. What is the default meter in Pro Tools? How would you go about changing the meter? (See "Setting the Base Meter" beginning on page 126.)

7. What is the default tempo in Pro Tools? (See "Setting the Base Tempo" beginning on page 127.)

8. What physical connections can you use to connect a MIDI controller to your system for recording on a MIDI or Instrument track? (See "Connecting a MIDI Device" beginning on page 128.)

9. Give some examples of virtual instrument plug-ins that are installed as standard components of Pro Tools. On which track types are virtual instrument plug-ins typically placed? (See "Using Virtual Instruments" beginning on page 133.)

10. How many parts can be included in an Xpand!2 patch? How can each part be turned on/off? (See "Using Xpand!2" beginning on page 134.)

11. What kind of virtual instrument is Boom? What does the Boom Matrix Display show? (See "Using Boom" beginning on page 135.)

12. What track views are available for MIDI data in the Edit window? Which view allows you to scroll up or down to see notes at different pitches? (See "Viewing MIDI Data on MIDI-Compatible Tracks" beginning on page 139.)

13. What track types can display data in MIDI Editor windows? (See "MIDI Editor Window Views" beginning on page 141.)

14. What is the Notation Display Enable button used for in the MIDI Editor window? (See "MIDI Editor Window Views" beginning on page 141.)

To review additional material from this chapter, see the PT101 Study Guide module available through the ElementsIED online learning platform at ElementsED.com.

EXERCISE 7

Working with MIDI

In this exercise tutorial, you will set the session tempo, create a click track, create an Instrument track, assign the Xpand!2 virtual instrument to the track, optionally record a MIDI performance using Input Quantize, and import existing MIDI clips to supplement or replace your MIDI recording.

Duration: 10 to 15 minutes

Media: Beat Waves.mid

> ### Media Files
>
> To complete this exercise, you will need to use the MIDI file included in the PT101 Download Media. You should have downloaded the media files in Exercise 4.
>
> If needed, you can re-download the media files by pointing your browser to http://alpp.us/PT101-128.
>
> *Note: The above URL is **case sensitive**.*

Getting Started

You will start by opening the Pro Tools session you completed in Exercise 6. If that session is not available, use the Exercise06 Sample file in the Completed Exercises folder within the PT101 Download Media folder.

Open the session and save it as Exercise 7:

1. Open the session file that you created in Exercise 6 (Storage Drive/Folder > PT101-XXX > Exercise06-XXX.ptx).

   Alternatively, you can use the Exercise06 Sample file (PT101 Download Media > 03. Completed Projects > Exercise06 Sample.ptx).

2. Choose FILE > SAVE AS and name the session *Exercise07-XXX*, keeping the session inside the original session folder (if working from your previous session) or moving the session into your PT101-XXX folder (if working from the sample file).

3. Click the MUTE button (M) on each of the existing tracks to temporarily mute them.

Press OPTION (Mac) or ALT (Windows) while clicking the Mute button on any unmuted track to mute all of the tracks at once.

Configuring the Session

In this part of the exercise, you will configure various settings in the Pro Tools Edit window and set the session tempo.

Configure the session:

1. Click on the **HORIZONTAL ZOOM IN** button on the toolbar to zoom in a level for a better view.

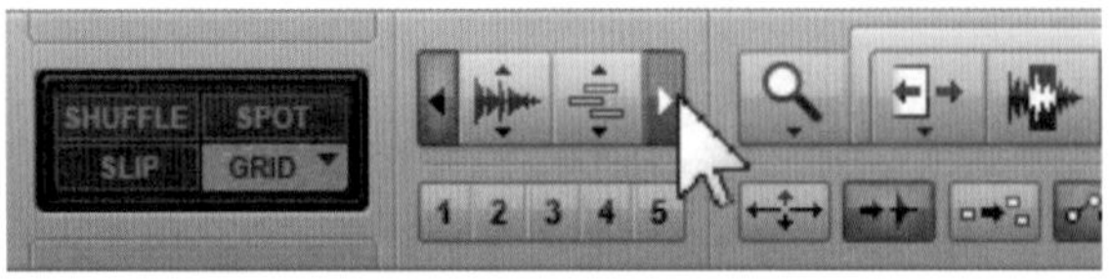

Figure 7.28 Clicking on the Horizontal Zoom In button on the Edit window toolbar

2. Choose **VIEW > RULERS > TEMPO** to display the Tempo Ruler, if not already shown.
3. Double-click on the red tempo event at the start of the Tempo Ruler. The Tempo Change dialog box will open.

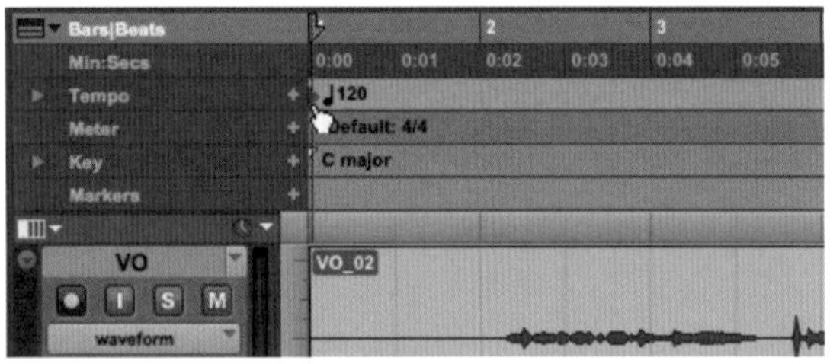

Figure 7.29 Double-clicking on the red tempo event on the Tempo Ruler

4. Change the session tempo in the dialog box to **123 BPM** and click **OK**. The tempo event will update to reflect the change.

Creating New Tracks

In this part of the exercise, you will create an Instrument track and assign the Xpand!2 plug-in to the track. You will also create a click track and configure the click settings.

Create an Instrument track:

1. Choose **TRACK > NEW** or press **COMMAND+SHIFT+N** (Mac) or **CTRL+SHIFT+N** (Windows) to open the New Tracks dialog box.
2. Configure the dialog box for a single stereo Instrument track and click **CREATE**. A new Instrument track will be added to your session.
3. Double-click the track nameplate. In the resulting dialog box, rename the track Beat Wave and click **OK**.

Assign a virtual instrument to the Instrument track:

1. Choose **WINDOW > MIX** or press **COMMAND+=** (Mac) or **CTRL+=** (Windows) to display the Mix window.
2. Click on **INSERT SELECTOR A** for the Beat Wave track and choose **MULTICHANNEL PLUG-IN > INSTRUMENT > XPAND!2 (STEREO)**. The Xpand!2 plug-in window will display.

3. Click on the **Librarian Menu** (displaying <factory default>) and select **04 Action Pads > 44 Space Race**.

Figure 7.30 The Xpand!2 plug-in window

> **You will have to scroll down past the "+##" presets to reach the 44 Space Race preset, near the bottom of the list.**

4. When finished, close the Xpand!2 plug-in window.

Create a click track for the session:

1. Choose **Track > Create Click Track**. An Aux Input track named Click will be added to your session.
2. Open the Transport window, if not already displayed, by choosing **Window > Transport.**
3. Click on the **Transport Window pop-up** menu and verify that **MIDI Controls** and **Expanded Transport** are enabled.

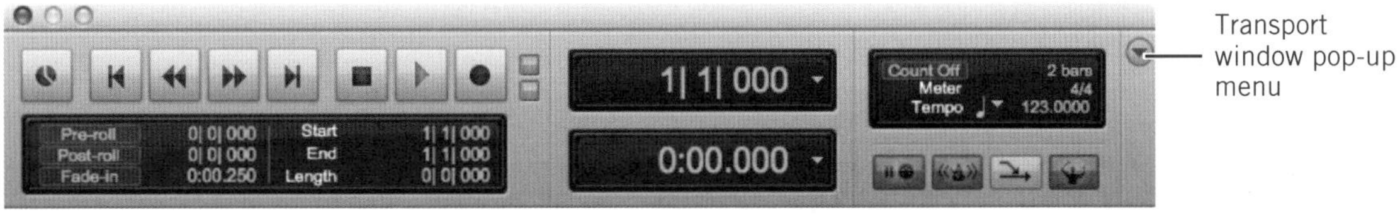

Figure 7.31 MIDI Controls and Expanded Transport enabled in the Transport window

4. In the MIDI Controls section of the Transport window, verify that the **Wait for Note** and **Metronome** (click) buttons are both enabled (blue).

Recording a MIDI Performance (Optional)

In this part of the exercise, you will record a MIDI performance on the Beat Wave Instrument track. If you do not have an available MIDI keyboard, you can skip this section and proceed to the next section.

Prepare for recording MIDI:

1. Verify that the MIDI device you will be using is powered on and connected to your system through an available MIDI In port or USB port.
2. Choose **SETUP > PLAYBACK ENGINE** and verify that the H/W Buffer Size setting is set low to minimize latency while recording.

For best results, use a H/W Buffer Size setting of 128 Samples or lower. Increase this setting only if Pro Tools gives you frequent error messages during recording or playback.

3. Choose **EVENT > EVENT OPERATIONS > INPUT QUANTIZE** to open the Input Quantize window.
4. Configure the Input Quantize settings as follows:
   - Check (select) the options for **ENABLE INPUT QUANTIZE**, **NOTE ON**, and **NOTE OFF**.
   - Set the **QUANTIZE GRID** to **1/4 NOTE**. Leave all other options unchecked.

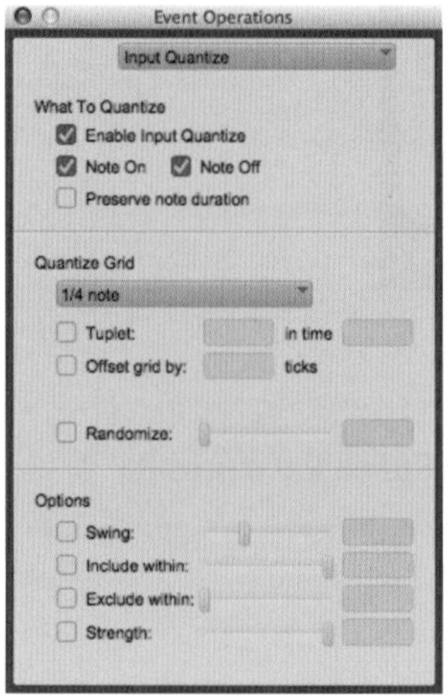

Figure 7.32 Input Quantize settings for recording on the Beat Wave track

5. Close the Input Quantize window; then choose **WINDOW > EDIT** or press **COMMAND+=** (Mac) or **CTRL+=** (Windows) to toggle to the Edit window.

Make an 8-bar record-selection and activate Wait for Note recording:

1. Verify that the session is in Grid mode (Grid button highlighted on the left side of the toolbar), and set the grid to 1/4 notes (0|1|000) using the Grid Value pop-up selector on the right side of the toolbar.

Figure 7.33 Grid mode enabled (left); Grid value set to quarter notes (right)

2. Using the **SELECTOR** tool, make a selection on the Beat Wave track, extending from Bar 2 to Bar 10 (2|1|000 to 10|1|000).

Use the Start, End, and Length fields in the Counter area to verify your selection.

3. Record-enable the Beat Wave track by clicking the **RECORD ENABLE** button at the head of the track.
4. Click the **RECORD** button in the Transport window to enable **WAIT FOR NOTE** MIDI recording.

   The Stop, Play, and Record buttons will begin to flash, and you will hear the metronome click begin to sound.

Record the selection:

1. When ready, press and hold the A2 key on your MIDI keyboard to begin recording.

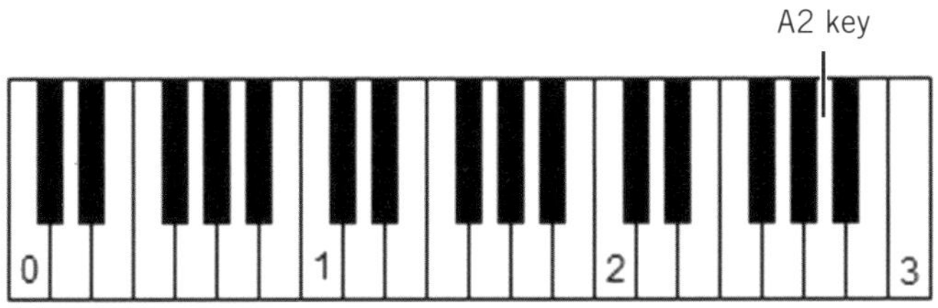

Figure 7.34 The A2 note on a standard piano keyboard

2. Hold the note steady for almost 2 full bars (around 7 beats); then release the note and play it again at Bar 4, holding it for another 7 beats or so.
3. Repeat the process, playing the note at Bar 6 and again at Bar 8.

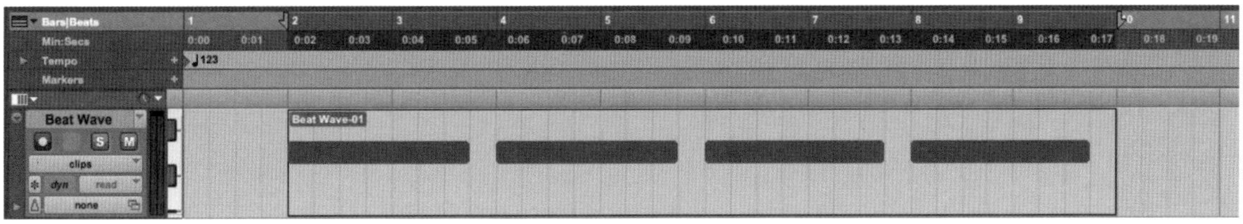

Figure 7.35 Desired end result after completing the 8-bar recording

   For this recording, the timing does not need to be exact. The Input Quantize function will ensure that each note begins and ends on a beat. If you are having difficulty with the timing, you can simply play the note at the start of the recording and hold it for the entire 8 bars.

4. When finished, review the results. If you are not happy with the recording, choose **EDIT > UNDO MIDI RECORDING** and try again.
5. When you're satisfied with the results, click the **RECORD ENABLE** button on the Beat Wave track to disable recording.
6. Next, disable the **WAIT FOR NOTE** and **METRONOME** buttons in the Transport window.

Importing MIDI Clips

In this section, you will import MIDI clips from the *Beat Waves.mid* file provided with the PT101 Download Media. You will use these clips to finish the performance on the Beat Wave track.

Import MIDI to the session:

1. Choose **FILE > IMPORT MIDI** and navigate to the Exercise Media folder from your downloaded files (PT101 Download Media > 02. Exercise Media).
2. Select the *Beat Waves.mid* file and click **OPEN**. The MIDI Import Options dialog box will appear.

3. In the MIDI Import Options dialog box, select **CLIP LIST** as the destination and click **OK**. (See Figure 7.36.) Two new clips will be placed in the Clip List (1st Wave-01 and 2nd Wave-01).

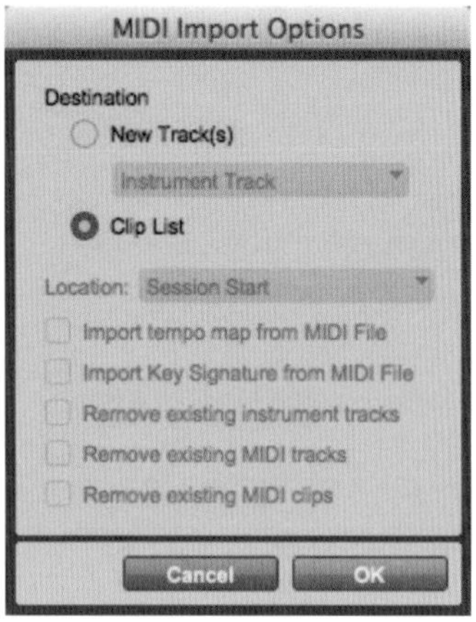

Figure 7.36 The MIDI Import Options dialog box with Clip List selected as the destination

Place MIDI clips on the Beat Wave track to finish the performance:

1. If you did not complete the MIDI recording steps in the previous section, or if you'd like to replace your recorded MIDI with the MIDI you've imported, do the following:
   - Using the **GRABBER** tool, select just the 1st Wave-01 MIDI clip in the Clip List.
   - Drag the clip to the start of the Beat Wave track.
2. With the **GRABBER** tool, select just the 2nd Wave-01 clip in the Clip List.
3. Drag the clip onto the Beat Wave track and position it to start at Bar 10.

Finishing Up

To complete this exercise tutorial, you will need to save your work and close the session. You will be reusing this session in Exercise 8, so it is important to save the work you've done.

You should also listen to your progress thus far before exiting.

Review and save your work:

1. Press **ENTER** or **RETURN** to place the cursor at the beginning of the session.
2. **OPTION-CLICK** (Mac) or **ALT-CLICK** (Windows) on the mute control of any muted track to unmute all of the tracks. Then re-enable the Mute control on the Fire FX track.
3. Press the **SPACEBAR** to play back the session and review your results.
4. Press the **SPACEBAR** a second time when finished.
5. Choose **FILE > SAVE** to save the session.
6. Choose **FILE > CLOSE SESSION** to close the session.

Remember that you cannot close a Pro Tools session by closing its windows. You must choose CLOSE SESSION from the FILE menu.

LESSON 8

Selecting and Navigating

This lesson covers various selection and navigation techniques that are available in Pro Tools. It includes descriptions of how to use Timeline and Edit selections, how to modify your session view (including setting track sizes and zoom displays), and how to create and use markers to quickly navigate your session.

Duration: 120 Minutes

GOALS

- Navigate a session with the Universe view
- Recognize the difference between a Timeline selection and an Edit selection
- Mark and adjust selection in and out points
- Use the Tab key to navigate a Track Playlist
- Adjust the session view for different needs
- Add, delete, and work with location markers

Key topics from this lesson are included in the *Pro Tools 12 Essential Training: 101* course on Lynda.com.

Understanding selection and navigation techniques can dramatically improve your efficiency when working with Pro Tools. Whether you need to audition material you have just added or you need to edit a transition between clips, being able to quickly find and select the right material is key. The sections in this lesson introduce you to various processes that you can use to streamline your work in all phases of your project.

Using the Universe View

Pro Tools provides a Universe view that can be displayed at the top of the Edit window. The Universe view displays an overview of your entire session, providing a miniature representation of all video, audio, and MIDI material on your displayed tracks.

Material residing on each track is represented by a single horizontal line in the Universe view, in the same color as the clips on the track. Since Aux Inputs, VCA tracks, and Master Faders do not contain any audio, they are represented as blank areas in the Universe view.

To toggle the display of the Universe view, do the following:

- Choose VIEW > OTHER DISPLAYS > UNIVERSE.

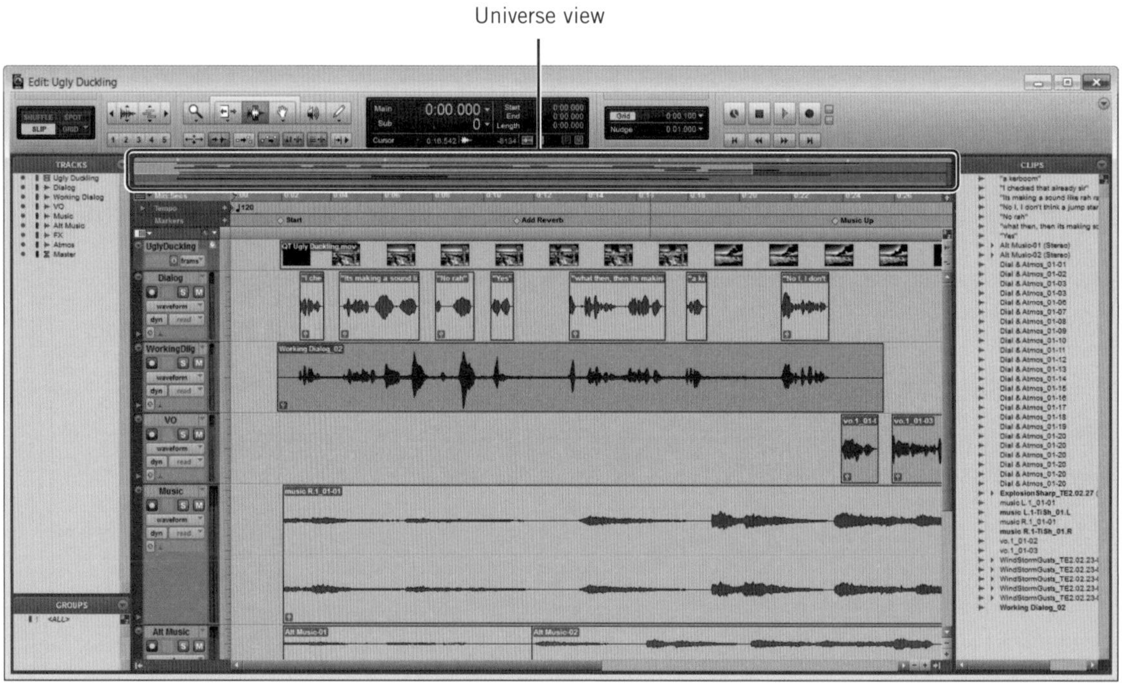

Figure 8.1 Universe view in the Edit window

Resizing the Universe

You can adjust the height of the Universe view to fit more tracks in the display or to allocate more room to the Edit window tracks display, as needed.

To resize the Universe view, do the following:

1. Click the area between the bottom of the Universe view and the top of the Timebase Rulers. The cursor will change to a double-headed arrow, indicating that you can adjust the Universe view area.
2. Drag up or down to change the height of the Universe view.

If you resize the Universe view to less than its minimum size, the view will toggle off. This provides another method of hiding the view. When you toggle the view on again, it will restore to its previous height.

The Current View Indicator

The track area currently displayed in the Edit window is represented by a white rectangular frame in the Universe view.

If you change the display in the Edit window—by zooming, scrolling, hiding or showing tracks, or changing track heights—the framed area in the Universe view will relocate and resize accordingly. During playback, if the Edit window is set to scroll, the framed area in the Universe view will also scroll.

Figure 8.2 Framed area in the Universe view

Moving and Scrolling from the Universe View

By clicking in the Universe view, you can scroll the Edit window horizontally, vertically, or both. This provides a simple method of navigating within your session and controlling which sections of your tracks are visible in the Edit window.

To navigate the session using the Universe view, do the following:

1. If the Universe view is not currently displayed, choose VIEW > OTHER DISPLAYS > UNIVERSE.
2. Do one of the following:
   - Click anywhere in the Universe view to move the framed area. The Edit window will update accordingly, jumping to the framed location.
   - Click and drag on the framed area. The Edit window will scroll in real time to match your movements in the Universe view.

Types of Selection

Once you've navigated to the area where you would like to work, you will often need to make a specific selection. As discussed in Lesson 4, Pro Tools provides two types of selections: *timeline selections* and *edit selections*. Timeline selections can be made from any Timebase Ruler and are used to set a playback or record range. Edit selections can be made in any track or in multiple tracks and are used to set an edit range.

Creating Timeline Selections

At any time while working in your Pro Tools session, you can create a timeline selection. Timeline selections are frequently made by dragging with the SELECTOR tool and can also be created or adjusted using the TIMELINE SELECTION fields in the Transport window or the TIMELINE SELECTION IN/OUT POINTS in the Main Timebase Ruler.

With LINK TIMELINE AND EDIT SELECTION enabled, a Timeline selection is also made whenever you select audio or MIDI data on a track. See "Creating Edit Selections" later in this lesson.

Selecting with the Timebase Rulers

To make a timeline selection with the Rulers, do the following:

1. With any tool selected, move your pointer over a **TIMEBASE RULER** in the Edit window. The Selector tool will become active.
2. Click and drag with the **SELECTOR** tool in any Timebase Ruler to select the desired area of the Timeline.

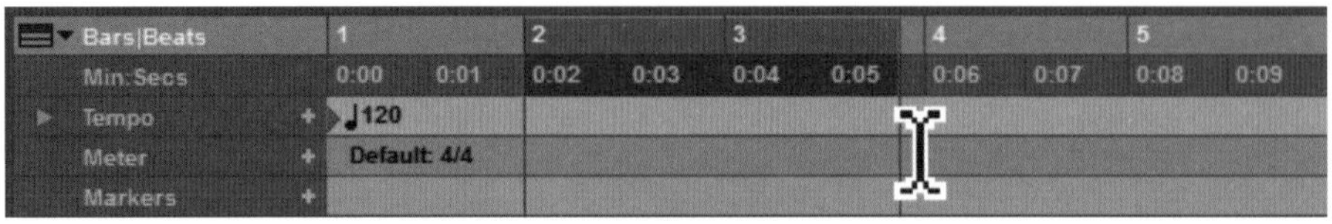

Figure 8.3 Making a Timeline selection with the Selector tool

The timeline selection is indicated in the Main Timebase Ruler by blue Timeline Selection In/Out Points (red if a track is record-enabled). The start, end, and length values for the timeline selection are also displayed in the Timeline Selection fields in the Transport window.

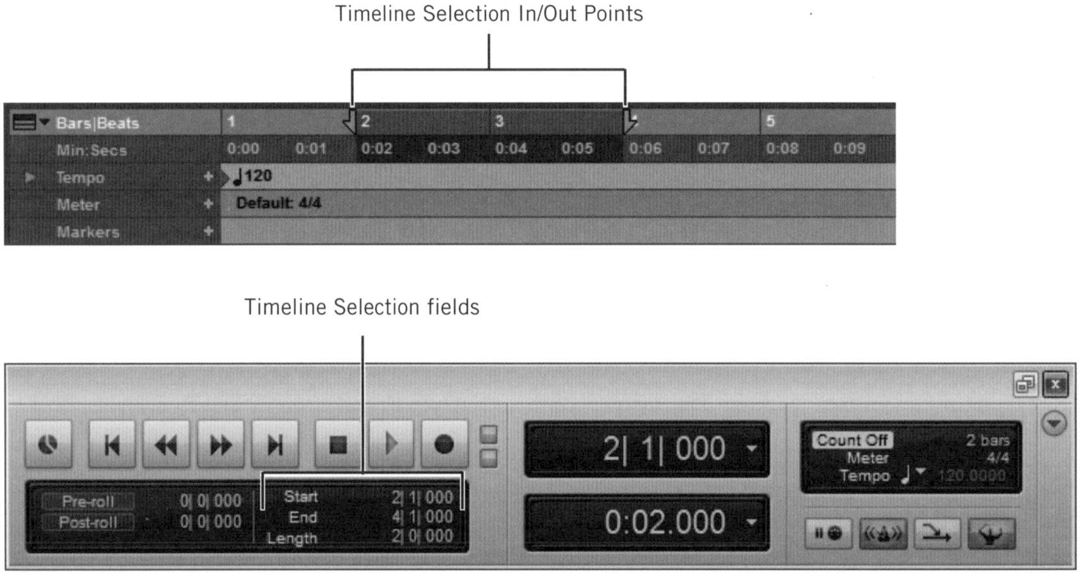

Figure 8.4 Timeline selection as indicated in the Timebase Rulers (top) and the Transport window (bottom)

Selecting with the Timeline Selection Fields (Transport Window)

You can use the Timeline Selection fields in the Transport window to create a new selection or to adjust a selection numerically from the keyboard.

To create a new selection using the Timeline Selection fields:

1. Click on the first field in the **START** Location Indicator to activate it. The selected field will become highlighted. (See Figure 8.5.)

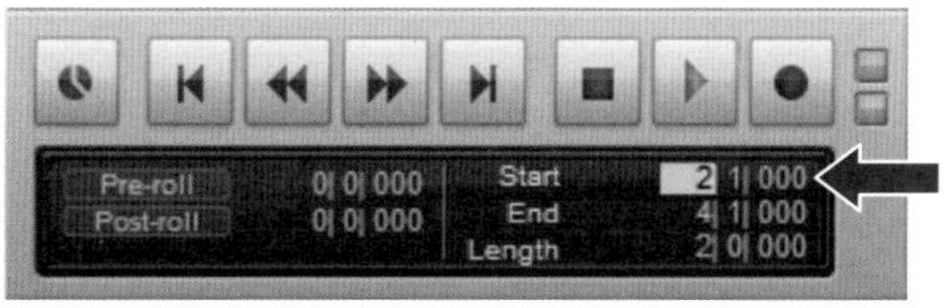

Figure 8.5 Start field selected in the Transport window

2. Enter the desired value or use the Up or Down arrow keys on the keyboard to increment or decrement the value one unit at a time.
3. Click on each successive field to select it (or use the Left and Right arrow keys on the keyboard to cycle through the fields).
4. Enter the desired value in each field or select a value using the Up or Down arrow keys.
5. Press Return or Enter to confirm your entry and move the insertion point to the specified location.
6. Do one of the following to complete the selection:
   - Repeat this process, using the End fields to specify the end point for the Timeline selection. The Length indicator fields will update accordingly.
   - Repeat this process, using the Length fields to specify the duration of the Timeline selection. The End indicator fields will update accordingly.

When you type a value in a Timeline Selection field or an Edit Selection field, Pro Tools will zero out all fields to the right of the changed field. To change a value without affecting the other fields (to move to a different bar but retain the beat and tick number, for example), select the value and press the Up or Down arrow key as needed.

The plus (+) and minus (–) keys provide a calculator-like function, allowing you to add or subtract a number to offset the current field. To add to or subtract from a field, press Plus or Minus in any field, followed by the desired offset. Press Return or Enter to calculate the new value or press Escape to cancel.

Selecting with the Timeline Selection In/Out Points

You can also use the Timeline Selection In Point and Out Point on the Main Timebase Ruler to create a new selection or to adjust an existing selection.

To set the timeline selection by dragging the Timeline Selection In/Out Points, do the following:

1. With any tool selected, move your pointer over the Timeline Selection In Point or Out Point in the Main Timebase Ruler. The Time Grabber tool will become active.
2. Drag the Timeline Selection In Point to set the selection start.
3. Drag the Timeline Selection Out Point to set the selection end.

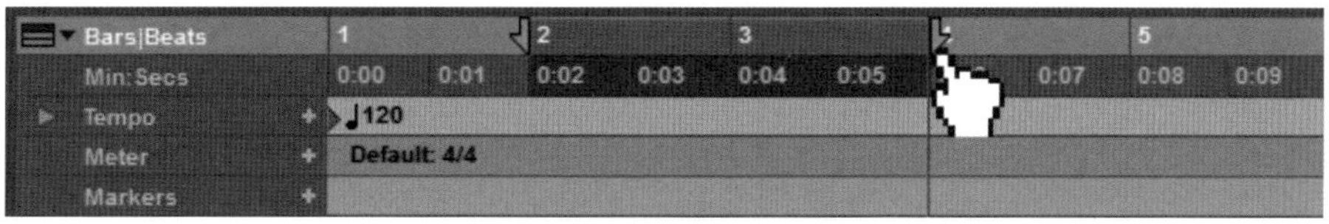

Figure 8.6 Dragging the Timeline Selection Out Point

Creating Edit Selections

When you are working with audio or MIDI data in Pro Tools, you can create an Edit selection to work with a portion of the material on a track. Edit selections are frequently made using the Grabber tool or the Selector tool. Edit selections can also be created or adjusted using the Edit Selection fields in the Edit window.

With LINK TIMELINE AND EDIT SELECTION enabled, an Edit selection is also made on all tracks whenever you select an area on a Timebase Ruler. See "Creating Timeline Selections" earlier in this lesson.

Selecting with the Grabber Tool

You can use the Grabber tool to make an Edit selection on any clip that exists on a Track Playlist. To select a clip with the Grabber tool, click once on the clip you want to select. The selected clip will be highlighted. To select multiple clips, click on the first of the clips you want to select and then SHIFT-CLICK on another clip. Both clips will be selected, along with all clips in between them.

Selected clips can be moved, copied, cut, or deleted (cleared) from the track.

When MIDI and Instrument tracks are set to Notes view, the Grabber tool selects individual MIDI notes or note ranges. To select MIDI clips, first set the track to Clips view (see "MIDI Clips View" in Lesson 7) and then click on a clip to select it.

Selecting with the Selector Tool

Using the Selector tool, you can select any portion of audio or MIDI data on your tracks for editing.

To make an Edit selection with the Selector tool, do one of the following:

- Click and drag across the area on the track that you want to select.
- Click once to define a starting point for the selection and then SHIFT-CLICK to define an ending point for the selection.

The selected area is indicated by a dark highlight on the track. The selected media can be moved, copied, cut, or deleted (cleared) from the track.

Double-clicking with the Selector tool will select an entire clip; triple-clicking will select the entire Track Playlist.

Selecting with the Edit Selection Fields (Edit Window)

You can use the Edit Selection fields in the Edit window to create a new selection or to adjust a selection numerically from the keyboard.

Figure 8.7 The Edit Selection fields in the Edit window

To create a new selection using the Edit Selection fields:

1. Click on the first field in the Start Location Indicator to activate it. The selected field will be highlighted.
2. Enter the desired value or use the Up or Down arrow keys on the keyboard to adjust the value one unit at a time.
3. Click on each successive field to select it (or use the Left and Right arrow keys to cycle through fields).
4. Enter the desired value in each field or select a value using the Up or Down arrow keys.
5. Press Return or Enter to confirm your entry and move the insertion point to the specified location.

Use the slash key (/) to move between the Start, End, and Length values. This shortcut also works for the Timeline Selection fields (Transport window).

6. Do one of the following:
   - Repeat this process, using the End fields to specify the end point for the Edit selection. The Length indicator fields will update accordingly.
   - Repeat this process, using the Length fields to specify the duration of the Edit selection. The End indicator fields will update accordingly.

Working with Selections

Pro Tools provides various ways of making selections and adjusting the selection boundaries. The following sections describe some common selection techniques.

Creating Separate Timeline Selections and Edit Selections

The default setting in Pro Tools links timeline selections and edit selections together. This means that whenever you select an area on a track, you simultaneously select the same area in the Timeline. This is often the easiest way to work because it allows you to easily play back selected areas as you adjust your edit selection.

However, in advanced workflows, you might encounter situations in which you want to unlink the Timeline selection from the Edit selection. You can link and unlink the Timeline selection and Edit selection using the Link Timeline and Edit Selection toggle button in the Edit window. This button is blue when the Timeline and Edit selections are linked.

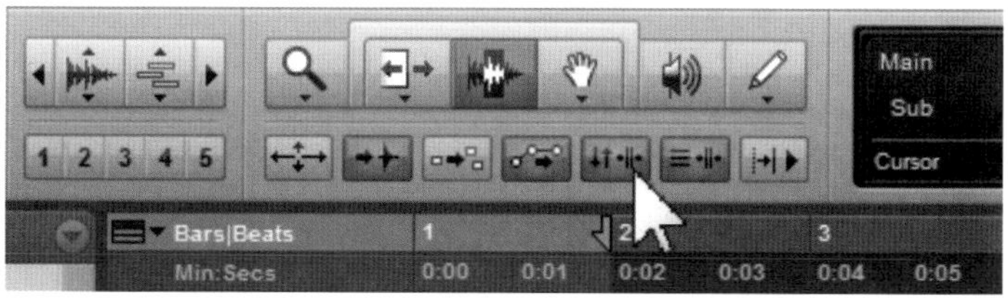

Figure 8.8 Using the toggle button to link/unlink the Timeline and Edit selections

For the purposes of this book, we assume that selections are made with the Timeline and Edit selections linked. Workflows that require unlinking the Timeline and Edit selections are introduced in later courses.

Making Selections on Multiple Tracks

Edit selections can be extended across multiple tracks in several different ways. The method you use will depend on the needs of the situation.

Selecting Material on Adjacent Tracks

When you create a selection with the Selector tool, you can drag vertically to select the same area across several adjacent tracks.

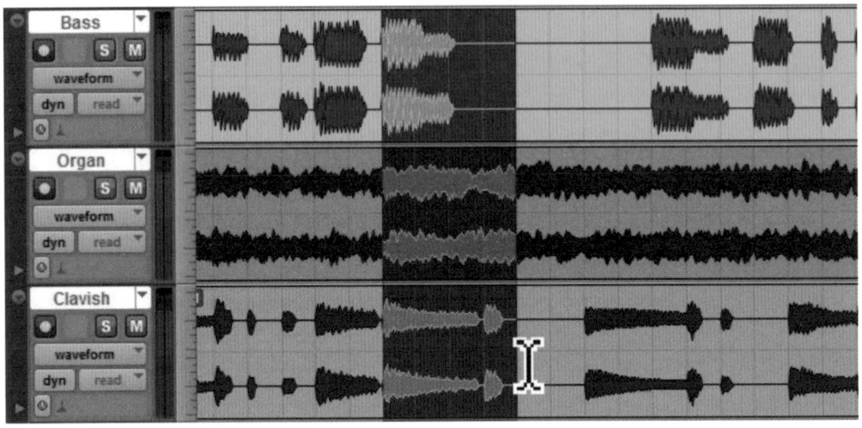

Figure 8.9 Making a selection across multiple tracks using the Selector tool

Selecting Material on Nonadjacent Tracks

Selecting material on nonadjacent tracks is a two-step process. After creating a selection on one or more tracks, you can add the selection to a nonadjacent track by Shift-clicking on the Track Playlist with the Selector tool.

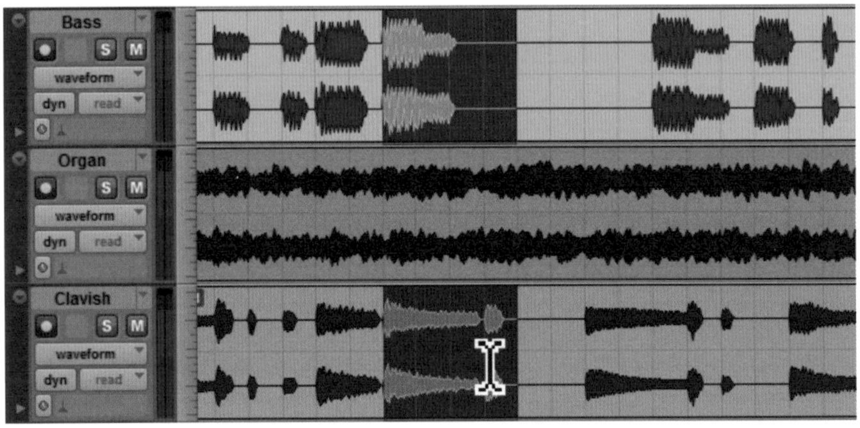

Figure 8.10 Making a selection across nonadjacent tracks by Shift-clicking on a Track Playlist

Selecting Material Based on Selected Tracks

The LINK TRACK AND EDIT SELECTION setting in Pro Tools provides an option for sharing Edit selections among tracks by selecting or deselecting the tracks themselves. This option allows you to copy a selection to another track, remove a selection from an individual track, and move a selection among tracks by selecting or deselecting track nameplates as needed.

Enabling Link Track and Edit Selection

In normal operation, selecting a track in Pro Tools brings that track into focus for certain track-level operations, such as grouping, hiding, duplicating, making active/inactive, deleting, and so forth. To select a track, you simply click on the track nameplate in the Edit or Mix window. The track nameplate becomes highlighted to indicate that the track is selected.

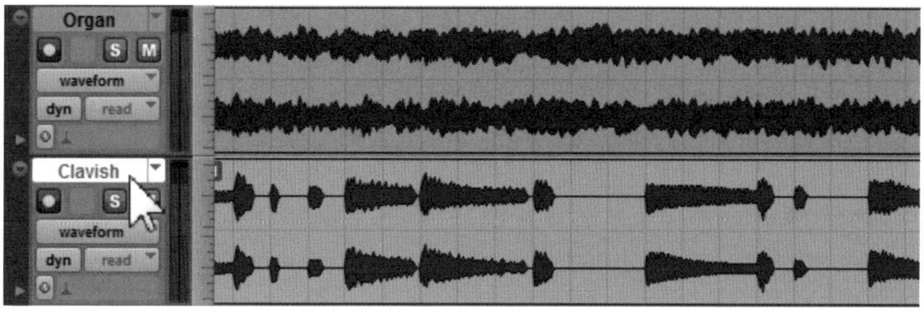

Figure 8.11 Selecting a track in the Edit window by clicking the nameplate

By enabling the Link Track and Edit Selection setting, tracks that receive an edit selection become selected automatically. Conversely, tracks that are selected after an edit selection is made will inherit the edit selection.

The Link Track and Edit Selection option can be activated by choosing **Options > Link Track and Edit Selection**. Alternatively, this option can be enabled using the **Link Track and Edit Selection** toggle button in the Edit window. This button turns blue when active.

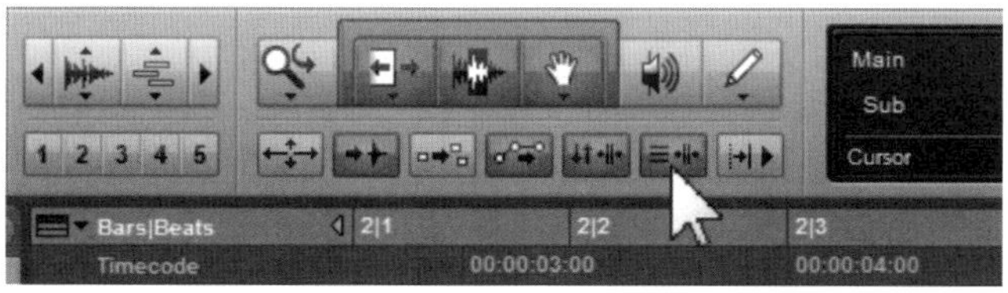

Figure 8.12 Using the toggle button to link the track and edit selections

Using Link Track and Edit Selection to Modify Playlist Selections

To copy an Edit selection (or playlist selection) to additional tracks with **Link Track and Edit Selection** enabled, do one of the following:

- To select a range of adjacent tracks, **Shift-click** on the nameplate of the last track in the range. All tracks in the range will be selected and will inherit the Edit selection.
- To select nonadjacent tracks, **Command-click** (Mac) or **Ctrl-click** (Windows) on the nameplates of the desired tracks. Each clicked track will be selected and will inherit the Edit selection.

To remove an Edit selection from a track while retaining it on others, **Command-click** (Mac) or **Ctrl-click** (Windows) on the nameplate of the unwanted track to deselect it. The Edit selection will be removed from the deselected track.

To move a selection to a different track, click on the nameplate of the desired destination track to select it. The Edit selection will be removed from the previously selected track(s) and placed on the newly selected track.

Using the Tab Key

When working in a track, you can use the Tab key to move the cursor or extend a selection to a clip boundary.

Moving the Cursor to Clip Boundaries

To advance the cursor to the next adjacent clip boundary to the right, press the **Tab** key. To withdraw the cursor to the previous clip boundary to the left, press **Option+Tab** (Mac) or **Ctrl+Tab** (Windows). With each press of the Tab key, the cursor will move to the next successive clip boundary.

Making Selections to Clip Boundaries

Using the Tab key to make selections can be quite useful when you want your selection to start or end exactly on a clip boundary, because it allows you to precisely locate the cursor to any clip start or end point.

- To select from the current cursor position or extend a selection to the next clip boundary to the right, press **Shift+Tab**.
- To select from the current cursor position or extend a selection to the previous clip boundary to the left, press **Option+Shift+Tab** (Mac) or **Ctrl+Shift+Tab** (Windows).

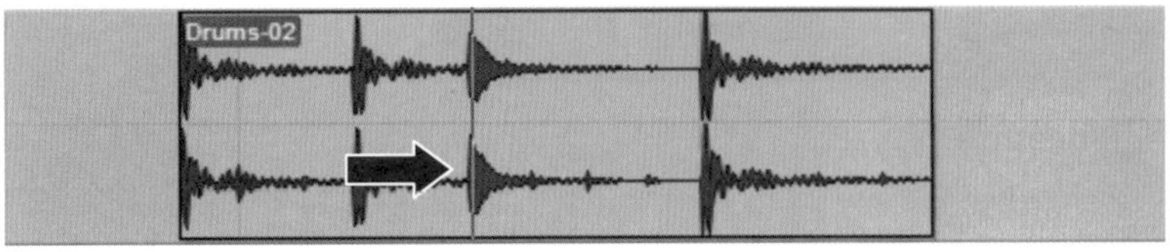

Figure 8.13 Starting cursor position

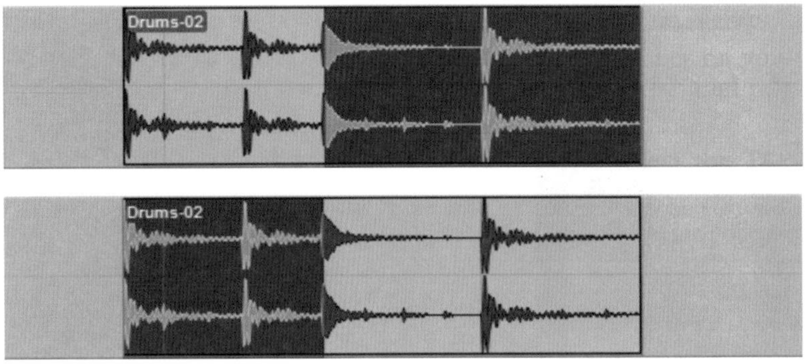

Figure 8.14 Result of pressing Shift+Tab (top) or Option+Shift+Tab/Ctrl+Shift+Tab (bottom)

The Tab key is a repeater key; do not hold it down. Doing so will cause your selection to tab rapidly to successive clip boundaries.

Tabbing to Transient Points

A variation on the standard Tab key behavior is provided by the Tab to Transients function. This function is extremely useful for finding the initial peak or modulation in an audio waveform, saving you time and hassle when locating the exact starting point of a sound or louder transition.

Enabling Tab to Transients

The Tab to Transients function can be toggled on/off selectively, as needed.

To use the Tab to Transients function, do the following:

1. Enable **Tab to Transients** under the **Options** menu, or click on the **Tab to Transients** toggle button in the Edit window toolbar so that the button becomes highlighted in blue.

Figure 8.15 Enabling the Tab to Transients function

2. Press the **Tab** key to move the cursor forward to the next transient to the right. Press **Option+Tab** (Mac) or **Ctrl+Tab** (Windows) to move the cursor backward to the previous transient to the left.

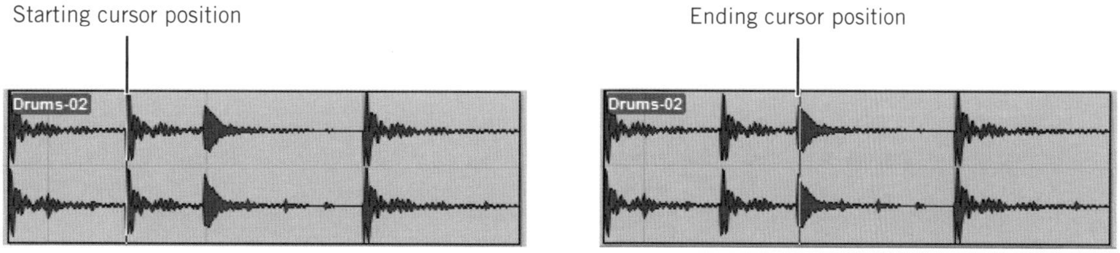

Figure 8.16 Advancing the cursor to the next drum hit using Tab to Transients: before (left) and after (right)

The Tab to Transients threshold is set by Pro Tools and is not user-adjustable.

Making Selections Based on Transients

Using the Tab to Transients function is an easy way to make selections that start or end on a sound, because it allows you to locate the cursor to an audio peak. You can make selections by holding **Shift** while tabbing.

- To select from the current cursor position or extend a selection to the next transient to the right, press **Shift+Tab**.
- To select from the current cursor position or extend a selection to the previous transient to the left, press **Option+Shift+Tab** (Mac) or **Ctrl+Shift+Tab** (Windows).

To disable the Tab to Transients function (so that the Tab key again moves to clip boundaries), click the **Tab to Transients** toggle button so that it is no longer lit blue.

Press Command+Option+Tab (Mac) or Ctrl+Alt+Tab (Windows) to toggle the Tab to Transients function on and off.

Adjusting the Session View

Pro Tools enables you to customize many aspects of your session display. You can change the display size of individual tracks, change the order in which tracks are displayed, change the Zoom settings for the current view, and create Zoom Presets to store and recall commonly used magnification settings.

Adjusting Track Height

Pro Tools allows you to change the size of the track display in the Edit window by adjusting the track height. Track height can be adjusted on a track-by-track basis, allowing each track to be displayed at any of the following sizes:

- Micro
- Mini
- Small
- Medium
- Large

- Jumbo
- Extreme
- Fit to Window

Larger track heights are particularly useful for precision editing because they show more detail. Smaller track heights are useful for conserving screen space in large sessions.

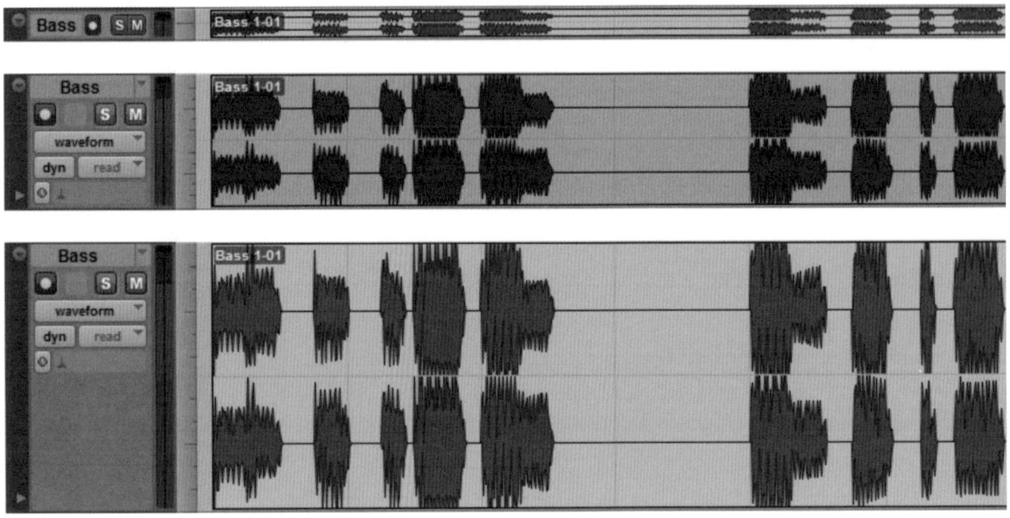

Figure 8.17 Bass track at different heights (mini, medium, and large track sizes shown)

Due to their small size, tracks using the small, mini, or micro display options do not show all of their controls. Hidden controls are available from the Track Options menu.

You can select a track height at any time by clicking on the Track Options menu or the amplitude scale area of the track, or you can adjust the height incrementally by dragging the lower boundary of the track.

To select a track height from a pop-up menu:

1. Click anywhere within the amplitude scale area immediately to the right of the track meter or click directly on the TRACK OPTIONS MENU button to the left of the track name.

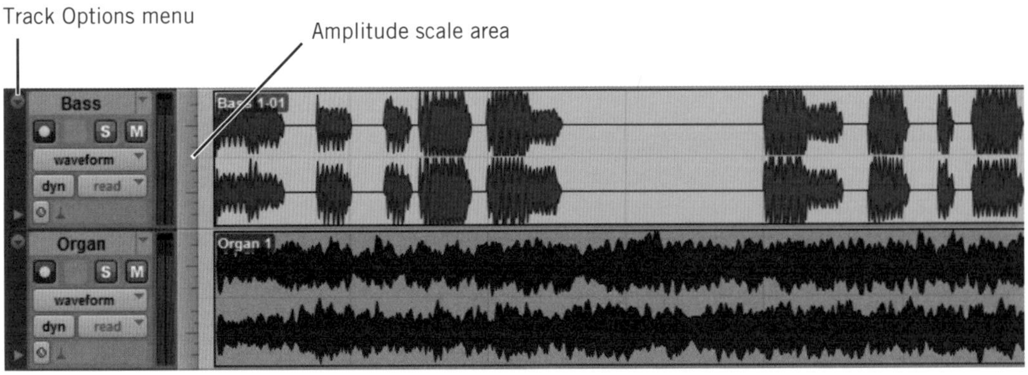

Figure 8.18 The Track Options menu button and amplitude scale area at the head of a track

2. Choose the desired height from the Track Height menu. (See Figure 8.19.) This menu may appear as a submenu at smaller track heights.

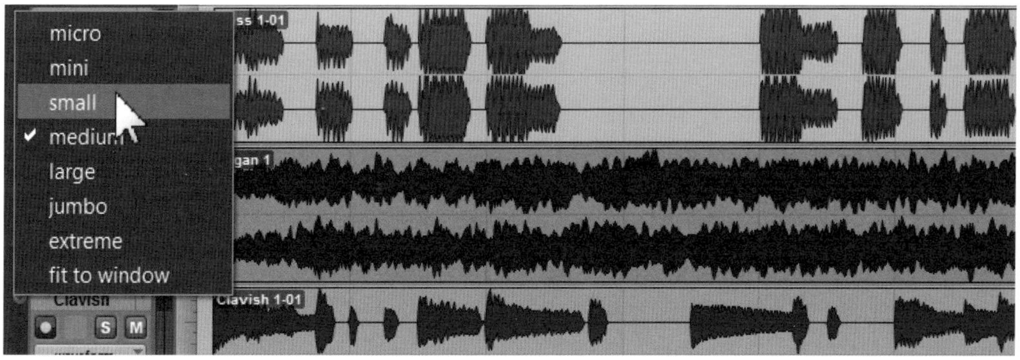

Figure 8.19 The Track Height pop-up menu

To set all tracks in the session to the same height, press the OPTION key (Mac) or ALT key (Windows) while selecting the desired height on any track.

To incrementally resize the track height using the lower boundary of the track:

1. Position your pointer over the lower boundary at the head of any track; the cursor will change into a double-headed arrow.
2. Click on the track boundary and drag up or down. The track height will change in increments.

Press and hold COMMAND (Mac) or CTRL (Windows) while adjusting track height for continuous, non-incremental adjustment.

Changing the Track Order

Pro Tools allows you to change the order of tracks in your session at any time to customize the onscreen layout. Changing the track order affects both the Mix and Edit windows, as well as the track layout on any connected control surface.

Arranging tracks in a logical order can simplify your navigation. This can be true even in relatively small sessions. Consider arranging the tracks in your session such that related tracks are displayed together, instruments are displayed in a logical order, or commonly used tracks are presented at the top. The order can be rearranged as needed as you work your way through the editing process.

To change the session's track order, do any of the following:

- In the Edit window, click on the track nameplate and drag the track above or below other tracks in the session.
- In the Mix window, click on the track nameplate and drag the track to the left or right of other tracks in the session. (See Figures 8.20 and 8.21.)
- In the Track List, click on the track name and drag it to a higher or lower position in the list.

Figure 8.20 Clicking on a track nameplate and dragging the track to a new position (Mix window)

Figure 8.21 Track order after repositioning the track

Using the Zoomer Tool

The Zoomer tool can be used to examine a waveform up close for precision editing.

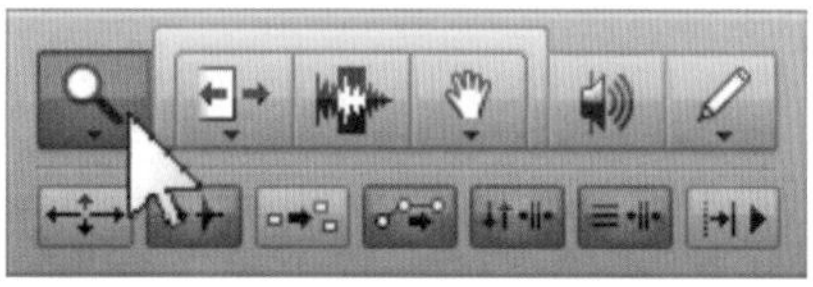

Figure 8.22 The Zoomer tool

Zooming In and Out

To zoom in, centering on a certain point in a track, do the following:

1. If it is not already selected, click the ZOOMER tool. The pointer will display a magnifying glass with a plus sign when positioned over a track.

2. Click once at the desired point within the track. The waveform will enlarge within the track display, with the zoom point centered horizontally in the Edit window.
3. To zoom in further, click multiple times. Each successive click zooms in by one additional level.

To zoom back out, do the following:

1. OPTION-CLICK (Mac) or ALT-CLICK (Windows) with the ZOOMER tool. The cursor will display a magnifying glass with a minus sign when positioned over a track while holding OPTION/ALT.

2. To zoom out further, click multiple times while holding OPTION/ALT. Each successive click zooms out by one additional level, with the zoom point centered horizontally in the Edit window.

Double-click on the ZOOMER tool button in the toolbar to zoom all the way out. This displays a full track view that fits the longest displayed track onto the screen.

Zooming In on a Range

The Zoomer tool can also be used to zoom in on a particular range, enlarging the range to fill the visible area of the track.

To zoom into a range, do the following:

1. If it is not already selected, click the ZOOMER tool to select it.
2. Click and drag with the magnifying glass over the horizontal portion of a track that you want to view up close. (To zoom horizontally and vertically, COMMAND-DRAG [Mac] or CTRL-DRAG [Windows]). As you drag, a dashed box will appear, indicating the range that you will be zooming in on.
3. Release the mouse. The display will fill the screen with the portion of the waveform you selected, zooming in horizontally to the same level on all tracks simultaneously.

Using Zoom Toggle

The Zoom Toggle button is located immediately beneath the Zoomer tool in the toolbar area. Use the ZOOM TOGGLE button to toggle the view between the current zoom state and a preset/predefined zoom state.

Figure 8.23 Zoom Toggle button

When Zoom Toggle is enabled, the Edit window displays the stored zoom state, as specified in the Zoom Toggle preferences. When Zoom Toggle is disabled, the Edit window reverts to the pre–Zoom Toggle view.

Zoom Toggle behavior varies, based on the Zoom Toggle settings selected in the Editing Preferences page (SETUP > PREFERENCES).

Changing the Horizontal and Vertical Zoom

The Edit window includes Zoom buttons in the toolbar area that allow you to adjust the track waveform or MIDI view without using the Zoomer tool. These buttons adjust the display zoom levels, keeping the insertion cursor or selection start point centered as it changes. Like the Zoomer tool, the Zoom buttons change only the display of the data and do not affect playback.

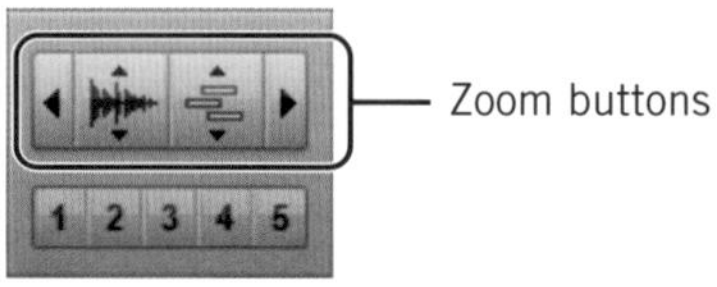

Figure 8.24 The Zoom buttons in the Edit window toolbar

From left to right, the Zoom buttons are as follows:

- **Horizontal Zoom Out button.** This button changes the time display of all tracks in the session by shrinking the track Timeline, audio waveform views, and MIDI displays to show more time on screen, with less detail. This adjustment is useful for obtaining a "big-picture" view of your Track Playlists.
- **Audio Zoom In and Out button.** This button changes the waveform amplitude display of all Audio tracks in the session by enlarging or shrinking the track waveform views vertically, making the waveforms appear taller or shorter. Zooming in is useful to distinguish low-amplitude audio waveforms; zooming out is useful to distinguish high-amplitude audio waveforms.
- **MIDI Zoom In and Out button.** This button changes the display of MIDI data on all MIDI-compatible tracks in the session by modifying the note range shown in the track (represented by the track's mini-keyboard). Zooming in shows a narrower range of notes, with each note appearing fatter; zooming out shows a broader range of notes, with each note appearing thinner.

The MIDI Zoom buttons do not affect tracks in Clips view. To see the effect of MIDI Zoom, switch your MIDI or Instrument tracks to Notes view.

- **Horizontal Zoom In button.** This button changes the time display of all tracks in the session by enlarging the track Timeline, audio waveform views, and MIDI displays to show less time across the screen, with greater detail. This adjustment is useful for distinguishing precise edit points and magnifying the Edit window display to a very high resolution.

Click and drag on any of the Zoom buttons for continuous zooming.

OPTION-CLICK (Mac) or ALT-CLICK (Windows) on any Zoom button to return to the previous zoom magnification.

Storing and Recalling Zoom Presets

Directly beneath the Zoom buttons are five buttons numbered 1 through 5. These are the Zoom Preset buttons, which are used to store and recall commonly used zoom magnifications. Each Zoom Preset can be updated to store a zoom setting of your choice. Custom presets are saved with your session.

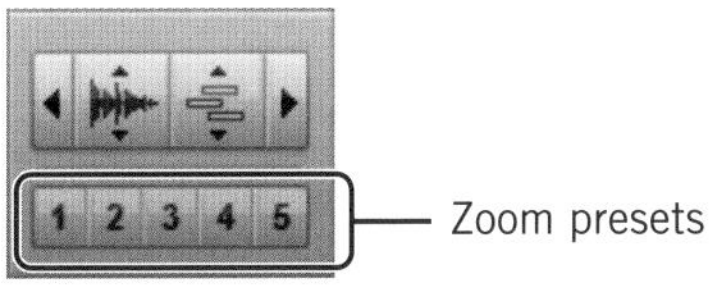

Figure 8.25 Zoom Preset buttons 1 through 5

To store a zoom setting as a Zoom Preset, do the following:

1. Using either the **ZOOM** buttons or the **ZOOMER** tool, set the screen to the desired zoom display.
2. While pressing the **COMMAND** key (Mac) or **CTRL** key (Windows), click one of the five **ZOOM PRESET** buttons, or click and hold a button and select **SAVE ZOOM PRESET** from the pop-up menu.

To recall a Zoom Preset, click your mouse directly on the preset number you want to recall. The zoom setting will be instantly recalled.

You can also recall Zoom Presets 1 through 5 by holding the CONTROL key (Mac) or START key (Windows) and pressing a numeral key (1 through 5) on your computer's alpha keyboard.

Adding Markers to Your Session

Markers can be used to bookmark locations in your session for quick recall. The following sections describe how to add and delete markers, how to use the Memory Locations window and other techniques to recall marker locations, and how to create selections using marker locations.

About Memory Locations

Pro Tools provides up to 999 memory locations for each session, which can be used to store and recall a variety of commonly used display settings. Like Zoom Presets, memory locations can store horizontal and vertical screen magnification settings. However, memory locations can also do much more.

Memory locations come in two main varieties: markers and selections. Markers are used to store locations on the Timeline (playback locations), while selections are used to store edit selections (edit locations). In this lesson, we will work only with markers.

In addition to storing a timeline selection, a marker can store a variety of additional information, such as the current zoom setting, track height settings, track show/hide status, and more. Timeline locations and other settings stored with a marker memory location are reestablished when the memory location is later recalled.

Creating a Marker

Markers can be added to a session at any time. Often you will be able to set markers at specified points when playback is stopped. Other times, you might find it useful to add markers on the fly during playback or recording.

Adding Markers at Specified Points

Markers are commonly used to map out the song structure. This can be done while playback is stopped, by locating to the beginning of each song section and adding a marker at that point.

To create a marker at a specified point, do the following:

1. If it is not already displayed, choose **VIEW > RULERS > MARKERS** to display the Markers Ruler.
2. Place the cursor at the desired location on a track or in the Timeline.
3. Click the **ADD MARKER/MEMORY LOCATION** button (plus sign) at the head of the Markers Ruler. The New Memory Location dialog box will appear.

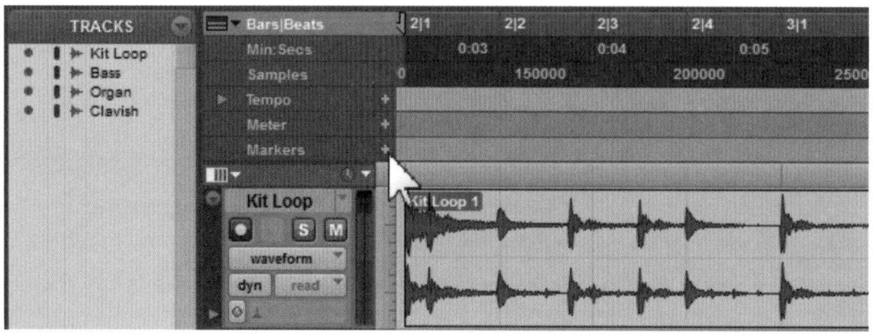

Figure 8.26 Adding a new marker using the plus sign at the head of the Markers Ruler

> **You can also add a marker at the cursor location by pressing ENTER on the numeric keypad to access the New Memory Location dialog box.**

4. Give the marker a descriptive name. You can also change the marker number, if desired. (See Figure 8.27.)
5. In the Time Properties section of the dialog box, select **MARKER**, if not already enabled.

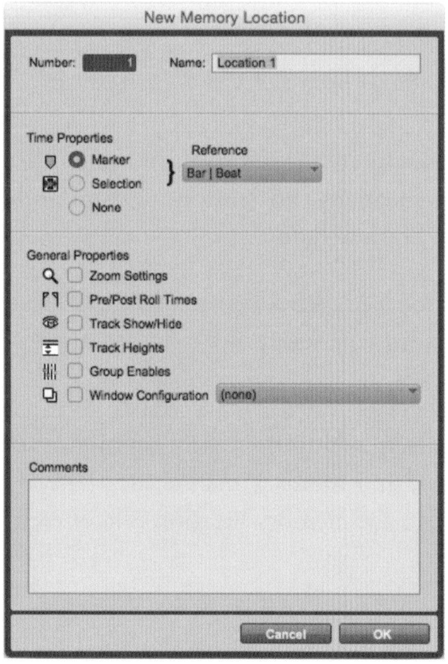

Figure 8.27 The New Memory Location dialog box

6. In the Reference pop-up menu, choose one of the following two options:

   - **Absolute.** This option sets the marker at a sample-based location on the Timeline. The marker will remain at a fixed location in time, regardless of session meter or tempo changes.
   - **Bar|Beat.** This option sets the marker at a tick-based location on the Timeline. The marker will maintain its relative position with respect to the bars and beats in the session, adjusting its absolute location with session meter or tempo changes.

7. (Optional) Under General Properties, select any options you wish to associate with the marker. For basic marking, the optional selections can all remain unchecked.

8. Click **OK**. A small yellow marker symbol corresponding to the memory location will appear in the Markers Ruler at the selected location.

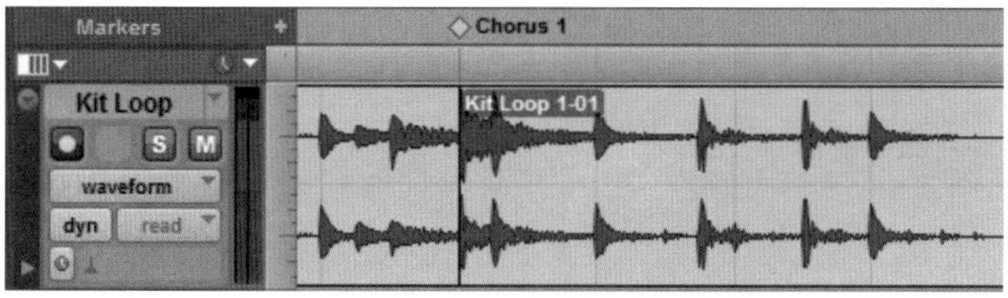

Figure 7.28 Absolute marker symbol on the Markers Ruler

Adding Markers during Playback and Recording

Memory locations can be added during real-time playback and recording in much the same way as when playback is stopped. When added this way, the marker stores the cursor position at the time that the operation is initiated.

To create a marker during playback (or recording), do the following:

1. If it is not already displayed, choose **VIEW > RULERS > MARKERS** to display the Markers Ruler.
2. Start playback (or record) from the desired starting position.
3. Click the **ADD MARKER/MEMORY LOCATION** button (plus sign) at the head of the Markers Ruler. The New Memory Location dialog box will appear.
4. Select the desired options (see Steps 4 through 7 in the previous section) and click **OK**.

You can also add markers on the fly by pressing ENTER on the numeric keypad during playback or recording.

The Memory Locations Window

The Memory Locations window can be used to view all markers and other memory locations that you have stored. To access the Memory Locations window, choose **WINDOW > MEMORY LOCATIONS**. The Memory Locations window will open. (See Figure 8.29.)

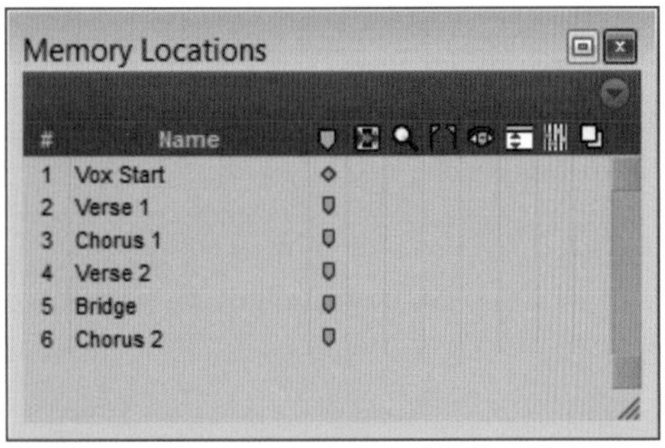

Figure 8.29 The Memory Locations window

Recalling a Marker Location

Pro Tools provides several options for recalling marker memory locations. You can use any of these techniques at any time; however, you will likely find the numeric keypad option to be the fastest in most cases.

To recall a marker location, do one of the following:

- Click the corresponding marker symbol in the Markers Ruler.
- In the Memory Locations window, click the entry for the desired marker location.
- On the numeric keypad, type a period, followed by the marker location number (1 through 999) and another period.

The marker location will be instantly recalled, and the playback cursor will be positioned at the associated location on the timeline.

Deleting a Marker Location

Pro Tools also provides options for deleting markers that you no longer need.

To delete a marker, do the following:

1. Display the Memory Locations window (**WINDOW > MEMORY LOCATIONS**).
2. Click on the entry that you want to delete.
3. Click on the Memory Locations menu button and choose **CLEAR "MARKER NAME"** from the pop-up menu. The selected marker will be deleted.

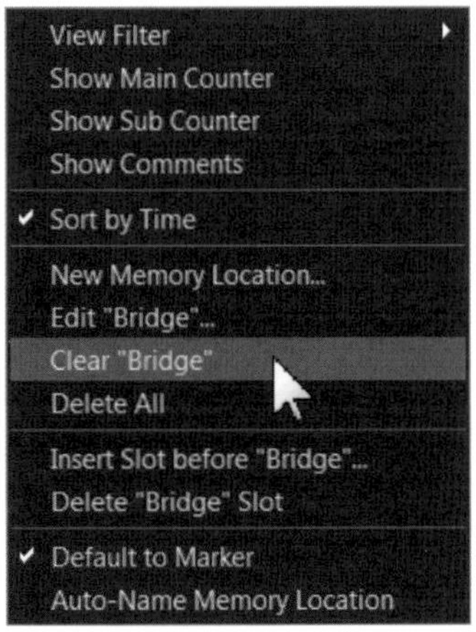

Figure 8.30 Removing the Bridge marker

OPTION-CLICK (Mac) or ALT-CLICK (Windows) on any entry in the Memory Locations window (or in the Markers Ruler) to instantly delete it.

Creating a Selection Using Markers

You can easily select between two previously created markers. This can be handy for quickly selecting song sections that you have marked, such as a verse, chorus, bridge, or guitar solo, for example.

To make a selection between two marker locations, do the following:

1. Click the first marker (or use another recall method) to recall the stored location.
2. Hold the SHIFT key and click the second marker (or use another recall method). The area between the two markers will become selected.

Review/Discussion Questions

1. What does the Universe view display? How can you use this view to scroll the Edit window display? (See "Using the Universe View" beginning on page 152.)

2. How can you adjust a selection using the Timeline Selection In/Out Points? (See "Selecting with the Timeline Selection In/Out Points" beginning on page 155.)

3. How can you make an Edit selection using the Grabber tool? (See "Selecting with the Grabber Tool" beginning on page 156.)

4. Describe two ways to make an Edit selection using the Selector tool. How can the Selector tool be used to easily select an entire clip? (See "Selecting with the Selector Tool" beginning on page 156.)

5. How can you make a selection on adjacent tracks using the Selector tool? How can you make a selection on nonadjacent tracks? (See "Making Selections on Multiple Tracks" beginning on page 158.)

6. What does the Link Track and Edit Selection setting do? (See "Selecting Material Based on Selected Tracks" beginning on page 158.)

7. How does the Tab key affect the cursor position when working in a track? How does this behavior change when the Tab to Transients button is active in the Edit window? (See "Using the Tab Key" and "Tabbing to Transient Points" beginning on page 159.)

8. How can the track height be adjusted for a track? How can all tracks be set to the same height? (See "Adjusting Track Height" beginning on page 161.)

9. Describe three ways to change the order of tracks in Pro Tools. (See "Changing the Track Order" beginning on page 163.)

10. Describe the button in the Edit window that activates Zoom Toggle. What does the Zoom Toggle function do? (See "Using Zoom Toggle" beginning on page 165.)

11. What is the function of the buttons numbered 1 through 5 beneath the Zoom buttons? (See "Storing and Recalling Zoom Presets" beginning on page 167.)

12. What are the two main types of memory locations provided in Pro Tools? How many memory locations can you add to a session? (See "About Memory Locations" beginning on page 167.)

13. How can you add a marker at the current cursor location? How can you add markers on the fly during playback? (See "Adding Markers at Specified Points" and "Adding Markers during Playback and Recording" beginning on page 168.)

14. Describe three ways to recall a memory location. (See "Recalling a Marker Location" beginning on page 170.)

To review additional material from this chapter, see the PT101 Study Guide module available through the ElementsIED online learning platform at ElementsED.com.

EXERCISE 8

Configuring the Session and Adding Memory Locations

In this exercise tutorial, you will configure options to help navigate the session. You will then identify key locations in the session and create memory locations to mark these points. You will use these memory locations in the next exercise to edit the voiceover and position the Fire FX clip.

Duration: 10 to 15 minutes

Media: None required

> **Media Files**
>
> To complete this exercise, you will need to have access to the audio files that you downloaded and imported previously. If needed, you can re-download the media files by pointing your browser to http://alpp.us/PT101-128.
>
> *Note: The above URL is **case sensitive**.*

Getting Started

You will start by opening the Pro Tools session you created in Exercise 7. If that session is not available, use the Exercise07 Sample file in the Completed Exercises folder within the PT101 Download Media folder.

Open the session and save it as Exercise 8:

1. Open the session file that you created in Exercise 7 (Storage Drive/Folder > PT101-XXX > Exercise07-XXX.ptx).

   Alternatively, you can use the Exercise07 Sample file (PT101 Download Media > 03. Completed Projects > Exercise07 Sample.ptx).

2. Choose **FILE > SAVE AS** and name the session *Exercise08-XXX*, keeping the session inside the original session folder (if working from your previous session) or moving the session into your PT101-XXX folder (if working from the sample file).

Configuring the Session

In this part of the exercise, you will configure various settings in the Pro Tools Edit window toolbar and rearrange the order of tracks in the session. You will also verify the Preferences setting for the Scrubber tool behavior.

Configure the session:

1. Enable the following options, as needed, by clicking the associated buttons in the Edit window toolbar (buttons should be lit blue, as shown in Figure 8.31):
   - Tab to Transients
   - Link Timeline and Edit Selection
   - Link Track and Edit Selection

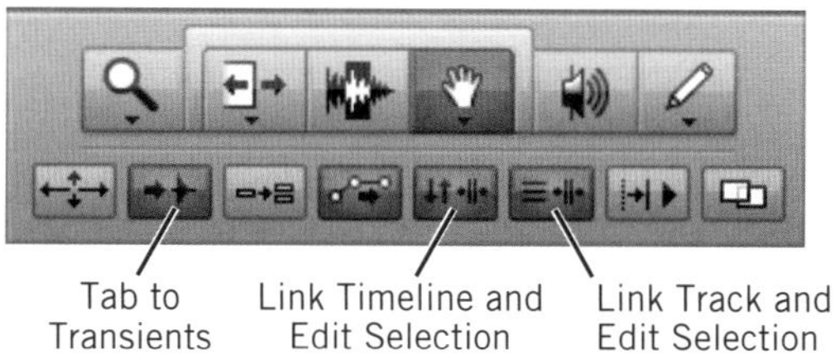

Figure 8.31 Options configured in the Edit window toolbar

2. Click and drag on the track nameplate for the Guitar track to move it below the Bass track.
3. Click and drag on the track nameplates for the other tracks, as needed, to arrange your track order as follows, from top to bottom: VO, Drums, Bass, Guitar, Beat Wave, Beach FX, Fire FX, Click, and Master 1.

Set the Scrubber tool behavior:

1. Choose SETUP > PREFERENCES to open the Preferences dialog box.
2. Select the OPERATION tab.
3. Enable EDIT INSERTION FOLLOWS SCRUB/SHUTTLE in the Transport section at the top left of the page.

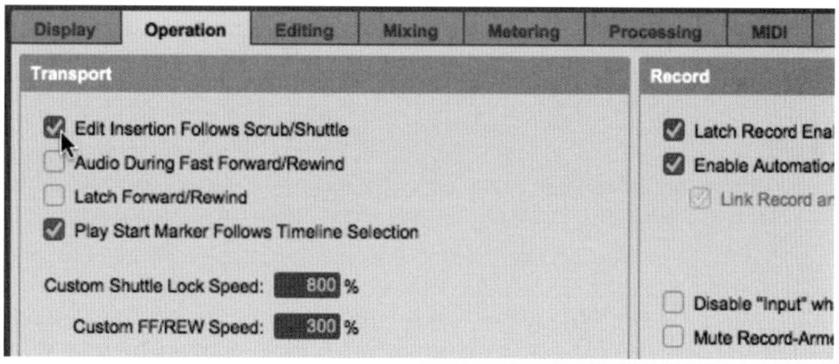

Figure 8.32 Enabling the Scrubber tool setting in Preferences

4. Click OK to accept the change and close the dialog box.

Creating Memory Locations

In this part of the exercise, you will use the Tab to Transients function to locate the start of the voiceover on the VO track and mark that point with a memory location. You will also use the Scrubber tool to locate the position for the fire sound effect, and then mark that point with a second memory location.

Mark the voiceover start location:

1. Choose VIEW > RULERS > MARKERS to display the Markers Ruler, if not already shown.
2. Select the VO track by clicking on the track nameplate so that it becomes highlighted.
3. Press RETURN (Mac) or ENTER (Windows), if needed, to return the cursor to the start of the track.
4. Tab to the first major transient on the track to locate the start of the voiceover. This should be 2 to 3 seconds into the track.
5. If needed, press the SPACEBAR to audition the track and verify the location. Press the SPACEBAR a second time to end the audition.
6. Click the plus sign (+) at the head of the Markers Ruler or press [ENTER] on the numeric keypad to display the New Memory Location dialog box.
7. In the dialog box, change the marker name to VO Start and click OK. The new marker will appear on the Markers Ruler.

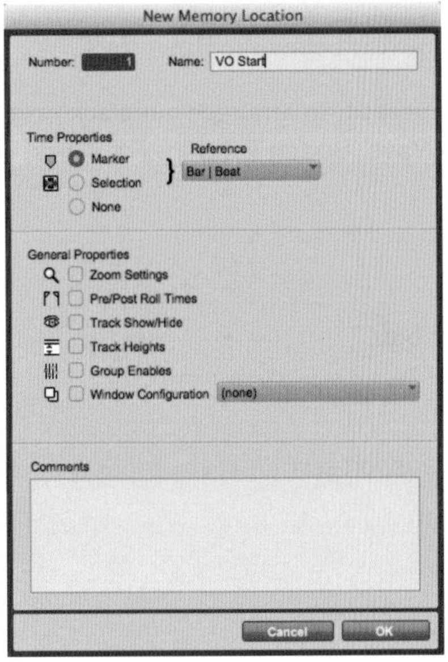

Figure 8.33 New Memory Location dialog box configured for the VO Start marker

Mark the location for the Fire FX clip:

1. Using the Scrubber tool, click and drag across the VO track around Bar 6 or 7. Listen for the words "so you don't get baked by the sun."
2. Scrub back and forth to locate the start of the word "baked" and release the mouse at that position. The edit cursor will be placed at the released location.
3. Once again, click the plus sign (+) at the head of the Markers Ruler or press [ENTER] on the numeric keypad to open the New Memory Location dialog box.
4. This time name the marker Sun Bake and click OK. The new marker will appear on the Markers Ruler.
5. Press ENTER (Windows) or RETURN (Mac) to return the cursor to the start of the track.

Finishing Up

To complete this exercise tutorial, you will need to save your work and close the session. You will be reusing this session in Exercise 9, so it is important to save the work you've done.

1. Choose FILE > SAVE to save the session.
2. Choose FILE > CLOSE SESSION to close the session.

Remember that you cannot close a Pro Tools session by closing its windows. You must choose CLOSE SESSION from the FILE menu.

Editing Your Media

This lesson covers the basics of editing audio and MIDI data in Pro Tools. It provides details on playback options, Edit modes, Edit menu commands, and moving and trimming operations. It also introduces techniques for creating fades and for undoing edit actions.

Duration: 120 Minutes

GOALS

- Set options for scrolling and looping during playback
- Understand the Pro Tools Edit modes
- Recognize the difference between Absolute Grid mode and Relative Grid mode
- Configure Grid and Nudge values
- Use standard editing commands to modify your playlists
- Understand the effects of Edit modes on moving and trimming operations
- Create fade-in, fade-out, and crossfade effects on your tracks

Key topics from this lesson are included in the *Pro Tools 12 Essential Training: 101* course on Lynda.com.

Any time you add audio or MIDI data to the tracks in your session, you are likely to need to do some editing. Whether you need to adjust timing, smooth out a transition, or improve a performance, editing techniques will play a large part in transforming a session from a basic recording to a polished final product. The processes described in the following sections will help you make that transformation, enabling your recordings and compositions to sound their best.

Selecting Playback Options

To simplify your navigation and workflow, Pro Tools provides various playback options to choose from while working on your sessions. Two settings you will likely want to explore include the scrolling mode and the Loop Playback option.

Scrolling Modes

As discussed in Lesson 4, Pro Tools offers various scrolling modes that determine how the contents of the Edit window are displayed during playback and recording. Available scrolling options include the following:

- **No Scrolling.** This option prevents the screen from following the position of the playback cursor. Use this option to keep the display located on an area that you are editing while playing back an area that starts or ends off screen.
- **After Playback.** This option scrolls the screen to the point where playback ends, centering the end point on the screen. Use this option to locate an area that needs editing by auditioning your tracks. By stopping playback when you hear something amiss, your screen will automatically be scrolled to the area needing attention.
- **Page Scrolling.** This option scrolls the screen one page at a time during playback. Use this option to view the contents of your tracks as they are played back.
- **Continuous.** This option scrolls the screen continuously during playback, keeping the playback cursor centered on the screen. This option works best at lower zoom settings.

The active scrolling option is set under OPTIONS > EDIT WINDOW SCROLLING.

Loop Playback

During editing, you will often want to listen to a selection repeatedly. Loop Playback allows you to repeat your selection continuously, looping from the end of the selection back to the start without interruption. This allows you to easily review the continuity of an edit or transition point.

To use Loop Playback, do the following:

1. Select the desired audio or MIDI data.
2. Choose OPTIONS > LOOP PLAYBACK. The Playback button in the Edit window and Transport window will change to show a loop arrow. (See Figure 9.1.)
3. Click PLAY or press the SPACE BAR to start continuous looped playback.

Figure 9.1 Transport window with Loop Playback active

You can adjust the start and end points of the loop during playback by modifying your selection, as discussed in Lesson 8. By dragging the corresponding In/Out Points in the Timeline Rulers, for example, you can resize your loop on either side.

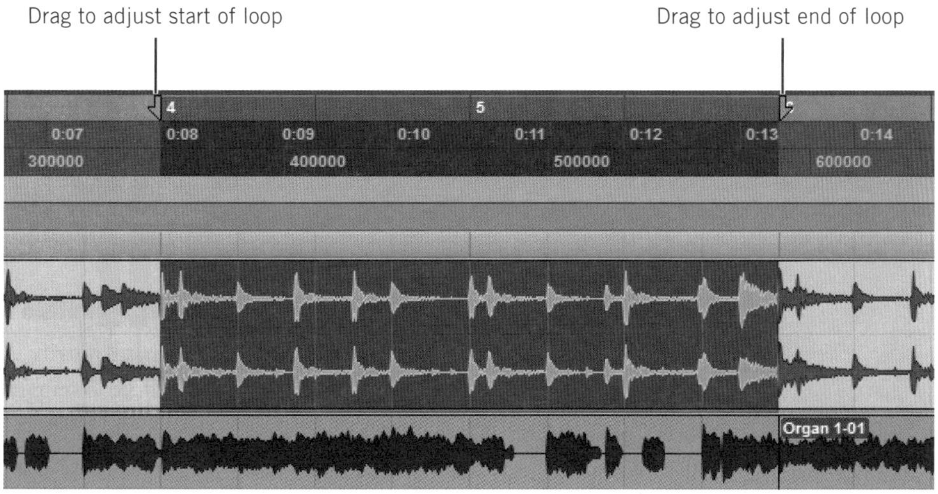

Figure 9.2 Area selected for Loop Playback

Loop Playback requires a selection at least 0.5 seconds in length.

Using the Edit Modes

As you learned in Lesson 3, Pro Tools provides four Edit modes: Shuffle, Spot, Slip, and Grid. The Edit modes affect the movement and placement of audio and MIDI clips, the results of certain Edit commands, and the functions of the Edit tools. Each Edit mode is useful for different purposes while editing.

- **Shuffle.** This mode allows you to shuffle the order of adjacent clips without adding space between them or having them overlap and to remove unwanted parts without leaving gaps. Use Shuffle mode to rearrange consecutive parts in your session and to shorten a performance by removing material.
- **Slip.** This mode allows you to place a clip anywhere on a track without affecting the placement of other clips, leaving space between clips or overlapping clips as desired. Use Slip mode to move or arrange the parts of your session freely and to place material anywhere on the timeline.
- **Spot.** This mode allows you to specify exact locations using numerical values when moving, placing, or trimming clips. Use Spot mode to move the parts of your session to specific known destinations.
- **Grid.** This mode allows you to snap clips and MIDI notes to the nearest time increment on a grid, based on the currently selected grid increment and Time Scale. Use Grid mode for precise timing by aligning parts using defined timing intervals. This is especially useful for aligning musical material to bar|beat locations.

Pro Tools also provides a combo-mode feature called Snap To Grid. This feature allows you to make selections based on the grid while editing in Shuffle, Slip, or Spot mode.

You can activate the desired Edit mode at any time by clicking on the corresponding mode button in the toolbar area of the Edit window. (See Figure 9.3.) To activate Snap To Grid, SHIFT-CLICK on the Grid mode button when in any other mode.

Figure 9.3 The Edit mode buttons (Slip mode selected)

Shuffle, Slip, and Spot modes have only one option each and do not require any additional configuration before you use them. Grid mode provides two options to choose from, Absolute Grid and Relative Grid. The functions of both options are affected by the Grid setting. (See "Configuring the Grid" later in this lesson.)

Editing in Shuffle Mode

In Shuffle mode, when you move or place clips on a track, their placement is constrained by other clips. Similarly, any edits you make to a clip will affect the placement of subsequent clips on the track. When you move or place a clip, it will automatically snap to the end of the preceding clip, causing the two clips to butt up against each other.

If you insert a clip between two existing clips, all subsequent clips on the track will move to the right to make space for the inserted clip. Conversely, if a clip is removed from between two existing clips, the subsequent clips on the track will move to the left to close up the space.

You can "shuffle" the order of clips in this mode, but you cannot separate clips from each other or add space between them, and you cannot make clips overlap as in Slip mode. However, any existing space between clips is maintained when the clips move as a result of insertions, deletions, or edits made earlier in the track.

When using the Trim tool in Shuffle mode, changing a clip's start or end point will automatically move the subsequent clips by the amount added to or trimmed from the edited clip.

The placement and insertion of individual MIDI notes is not affected by Shuffle mode.

To activate Shuffle mode, click on the **SHUFFLE** button in the Edit window or press function key **F1**.

Editing in Slip Mode

In Slip mode, when you move, trim, cut, or paste clips, their placement is unconstrained by other clips on the track. Editing a clip has no effect on subsequent clips, unless the edit causes clips to overlap, in which case the underlying clip is trimmed or obscured by the overlying clip.

To activate Slip mode, click on the **SLIP** button in the Edit window or press function key **F2**.

Editing in Spot Mode

In Spot mode, you can move or place clips within a track at precise locations by specifying the desired destination numerically. As in Slip mode, edit operations do not affect the placement of other clips on the track.

Spot mode allows you to specify a destination based on any time format. You can also use Spot mode to capture an incoming timecode address or to spot a clip using its time stamps as reference points. This can be particularly useful for post-production tasks involving SMPTE frame locations.

When Spot mode is enabled, Pro Tools prompts you with a dialog box whenever a clip is dragged from the Clip List or a Workspace browser or whenever you click on a clip with the Grabber or Trim tool.

When placing or moving a clip, you specify a destination location for the clip by entering a value in the Start, Sync Point, or End field in the Spot dialog box. When trimming a clip, you specify the start or end point for the trim using the Start or End field in the dialog box, respectively.

To activate Spot mode, click on the SPOT button in the Edit window or press function key F3.

Editing in Grid Mode

In Grid mode, you can make edits based on the timing interval defined by the grid. (See "Configuring the Grid" below.) Selections and insertion points snap to grid intervals, which in turn affects cut, copy, and paste operations. Move and trim operations either align to the grid or move in grid increments relative to their origination point, depending on the option selected (Absolute or Relative).

- In Absolute Grid mode, moving any clip snaps the clip start to the grid; trimming a clip snaps the trimmed edge to the grid. If a clip's start point falls between grid lines, moving the clip will snap its start time to the nearest grid line; trimming it will align the trimmed edge to the nearest grid line. This mode is commonly used to ensure that clips start or end cleanly on the beat or on a subdivision of the beat.
- In Relative Grid mode, clips are moved and trimmed by grid units. If a clip's start point falls between grid lines, the clip will move in grid increments, preserving its offset from the grid. Likewise, the Trim tool will trim in grid increments, preserving the starting point or ending point offset. This mode is commonly used to move clips by bars or beats while maintaining any offset relative to the beat.

To activate Grid mode using the last-used option, click the GRID button in the Edit window or press function key F4. To change the Grid mode from the last-used option, click and hold the GRID button and select the desired option from the pop-up selector, or press F4 a second time to toggle the mode.

You can temporarily suspend the Grid and use Slip mode behavior by holding down the COMMAND key (Mac) or CTRL key (Windows). The same modifiers work to temporarily enforce the Grid when working in any other Edit mode.

Using the Snap To Grid Function

The Pro Tools Snap To Grid feature lets you make grid-based selections while working in Shuffle, Slip, or Spot mode. With Snap To Grid enabled, Edit selections are constrained by the grid, while edit operations are based on the other selected Edit mode.

For example, in Shuffle mode with Snap To Grid enabled, any selections you make on audio clips will snap to grid boundaries; however, if you cut a selection of audio, any clips to the right of the edit will shuffle to the left as normal in Shuffle mode.

To enable Snap To Grid, do the following:

1. Activate the Edit mode you wish to work in (Shuffle, Slip, or Spot).
2. Shift-click on the GRID mode button or press SHIFT+F4.

Figure 9.4 Snap To Grid in Shuffle mode

Press F1+F4 to enable Snap To Grid and Shuffle mode, press F2+F4 to enable Snap To Grid and Slip mode, and press F3+F4 to enable Snap To Grid and Spot mode.

Configuring the Grid

Pro Tools allows you to set a timing grid, based on an interval of your choosing, to help maintain the timing of clips, notes, events, and selections as you edit your track material. The grid settings affect edit operations in Grid mode. (See the preceding "Editing in Grid Mode" section.) The grid can also be used for display purposes, allowing it to serve as a visual reference whether or not Grid mode is active.

Grid boundaries can be based on frames, bar and beat values, minutes and seconds, or a specified number of samples.

To configure the grid, do the following:

1. Click the GRID VALUE pop-up selector in the toolbar area of the Edit window.

Figure 9.5 Grid Value pop-up selector

2. From the Grid Value pop-up menu, choose an appropriate Time Scale. (See Figure 9.6.) The menu will close after you make a selection.

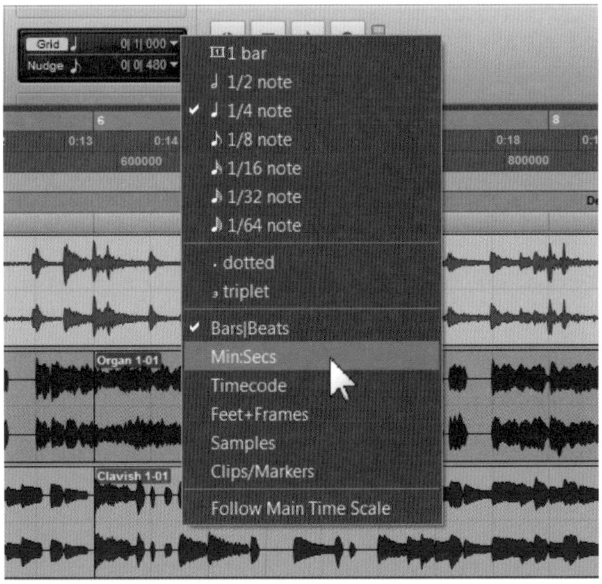

Figure 9.6 Selecting a Time Scale for the grid

3. Click the GRID VALUE pop-up selector again to choose a corresponding grid size; the options available will vary depending on the Time Scale selected in Step 2. (See Figure 9.7.)

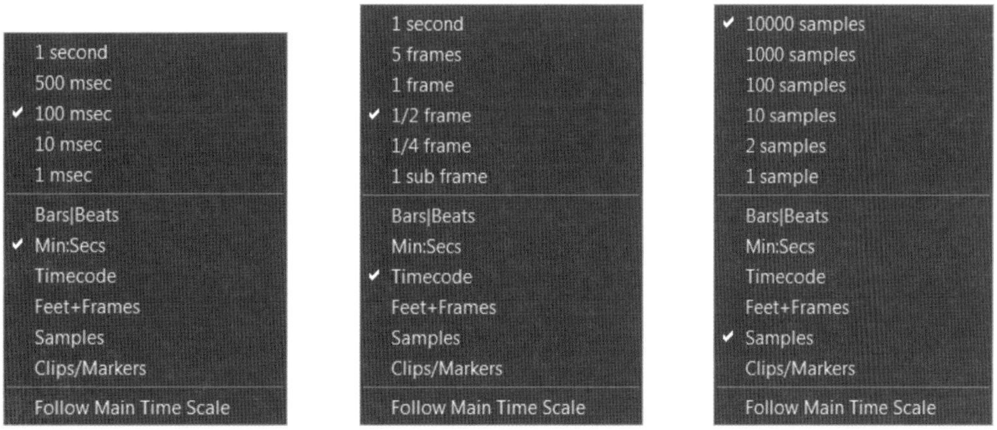

Figure 9.7 Grid-size options for various Time Scales

> **The Follow Main Time Scale option at the bottom of the Grid Value pop-up menu causes the grid to change automatically whenever the Main Time Scale is changed, using the grid size last set for each Time Scale.**

Once you set the grid to an appropriate Time Scale and size, you will have the option of displaying the grid lines in the Edit window to serve as a visual reference.

To display or hide grid lines, click at the head of the currently selected main Timebase Ruler or click on the Grid indicator in the toolbar. (See Figure 9.8.) The Grid lines will toggle on or off, and the Grid indicator light (green highlight) will toggle on or off, correspondingly.

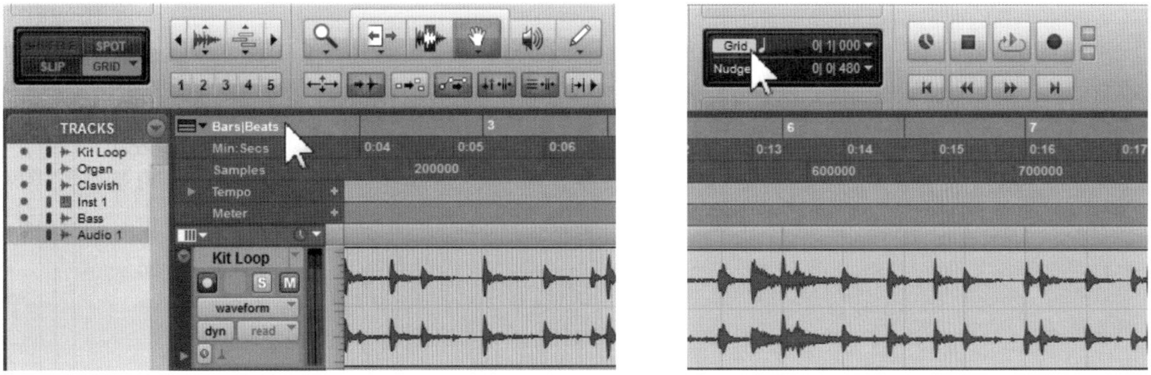

Figure 9.8 Click on the main Timebase Ruler (left) or on the Grid indicator (right) to toggle the grid-line display.

Editing Clips

Pro Tools offers a variety of common editing commands—such as Copy and Paste—as well as application-specific commands—such as Separate Clip and Heal Separation—that affect clips.

As discussed in Lesson 5, Pro Tools distinguishes between subset clips (portions of an audio file) and whole-file clips (entire parent audio files). The editing techniques described in this section apply to both types of clips, unless otherwise specified.

Basic Editing Commands

Like most commercial applications, Pro Tools offers standard Cut, Copy, Paste, and Clear (delete) commands. The Pro Tools Duplicate and Repeat commands also offer functionality similar to that found in other media applications. Pro Tools performs each of these editing functions nondestructively, meaning that the operations do not alter the original media files.

Each of these commands can be performed on a single track or on multiple tracks simultaneously, depending on the selection or the Clipboard contents. Edits can apply to the following material:

- Part of a clip or parts of multiple clips (selected with the Selector tool)
- A whole clip or multiple whole clips (selected with the Grabber tool)

Selections can cross multiple clip boundaries, can include entire clips or partial clips, and can even include silence, if desired.

When you use any of these editing commands on audio selections within a clip or clips, Pro Tools creates byproduct clips and automatically adds them to the Clip List.

The Cut Command

Using the Cut command, you can remove selected material from its current position and place it on the Clipboard (in the computer's RAM) to be pasted elsewhere.

To cut a selection and place the material on the computer's Clipboard, do the following:

1. Make a selection of any length on a single track or multiple tracks.
2. Choose EDIT > CUT, or press COMMAND+X (Mac) or CTRL+X (Windows). The selected audio and/or MIDI data will be removed from the original location and copied to the Clipboard.

When you cut or clear a selection in Shuffle mode, all audio to the right will slide over by the amount of time removed so that no gap remains.

The Copy Command

The Copy command is much like the Cut command, but instead of removing the selected range, it leaves the original and places a copy of it on the Clipboard so that you can paste it elsewhere.

To copy a selection, do the following:

1. Make a selection of any length on a single track or multiple tracks.
2. Choose EDIT > COPY, or press COMMAND+C (Mac) or CTRL+C (Windows). The selected audio and/or MIDI data will be copied to the Clipboard.

When you place a selection on the computer's Clipboard using a Cut or Copy command, you replace any material previously stored on the Clipboard.

The Paste Command

Using the Paste command, you can insert the contents of the Clipboard at a location that you have chosen with the Selector tool. You can paste data only after something has been cut or copied to the Clipboard.

To use the Paste command, do the following:

1. Select the desired paste destination using one of the following methods:
   - Place the cursor (insertion point) on the desired destination track or tracks at the location where you want the start of the paste to occur.

- Make a selection of any length on the desired destination track or tracks, with the beginning of the selection at the location where you want the start of the paste to occur.

To paste on multiple tracks, you must make an insertion point or selection on each of the desired destination tracks.

2. Choose EDIT > PASTE, or press COMMAND+V (Mac) or CTRL+V (Windows). The material on the Clipboard will be pasted in, beginning at the selected start point.

If the Clipboard contains material from multiple tracks, the data will be pasted starting with the topmost track; the selected destination tracks will be filled from top to bottom.

To paste data immediately after a clip, use the TAB key (with the Tab to Transients function turned off) to place the cursor exactly at the clip's end.

The Clear Command

The Clear command allows you to remove any selected material without placing it on the Clipboard.

To clear a selection, do the following:

1. Make a selection of any length on a single track or multiple tracks.
2. Choose EDIT > CLEAR, or press COMMAND+B (Mac) or CTRL+B (Windows). This command has the same result as pressing the Delete key on the keyboard.

The Duplicate Command

The Duplicate command makes a copy of any selected material and places it immediately after the end of the selection. This command provides a quick way to repeat a selection, extend a sound, or create a simple looping effect—it is faster and more convenient than copying and pasting data to achieve the same result.

For advanced looping effects, use the clip looping features in Pro Tools.

Clip looping is covered in the Pro Tools 110 course.

To duplicate audio or MIDI data, do the following:

1. Make a selection of any length and content on one or more tracks.
2. (Optional) Play the selection using Loop Playback to ensure that it plays smoothly in succession. If the selection plays smoothly when it loops, you can duplicate it without creating an audible edit point.
3. Adjust the selection as needed to create a smooth loop transition. You might want to zoom in to position the start and end of the selection on a zero crossing (a point of no amplitude in a waveform).
4. After you are satisfied with the selection, choose EDIT > DUPLICATE or press COMMAND+D (Mac) or CTRL+D (Windows). The selection will be duplicated and pasted at the end of the selected area or clip.

The Repeat Command

The Repeat command is similar to Duplicate, but it allows you to specify the number of times the selected material will be duplicated.

To repeat a selection of audio or MIDI data multiple times, do the following:

1. Make a selection of any length and content on one or more tracks.
2. Choose EDIT > REPEAT or press OPTION+R (Mac) or ALT+R (Windows). The Repeat dialog box will open.

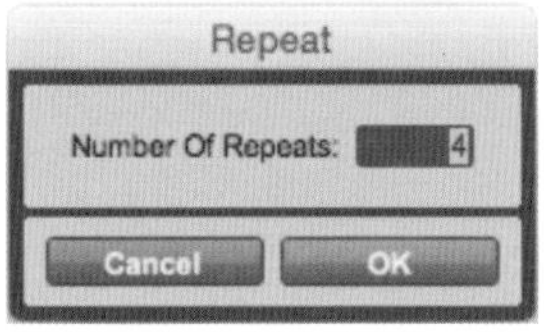

Figure 9.9 Repeat dialog box

3. Enter the desired number of repeat iterations and click OK. The selected material will be duplicated in succession immediately following the selection's end point, as specified in the Repeat dialog box.

Special–Purpose Editing Commands

Pro Tools includes a number of editing commands that are specific to the needs of audio and MIDI production. The following sections introduce commands for separating clips and restoring separated clips.

The Separate Clip Command

Separating a clip is the process of breaking a clip in two or separating a selection as a new, independent clip.

You can separate a clip for one of several purposes:

- To split a clip into two separate clips at the insertion point. Use this process to divide a source clip into two new clips on a track, adding both to the Clip List. (See Figure 9.10.)
- To separate a selection from a parent clip or from the material on either side. Use this process to create a clip from a selection, creating new byproduct clips on either side. (See Figure 9.11.)
- To create multiple new clips from a selection, dividing the selection at Grid intervals or at transients. Use this process to slice up a clip at Grid lines or transient locations within the clip. (See Figure 9.12.)

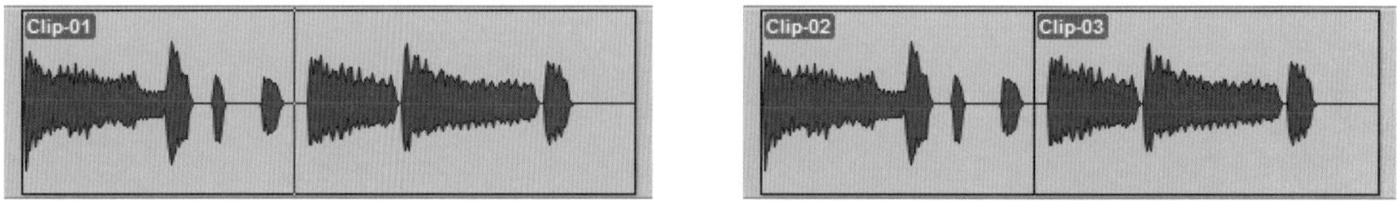

Figure 9.10 Separating a clip at the insertion point: before (left) and after (right)

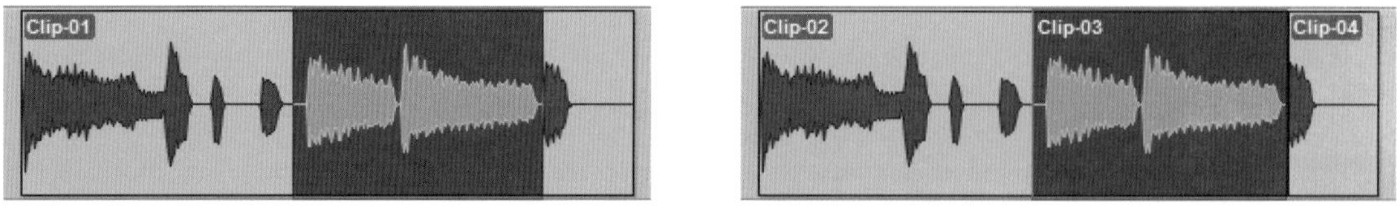

Figure 9.11 Separating a selection as a new clip: before (left) and after (right)

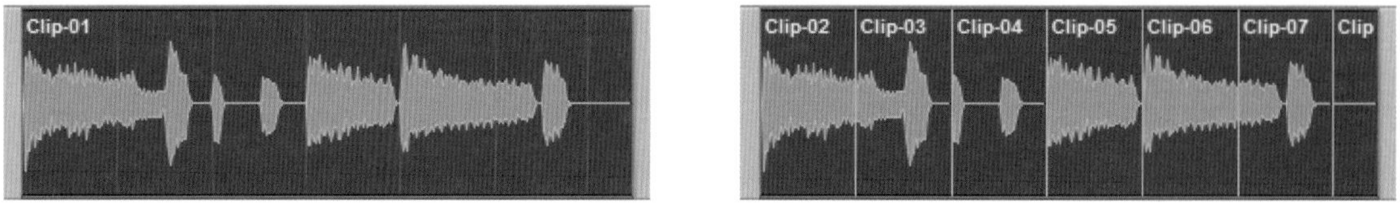

Figure 9.12 Separating a selection into new clips at Grid intervals (before and after)

When you separate clips, you create *byproduct* clips from the material on either side of the selection. These new byproduct clips appear on the track and in the Clip List with new edit numbers appended to their names.

To separate a clip, do the following:

1. Make a selection of any length within a clip or across multiple clips, or place the cursor (insertion point) at the location where you want a split to occur.
2. Do one of the following:
   - To create a separation at the insertion point or selection boundaries, choose **EDIT > SEPARATE CLIP > AT SELECTION** or press **COMMAND+E** (Mac) or **CTRL+E** (Windows).
   - To create separations at each Grid boundary or transient, choose **EDIT > SEPARATE CLIP > ON GRID** or **AT TRANSIENTS**, respectively. The Pre-Separate Amount dialog box will open.

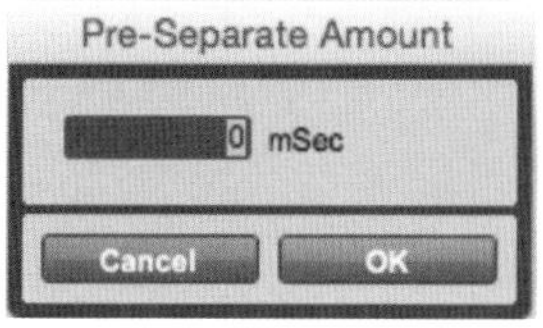

Figure 9.13 The Pre-Separate Amount dialog box

3. Enter the pre-separate amount in the dialog box, if needed, and click **OK**. This specifies the amount of pad time Pro Tools will include in the new clips before each Grid boundary or transient point.

Pro Tools creates new clips based on the selection start and end points. If the **ON GRID** or **AT TRANSIENTS** option is chosen, additional clips will be created within the selection at each Grid line or transient point. All resulting new clips will have the next available edit number appended to the end of the original clip name.

The Heal Separation Command

If you've separated a clip and you later decide to undo the separation, you can repair the clip and restore the original unedited material using the Heal Separation command. The Heal Separation command works across separated clip components, provided that the pieces are contiguous and their relative start and end points haven't changed since the separation.

To heal a separation between two or more contiguous clips, do the following:

1. Create a selection across the separation points that you wish to repair.

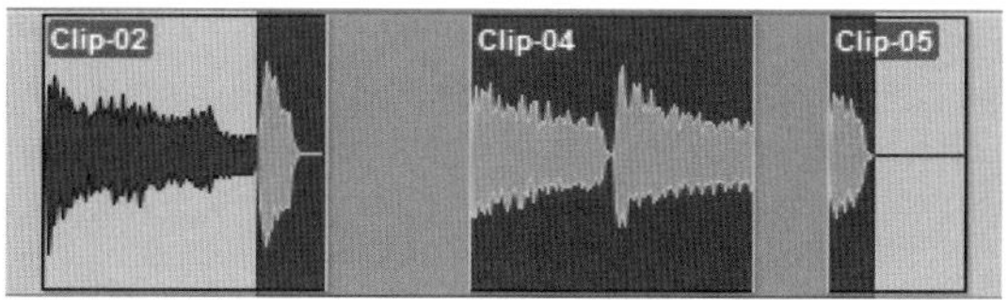

Figure 9.14 Selecting across separation points

2. Choose **EDIT > HEAL SEPARATION** or press **COMMAND+H** (Mac) or **CTRL+H** (Windows).

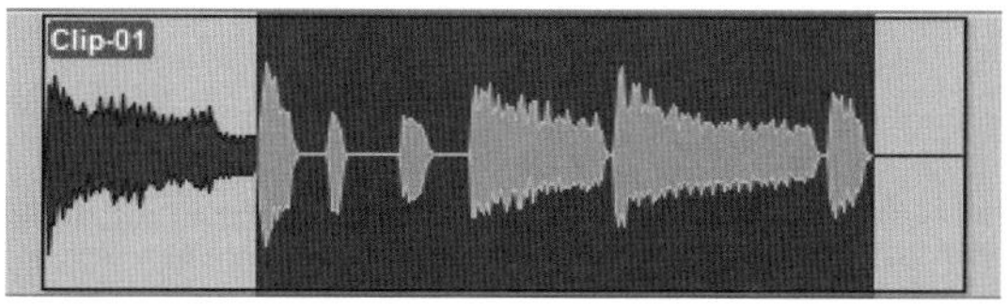

Figure 9.15 Selection after separations are healed

Moving and Trimming Clips

The following sections describe techniques for moving and trimming clips and discuss the effects of the Edit modes on these operations. The Nudge function is also introduced, along with the process for setting the Nudge value.

Using the Grabber Tool

The Grabber tool can be used to drag a clip from the Clip List or from an existing location on a Track Playlist. You can drag a clip to a different location within the same track or to a different track.

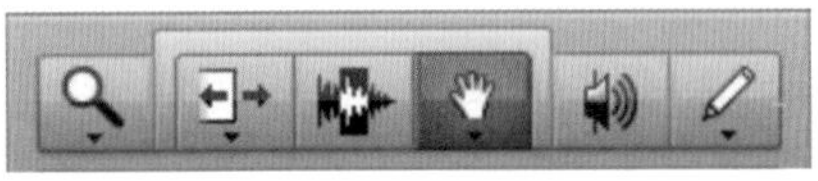

Figure 9.16 The Grabber tool selected in the Edit window toolbar

Moving Clips in Slip Mode

In Slip mode, you can move clips freely using the Grabber tool. You can place clips so that they overlap or so that they have space between them on a track. During playback, you will hear silence in any open areas.

To move a clip in Slip mode, do the following:

1. Select the GRABBER tool. The cursor will change into a hand icon when placed over a Track Playlist.
2. Click on the clip and drag it to the desired destination. A preview of the clip will appear as you drag it.
3. Release the mouse to position the clip.

As you drag clips, the Start, End, and Length Selection indicator boxes dynamically update to show you the result of the movement.

Moving Clips in Grid Mode

When using the Grabber tool in Grid mode, moving and dragging clips is constrained by the current Grid setting as configured in the Grid Value pop-up menu.

To move a clip in Grid mode, do the following:

1. Verify that the Grid value has been set as desired. (See "Configuring the Grid" earlier in this lesson.)
2. Select the GRABBER tool. The cursor will change into a hand icon when placed over a Track Playlist.
3. Click and drag the clip to the desired destination. A preview of the clip will appear on the track, snapping to each successive grid line as you drag the clip.
4. Release the mouse to position the clip.

Moving Clips in Shuffle Mode

In Shuffle mode, clip movement is constrained by other clips. When you move a clip, it automatically snaps to an adjacent clip. You can shuffle the clip order, but you cannot leave space between clips or overlap them.

To move a clip in Shuffle mode, do the following:

1. Select the **GRABBER** tool. The cursor will change into a hand icon when placed over a Track Playlist.
2. Drag a clip to the desired destination. The clip preview will snap between the start and end points of existing clips on the track as you drag.
3. Release the mouse to position the clip. Adjacent clips will reposition themselves as needed to accommodate the clip and to close up the space left at its point of origin.

Moving Clips in Spot Mode

Spotting is the process of placing clips at known time locations within your tracks based on exact Time Scale units, such as Min:Secs, Bars|Beats, or SMPTE timecode.

To move and place a clip in Spot mode, do the following:

1. Select the **GRABBER** tool. The cursor will change into a hand icon when placed over a Track Playlist.
2. Click on the desired clip on a track (or drag it from the Clip List). The Spot dialog box will appear.

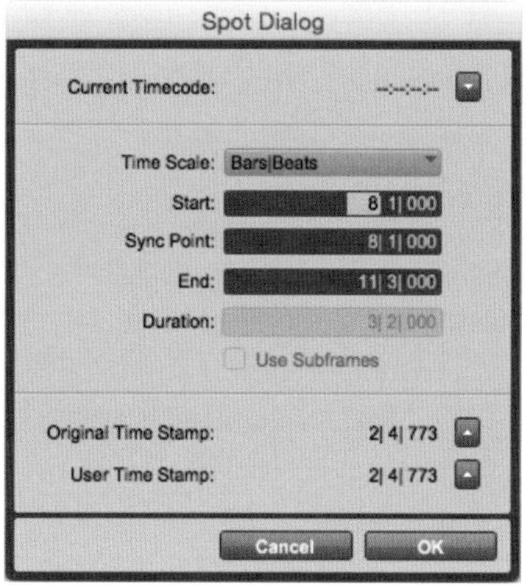

Figure 9.17 The Spot dialog box

3. Choose the desired **TIME SCALE** from the Time Scale pop-up menu.
4. Enter the new location in either the **START** or **END** field and click **OK**. The clip's start or end point will align to the specified location.

Using the Trim Functions

Clips can be trimmed using either the Trim tool or the Trim command. The Trim functions allow you to shorten or lengthen clips as desired by trimming their heads or tails.

The Trim Tool

The Trim tool can be used to dynamically adjust the length of a clip. By trimming the head or tail of an audio clip, you can eliminate unwanted material that precedes or follows any audio that you want to retain.

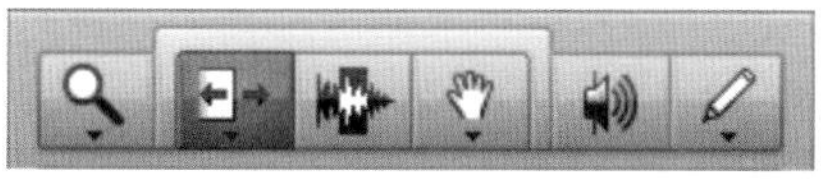

Figure 9.18 The Trim tool selected in the Edit window toolbar

To trim a clip, do the following:

1. If needed, use the **ZOOMER** tool to zoom in on the area you want to trim.
2. Click the **TRIM** tool (standard).
3. Position the cursor over the audio clip you want to trim. The cursor will change to a left trim shape or a right trim shape on either side of the clip's midpoint. (See Figure 9.19.)

> **The Trim tool must be placed within a clip to be active. You cannot click outside of a clip and drag into it to trim the clip.**

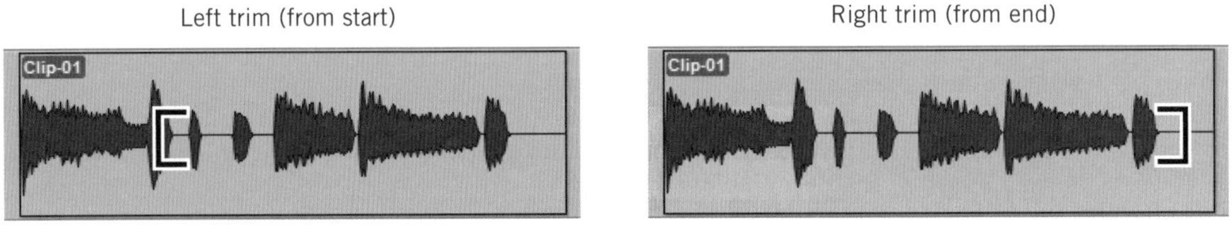

Figure 9.19 Trim tool, as displayed on either side of the clip midpoint

4. Click the cursor in the front half to trim the clip start or in the back half to trim the clip end; click and drag to adjust the trim location in either direction.
5. Release the mouse button at the desired location to complete the trim.

> **To reverse the Trim tool so that you can trim in the opposite direction without having to trim past the midpoint, press OPTION (Mac) or ALT (Windows) before trimming a clip.**

The Trim Clip Command

The Trim Clip command in the Edit menu allows you trim a clip to the boundaries of a selection or to trim a clip on either side of the insertion point.

To use the Trim Clip command based on a selection, do the following:

1. Select the portion of a clip you want to retain.

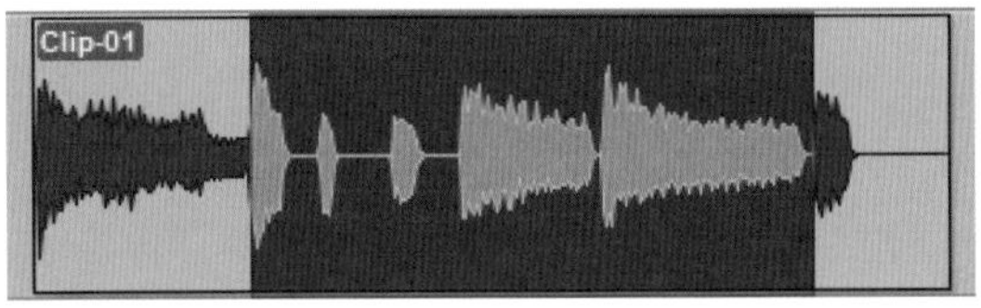

Figure 9.20 Audio selected for trimming

2. Choose **EDIT > TRIM CLIP > TO SELECTION**. The portion of the clip outside of the selection will be deleted.

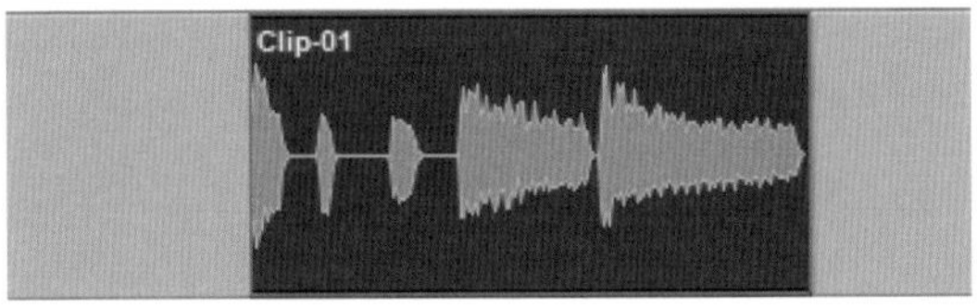

Figure 9.21 Selection after trimming

You can also press COMMAND+T (Mac) or CTRL+T (Windows) to trim a clip to a selection.

To use the Trim Clip command to clear audio preceding or following the insertion point, do the following:

1. Position the insertion point within a clip where you want the clip to start or end.
2. Choose EDIT > TRIM CLIP > START TO INSERTION or EDIT >TRIM CLIP > END TO INSERTION to trim all audio before the insertion point or after the insertion point, respectively.

Using the Nudge Function

Pro Tools allows you to adjust the placement of clips and selections in small, precise Nudge increments using the keyboard. The size of these increments, known as the *Nudge value*, is set much like the Grid size. Nudging a clip allows you to move the clip incrementally by predefined units.

You can use the Nudge function in any of the four editing modes. Nudging will always move the selected clip or clips without constraints and without causing adjacent clips to move, regardless of Edit mode.

Configuring the Nudge Value

The Nudge value can be based on frames, bar and beat values, an absolute time measurement (in milliseconds), or a specified number of samples, depending on the Time Scale selected.

To configure the Nudge value, do the following:

1. Click the NUDGE VALUE pop-up selector in the toolbar area of the Edit window.

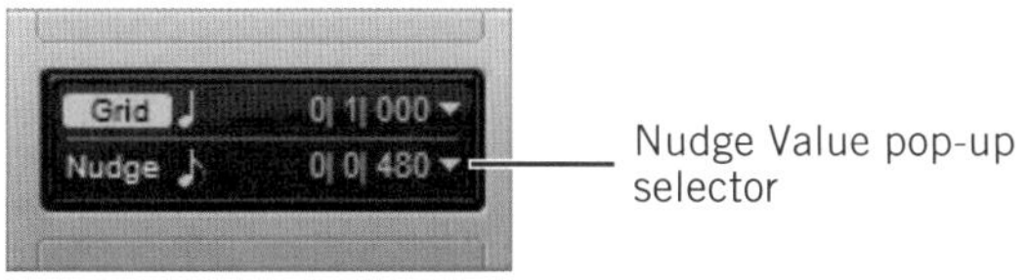

Figure 9.22 Nudge Value pop-up selector in the Edit window toolbar

2. From the NUDGE VALUE pop-up menu, choose the desired Time Scale. The menu will close after you make a selection.

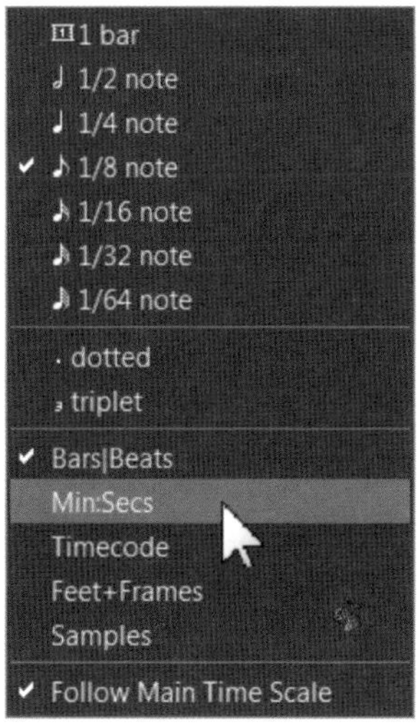

Figure 9.23 Selecting a Time Scale for the Nudge

3. Click the **Nudge Value** pop-up selector again to choose a corresponding Nudge size; the options available will vary depending on the Time Scale selected in Step 2.

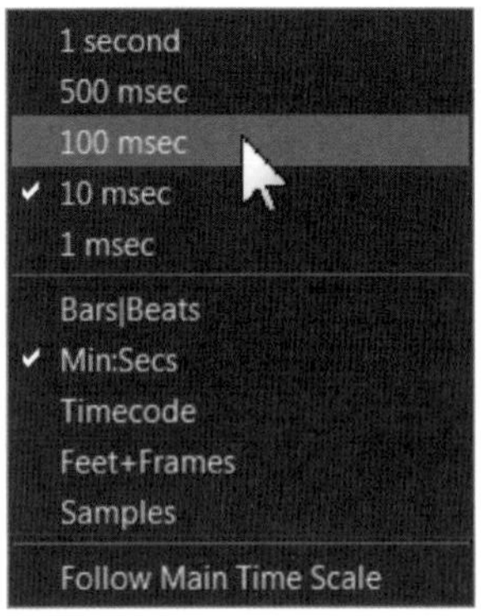

Figure 9.24 Selecting a Nudge size

The Follow Main Time Scale option at the bottom of the Nudge Value pop-up menu enables the Nudge value to change automatically whenever the Main Time Scale is changed, adopting the last used value for that Time Scale. To maintain the Nudge in a Time Scale that is different from your Main Time Scale, deselect this option.

Nudging Clips

To nudge a single clip or multiple clips, do the following:

1. Verify that the Nudge Time Scale and size have been set as desired. (See "Configuring the Nudge Value" above.)
2. With the **Grabber** tool, select the clip or clips you want to nudge.
3. On the numeric keypad, press the **Plus** key **[+]** to move the clip(s) later in the track or the **Minus** key **[–]** to move the clip(s) earlier in the track. The clips will move incrementally by the Nudge value.

If you are using a laptop computer that does not have a numeric keypad, you can use the Function key (marked Fn) and the corresponding +/– keys to nudge clips.

You can also activate the Nudge functions by holding the Control key (Mac) or Start key (Windows) while pressing the < and > keys (comma and period, respectively).

Nudging Selections

In addition to nudging clips, you can also nudge selections using the **Plus** **[+]** and **Minus** **[–]** keys on the numeric keypad.

To nudge a selection, do the following:

1. Make a selection on any track or tracks that does not encompass an entire clip.
2. On the numeric keypad, press the **Plus** key **[+]** to move the selection later or the **Minus** key **[–]** to move the selection earlier. The selection will move incrementally by the Nudge value.

To nudge a selection that includes one or more clips without nudging the clips, do the following:

- Hold the **Shift** key while pressing the **Plus** key **[+]** or the **Minus** key **[–]** on the numeric keypad. The selection will move incrementally by the Nudge value without affecting the underlying clips.

> **Adding the Shift Key to Freely Nudge Any Selection**
>
> When a selection encompasses one or more entire clips, nudging will cause the underlying clip(s) to move with the selection. By holding Shift while nudging, you can nudge the selection independently, without affecting the underlying clip(s).

Creating Fade Effects

A *fade* is a steady volume ramp that you create on a clip boundary. Fades have many different applications, from smoothing out an edit, to creating seamless clip overlaps, to building volume fade-ins and fade-outs for music and sound effects. This section covers the process of creating simple fade-ins, fades-outs, and crossfades.

Applying Fade-Ins and Fade-Outs

Fade-in and fade-out effects can be created at the beginning or ending of any audio clip, respectively, using a selection that touches or crosses the clip boundary.

Following are some basic guidelines for creating fades:

- Make your selection to match the desired fade; the length of the fade is determined by the selection length.
- Make a selection that touches or crosses an open clip boundary (not adjacent to another clip); selecting across adjacent clips will create a crossfade. (See the "Applying Crossfades" section that follows.)
- To create a fade-in, select from at or before the beginning clip boundary; to create a fade-out, select up to or across an ending clip boundary.
- Fade-ins always begin at the head boundary, and fade-outs always end at the tail boundary. Extending a selection into a blank area beyond a clip's boundaries will not change the fade length.

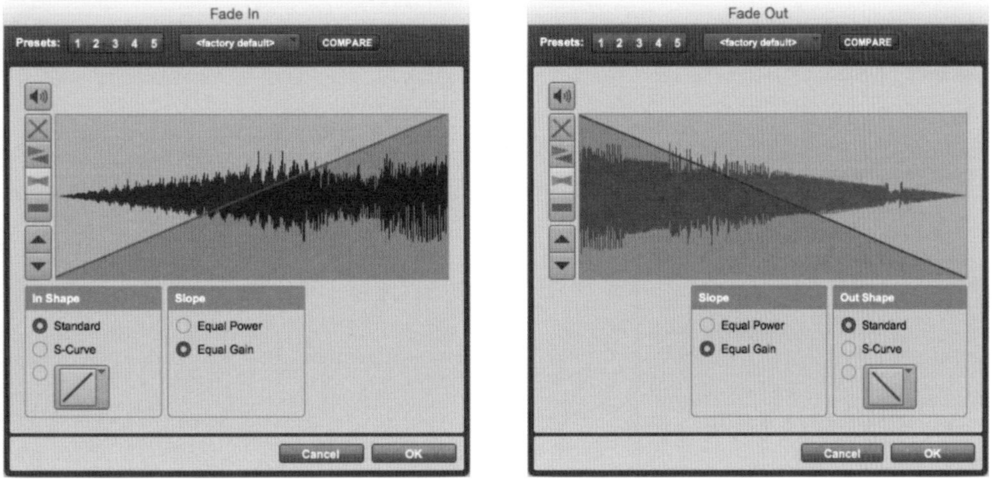

Figure 9.25 The Fade-In and Fade-Out dialog boxes

To create a fade, do the following:

1. Select the beginning or ending of a clip. (**SHIFT-CLICK** additional tracks to create fades on multiple tracks whose clips begin or end simultaneously.)
2. Choose **EDIT > FADES > CREATE** or press **COMMAND+F** (Mac) or **CTRL+F** (Windows). The corresponding Fade-In or Fade-Out dialog box will appear. (See Figure 9.25.)
3. Choose the desired settings in the dialog box (see "Fade Settings" later in this lesson) and click **OK**. The fade will be appear in the Track Playlist at the head or tail of the source clip.

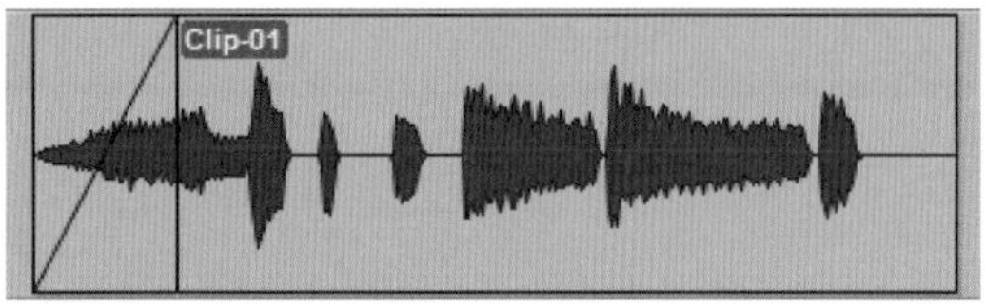

Figure 9.26 Fade-in at the head of a clip

Applying Crossfades

Pro Tools allows you to create crossfades between any two adjacent audio clips that have sufficient underlying audio in their parent audio files. *Crossfading* is essentially the process of overlapping two audio sources and fading out the first source while simultaneously fading in the second source. Pro Tools achieves this effect using the underlying audio on either side of the boundary between adjacent subset clips.

Both clips must be subset clips with sufficient underlying audio to extend across the length of the selection.

To create a crossfade between two adjacent clips, do the following:

1. Make a selection across the boundary between the clips.

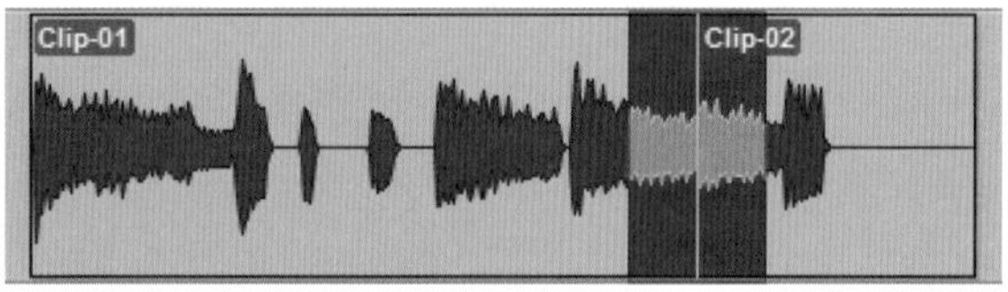

Figure 9.27 Area for crossfade selected in the Edit window

2. Choose **EDIT > FADES > CREATE** or press **COMMAND+F** (Mac) or **CTRL+F** (Windows). The Crossfade dialog box will open.

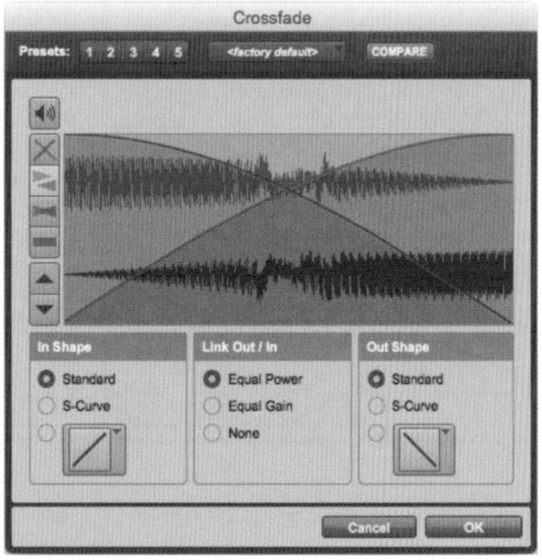

Figure 9.28 The Crossfade dialog box

3. Choose the desired settings in the Fades dialog box (see the "Fade Settings" section that follows) and click **OK**. If sufficient underlying audio is available, the crossfade will be applied and will appear in the Track Playlist.

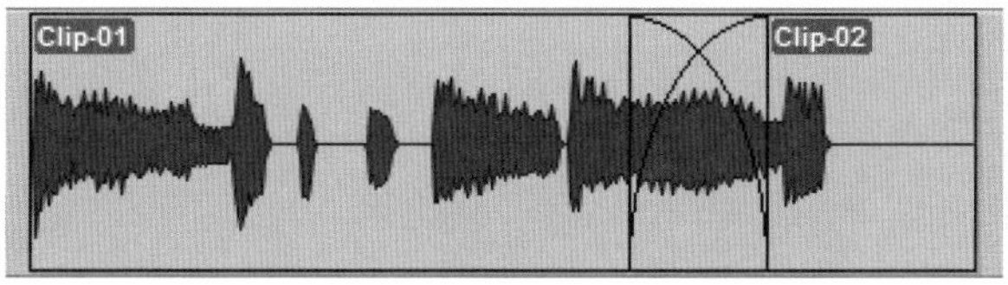

Figure 9.29 Crossfade applied between clips

You can audition and preview the resulting crossfade before applying it by clicking the corresponding icons on the left edge of the Crossfade dialog box.

If either or both source clips lack sufficient underlying audio to generate a crossfade across the selection, a warning will display after you click **OK** in the Fades dialog box. The warning serves to alert you that the attempted crossfade is invalid.

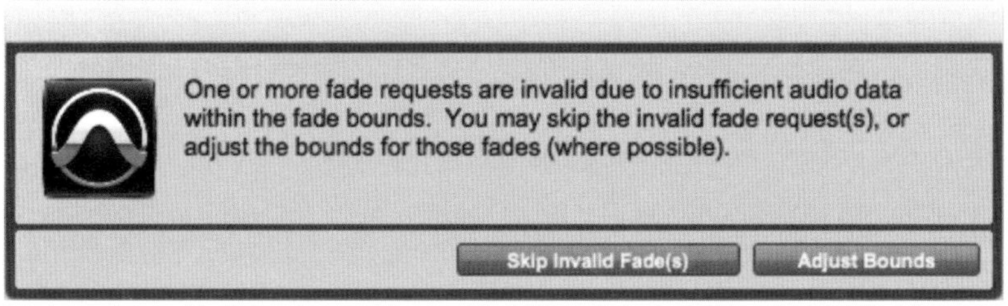

Figure 9.30 Invalid fade warning

Clicking the **Adjust Bounds** button in this warning box will adjust the placement and length of the fade to fit the available audio from the incoming or outgoing clip. If insufficient audio is available to overlap the clips at all, no fade will be created.

Fade Settings

The Fade dialog boxes display fade-in shapes in red and fade-out shapes in blue. Either shape can be changed by choosing from the presets in the Shape drop-down selectors or by choosing between the Standard or S-Curve fade shapes using the radio buttons.

The curve shapes determine how the amplitude of the clip's audio will change over the course of the fade.

Undoing Your Work

Often your editing tasks will involve performing a series of related steps to achieve a desired effect. Along the way, you might at times need to revert to an earlier point, either to start over or to do a before-and-after comparison. Fortunately, Pro Tools provides rich undo options that give you the flexibility to work without constraints.

Using Multi-Level Undo

Multi-level undo operations make it possible to return to earlier stages of work during the editing process. This lets you work and experiment with confidence, knowing that you can back out of changes if you are not satisfied with the results.

Pro Tools 12 provides up to 64 levels of undo operations. All commands that are undoable are stored sequentially in an undo queue. However, certain commands cause changes that are not undoable. Any of these events will clear the undo queue.

Some common actions that *cannot* be undone include the following:

- Deleting tracks
- Closing a session and/or quitting Pro Tools
- Clearing audio from the Clip List
- Recording in Destructive Record mode (covered in advanced courses)

Changing the Levels of Undo

Pro Tools' default settings provide the maximum supported levels of undo operation. If available memory (RAM) for your system is running low, you can reduce this setting to free up memory. (Large undo queues require more RAM and can affect performance under certain conditions, where the available RAM is insufficient.)

To change the number of levels of undo, follow these steps:

1. Choose **SETUP > PREFERENCES** and then click the **EDITING** tab. (See Figure 9.31.)
2. At the bottom of the dialog box, enter the desired undo setting (between 1 and 64).
3. Click **OK** to accept the change and close the Preferences dialog box.

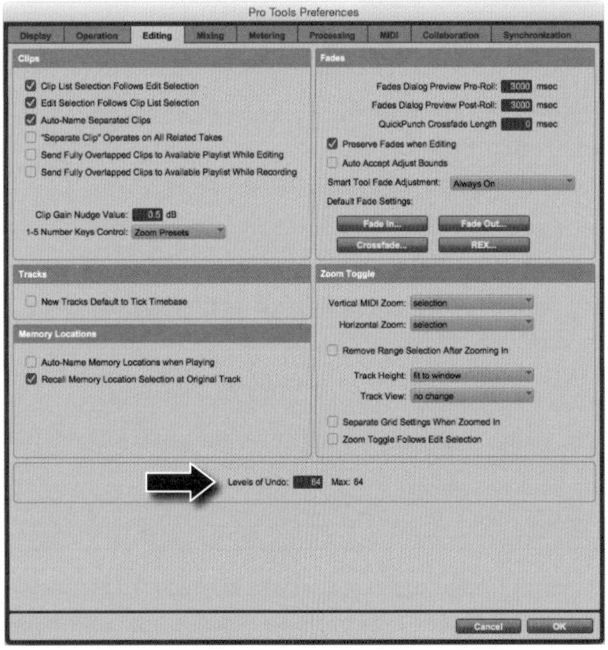

Figure 9.31 Levels of undo setting in the Preferences dialog box

Using the Undo and Redo Commands

To access the Undo command, choose **EDIT > UNDO** or press **COMMAND+Z** (Mac) or **CTRL+Z** (Windows). The Undo command in the Edit menu lists the action to be undone along with the command name. (See Figure 9.32.)

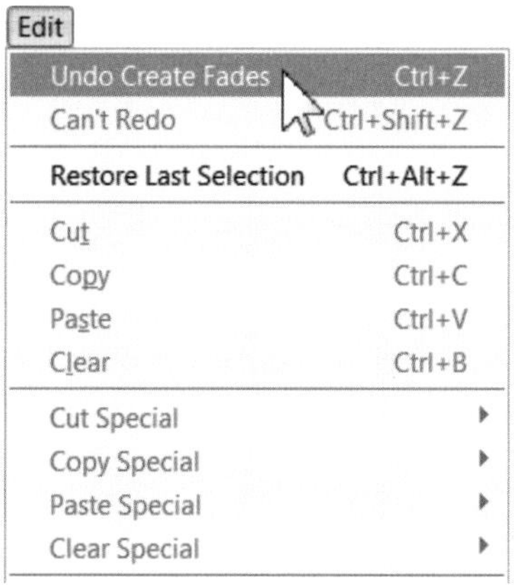

Figure 9.32 The Undo command in the Edit menu, showing the action that will be undone

To perform multiple undo operations, repeat the above process as needed, up to the limit set on the Editing Preferences page.

If you undo an action that you want to keep, you can reinstate the action using the Redo command. To access the Redo command, choose EDIT > REDO or press COMMAND+SHIFT+Z (Mac) or CTRL+SHIFT+Z (Windows). Like the Undo command, the Redo command lists the action that it will affect.

Using the Undo History Window

The Undo History window displays the Undo Queue, showing up to the last 64 actions that can be undone. You can use this window to view the recent actions taken and the sequence of those actions, as well as any actions recently undone.

To show the Undo History window, choose WINDOW > UNDO HISTORY. The Undo History window will display, showing undoable operations in bold and operations that have already been undone in italics.

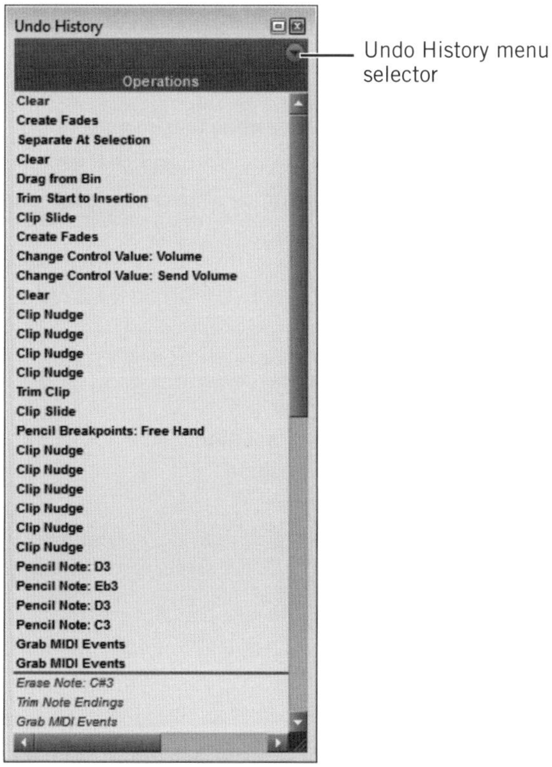

Figure 9.33 The Undo History window

The Undo History window allows you to instantly return to any previous state from the actions listed. This window can also show the creation time of each action, enabling you to revert to the state a session held at a particular time.

The following actions can be performed using the Undo History window:

- **Multiple simultaneous undos.** To undo multiple operations in the Undo History window, click on the last bold operation that you want to undo in the list. The selected operation and all operations performed after it will be undone; the undone operations will display in italics.

> **Undoable actions are stored sequentially in the queue, with the most recent action at the front of the queue (bottom of the list). Actions must be undone in consecutive order; you cannot undo an individual action out of sequence.**

- **Multiple simultaneous redos.** To redo multiple operations in the Undo History window, click the last italicized operation that you want to redo in the list. The selected operation and all operations that precede it in the list will be redone; the redone operations will again display in bold.
- **Undo all.** To undo all the operations in the undo queue, click the UNDO HISTORY MENU selector and choose UNDO ALL from the pop-up menu.
- **Redo all.** To redo all the operations in the redo queue, click the UNDO HISTORY MENU selector and choose REDO ALL.
- **Clear the queue.** To clear the undo queue, click the UNDO HISTORY MENU selector and choose CLEAR UNDO QUEUE. When you select this option, a dialog box opens, verifying the action; click YES to complete the command.

When the number of operations in the Undo History exceeds the limit set in the Edit Preferences, the oldest operations (at the top of the list) are removed. The operation next in line to be pushed out of the queue is shown in red.

Using Restore Last Selection

Selections are not stored in the undo queue. Therefore, if you accidentally drop a selection, you cannot choose EDIT > UNDO to restore the dropped selection. However, Pro Tools provides a separate command that enables you to restore your last Edit or Timeline selection. This command is very useful in the event that you accidentally lose a selection or find that you need to reuse a selection you just dropped.

To restore the last selection, choose EDIT > RESTORE LAST SELECTION or press COMMAND+OPTION+Z (Mac) or CTRL+ALT+Z (Windows).

> **The Restore Last Selection command has only a single level of restore. If you accidentally drop a selection, you MUST restore it before moving the cursor position. Otherwise, the cursor position from the dropped selection will be restored instead.**

Using Revert to Saved

If you need to undo changes that are no longer available in the Undo History, you can use the Revert to Saved command to restore the last saved version of your session. Reverting to the last saved version has the same effect as closing the session without saving changes and then reopening it.

To revert to the last saved version of your session, do the following:

1. Choose FILE > REVERT TO SAVED. A dialog box will display to verify that you want to revert the session.

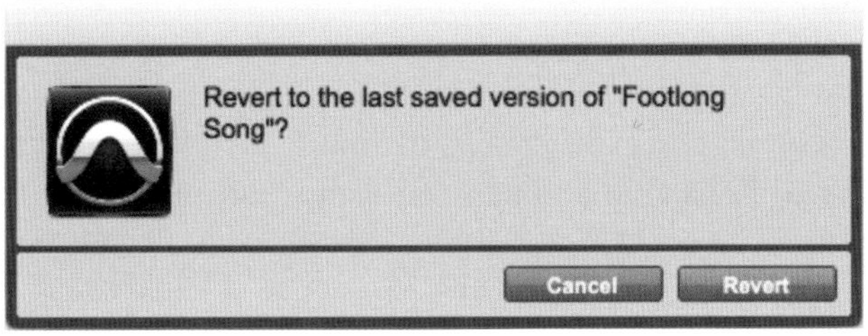

Figure 9.34 Revert to Saved dialog box

2. Click REVERT to continue.

Restoring from Session Backups

Although the Revert to Saved command is convenient, it is not always able to restore your session to the desired earlier state. If you have saved your work after the point that you wish to restore, Revert to Saved may not take you back far enough. Conversely, if you have made many changes since the last save, but you need to undo only some of those changes (including changes no longer in the undo queue), Revert to Saved will take you back too far.

In these cases, restoring from a session backup may be a better option.

If the Auto Backup function has been enabled in Preferences, your Session File Backups folder will include multiple backups saved periodically from earlier stages. (See "Session File Backups" in Lesson 2.)

Opening a session file backup is similar to opening an earlier saved copy of the session. However, the session will open with a *.recovered* extension added.

To restore your session from a backup, do the following:

1. Choose FILE > OPEN SESSION and navigate to the Session File Backups folder within your main session folder.
2. Select a backup session based on the modification date and time.
3. Once the session opens, verify that the backup file represents the desired stage of the session.
4. Select FILE > SAVE AS to save the restored session with an appropriate name.

Review/Discussion Questions

1. What does the Loop Playback option do? What is the minimum loop length required for loop playback? (See "Loop Playback" beginning on page 180.)

2. What happens when you delete a clip from between two existing clips in Shuffle mode? What happens when you do the same thing in Slip mode? (See "Editing in Shuffle Mode" and "Editing in Slip Mode" beginning on page 182.)

3. What happens when you move a clip whose start point falls between Grid lines in Absolute Grid mode? What happens when you do the same thing in Relative Grid mode? (See "Editing in Grid Mode" beginning on page 183.)

4. How can you configure the size of the Grid increments used in Grid mode? How can you display or hide the Grid lines in the Edit window? (See "Configuring the Grid" beginning on page 184.)

5. Name some common editing commands provided in Pro Tools. (See "Basic Editing Commands" beginning on page 185.)

6. What are some operations that the Separate Clip command can be used for? (See "The Separate Clip Command" beginning on page 188.)

7. What happens when you click on a clip with the Grabber tool in Spot mode? (See "Moving Clips in Spot Mode" beginning on page 191.)

8. What is the Trim tool used for? What modifier can you use to reverse the direction of the Trim tool? (See "The Trim Tool" beginning on page 191.)

9. What is the Nudge value used for? In what Edit modes can the Nudge function be used? (See "Using the Nudge Function" beginning on page 193.)

10. What keys are used to nudge a clip or selection earlier or later on a track? (See "Nudging Selections" beginning on page 194.)

11. How would you go about creating a fade-out at the end of a clip? How would you go about creating a crossfade between two adjacent clips? (See "Applying Fade-Ins and Fade-Outs" and "Applying Crossfades" beginning on page 195.)

12. How many levels of operations can you undo in Pro Tools 12? What are some operations that cannot be undone? (See "Using Multi-Level Undo" beginning on page 197.)

13. How can you display the Undo History window? What are some actions available in this window? (See "Using the Undo History Window" beginning on page 199.)

14. What are some available options for undoing changes that are no longer available in the Undo History window? When would each option apply? (See "Using Revert to Saved" and "Restoring from Session Backups" beginning on page 200.)

To review additional material from this chapter, see the PT101 Study Guide module available through the ElementsIED online learning platform at ElementsED.com.

EXERCISE 9

Editing Audio

In this exercise tutorial, you will use the memory locations you created in Exercise 8 to clean up the VO track and add a fire effect. You will also shorten the music tracks to fit within the 30-second target ad length.

Duration: 10 to 15 Minutes

Media: Fire FX.wav

> **Downloading the Media Files**
>
> To complete this exercise, you will need to have access to the audio files that you downloaded and imported previously. If needed, you can re-download the media files by pointing your browser to http://alpp.us/PT101-128.
>
> *Note: The above URL is **case sensitive**.*

Getting Started

You will start by opening the Pro Tools session you created in Exercise 8. If that session is not available, use the Exercise08 Sample file in the Completed Exercises folder within the PT101 Download Media folder.

Open the session and save it as Exercise 9:

1. Open the session file that you created in Exercise 8 (Storage Drive/Folder > PT101-XXX > Exercise08-XXX.ptx).

   Alternatively, you can use the Exercise08 Sample file (PT101 Download Media > 03. Completed Projects > Exercise08 Sample.ptx).

2. Choose **FILE > SAVE AS** and name the session *Exercise09-XXX*, keeping the session inside the original session folder (if working from your previous session) or moving the session into your PT101-XXX folder (if working from the sample file).

Configure the session:

- Click on the **GRID VALUE** pop-up selector in the toolbar and set the Grid to 0|1|000 (1/4 note), if not already selected.

Figure 9.35 Clicking the Grid Value pop-up selector in the Edit window

Editing the Voiceover and Placing the Fire Sound Effect

In this part of the exercise, you will use the memory locations you created earlier to edit the session audio. First you will remove the background noise from the beginning of the VO track. Then you will place the Fire FX clip at the proper location.

Remove noise before the voiceover starts:

1. Recall the VO Start memory location by clicking on it in the Markers ruler.
2. Select the VO track by clicking on its nameplate. The Edit cursor will appear on the track.
3. Choose EDIT > TRIM CLIP > START TO INSERTION to remove the portion of the clip before the memory location.

Place the Fire effect:

1. Click on the SLIP mode button on the left side of the Edit window toolbar to place the session into Slip mode. The Slip button will be lit green when active.

Figure 9.36 Enabling Slip mode in the Edit window

2. Using the GRABBER tool, select the clip on the Fire FX track.
3. Drag the clip to the right so that the start of the clip lines up with the Sun Bake memory location. Note that the clip placement does not need to be exact.

A vertical yellow line will be visible on the track at the marker location. Use this line as a visual guide when placing the clip.

4. Unmute the Fire FX track so that the fire effect becomes audible in the mix.

Shortening the Music Tracks

In this section of the exercise, you will remove a portion of the Drums, Bass, GTR, and Beat Wave tracks to fit the music within a 30-second radio ad spot.

Select the audio and MIDI data to remove:

1. Click on the GRID button in the Edit window toolbar to activate Grid mode. The Grid button will light blue when active.
2. Activate the SELECTOR tool in the Edit window toolbar.

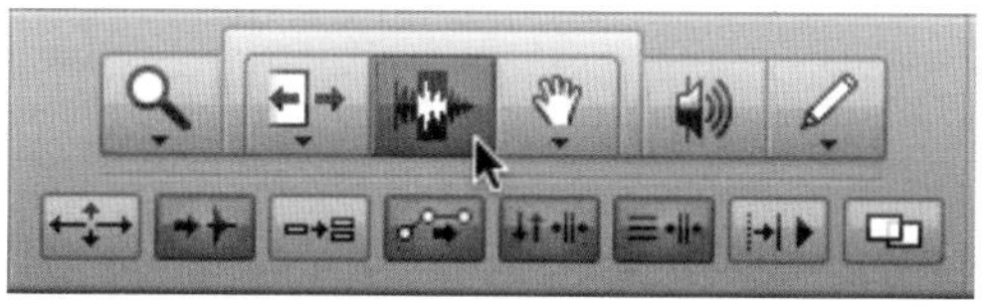

Figure 9.37 Enabling the Selector tool in the Edit window toolbar

3. Make a selection on the **Drums** track from Bar 16 to Bar 18 (**16|1|000** to **18|1|000**).

Figure 9.38 Two-bar selection on the Drums track, starting at Bar 16

4. Extend the selection across the **Bass**, **GTR**, and **Beat Wave** tracks by Shift-clicking on the nameplate of the **Beat Wave** track.

Remove the selected media:

1. Put the session into **SHUFFLE** mode by clicking on the Shuffle button in the toolbar. The Shuffle button will light red when active.
2. Press the **DELETE** or **BACKSPACE** key. The selected audio and MIDI material will be removed, and the remaining material on the tracks will slide over to close up the gap.
3. Return the session to **GRID** mode when finished.
4. Next, double-click on the **ZOOMER** tool icon to zoom out and view the entire session.
5. Activate the **SELECTOR** tool when finished.

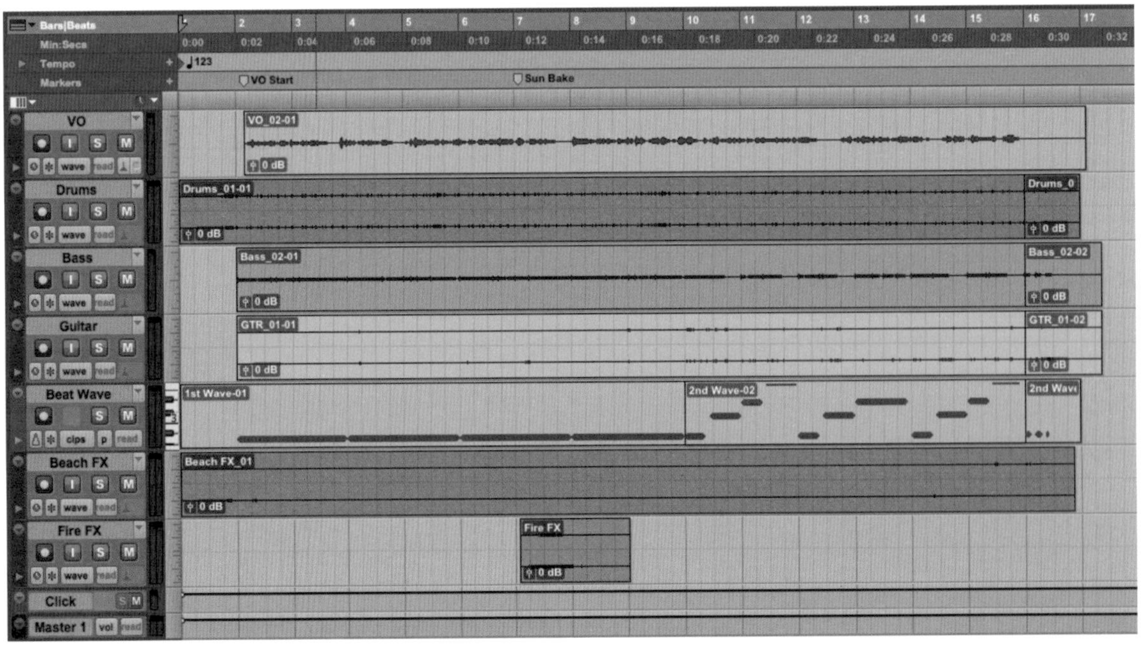

Figure 9.39 Tracks in the Edit window after editing

Finishing Up

To wrap up this exercise tutorial, you can listen to the work you've completed up to this point. Then be sure to save your work before closing the session. You will be reusing this session in the next exercise, so it is important to save the work you've done.

Review and save your work:

1. Press ENTER (Windows) or RETURN (Mac) followed by the SPACEBAR to begin playback from the session start and hear the results of your edits.
2. After listening through the session, press the SPACEBAR a second time to stop playback.
3. When finished, save and close the session.

Remember that you cannot close a Pro Tools session by closing its windows. You must choose CLOSE SESSION from the FILE menu.

LESSON 10

Mixing and Creating a Bounce

This lesson covers basic mixing techniques and processes as they are performed in a Pro Tools environment. It includes discussions of mixer terminology, Mix window configuration (including configuring inserts, sends, and returns), basic automation, and real-time plug-ins. The lesson also covers techniques for finishing your work, including creating a session back-up/archive and mixing down your session to a stereo file.

Duration: 120 Minutes

GOALS

- Recognize common mixer terminology
- Understand how inserts and send-and-return paths are used to add signal processing to your tracks
- Configure the Inserts and Sends views in the Mix window
- Record and edit basic automation for your mix
- Add plug-ins to your tracks for internal effects processing and sound shaping
- Understand the purpose of the Save Copy In command and recognize situations in which you should use it
- Select appropriate options for your stereo mix when using Bounce to Disk

Key topics from this lesson are included in the *Pro Tools 12 Essential Training: 101* course on Lynda.com.

With all of your tracks recorded and edited, it's time to start thinking about how to create a good balance between the audio elements, adding emphasis where it's needed and creating the subtle touches required for a professional–sounding result. Setting levels, adding signal processing, and creating dynamic automation are all parts of this process.

Once the mix sounds the way you want it, you will be ready to output the finished product as a stereo file. This lesson outlines the essential concepts and techniques required to complete all of these mixing tasks.

Basic Mixer Terminology

The fundamental job of any audio mixer is to route incoming and outgoing audio via the mixer's inputs and outputs. Additional signal routing and processing can be achieved using the mixer's inserts and send and return functions. These terms are defined in this section as they apply to general audio mixing; specific Pro Tools applications of these concepts are described under "Working in Mix Window" later in this lesson.

Inputs

The term *input* refers to an audio signal traveling into an audio hardware device, such as a mixer or an audio interface. The inputs available in Pro Tools vary depending on the system and the audio interface(s) in use.

Outputs

The term *output* refers to an audio signal traveling out of an audio hardware device. The outputs available in Pro Tools also vary depending on the system and the audio hardware in use. In standard Pro Tools, all tracks will route to the main stereo outputs (left and right) by default.

Inserts

Most mixers have a feature known as a *channel insert*. An insert is an audio patch point that allows a signal processor to be placed directly into the signal path of the audio channel.

Pro Tools provides 10 insert positions per track, allowing you to process a track's signal through multiple software plug-ins and/or external effects loops in series.

Sends and Returns

The term *send* refers to a signal path carrying a mix output of one or more channels (or tracks) routed for parallel processing. The send may route to an external receiving device, such as a hardware effects unit, or to an internal processor, such as a software plug-in.

Pre-Fader versus Post-Fader Sends

Sends can be *pre-fader*, meaning the send level is independent of the source track's fader level, or *post-fader*, meaning the send level is affected by changes you make to the fader on the source track. In Pro Tools, sends are post-fader by default; however, you can set a send to pre-fader at any time, as needed.

Send and Return Processing

When using a send for external processing, the signal is routed out of the mixer, through an external device where some type of processing is added, and then returned to the mixer through an *auxiliary input* (sometimes called an *auxiliary return*). When using a send for internal processing in Pro Tools, effects are added using a plug-in applied to the returned signal on the destination track (an Aux Input track).

The return channel in the mixer provides level and pan controls, allowing precise control over how the reintroduced signal combines with other audio in the system.

Working in the Mix Window

Pro Tools' mixing operations and functions are typically performed using the Mix window. The Mix window is similar to a standard mixing console. This window offers a variety of display options, many of which can also be customized.

The Mix window can be displayed or hidden as needed. To view the Mix window, choose WINDOW > MIX. If the Mix window is already open but is inactive (such as when it is hidden behind another window), this command will make it active, bringing it to the front of the display.

Press COMMAND+= (Mac) or CTRL+= (Windows) to toggle between the Mix and Edit windows.

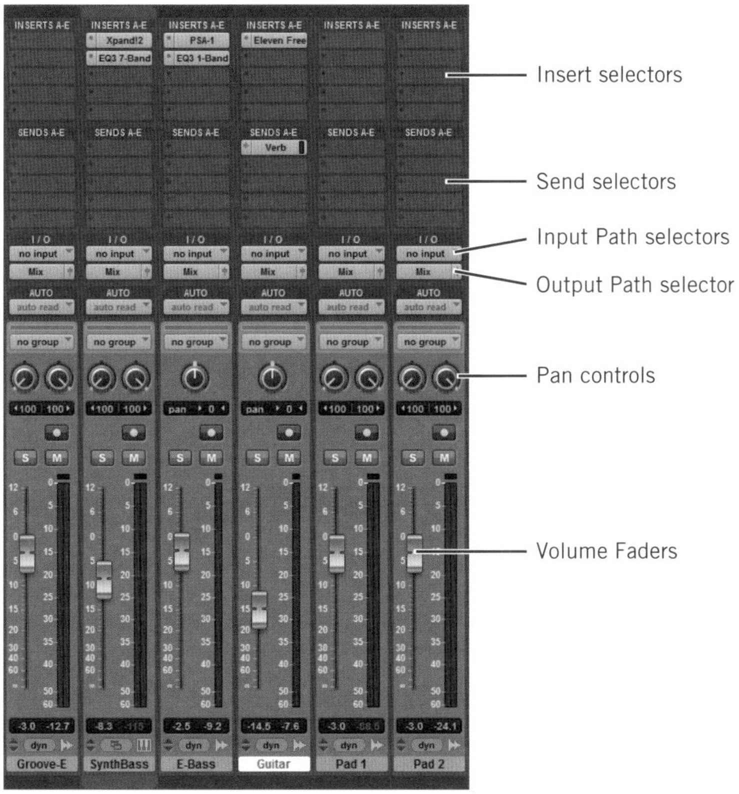

Figure 10.1 Mix window controls

Configuring the Mix Window

The Mix window includes several component parts and controls. Among the controls that you will use to create your mix are Volume Faders, Pan controls, I/O selectors, and Insert and Send selectors.

The Input and Output selectors (I/O selectors) include Audio Input Path selectors and Audio Output Path selectors, as well as MIDI Input selectors and MIDI Output selectors (MIDI and Instrument tracks only).

To create a session mix, you will set the Volume Faders for each track to achieve an appropriate blend of audio levels and set the Pan controls to achieve the desired positioning of sounds within the stereo field. You can make changes in real time during playback, either by manually adjusting the controls or by using automation. (See "Using Basic Automation" later in this lesson.)

The Input and Output selectors are used to route signals to and from your tracks. Often the basic I/O routing for your mix will already be in place, based on the work you have done up to this point. However, if needed, you can use these selectors to configure different signal routing for your mix.

Mixing also often involves using inserts and sends to add various types of signal processing to the audio on a session's tracks. You can use the Insert and Send selectors in the Mix window to achieve these operations.

Input and Output Selectors

The Mix window displays the main Input and Output selectors for each track in the session by default. Though much of your signal routing might have been set up during the recording and editing stages of your project, it is always a good idea to double-check the I/O settings when you begin mixing.

Input Paths

For tracks that are playing back material already on the track, no input routing is necessary. Tracks that are receiving live input from other sources will need to have their inputs set accordingly.

When modifying or setting up tracks for mixing, pay particular attention to the Audio Input Path selector settings for any Aux Input tracks in your session. These tracks are often used to route audio from a send or submix. Aux Inputs may also be used to receive live audio from an external source.

In these cases, the Input routing must be configured accordingly.

The diagram in Figure 10.2 shows how the Audio Input Path selector for an Aux Input track corresponds to the input connectors of an Mbox used to route live input from a synthesizer.

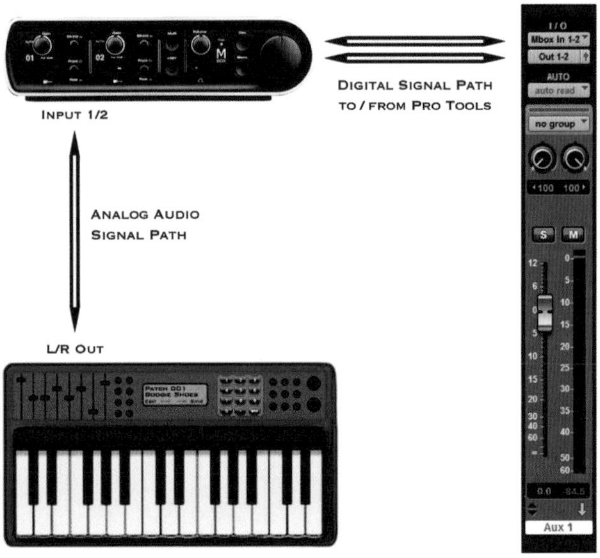

Figure 10.2 Common signal flow using an Aux Input track for live input through an Mbox

Output Paths

Pro Tools enables you to route the output of each track to any hardware output or bus. For the purposes of creating a stereo mix, you will generally use the main stereo outputs of your audio interface (default).

To set up a basic stereo mix, verify that the Audio Output Path selectors for the tracks in your session are set to the main outputs of your audio interface, as appropriate, so that the audio from each track is included in the stereo playback. This is typically done through an output path labeled Output 1-2, Analog 1-2, or similar.

If needed, use the Audio Output Path selector to select the desired output path for your tracks.

Inserts and Sends Views

The Mix window has independent view areas for the track inserts and sends. These view areas can each be toggled on or off in the Mix window.

- **Inserts view.** The two Inserts view areas (Inserts A–E and Inserts F–J) allow you to access and view the 10 track Insert selectors. (Five are displayed in each view area.)

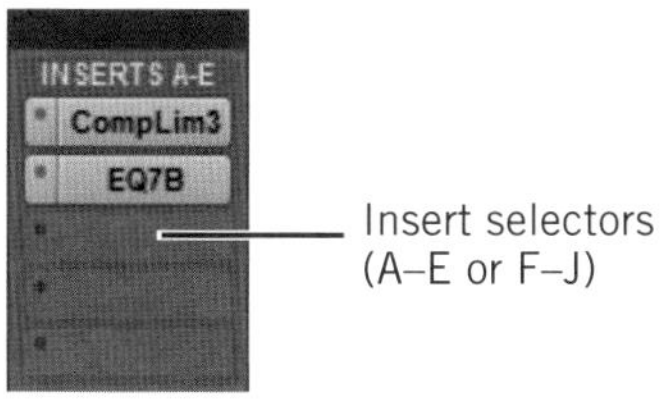

Figure 10.3 Inserts view area in the Mix window

- **Sends view.** The two Sends view areas (Sends A–E and Sends F–J) allow you to access and view the 10 track Send selectors. (Five are displayed in each view area.)

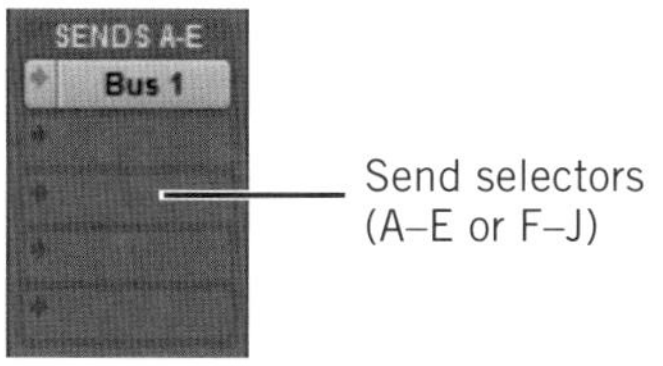

Figure 10.4 Sends view area in the Mix window

To toggle the display of an Inserts or Sends view area in the Mix window, choose VIEW > MIX WINDOW VIEWS and click an option in the submenu to select or deselect it.

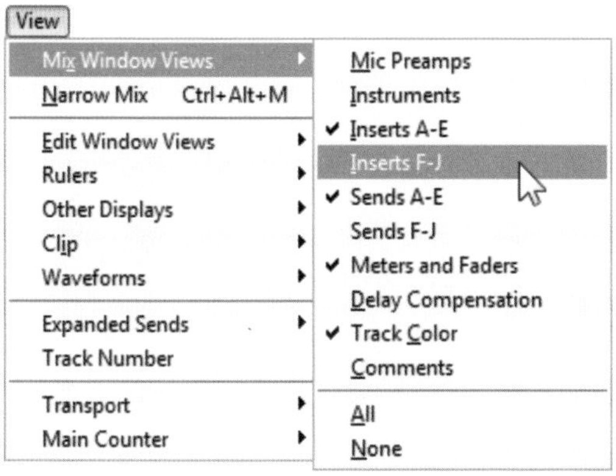

Figure 10.5 Toggling the Inserts F–J view area from the Mix window submenu

The Inserts and Sends view areas are available in both the Mix and Edit windows and can be shown or hidden independently in each window.

Configuring Inserts

With an Inserts view area displayed in the Mix window, you can add an insert processor to any track. To add an insert processor, click on the Insert selector and choose a plug-in option or an I/O option from the pop-up menu. Plug-ins provide software-based signal processing, while I/O routing creates an effects loop for an external hardware device.

Plug-In Inserts

Plug-in inserts route audio through a software add-on from within a track in the Mix window. Choose a plug-in insert to add a software signal processor, such as an EQ plug-in, directly into the signal path of the channel.

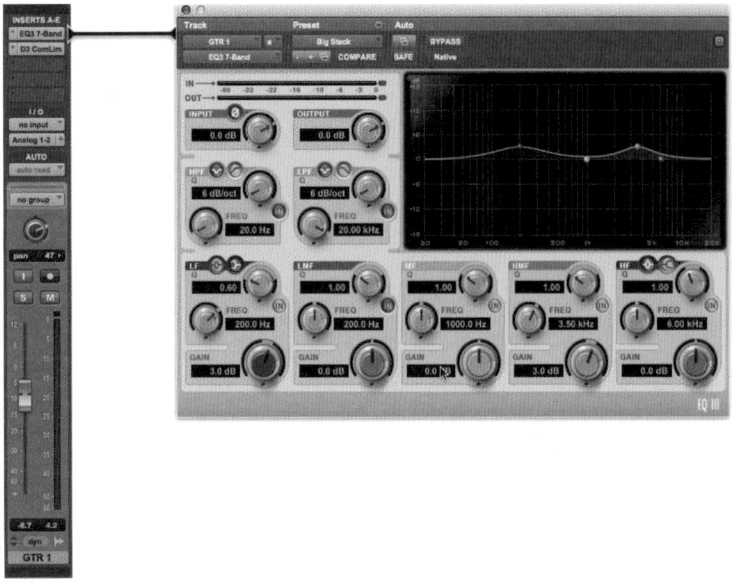

Figure 10.6 EQ plug-in on Insert A of a guitar track

Hardware Inserts

I/O inserts route audio through an external hardware device using parallel inputs and outputs of an audio interface. This option requires an audio interface with sufficient I/O capacity to support hardware inserts in addition to stereo playback through the main left-right outputs.

Hardware inserts are covered in advanced courses.

Configuring Sends and Returns

Sends are used to route a track's signal to a secondary path for parallel processing (internal or external) without interrupting the signal flow through the originating track. To add the processed signal back into the mix, it is typically returned via an Aux Input.

To route a send to an external device, choose **OUTPUT** from the Send selector and select the appropriate output path on your audio interface. Connect this output to the external device, and return the processed signal from the device to an available input on your audio interface. This signal is the return, which then must be routed to the Audio Input of an Aux Input track.

To route a send to an internal processor, such as a plug-in on an Aux Input track, choose **BUS** from the Send selector and select an appropriate bus for routing the signal. This bus will also need to be routed to the input of the Aux Input track.

Using Basic Automation

For a simple mix, you can often set the Volume Faders and Pan controls as desired and leave them unchanged from the start of the mix to the end. For a more complex mix that requires dynamic changes during the course of playback, you can use track automation. Pro Tools allows you to record any real-time changes you make as automation on your tracks. Automatable controls include volume, pan, mute, send levels, and more.

Tracks in Pro Tools use *automation modes* to determine how automation features work on the track. You can set the automation mode for each track independently. The following sections discuss the three basic automation modes—Write, Read, and Off—to illustrate real-time automation in Pro Tools.

Recording Automation (Write Mode)

By setting automation on a track to Write mode, you can record the changes you make to enabled controls on the track in real time. The basic steps for recording automation in Write mode are as follows:

1. Enable the automation type that you want to record, such as volume or pan, as follows:

   a. Choose **WINDOW > AUTOMATION**. The Automation window will open.

   b. Click on each automation parameter to set its state as desired (enabled versus disabled). Parameters display in red when enabled, or gray when disabled.

Figure 10.7 Toggling an automation parameter in the Automation window

2. Put the track in an automation-writing mode by choosing **WRITE** from the Automation Mode selector in the Mix or Edit windows.

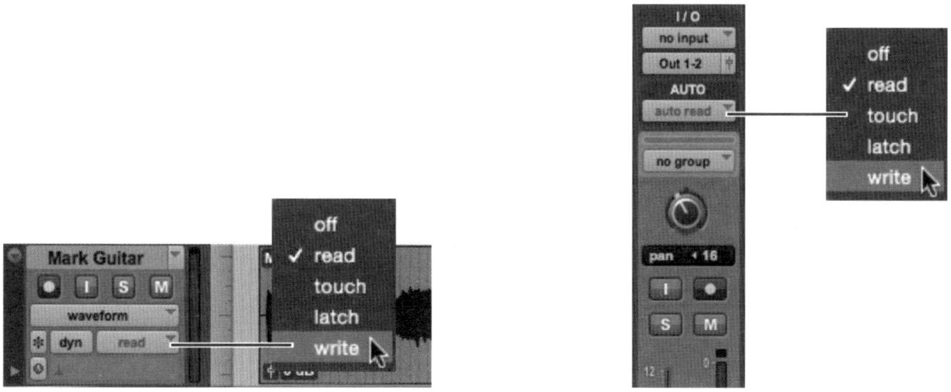

Figure 10.8 Selecting Write mode from the Automation Mode selector: Edit window (left) and Mix window (right)

3. Begin playback to start writing automation, and adjust controls as needed. Pro Tools will record all adjustments performed on enabled controls.

If you are not satisfied with the changes you've written during an automation pass, you can undo the pass or simply repeat these steps to write new automation over the previous data.

Playing Back Automation (Read Mode)

The default automation mode for a track is Read mode. In this mode, the automation playlist is used to play the automation data that has been written for a track. Automation cannot be written in Read mode, but the automation playlist can be edited with the Edit tools. (See "Viewing and Editing Breakpoint Automation" later in this lesson.)

To return to Read mode when a different mode has been activated, click the **AUTOMATON MODE SELECTOR** and choose **READ**.

Use Read mode to play back automation after a write pass without running the risk of recording over the automation.

Turning Automation Off (Off Mode)

The Off mode turns off automation for all automatable parameters on the track, regardless of their status in the Automation window.

In Off mode, no automation is recorded during playback, and any existing automation data for the track is ignored during playback. To turn off automation so that it neither records nor plays back, click the **AUTOMATION MODE SELECTOR** and choose **OFF**.

Viewing Automation Playlists

Each automatable parameter on a track has an associated automation playlist. The automation playlist (or automation graph) can be displayed in the Edit window, allowing you to see the automation changes. When displayed, the automation playlist can also be edited and refined using Edit tools, such as the Grabber.

To display an automation playlist, do the following:

1. Click on the **TRACK VIEW SELECTOR** in the Edit window.

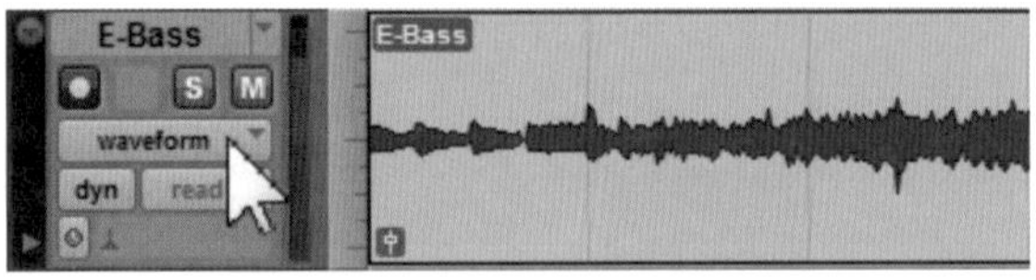

Figure 10.9 Clicking a Track View selector in the Edit window

2. Select the automation playlist that you want to display from the pop-up menu. The automation graph will be displayed as a black line, superimposed on the track audio or MIDI data.

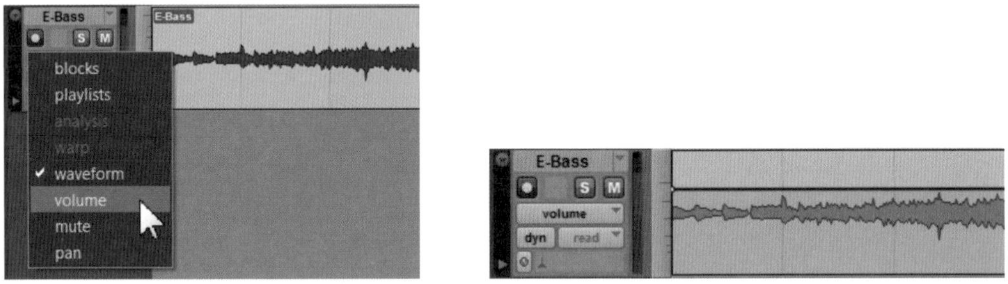

Figure 10.10 Selecting the Volume automation view (left); the Volume automation graph displayed (right)

Pro Tools also allows you to display automation playlists by clicking on the **SHOW/HIDE AUTOMATION LANES** button (triangle) at the head of a track. The Volume automation lane will appear beneath the parent track. Additional automation lanes can be displayed by clicking on the plus sign (+) within the displayed lane. (See Figure 10.11.)

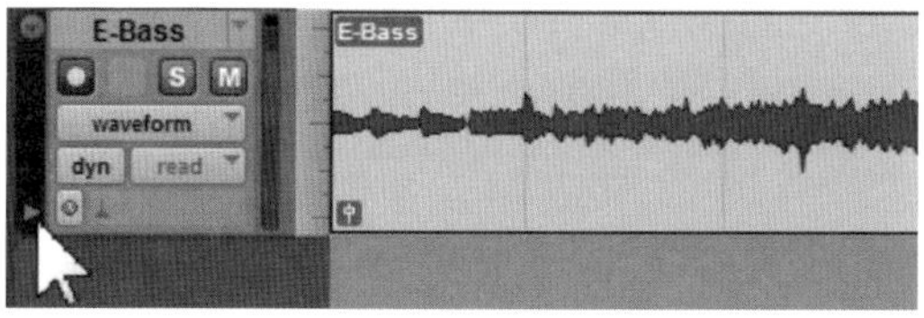

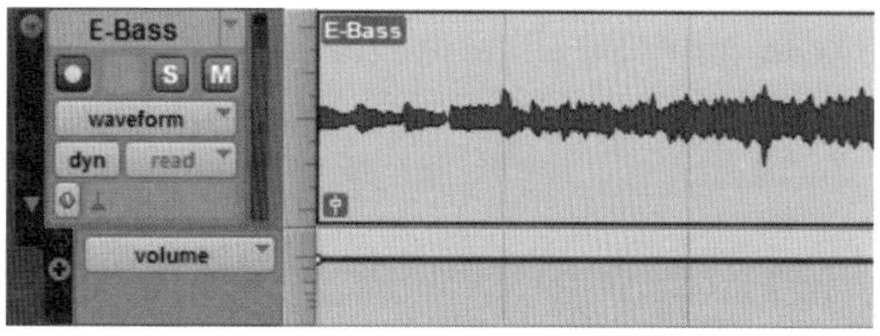

Figure 10.11 Clicking the Show/Hide Automation Lanes button (left); Volume automation lane displayed (right)

Editing Breakpoint Automation

You can edit an automation playlist by adding, moving, or deleting breakpoints using the Grabber tool. To edit a playlist with the Grabber tool, do any of the following:

- Click on the automation graph line to add a breakpoint.
- Click and drag an existing breakpoint to adjust its position.
- OPTION-CLICK (Mac) or ALT-CLICK (Windows) on an existing breakpoint to remove it.

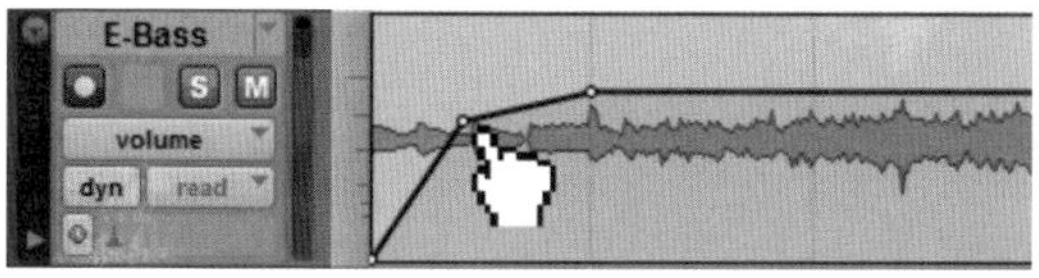

Figure 10.12 Editing the Volume playlist using the Grabber tool

Automation playlists can also be edited using other Edit tools. Additional information on using and editing automation is provided in advanced courses.

Using Plug-In Processors

As you learned in earlier lessons, plug-ins are software add-ons for Pro Tools that provide added functionality such as effects processing or a virtual instrument sound source for a track.

Pro Tools provides two main categories of plug-ins:

- Real-time processing, provided by AAX plug-ins (Native and DSP)
- File-based processing (non-real-time), provided by AudioSuite plug-ins

Details on using AudioSuite plug-ins are provided in the Pro Tools 110 course.

The following sections focus on real-time plug-ins in standard Pro Tools.

Real-Time Plug-In Formats

Plug-ins can be used in mono, multi-mono, or multi-channel formats (limited to stereo in standard Pro Tools.) The plug-in formats available depend on the selected plug-in and the track format (mono or stereo).

You will generally want to use multi-channel plug-ins for linked processing on stereo tracks. If no multi-channel version is available, you can use a multi-mono version instead.

- **Mono plug-ins.** Plug-ins in this format are available for use on mono tracks. Some mono plug-ins can generate stereo output from a mono channel.

- **Multi-mono plug-ins.** Plug-ins in this format can be used on stereo tracks and will process each channel independently. The left and right channels will be linked by default but can be unlinked if desired to adjust the channels independently.
- **Multi-channel plug-ins.** Plug-ins in this format are designed for use on stereo tracks. Controls for the left and right channels are always linked together in a multi-channel plug-in.

Plug-Ins Provided with Pro Tools

Pro Tools comes bundled with a variety of plug-in options. These include the Avid Pro Tools plug-ins listed in Appendix B and the AIR effects and instrument plug-ins listed in Appendix C. Among these bundles you will find dynamics processors, EQs, reverbs, delays, flangers, choruses, and more.

Two commonly used types of processing for Audio tracks are dynamics processors (such as compressors and gates) and equalizers (graphic and parametric EQs). Popular plug-ins in these categories include the following:

- Avid EQ III
- Avid Dynamics III
- Avid Channel Strip

Avid EQ III

The Avid EQ III is an equalizer plug-in for adjusting the frequency spectrum of audio material in Pro Tools. This plug-in can be added to a track in a 1-band or 7-band parametric EQ configuration.

To add the EQ III plug-in to a Pro Tools track, click on an INSERT SELECTOR and choose PLUG-IN > EQ. Then select either the EQ3 1-Band or EQ3 7-Band, as desired. The EQ III plug-in window will open.

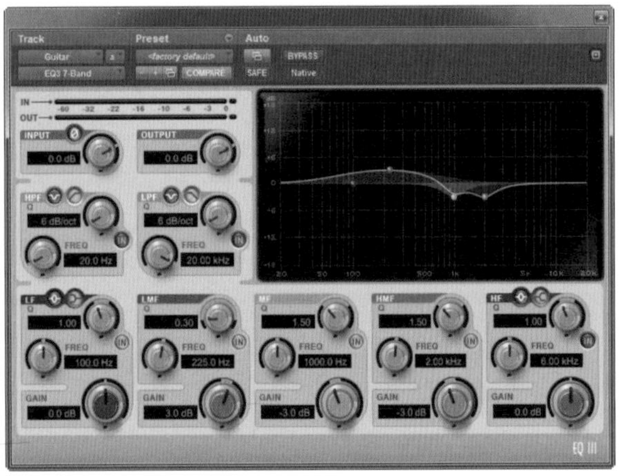

Figure 10.13 The EQ III 7-band equalizer plug-in window

Avid Dynamics III

The Avid Dynamics III plug-in provides a suite of dynamics processors, including a Compressor/Limiter, an Expander/Gate, and a De-Esser.

The Compressor/Limiter plug-in can be used to control dynamic levels, using standard attack, release, threshold, and ratio controls. The Expander/Gate plug-in can be added to a track to eliminate unwanted background noise in quiet areas by fine-tuning the ratio, attack, hold, release, and range. The De-Esser can be used to reduce sibilants, using frequency and range controls.

To add a Dynamics III plug-in to a track, click on an **Insert selector** and choose **Plug-In > Dynamics**. Then select the Dyn3 Compressor/Limiter, Dyn3 De-Esser, or Dyn3 Expander/Gate, as desired. The selected plug-in window will open.

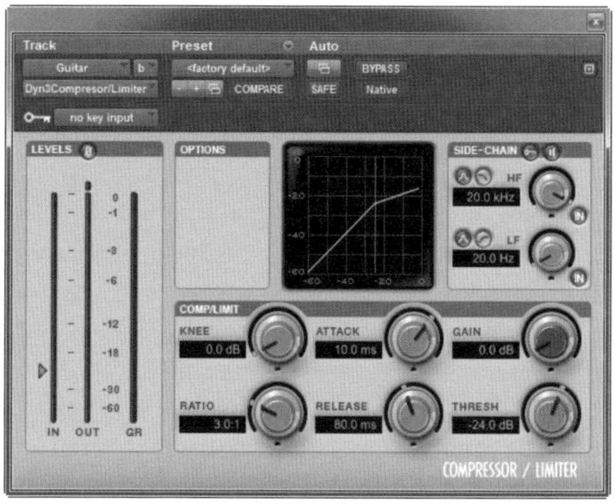

Figure 10.14 The Dynamics III Compressor/Limiter plug-in window

Avid Channel Strip

The Avid Channel Strip plug-in combines EQ, Dynamics, Filter, and Gain effects processing in a single user interface. Channel Strip also provides a gain transfer graph for the Expander/Gate and Compressor/Limiter effects, and a Frequency Graph showing the response curve for the current EQ settings.

To add the Channel Strip plug-in to a track, click on an **Insert selector**, choose either **Plug-In > EQ** or **Plug-In > Dynamics**, and then select **Channel Strip**. The Avid Channel Strip plug-in will open.

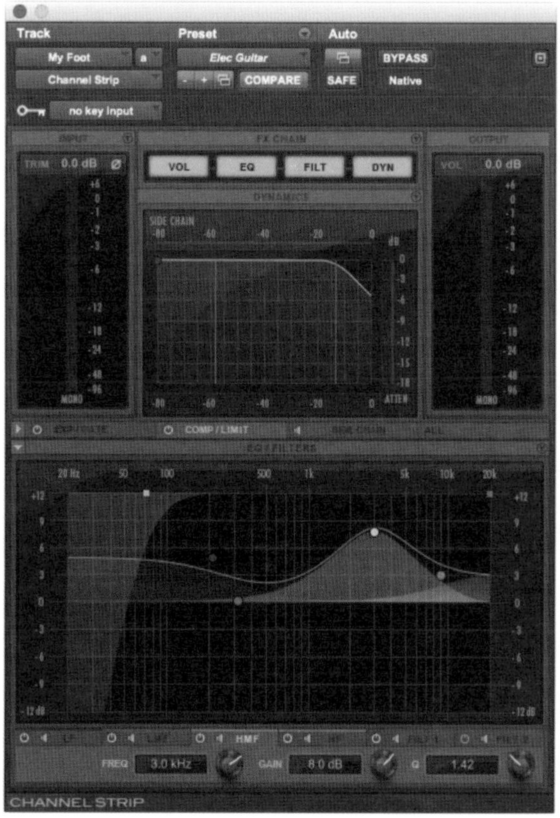

Figure 10.15 The Avid Channel Strip plug-in window

Backing Up Your Session

Once you've finished crafting your mix with automation and plug-in processing, you can safeguard your work by creating a backup copy. Creating backups is critical for archival and disaster-recovery purposes. Because Pro Tools sessions are stored electronically, it is possible to accidentally lose your work by deleting or overwriting files, having a file become corrupt, encountering a virus, or having a drive fail.

Considerations for Backup and Archive Copies

Some of the best protection measures include creating multiple copies of your files, using a separate drive for backup copies, and storing copies in the cloud to protect against disasters such as fire or flood. The more valuable your sessions, the more robust your backup plans should be. At a minimum, you should create a backup session upon completing any work that would be difficult or time-consuming to re-create, especially if the recording has significant value or importance to you or your clients.

Whenever creating a backup or archive copy, be sure to include any media files (audio and video) that are referenced by the session. Keep in mind that these files may not be included in the original session folder.

Saving a Session Copy

One option you can use to create a copy of your session and all related files is the Save Copy In command. Unlike the Save As command, which creates a copy of the Pro Tools session file only, the Save Copy In command can be used to save all session media, allowing you to create a self-contained session folder in a separate location, such as on another drive.

The Save Copy In command saves a copy of your current session without closing the original session, meaning that as you continue to work, any subsequent changes are made in the original and do not affect the copy.

One key difference between the Save As command and the Save Copy In command is their effect on the open session. After a Save As operation, the open session will be the *renamed copy* that you created. By contrast, after a Save Copy In operation, the *original session* will remain open, not the copy.

Uses for the Save Copy In Command

When using the Save Copy In command, a number of options will be available that allow you to convert and consolidate session information. Some applications of the Save Copy In command include the following:

- Backing up an entire Pro Tools session and all of its associated files without leaving the original session.
- Creating multiple versions of a session at various stages of a project.
- Creating a session copy with a different bit depth, sample rate, and/or file format.
- Creating a session copy that is compatible with older Pro Tools systems.
- Converting a local session document to a cloud-enabled project document (or vice versa).

Applying the Save Copy In Command

The Save Copy In command is available under the File menu. The Save Copy In dialog box includes a variety of configuration choices.

To use the Save Copy In function, do the following:

1. Choose FILE > SAVE COPY IN. The Save Copy In dialog box will open. (See Figure 10.16.)

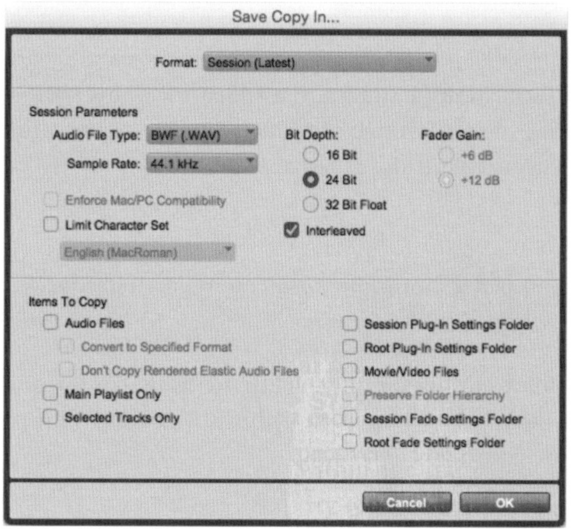

Figure 10.16 The Save Copy In dialog box

2. (Optional) In the Format drop-down menu, choose from among the available options to select a different document format, if desired.

Figure 10.17 Selecting an earlier Pro Tools version

3. (Optional) Modify the settings in the Session Parameters section of the dialog box, as desired. (The parameters default to match the settings of the source session or project.)

When using the SESSION (PRO TOOLS 5.1 -> 6.9) format with either AIFF or WAV audio files, the Enforce PC/Mac Compatibility checkbox will become available. This option ensures that all files are compatible with supported Mac and Windows systems.

4. In the Items to Copy section of the dialog box, enable additional options as desired.

   When creating a backup archive, be sure to enable the **AUDIO FILES** option here to include copies of all the audio files used in the session. If the session includes a Video track, you may also want to enable the **MOVIE/VIDEO FILES** option to include a copy of the video file in the new session location.

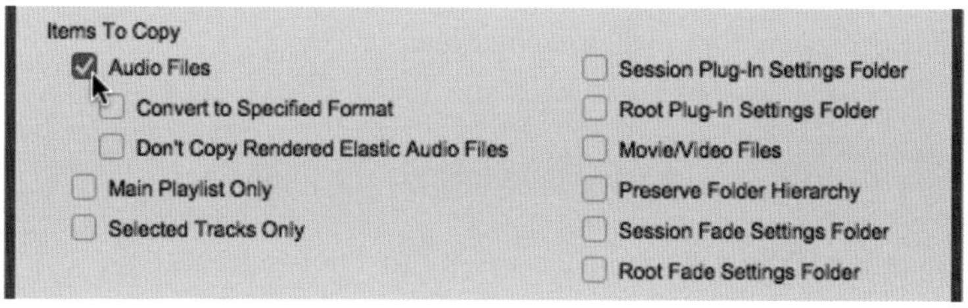

Figure 10.18 Optional items that can be copied with the session

5. Click **OK** when you are finished configuring the options as desired. The new session and any selected media files will be saved into the directory location you select.

Creating a Stereo Mixdown

Mixing down is the process of recording the output from multiple tracks to a stereo file. This process is also commonly referred to as *bouncing* the session. Mixing down is often the last phase of music production, although you can create a bounce at any time to create a complete mix as a stereo file.

Mixdown Options

The most commonly used mixdown option in Pro Tools is the Bounce to Disk command. This option is a fast and easy way to create a bounce, requiring little to no setup.

Advanced users also frequently use the *bounce to tracks* technique. Bouncing to tracks is the process of recording the output of any or all of the session tracks to a new stereo track within the session. This process is also commonly referred to as creating an internal bounce or internal layback.

For the purposes of this course, we will focus on the Bounce to Disk option.

Considerations for Bouncing Audio

When performing a bounce with Pro Tools, it is important to recognize that the bounce will capture all audible information in your mix just as you hear it during playback.

The following principles apply to bouncing in Pro Tools:

- **The bounce will include only audible tracks.** What you hear during playback is exactly what will be included in the bounce. Any tracks that are muted will not be included. Conversely, any tracks that are soloed will be the *only* tracks represented in the bounce.
- **The bounce will be based on the selected output path.** All source tracks for the bounce must be assigned to the same output path. Any audio not routed to the bounced output path will not be represented in the bounce file.
- **The bounced file will be a "printed" version of your session.** Inserts, sends, and external effects will be applied permanently in the bounce. Listen closely to your entire session prior to completing a bounce to ensure that everything sounds as it should. Pay close attention to levels, being sure to avoid clipping.
- **The bounce will be based on the Timeline selection.** If you have an active selection, Pro Tools will bounce for the length of the selection only. If no selection is present, the Bounce to Disk command will create a bounce from the start of the session to the end of the longest track.

Bouncing to Disk

The Bounce to Disk command allows you to mix your entire session directly to a stereo file on disk. The corresponding dialog box lets you set the bit depth, file format, and sample rate for the bounced file. You can also choose to perform an Offline Bounce for faster-than-real-time mixdown.

Supported File Types

The file types that you can create from the Bounce to Disk command include the following:

- **WAV.** This is the default file format for Windows- and Mac-based Pro Tools systems.
- **AIFF.** This file format is primarily used on Mac systems. Use the AIFF format if you plan to import the bounced audio into Mac applications that do not support the WAV format.
- **MP3.** This file format can create smaller audio files for Internet streaming and portable devices. Use this file format to balance file size against audio quality.

- **MXF.** MXF (*Material Exchange Format*) is a media file format designed for the interchange of audio-visual material with associated data and metadata. Use this format to prepare a bounce for import to applications such as Avid's Media Composer.

> **Bouncing to MXF requires enabling the ENFORCE MEDIA COMPOSER COMPATIBILITY option in the Bounce to Disk dialog box.**

Using the Bounce to Disk Command

The Bounce to Disk command combines the outputs of all currently audible tracks routed to a common output or output pair to create a new audio file on your hard drive.

To bounce all currently audible tracks, do the following:

1. Adjust track output levels and finalize an automated mix. Any inserts or effects settings that are active on your tracks will be permanently written to the bounced audio file.
2. Make sure that all of the tracks you want to include in the bounce are audible. To mix down all tracks in your session, verify that no tracks are soloed or muted.
3. Verify that the output of each track is routed to the same bus or output pair. Use the **AUDIO OUTPUT PATH SELECTOR** as needed to set the track outputs.
4. Choose **FILE > BOUNCE TO > DISK**. The Bounce dialog box will appear.

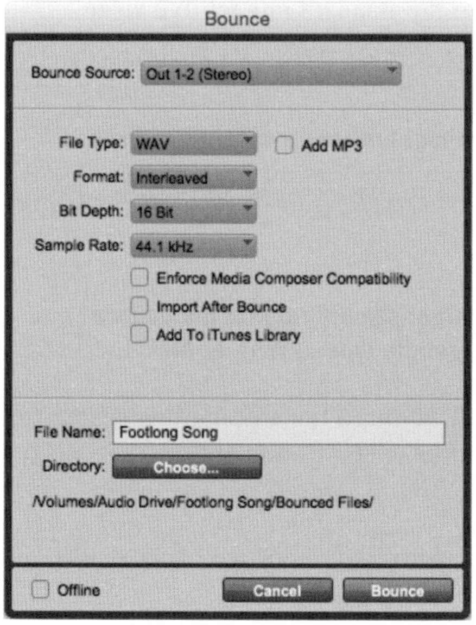

Figure 10.19 The Bounce dialog box

5. Select the output pair that you used in Step 3 from the **BOUNCE SOURCE** drop-down list, if needed. This option will default to the main stereo outputs.
6. Choose the desired file type for your bounce file from the **FILE TYPE** pop-up menu. Available options include WAV, AIFF, MP3, and MXF.

> **You can also bounce to a WAV, AIFF, or MXF file and simultaneously create an MP3 file. Select the format for your primary bounce from the FILE TYPE pop-up menu and enable the ADD MP3 checkbox next to the pop-up menu.**

7. Choose the file format for your stereo bounce from the **FORMAT** pop-up menu.
   - **Interleaved.** This option creates a single file containing both channels of a stereo mix. Interleaved files are compatible with most online services and music applications, including SoundCloud and iTunes.
   - **Multiple Mono.** This option creates two separate mono files for a stereo mix: one for the left channel and another for the right channel. This file format is required for MXF media files.

A third option, the Mono (Summed) format, provides a single audio file that is a summed mono mix of the bus path. Choose this option if you need to create a composite mix of mono tracks. All panning information will be disregarded.

8. Choose the desired bit depth for the bounced file(s) from the **BIT DEPTH** pop-up menu.
   - Choose 16 Bit if you plan to burn your bounce to CD without further processing.
   - Choose 24 Bit when you want to create a final mix that will be mastered separately.
   - Choose 32 Bit Float for ultra-high-resolution files that will undergo further processing or editing.

The standard bit depth resolution for compact discs is 16 bits.

9. Choose the desired sample rate for the bounce files from the **SAMPLE RATE** pop-up menu. Higher sampling rates will provide better audio fidelity but will also increase the size of the resulting file(s).

The standard sample rate for compact discs is 44.1 kHz; the standard rate for DVD video is 48 kHz.

If you plan to burn your bounced audio directly to CD without further processing, choose 44.1 kHz as the sample rate for the bounce.

10. Select other options as desired.

The Import After Bounce option is available only if the target sample rate for the bounce file matches the sample rate of your session and the target file type is WAV or AIFF.

11. If desired, specify a different file name and location for your bounced file(s) using the settings near the bottom of the Bounce dialog box. By default, the bounced file will be named after the session and placed in the Bounced Files folder inside the session folder.
12. For a faster-than-real-time bounce, enable the **OFFLINE** checkbox at the bottom of the dialog box.
13. After confirming your settings, click the **BOUNCE** button.

When performing a real-time bounce, the audio will play back as Pro Tools processes the bounce, and a countdown window will appear, displaying the time remaining for your bounce to complete. (See Figure 10.20.)

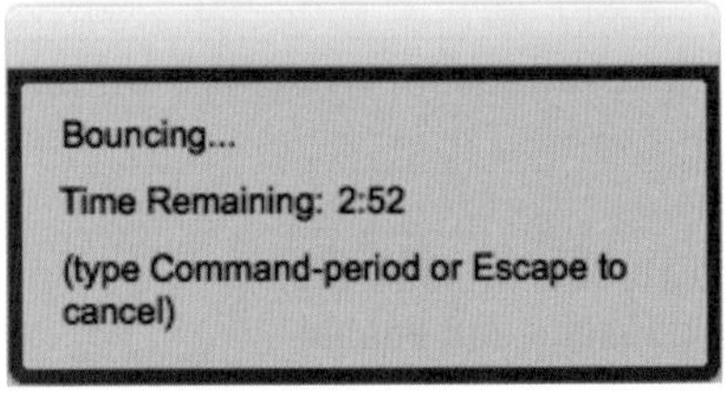

Bouncing...
Time Remaining: 2:52
(type Command-period or Escape to cancel)

Figure 10.20 The Bounce to Disk countdown window (real-time bounce)

You will not hear the bounce file play back in real time if you are not monitoring the bounce source.

When performing an offline bounce, Pro Tools processes the bounce without audio playback. A progress window will appear, displaying the Timeline processed amount, the total Timeline duration, and the bounce speed as a multiple of the real-time duration.

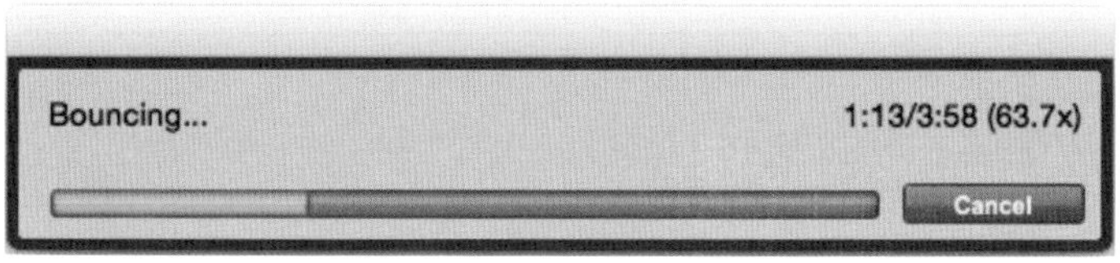

Figure 10.21 The Bounce to Disk progress window (offline bounce)

Adding a Bounce File to Your iTunes Library

If you plan to add your completed mix to an audio CD, one of your options is to use iTunes software to burn the CD. Pro Tools lets you bounce your mix directly to your iTunes library to simplify this process.

If iTunes is not already installed on your system, you can download a copy from the Apple website at www.apple.com/itunes.

To add a bounce file to your iTunes library, do the following:

1. Choose FILE > BOUNCE TO > DISK.
2. Set the Format to INTERLEAVED and configure other options as desired.
3. Enable the ADD TO ITUNES LIBRARY option near the middle of the dialog box.

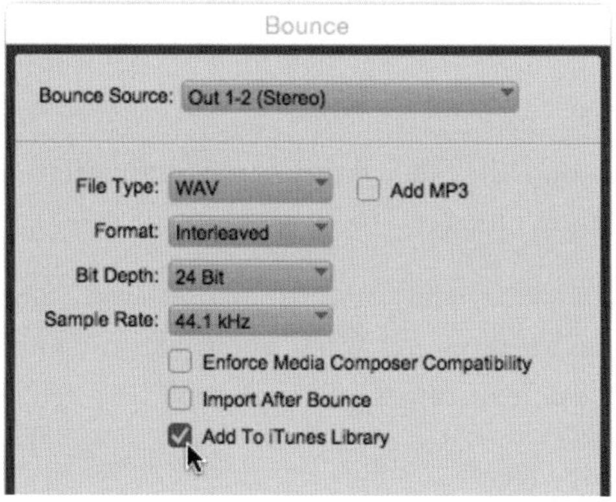

Figure 10.22 The Add to iTunes Library option in the Bounce dialog box

4. Click BOUNCE. The bounce process will proceed as described above, and a copy of your bounced file will automatically be imported into iTunes.

If iTunes is not installed on your computer, the Add to iTunes Library option does not do anything.

Review/Discussion Questions

1. What term is used to describe an audio patch point that applies a signal processor directly into the signal path on a track? How many of these patch points does Pro Tools provide on each track? (See "Inserts" beginning on page 210.)

2. What term is used to describe a signal path carrying a mix output of one or more tracks routed for parallel processing? How can this signal be returned to the sending device? (See "Sends and Returns" beginning on page 210.)

3. What menu would you use to display or hide the Mix window? What keyboard shortcut can you use to toggle between the Mix and Edit windows? (See "Working in the Mix Window" beginning on page 211.)

4. What menu command can you use to display or hide an Inserts or Sends view area in the Mix window? (See "Inserts and Sends Views" beginning on page 213.)

5. Which Pro Tools automation mode discussed in this lesson records changes to track controls in real time when playing back the session? (See "Recording Automation" beginning on page 215.)

6. What is the difference between Read mode and Off mode? Which mode allows you to play back existing automation on the track? (See "Playing Back Automation" and "Turning Automation Off" beginning on page 215.)

7. What track control can you use to display an automation playlist? What window are automation playlists displayed in? (See "Viewing Automation Playlists" beginning on page 216.)

8. What tool can you use to add, move, or delete automation breakpoints? What modifier can you use to delete a breakpoint by clicking on it? (See "Editing Breakpoint Automation" beginning on page 217.)

9. What type of plug-in provides real-time processing? What type provides non-real-time processing? (See "Using Plug-In Processors" beginning on page 217.)

10. What are some plug-in options that are available for EQ and dynamics processing? (See "Plug-Ins Provided with Pro Tools" beginning on page 218.)

11. Why is it important to back up your Pro Tools sessions? What are some ways in which your Pro Tools work can be lost accidentally? (See "Backing Up Your Session" beginning on page 220.)

12. How is the Save Copy In command different from the Save As command, in terms of the files that are saved? (See "Saving a Session Copy" beginning on page 220.)

13. Which session will be open after completing a Save Copy In operation: the original or the copy? How is this different from the Save As operation? (See "Saving a Session Copy" beginning on page 220.)

14. What command can you use to save a session with a different sample rate or bit depth? (See "Uses for the Save Copy In Command" beginning on page 220.)

15. What are some considerations for bouncing audio in Pro Tools? How is the bounce affected by soloed or muted tracks? How is it affected by the active selection? (See "Considerations for Bouncing Audio" beginning on page 222.)

16. What command lets you mix your entire session directly to a stereo file? What file types are supported for the bounce file with this command? (See "Bouncing to Disk" beginning on page 222.)

17. What bit depth and sample rate should you use when bouncing to disk if you plan to burn the file to CD without further processing? (See "Using the Bounce to Disk Command" beginning on page 223.)

18. How can you add audio files to iTunes for use in burning a CD? (See "Adding a Bounce File to Your iTunes Library" beginning on page 225.)

To review additional material from this chapter, see the PT101 Study Guide module available through the ElementsIED online learning platform at ElementsED.com.

EXERCISE 10

Automating Shared Effects and Creating a Stereo Bounce

In this exercise tutorial, you will finalize your session. You will start by creating a shared effect using a delay plug-in on an Aux Input track. Then you will automate the delay effect using send mute automation on the VO track. Next you will set basic levels for your tracks, and you'll finish by bouncing the mix to a stereo file.

Duration: 15 to 20 minutes

Media: None

> **Downloading the Media Files**
>
> To complete this exercise, you will need to have access to the audio files that you downloaded and imported previously. If needed, you can re-download the media files by pointing your browser to http://alpp.us/PT101-128.
>
> *Note: The above URL is* ***case sensitive.***

Getting Started

You will start by opening the Pro Tools session you created in Exercise 9. If that session is not available, use the Exercise09 Sample file in the Completed Exercises folder within the PT101 Download Media folder.

Open the session and save it as Exercise 10:

1. Open the session file that you created in Exercise 9 (Storage Drive/Folder > PT101-XXX > Exercise09-XXX.ptx).

   Alternatively, you can use the Exercise08 Sample file (PT101 Download Media > 03. Completed Projects > Exercise09 Sample.ptx).

2. Choose FILE > SAVE AS and name the session *Exercise10-XXX*, keeping the session inside the original session folder (if working from your previous session) or moving the session into your PT101-XXX folder (if working from the sample file).

Creating a Delay Effect

In this part of the exercise, you will create an Aux Input track to function as the delay return, assign a delay plug-in on the track, and create sends from the VO track and the Fire FX track to the delay effect.

Create a delay return:

1. Select the Fire FX track by clicking on its nameplate in the Edit window.
2. Choose **TRACK > NEW** and create a new stereo Aux Input track. A new track named Aux 1 will appear below the Fire FX track.
3. Double-click on the track nameplate for the Aux 1 track and rename it Delay.
4. Choose **WINDOW > MIX** or press **COMMAND+=** (Mac) or **CTRL+=** (Windows) to switch to the Mix window.

Configure the Delay track:

1. Click on the **AUDIO INPUT PATH SELECTOR** for the Delay track (the top selector under the I/O label) and select **BUS > BUS 1-2 (STEREO)**.

Figure 10.23 Audio Input Path selector on the Delay track

2. Click on **INSERT SELECTOR A** for the Delay track (under the Inserts A-E label) and choose **MULTICHANNEL PLUG-IN > DELAY > AIR DYNAMIC DELAY (STEREO)**. The plug-in window will open.
3. Select the **05 TWO AGAINST THREE** preset using the **LIBRARIAN** menu (displaying <factory default>).
4. Lower the **FEEDBACK** parameter to 40% and increase the **MIX** parameter to 100%.

Figure 10.24 The AIR Dynamic Delay plug-in configured for the session

5. Close the plug-in window when you're finished.

Assign sends on the VO and Fire FX tracks:

1. Click on **SEND SELECTOR A** on the Fire FX track (under the Sends A-E label) and select **BUS > BUS 1-2 (STEREO)**. The Send window will open.
2. **OPTION-CLICK** (Mac) or **ALT-CLICK** (Windows) on the Send fader for the Fire FX track to set it to 0.0 dB.
3. Close the Send window when finished.
4. Repeat the above process to assign a send on the VO track.
5. Raise the Send fader for the VO track to around -10.0 dB. Leave the send window open when finished.

Recording Automation and Setting Levels

In this part of the exercise, you enable send mute automation for the session and place the VO track into Write automation mode. Next you will record automation during playback, toggling the mute state on and off for the send from the VO track. Then you will set basic fader levels for all the tracks in your mix.

Prepare the session for automation:

1. Press **COMMAND+=** (Mac) or **CTRL+=** (Windows) to activate the Edit window.
2. Choose **WINDOW > AUTOMATION** to open the Automation window.
3. **OPTION-CLICK** (Mac) or **ALT-CLICK** (Windows) on any enabled (red) automation button in the Automation window to disable all parameters.
4. Next, click on the **SEND MUTE** button (S Mute) to enable only send mute automation for the session. The button will be lit red when enabled. (See Figure 10.25.)

Figure 10.25 Send mute automation enabled in the Automation window

5. Close the Automation window when finished.
6. Click the **MUTE** button (**M**) in the open send window to mute it at the session start.
7. Using the VO track's **AUTOMATION MODE SELECTOR**, put the track into Write automation mode.

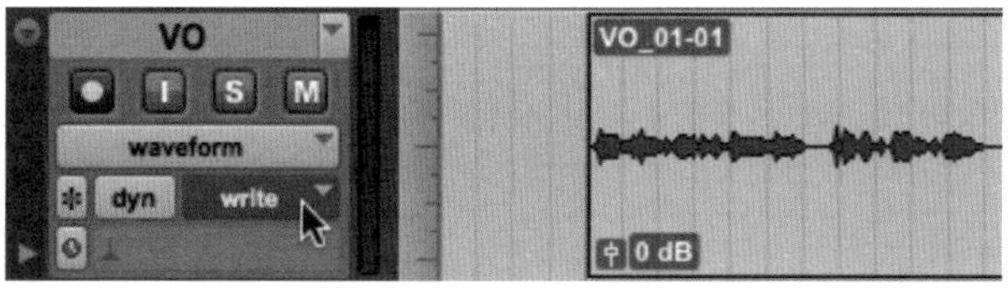

Figure 10.26 Automation Mode selector on the VO track set to Write mode

8. Press **RETURN** (Mac) or **ENTER** (Windows) to return to the session start.

In the next series of steps, you will be muting/unmuting the send on the fly during playback. You may need to practice the timing a few times to get the desired results.

To practice the timing without writing automation, you can keep the track in Read mode while playing through the session and toggling the mute control on/off. Switch back to Write mode when you're ready to record automation.

Record send mute automation:

1. Begin playback, keeping the send muted for approximately 10 seconds.
2. Unmute the send just before the words "baked by the sun." Re-enable the send mute after the word "sun."
3. Continue playback for another approximately 10 seconds with the send muted.
4. Unmute the send again just before the words "sand-free technology." Re-enable the send mute after the word "technology."
5. Continue playback for another 8 seconds or so with the send muted.
6. Unmute the send at the end of the phrase, "stop by Spiccoli's surf shop" as the voiceover reaches the word "today."
7. Allow playback to continue through the end of the session; then press the **SPACEBAR** to stop playback.

   If you are not satisfied with the results, you can place the track back into Write mode and try the automation pass again.

8. When finished, close the send window and set the **AUTOMATION MODE** selector for the VO track back to Read mode.

Set levels for your mix:

1. Press **COMMAND+=** (Mac) or **CTRL+=** (Windows) to activate the Mix window.
2. Begin playback and adjust the levels of each track to achieve a clear, intelligible ad with an appropriate music bed and background effects levels. Following are some suggestions:
   - The voiceover may be a bit low in the mix compared to other elements. Try raising the VO fader by around 2 or 3 dB.
   - The Xpand!2 synthesizer part is a bit too prominent and overpowers the guitar and bass tracks. Try lowering the fader on the Beat Wave track by 6 to 8 dB.
   - The fire sound comes in a bit too loud. Try lowering the fader on the Fire FX track by 4 to 5 dB.

Bouncing to Disk

In this part of the exercise, you will maximize the output levels for the mix using a maximize plug-in on the Master Fader track. Then you will use the Bounce to Disk function to create a stereo file from your session mix.

Maximize the mix output:

1. Click on **INSERT SELECTOR A** for the Master 1 track (under the Inserts A-E label) and choose **MULTICHANNEL PLUG-IN > DYNAMICS > MAXIM (STEREO)**. The plug-in window will open.
2. Press the **SPACEBAR** to begin playback.
3. In the Maxim plug-in window, set the **CEILING** slider around -0.5 dB. This sets the maximum allowable level for the plug-in, limiting the output levels to prevent clipping.
4. While listening to the mix, adjust the **THRESHOLD** slider to achieve a healthy output level without artificially compressing the dynamic range. A setting of around -5 to -7 dB will likely be adequate for this session.

Watch the histogram on the left side of the plug-in. Do not lower the Threshold beyond the top signal level shown in the histogram. (The level bars will turn red when the Threshold is set too low and can result in distortion.)

5. Close the Maxim plug-in window when done.

Bounce the session to a stereo file:

1. Press **COMMAND+=** (Mac) or **CTRL+=** (Windows) to activate the Edit window.
2. Click on the head of the **MIN:SECS** ruler so the ruler becomes highlighted, making it the main timebase.
3. Using the **SELECTOR** tool, make a selection on the VO track beginning at 1 second and extending to 31 seconds (0:01.000 to 0:31.000). Verify the selection using the **START** and **END** fields in the Counter display area.
4. Choose **FILE > BOUNCE TO > DISK** to open the Bounce dialog box.
5. Select the following options for your bounce:
   - File Type: WAV
   - Format: Interleaved

- Bit Depth: 16 Bit
- Sample Rate: 44.1 kHz
- File Name: YourName-SurfShop

6. Leave the other options set to their defaults (or as directed by your instructor) and click the **BOUNCE** button.

   Your stereo bounce will be created and saved in the Bounced Files folder within your session folder.

Finishing Up

Congratulations! Over the course of these exercises, you have created a session from scratch, imported and edited audio, recorded audio and MIDI, added effects, recorded automation, and bounced the result to a stereo file.

1. When your bounce completes, save your session and quit Pro Tools.
2. Verify the location of your bounced file.

   In classroom settings, your instructor may require that you copy this file and/or your session folder to a learning management system, flash drive, or shared network location to submit it for a grade.

For more hands-on experience, see the Music Hands-On Project and the Post Hands-On Project in Section II of this book.

SECTION II

Supplemental Projects

OVERVIEW

Section II of this course includes two supplemental projects (Lessons 11 and 12) that allow you to work with pre-recorded sessions and continue to work with Pro Tools. In theses lessons, you will work on session documents that include Audio, MIDI, and Video files.

Throughout this section, you will apply many of the concepts that you learned in Section I. The goal of the supplemental projects is to illustrate the concepts discussed earlier in the book using straightforward, practical workflows applied to common music and video post-production tasks.

The work you will do in these lessons may also involve advanced functionality not specifically covered earlier in this book. Getting some exposure to these techniques will help broaden your understanding of Pro Tools in the music and post-production environments.

The following pages describe the two supplemental projects included in this course and provide setup instructions for the work you will be doing. Included is a description of Pro Tools system requirements and recommended available disk space for completing the projects.

Getting to Know the Sessions

The mixes that you will complete use real-world sessions provided in incomplete form. You will have the opportunity to work on two different projects, one representing a music production scenario (Lesson 11) and one representing a video post-production scenario (Lesson 12). While these lessons remain focused on the core set of Pro Tools functions described in Section I of the book, you will find that the workflows occasionally introduce concepts that have not been covered. (These concepts are discussed in later courses.)

Project 1

Project 1, the Music Session, is a two-minute segment of a song by The Pinder Brothers. The session consists of 17 tracks in rough form. To complete this project, you will add Audio and Instrument tracks, supplement the drums using the Boom plug-in, add and edit audio and MIDI clips, add an extended intro, and use effects processing to polish the mix.

Project 2

Project 2, the Post Session, is a 45-second commercial spot for Glad Trash Bags consisting of 20 tracks in rough form. To complete this project, you will import video footage as a QuickTime movie, import additional music and sound effects files, make various improvements and enhancements to the audio, replace the music bed, and add effects processing to polish the mix.

Pro Tools System Requirements

To complete these projects, you will need a qualified computer with Pro Tools 12 software installed. Many parts of the projects can be completed using earlier Pro Tools versions with slight modifications in various steps; however, to complete the projects as written, you will need current software. The descriptions and screenshots in this section are based on standard Pro Tools 12.8 software. Some menu commands, preference options, dialog boxes, and user interface features may vary in different software versions.

The projects are designed for compatibility with Pro Tools 12 software using any qualified audio interface or supported built-in audio configuration. However, the projects have not been tested with all configurations.

The projects can also be completed using any current Pro Tools HD software or hardware system, although certain steps may vary slightly.

Media Files for Supplemental Projects

To complete the projects, you will need access to the 04.Hands-On Projects folder on a local hard drive. The Hands-On Projects folder is provided with the Download Media discussed earlier in this book. Files in this folder include session templates, audio files, MIDI files, and other media files required for the projects. If you have not already downloaded the course media files, see the "Download Instructions" section below.

Disk Space Requirements for Project Sessions

You will need space available on your destination drive to store the session files and related media. If possible, select a storage drive that is separate from your system drive to use as the destination for the session files.

The minimum recommended disk space for completing both projects is 1 GB:

- 300 MB for the Music project session files
- 300 MB for the Post project session files
- 300 MB available for recording and creating archive copies

To check the available space on your selected drive, do the following:

- In Windows, click on the **START** icon in the lower left and select **COMPUTER** to view information about the available drives.
- On a Mac, click on the selected drive icon from the desktop and choose **FILE > GET INFO** to display the Information window for the drive.

Download Instructions

If you have not already downloaded the media files for this course, do so before continuing to the projects:

1. Launch Internet Explorer, Safari, or another web browser of your choice.
2. Point the browser to http://alpp.us/PT101-128.

The web address used for downloading the course media files is case sensitive; be sure to enter it exactly as shown.

3. The PT101_DownloadMedia-v12.8.zip file will download; if needed, double click the zip file to extract the PT101 Download Media folder and its contents.
4. Locate the 04. Hands-On Projects folder within the PT101 Download Media folder.
5. If needed, copy the Project 1-Music Session and Project 2-Post Session folders to an appropriate location on a local storage drive.

LESSON 11

Project 1: Music Session

In this lesson, you will complete a session involving a two-minute song snippet. To complete this session, you will add Audio and Instrument tracks, import audio and MIDI clips, use the Boom and Mini Grand virtual instruments, and add EQ and effects processing to polish the mix.

Duration: 90 Minutes

The media files for this project are provided courtesy of Matt Pinder of The Pinder Brothers:

- SONG: Driving You Home (excerpt)
- PERFORMED BY: The Pinder Brothers
- WRITTEN BY: Michael Lee Pinder
- PRODUCED BY: Scott Reams and The Pinder Brothers ©2015

The audio files provided for this project are strictly for use to complete the exercises contained herein. No rights are granted to use the files or any portion thereof in any commercial or non-commercial production or performance.

Project Media Files

To complete this project, you will need to have access to the Download Media folder for this course. If needed, you can download the media files by pointing your browser to http://alpp.us/PT101-128.

*Note: The above URL is **case sensitive**.*

Powering Up

To get started on this project, you will need to power up your system. It is important to power up properly to avoid problems that could possibly damage your equipment.

When using audio equipment, you should power up components in the order that the audio signal will flow through them. The general process for powering up a Pro Tools 12 system is as follows (see your system documentation for powering up a system with HD Native or HDX hardware):

1. Power up external hard drives, if used.
2. Verify connections and power up any audio and/or MIDI interfaces.
3. Start the computer.
4. Launch Pro Tools.
5. Power up your monitoring system, if applicable.

Refer to Lesson 2 for more details on powering up your system.

Opening the Music Project

In this section of the lesson, you will open the session and prepare the files for the work you will be doing.

The session you will use for this project has been saved as a *session template*. When you open the session template, Pro Tools will create a new session based on the template, leaving the original template file unchanged. All existing tracks and audio files used in the template file will be duplicated in your new session.

Locate and Open the Session Template

Pro Tools provides a number of ways to open a session or session template. You can navigate to the session folder in your computer's Explorer or Finder window and double-click on the session or template file to open it. You can also locate and open the session or template file from the Workspace browser.

Locate and open the Music session template:

1. Do one of the following:
   - Navigate to your copy of the session template from the Dashboard or desktop and open it. The template file is located in the PT101 Download Media (v12.8) > 04. Hands-On Projects > Project 1 – Music Session folder and is named *Music Project-Starter.ptxt*.

   - Or -

   - Locate the session template using the Workspace browser inside of Pro Tools:
     a. If the Dashboard is displayed, click the **CANCEL** button to dismiss it.
     b. Choose **WINDOW > NEW WORKSPACE > DEFAULT.**
     c. Click the **ADVANCED SEARCH** button (magnifying glass with a plus sign) to display the advanced search settings.
     d. Type "Music Project-Starter" in the text field (including the quotes) and click the **ADD ROW** button (plus sign) to add a second search filter.

e. Specify [KIND] [IS] [SESSION FILE TEMPLATE] using the pop-up menus in the second row.

After a few moments the session template will display in the Workspace browser.

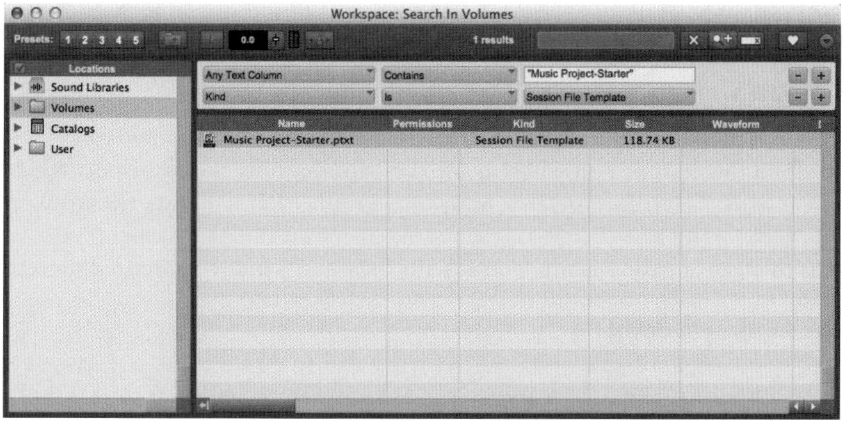

Figure 11.1 Session template displayed in a Workspace browser window

f. Double-click on the template file to open it.

A dialog box will open, displaying default parameters for the template.

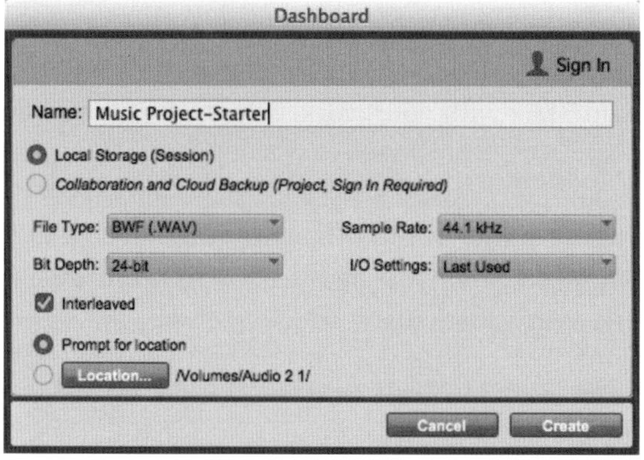

Figure 11.2 Parameters dialog box for the Music project

2. Name the session Music Project-XXX, replacing the Xs with your initials.

3. Click CREATE to accept the settings. A second dialog box will open, prompting you for a save location.

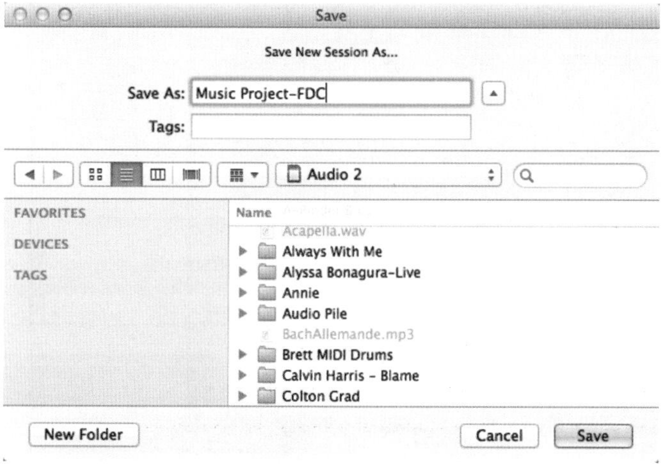

Figure 11.3 Save dialog box for the Music project

4. Navigate to an appropriate location and click **SAVE**. The session will open with the Edit window displayed.

Refer to Lesson 4 for additional information on locating and opening sessions.

Orient the Session Windows

When the session opens, the Edit window will be displayed on screen. You will use this window for much of the arranging and editing you do in this lesson. You will also use the Mix window, the Transport window, and the Score Editor window. As you work, you may need to reposition and resize the windows from time to time.

You can use the following steps to create a basic starting point, with the main windows cascaded on screen.

Set a starting position and size for the windows:

1. If you used the Workspace browser to open the session, close it by choosing **WINDOW > WORKSPACES > CLOSE ALL WORKSPACES.**
2. Open both the Mix window (**WINDOW > MIX**) and the Transport window (**WINDOW > TRANSPORT**).
3. Press **COMMAND+=** (Mac) or **CTRL+=** (Windows) to toggle to the Edit window and bring it to the front.
4. Choose **WINDOW > ARRANGE > CASCADE** to arrange the Mix and Edit windows in a cascading fashion.

   (Alternatively, you can maximize each window as you open them for full-screen views.)
5. Position the Transport window where it will least interfere with your work. Try the top or bottom of the screen.

The 17 tracks in the session are displayed horizontally (left to right) in the Mix window and vertically (top to bottom) in the Edit window. (See Figure 11.4.) From time to time, you might need to scroll each window and/or reposition the Transport window to view and work with a particular track.

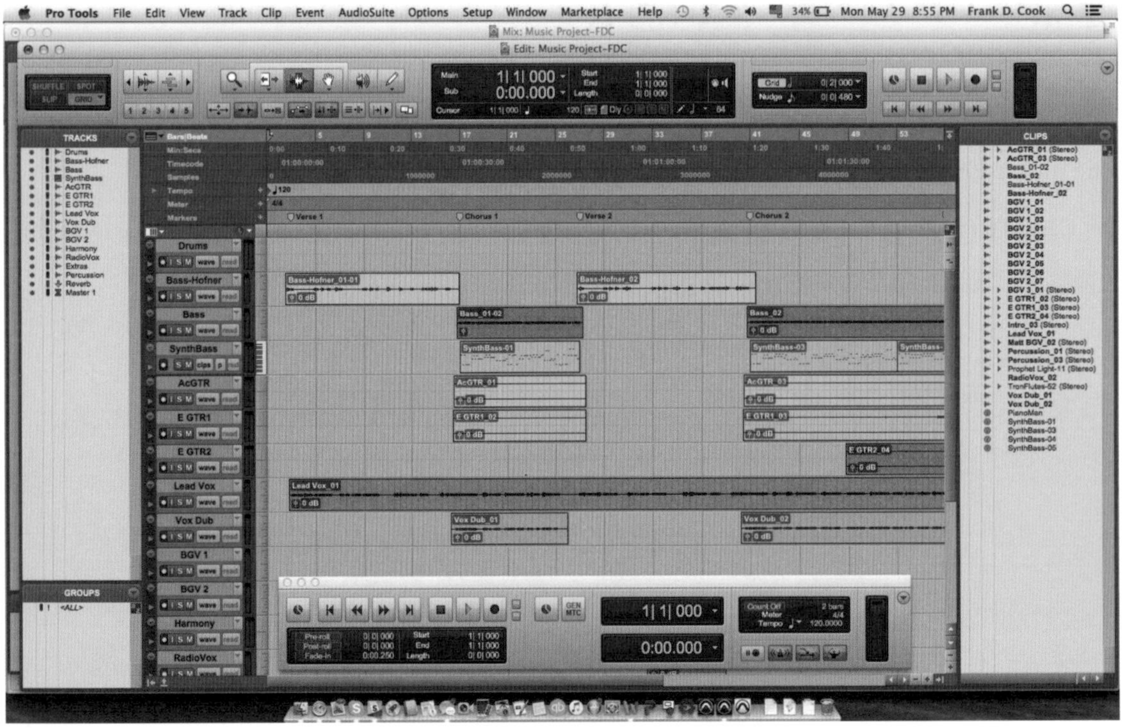

Figure 11.4 Session windows oriented for the start of the project

Set the Preferences

This project requires certain Preference settings. Before continuing, you will need to verify the Zoom Toggle Preference settings for your session. You will also need to ensure that the Link Track and Edit Selection option is on and Insertion Follows Playback is off. Pro Tools makes these options available under the Options menu as well as via buttons in the Edit window toolbar.

Check Preferences settings:

1. Choose **SETUP > PREFERENCES**. The Preferences dialog box will open.
2. Click on the **EDITING** tab.
3. In the **ZOOM TOGGLE** section of the Editing tab, select the following settings (see Figure 11.5):
   - Verify that both **VERTICAL MIDI ZOOM** and **HORIZONTAL ZOOM** are set to Selection.
   - Verify that **REMOVE RANGE SELECTION AFTER ZOOMING IN** is unchecked.
   - Set **TRACK HEIGHT** to Jumbo.
   - Set **TRACK VIEW** to Last Used.
   - Verify that **ZOOM TOGGLE FOLLOWS EDIT SELECTION** is unchecked.

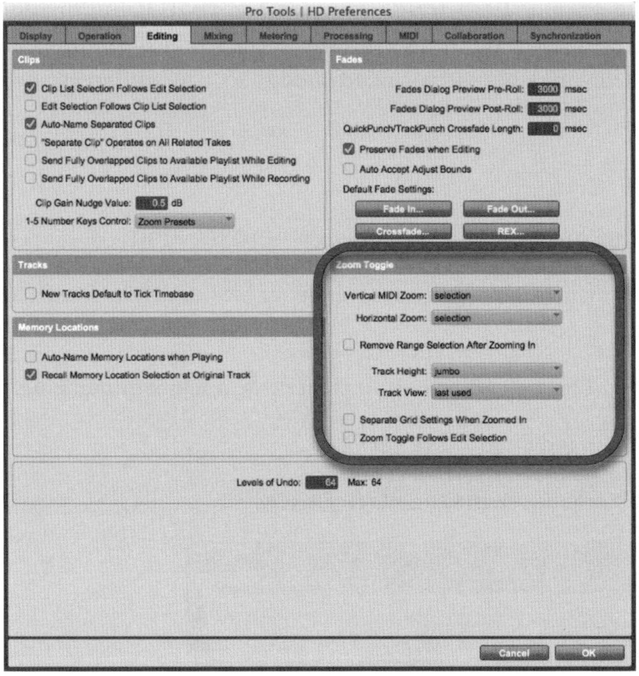

Figure 11.5 Preference settings for Zoom Toggle under the Editing tab

4. Click **OK** to close the Preferences dialog box.

Check other settings:

1. Verify that **LINK TRACK AND EDIT SELECTION** is enabled (checked) under the **OPTIONS** menu. The corresponding button will be lit blue in the Edit window toolbar (below the Scrubber tool on the left).
2. Verify that the **INSERTION FOLLOWS PLAYBACK** button is off (unlit) in the Edit window toolbar (below the Scrubber tool on the right).

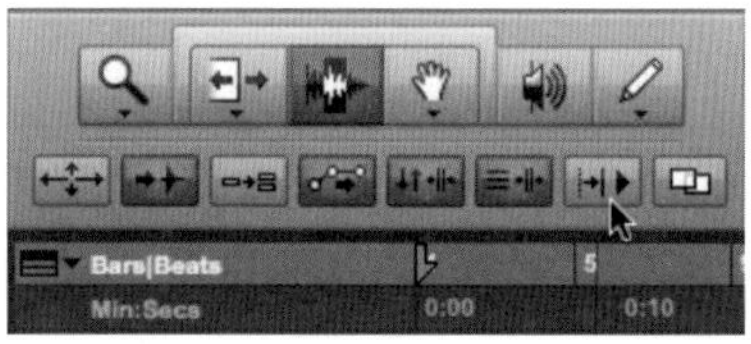

Figure 11.6 Insertion Follows Playback button in the Edit window (under the cursor)

Connect Monitoring Devices

If you have a monitoring system connected to the left and right outputs of your audio interface, you will use that to listen to the session playback. If you do not have a monitoring system, you can listen to the session playback using headphones on a compatible interface or on your computer (if using onboard sound output). Plug in your headphones to an available headphone jack and test the output and playback level.

Creating New Tracks

In this section of the project, you will create the new tracks needed for the session. Additional details on the commands and processes used in this section can be found in Lesson 4.

Create and Name Tracks

You will need to create two new tracks for the session. Both tracks will play back MIDI information using virtual instruments. When creating tracks, you will select the track type and format, based on how each track will be used. In this case, the tracks will be used for stereo virtual instruments, so you will create two stereo Instrument tracks.

Create new Instrument tracks:

1. If needed, activate the Edit window by clicking on it or by choosing WINDOW > EDIT.
2. Choose TRACK > NEW. The New Tracks dialog box will open, displaying Mono, Audio Track, and Samples as default selections from left to right.
3. Type the number **2** into the number field. This will allow you to create two tracks simultaneously.
4. Click on the TRACK FORMAT pop-up menu and choose STEREO.
5. Click on the TRACK TYPE pop-up menu and choose INSTRUMENT TRACK.

Figure 11.7 New tracks dialog box configured for adding Instrument tracks to your session

6. Click CREATE. The new tracks will be added to the session.

Name and reposition your new tracks:

1. Double-click on the nameplate of the first Instrument track (Inst 1) to open the Track Name dialog box.
2. Type BEATS in the Name the Track field.
3. Add comments to help identify the track function, such as "Instrument – Boom."

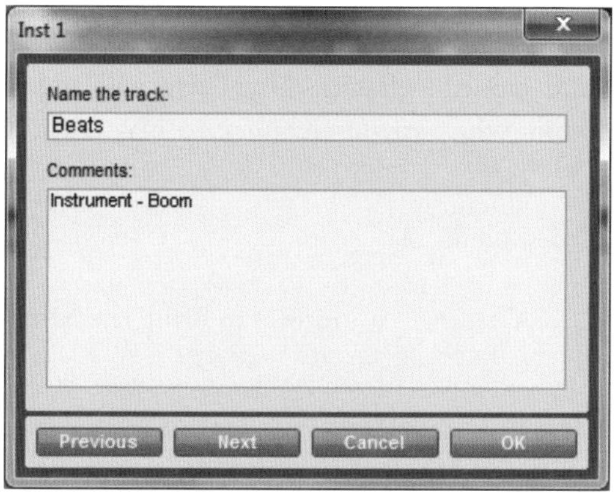

Figure 11.8 Naming the Beats track

4. Click the NEXT button. You will see Inst 2 displayed.
5. Type PIANO in the Name the Track field and add comments, such as "Instrument – Mini Grand."
6. Click OK. The tracks will display with their new names.
7. With both tracks still selected, click on the nameplate of the Beats track and drag the tracks to the top of the Tracks display area in the Edit window (above the Drums track).

Figure 11.9 New tracks positioned at the top of the Edit window

Save Your Session

After making any significant changes to a session, it is a good idea to save your work. Doing so will minimize any rework that you might have to do in the event of a disruption (such as a power outage or accident).

Save your work:

- Choose FILE > SAVE to save your progress up to this point.

Working with MIDI Data

For this section of the project, you will add the Boom and Mini Grand virtual instrument plug-ins to your Instrument tracks, add a MIDI clip from the Clip List, and create MIDI data using a variety of Edit tools.

Add a Virtual Instrument

In the previous section, you created an Instrument track and named it **Beats**. Now, you will add a virtual instrument to this track using the Boom plug-in. This will allow the Instrument track to play back an audio drum instrument triggered by MIDI data.

Insert Boom onto the Beats track:

1. Choose **WINDOW > MIX** or press **COMMAND+=** (Mac) or **CTRL+=** (Windows) to bring the Mix window forward and make it active.
2. Scroll the Mix window as needed to locate the **Beats** track.
3. Next, click on **INSERT SELECTOR A** on the **Beats** track.

Figure 11.10 Insert selector A on the Beats track at the top left (Mix window)

4. Choose **MULTICHANNEL PLUG-IN > INSTRUMENT > BOOM (STEREO)** from the pop-up list. The Boom plug-in window will appear on screen.
5. Click on the **LIBRARIAN** menu (currently set to **<factory default>**) and choose **068 - 085 > A BILLION 076**.

Figure 11.11 Selecting a preset for the Boom plug-in

6. Click on the **CLOSE** button in the upper-left corner (Mac) or upper-right corner (Windows) of the Boom window to close the plug-in.

Create a MIDI Clip

Pro Tools provides a variety of ways to create MIDI data. In this section, you will use the Pencil tool to trigger playback of the Boom virtual instrument.

Draw MIDI data to control pattern playback of Boom:

1. Press **COMMAND+=** (Mac) or **CTRL+=** (Windows) to toggle back to the Edit window.
2. Click in the piano roll area immediately to the right of the track meter on the Beats track. The Track Height pop-up menu will appear.

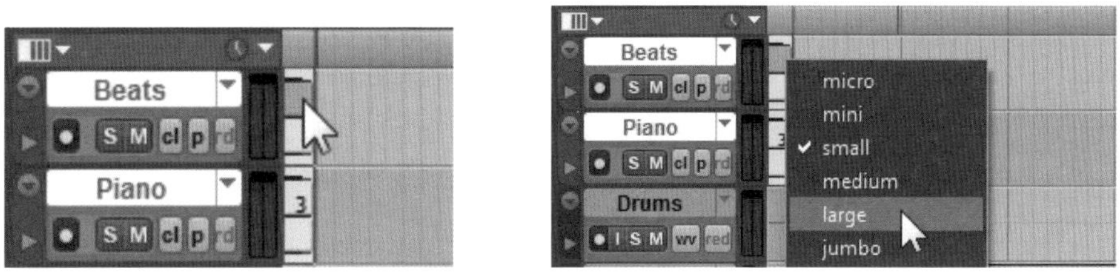

Figure 11.12 Clicking in the piano roll area of the Beats track (left) and choosing a track height (right)

3. Choose **LARGE** from the pop-up menu to set the track height for the Beats track.
4. Click on the **TRACK VIEW SELECTOR** of the Boom track (currently set to Clips) and choose **NOTES** from the pop-up menu.

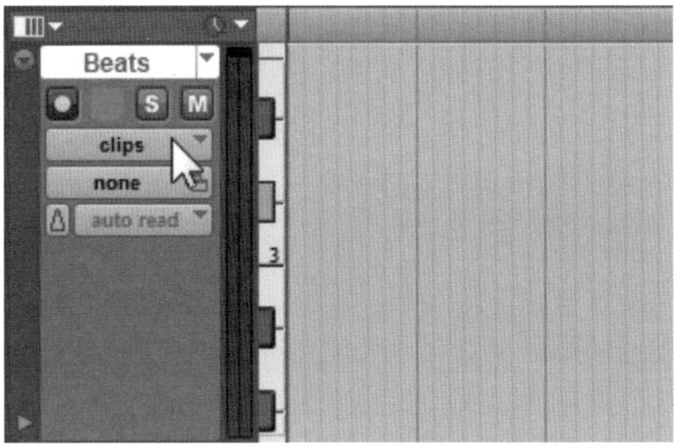

Figure 11.13 Clicking on the Track View selector to select Notes view

5. With the **PENCIL** tool, draw a note beginning at 41|1|000 and extending to 57|1|000. (Use the Bars|Beats ruler as a reference.) You may need to trim the note to get the perfect length.

MIDI notes in the range of C3 through D#4 each trigger a different pattern in Boom. You can drag the note up or down to select a different pattern.

6. Click and hold on the note to audition the current pattern; drag the note up or down to select the desired pattern. (The pattern at C3 will work well for this piece, but feel free to experiment.)

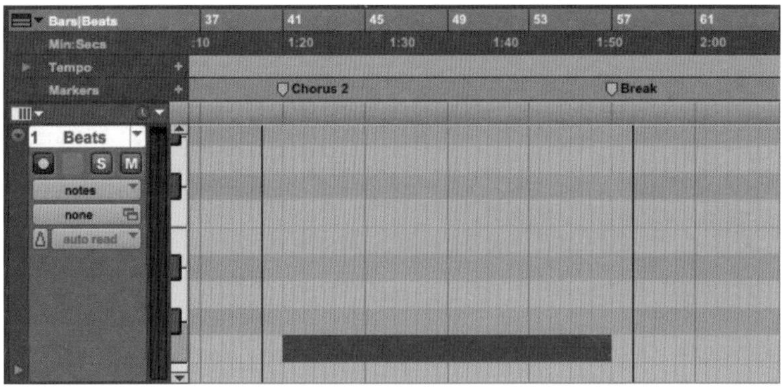

Figure 11.14 MIDI note on the Beats track

7. Press the SPACEBAR to audition the Boom drum pattern with your session. Press the SPACEBAR a second time to stop playback. If needed, adjust the note position to change the pattern and audition again until you're happy with the playback.

Add Another Virtual Instrument

In the previous section, you added a Boom virtual instrument plug-in to the Beats track. Now, you will add the Mini Grand virtual instrument plug-in to the Piano track.

Insert Mini Grand on the Piano track:

1. Choose **Window > Mix** or press **Command+=** (Mac) or **Ctrl+=** (Windows) to again activate the Mix window.
2. Click on **Insert Selector A** on the Piano track.
3. Choose **Multichannel Plug-In > Instrument > Mini Grand (Stereo)** from the pop-up list. The Mini Grand plug-in window will appear on screen.

Figure 11.15 The Mini Grand instrument plug-in

4. Click on the **Librarian** menu (currently set to <factory default>) and choose the **10 Soft Pop Piano** preset.

5. Click on the CLOSE button in the upper-left corner (Mac) or upper-right corner (Windows) of the Mini Grand window to close the plug-in.

Drag in a MIDI Clip

The session's Clip List includes a MIDI clip containing a previously recorded MIDI piano performance for this song. You will now bring it onto the Piano track.

Drag the PianoMan clip onto the Piano track:

1. Toggle back to the Edit window by choosing WINDOW > EDIT or pressing COMMAND+= (Mac) or CTRL+= (Windows).
2. Locate the PianoMan clip in the Clip List.
3. With the GRABBER tool, select the PianoMan clip and drag it from the Clip List onto the Piano track. Position the clip to start at the Verse 1 marker (3|1|000).
4. Solo the Piano track by clicking on the track's SOLO button (labeled "S") in the Edit window under the track name.

You can also toggle Solo mode on and off for any track containing the Edit cursor by pressing SHIFT+S on the computer's QWERTY keyboard.

5. Press the SPACEBAR to audition the MIDI piano for a few measures. Press the SPACEBAR a second time to stop playback.
6. Unsolo the Piano track and audition a few measures again, in context with the session, to verify the timing.
7. If necessary, adjust the clip placement to ensure that it begins at 3|1|000.

Edit a MIDI Performance

Next you need to edit the SynthBass track to help key passages stand out more. To do this, you will edit the velocities of the MIDI events on the SynthBass track.

View the MIDI velocity stalks on the SynthBass track:

1. Locate the SynthBass track in the Edit window.
2. With the GRABBER tool, select the first clip on the track (SynthBass-01).
3. Press CONTROL+E (Mac) or START+E (Windows) on your keyboard to activate Zoom Toggle. The selection will expand, filling the available space in the window.
4. Click on the TRACK VIEW SELECTOR for the SynthBass track and choose VELOCITY from the pop-up menu, if not already displayed.

Figure 11.16 Clicking on the Track View selector on the SynthBass track

The Velocity view displays velocity stalks associated with each MIDI note, representing their individual velocity values. (The taller the stalk, the higher the velocity value.)

Edit the velocities for the first clip:

1. Enable Loop Playback mode by choosing **OPTIONS > LOOP PLAYBACK**. A loop arrow will display on the Play button in the Transport window.
2. Press the **SPACEBAR** to play back the selection and allow it to continue playing throughout this section.
3. With the **GRABBER** tool, click any open area of the track to deselect all of the notes in the clip.
4. With the **GRABBER** tool still active, click on the diamond at the top of the last velocity stalk in the clip (at the right of the screen) so that it becomes selected.

   The diamond will turn white, and the corresponding note will become highlighted.
5. Press and hold the **SHIFT** key while clicking on each of the preceding five velocity stalks so that the last six velocity stalks are selected.
6. Click any selected velocity stalk and drag it upward to the top of the range. This will increase the velocity of all highlighted notes, making them more prominent.

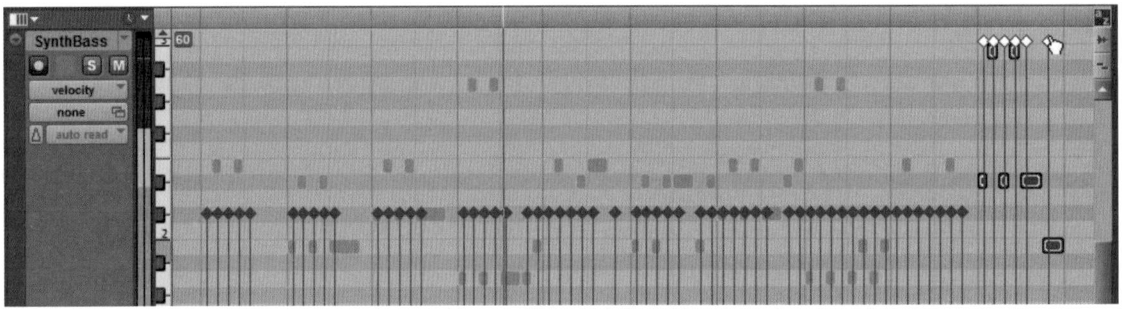

Figure 11.17 Raising velocity stalks of selected notes

7. When you are satisfied with the result, stop playback.
8. Press **CONTROL+E** (Mac) or **START+E** (Windows) on your keyboard to return the session to its previous view.

Next you will make a similar change at the end of the session.

Edit the velocities for the end of the session:

1. Click on **ZOOM PRESET 2** to zoom in a bit.
2. Scroll the Edit window horizontally as needed to locate the SynthBass-04 clip (second-to-last SynthBass clip on the track).
3. With the **GRABBER** tool, select the SynthBass-04 clip.
4. Press **CONTROL+E** (Mac) or **START+E** (Windows) to activate Zoom Toggle. The selection will expand, and the track will switch to Velocity view.
5. Click any selected velocity stalk and drag it upward to the top of the range to make the selected notes more prominent.
6. Press **CONTROL+E** (Mac) or **START+E** (Windows) to return the session to its previous view.

Save Work in Progress

As you complete each main portion of the project, you should save your work in progress. This will protect your work while the session is open.

Save your work:

- Choose FILE > SAVE to save your progress up to this point.

Working with Audio Data

In the next section of the project, you will use a variety of techniques to manipulate audio clips.

Import an Audio File to a Track

As you've already seen, the Workspace browser is a great resource for locating, opening, and importing all sorts of media files. For this part of the project, you will use a Workspace browser to import an audio file containing the drums for the song.

Arrange the Edit window for importing:

1. Press RETURN (Mac) or ENTER (Windows) to return to the start of the session.
2. Click on ZOOM PRESET 4 to zoom in a few levels.
3. Scroll the Edit window vertically so that the Drums track is positioned at the top of the window.
4. Click in the amplitude scale area immediately to the right of the track meter on the Drums track and choose LARGE from the pop-up menu.

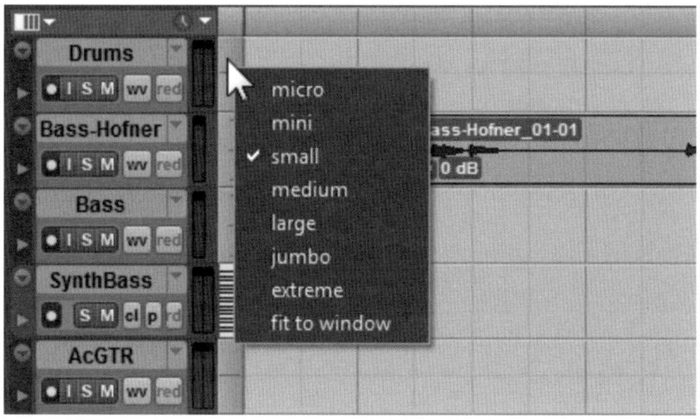

Figure 11.18 Track height pop-up menu for the Drums track

Locate the DrumMix audio file with a Workspace browser:

1. Choose WINDOW > NEW WORKSPACE > DEFAULT to open a Workspace browser window.

You can also press OPTION+I (Mac) or ALT+I (Windows) to open a new Workspace browser window.

2. Click the ADVANCED SEARCH button (magnifier with a plus) to display advanced search settings.
3. Type DrumMix in the text field and click the ADD ROW button (plus sign) to add a second search filter.

4. Specify **[KIND] [IS] [AUDIO FILE]** using the pop-up menus in the second row.

   After a few moments the DrumMix.wav file will appear in the Workspace browser.

Drag the audio file to the Drums Audio track:

1. Reposition the Workspace browser as needed so that you can see the Drums track above it in the Edit window.
2. Drag the DrumMix.wav audio file from the Workspace browser onto the Drums track.
3. Close the Workspace browser to reduce on-screen clutter.
4. Use the **GRABBER** tool to drag the DrumMix file to start at 10|1|000.

Use the Bars|Beats Ruler as a reference while positioning the DrumMix file.

5. Press the **SPACEBAR** to audition a few bars of the session with the drums. Press the **SPACEBAR** a second time when finished to stop playback.

Import a Clip Group to a Track

For this part of the project, we'll return to the Workspace browser to import a clip group. A clip group can be thought of as simply a collection of individual clips grouped together to look and act as a single, larger clip.

Scroll the BGV tracks into view:

- Scroll the Edit window vertically so that the BGV 1 and BGV 2 tracks are visible on screen.

Locate the Background Vocals clip group with the Workspace browser:

1. Choose **WINDOW > NEW WORKSPACE > DEFAULT** to open a Workspace browser.
2. Click the **ADVANCED SEARCH** button (magnifier with a plus) to display the advanced search settings.
3. Type BGVox in the text field and click the **ADD ROW** button (plus sign) to add a second search filter.
4. Specify **[KIND] [IS] [CLIP GROUP FILE]** using the pop-up menus in the second row.

   After a few moments the BGVox.cgrp file will appear in the Workspace browser.

Drag the clip group to the BGV 1 and BGV 2 Audio tracks:

1. Reposition the Workspace browser, if necessary, so you can see both the BGV 1 and BGV 2 tracks in the Edit window and the BGVox.cgrp clip group in the Workspace browser.
2. Drag the BGVox.cgrp file from the Workspace browser onto the BGV tracks in the Edit window. Be sure that both tracks are targeted destinations for the clip group as you drag.
3. Drop the clip group anywhere on the targeted tracks.
4. Close the Workspace browser to reduce on-screen clutter.
5. Use the **GRABBER** tool to drag the BGVox file to start at 16|1|000.

Listen to the progress so far:

1. Press RETURN (Mac) or ENTER (Windows) to go to the beginning of the session.
2. Press the SPACEBAR to begin playback.
3. When finished, press the SPACEBAR again to stop playback.

Insert Time

For this part of the project, we're going to add four bars to the start of the song.

Select the location to insert time at the beginning of the song:

1. Press RETURN (Mac) or ENTER (Windows) to set the Edit Selection Start to 1|1|000.
2. In the Edit Selection Length field at the top of the Edit window, enter **4|0|000**:
   - Click in the first field to activate it and type **4**. The remaining fields will zero out.
   - Press RETURN (Mac) or ENTER (Windows) to confirm the entry.

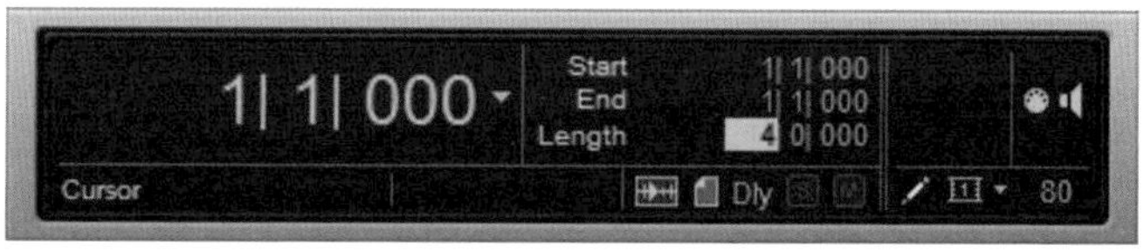

Figure 11.19 Entering the Edit Selection Length values

You will now have a four-bar selection spanning from Bar 1 to Bar 5.

Use the Insert Time operation to add the selected amount of time:

1. Choose EVENT > TIME OPERATIONS > INSERT TIME. The Time Operations window will appear on screen.
2. Verify that the Start, End, and Length times are correct. The values should be the following:
   - START: 1|1|000
   - END: 5|1|000
   - LENGTH: 4|0|000

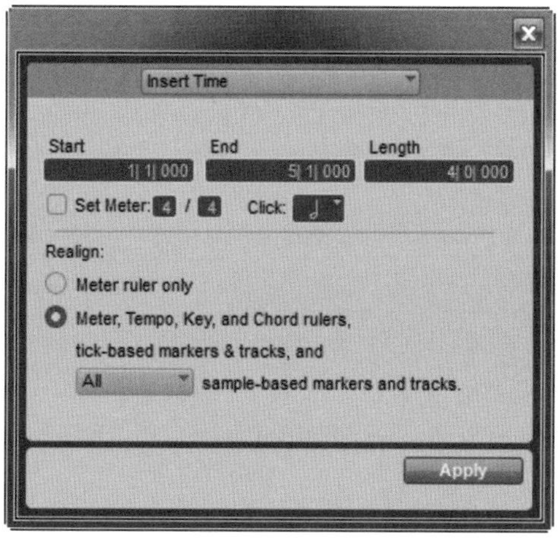

Figure 11.20 The Time Operations window

3. Click **APPLY**. Four bars will be added at the start of the session.
4. Close the Time Operations window.

Edit the Tracks

Next, we're going to edit the tracks to complete the audio arrangement.

Edit the Extras track:

1. If necessary, scroll the Edit window so that the Extras track is visible on screen.
2. Locate the Intro_03 clip in the Clip List and drag it to the start of the Extras track.

Edit the Harmony track:

1. Locate and select the Harmony track. The Edit selection will move to the selected track.
2. Press **OPTION+RETURN** (Mac) or **CTRL+ENTER** (Windows) to move to the end of the session.
3. Click the **SPOT** button in the upper-left corner of the Edit window to activate Spot mode.
4. Use the **GRABBER** tool to select the Matt BGV_02 clip at the end of the track. The Spot dialog box will open.
5. Set the Time Scale to **BARS|BEATS**, if needed.
6. In the Start field, type 34|1|000 and click **OK**. The clip will move to Bar 34.

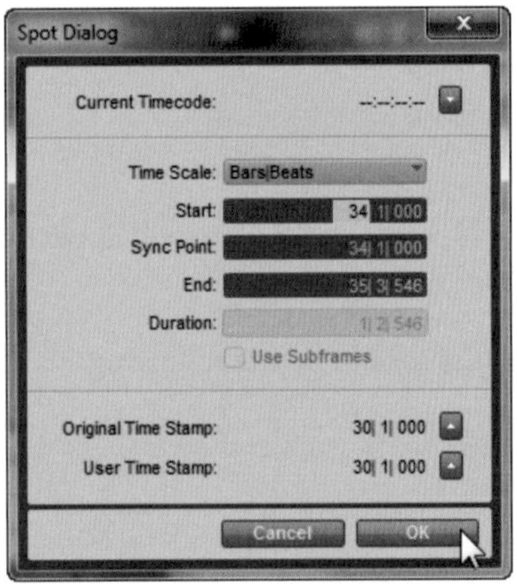

Figure 11.21 The Spot dialog box

7. Press the **LEFT** Arrow key to scroll to the clip and confirm its location.
8. Click the **GRID** button to reactivate Grid mode.

Listen to the edits:

1. Press **ENTER** (Windows) or **RETURN** (Mac) to go to the beginning of the session.
2. Double-click on **ZOOMER** tool to zoom all the way out.
3. Press the **SPACEBAR** to begin playback. Listen for the new intro on the Extras track and the harmony vocal part on the Harmony track.
4. Press the **SPACEBAR** a second time when finished.

Save Work in Progress

You have now imported and arranged all audio files and completed the editing tasks needed for the session. You should take this opportunity to save your work.

Save your work:

- Choose FILE > SAVE to save your progress up to this point.

Mixing in Pro Tools

Now that the editing is complete, you will use some of the mixing features in Pro Tools to add real-time processing to the project and blend the sound elements together. You will complete this work using the Mix window.

Add EQ

The SynthBass track has a little too much low end, causing it to overshadow the bass guitar and kick drum. To fix the problem, you will use the EQ III plug-in to roll off some of the low end.

Insert the 1-Band EQ III plug-in on the SynthBass track:

1. Scroll the Edit window vertically to display the SynthBass track. Then click on the SynthBass-01 clip on the track with the Grabber tool to select it.
2. Choose WINDOW > MIX or press COMMAND+= (Mac) or CTRL+= (Windows) to activate the Mix window.
3. Click on INSERT SELECTOR B of the SynthBass track.

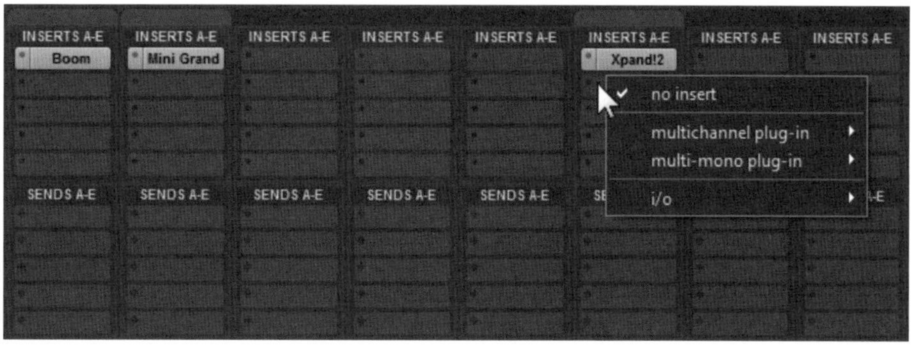

Figure 11.22 Selecting an amp type in the Eleven Free plug-in

4. Choose MULTICHANNEL PLUG-IN > EQ > EQ3 1-BAND (STEREO) from the pop-up menu. The 1-Band EQ III plug-in window will appear.
5. In the 1-Band EQ III plug-in window, select the HIGH-PASS filter type.

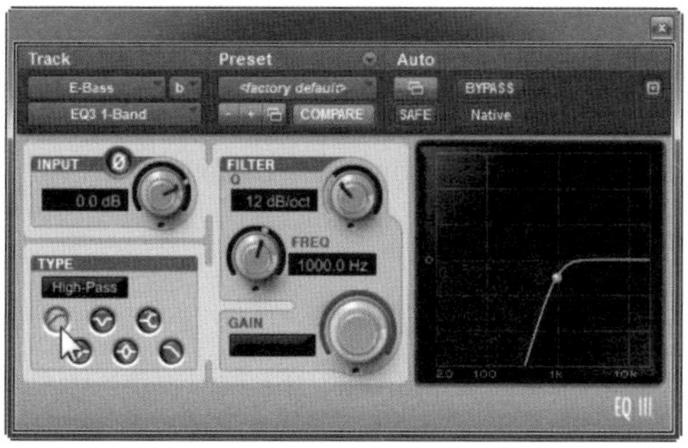

Figure 11.23 Using the High-Pass filter in the EQ III plug-in window

Adjust the EQ to roll off the low end:

1. Solo the SynthBass track by clicking on the **SOLO (S)** button just above the Volume Fader in the Mix window.
2. Press the **SPACEBAR** to initiate playback.
3. In the 1-Band EQ III plug-in window, drag the gray ball to the left or right until you hear the desired reduction in low frequencies when playing back (try around 95 to 125 Hz).
4. Unsolo the SynthBass track and listen to the EQ in context. Try toggling the **BYPASS** button on/off to hear the change.
5. Adjust the EQ frequency as needed; press the **SPACEBAR** when finished to stop playback.
6. Close the EQ III plug-in window to reduce on-screen clutter.

Add Effects to the RadioVox Track

In this part of the project, you will use an EQ plug-in along with the Eleven Free plug-in to emulate the sound of an old transistor radio on the RadioVox track.

Insert the 7-Band EQ III plug-in on the RadioVox track:

1. Scroll the Mix window as needed to locate the RadioVox track towards the right side of the window.
2. Click on **INSERT SELECTOR A** of the RadioVox track and choose **PLUG-IN > EQ > EQ3 7-BAND (MONO)** from the pop-up menu. The 7-Band EQ III plug-in window will appear.
3. In the 7-Band EQ III plug-in window, click on the **LIBRARIAN** menu (currently set to <factory default>) and choose **SPECIAL EFFECTS > TELEPHONE 2 – 7 BAND.**
4. Close the EQ III plug-in window to reduce on-screen clutter.

Insert the Eleven Free plug-in on the RadioVox track:

1. Click on **INSERT SELECTOR B** of the RadioVox track and choose **PLUG-IN > HARMONIC > ELEVEN FREE (MONO)** from the pop-up menu. The Eleven Free plug-in window will appear.
2. In the Eleven Free plug-in window, click on the Librarian Menu (currently set to <factory default>) and select the **DC VINTAGE CRUNCH** preset.

Adjust the Eleven Free settings:

1. Solo the Lead Vox and RadioVox tracks by clicking on the **SOLO (S)** buttons for each track, just above their Volume Faders in the Mix window.
2. Open the Memory Locations window (**WINDOW > MEMORY LOCATIONS**) and click on **NOW OR NEVER** to select an appropriate playback range for auditioning.

> **If needed, you can resize the Memory Locations window by clicking on any window border and dragging with the double-headed arrow.**

3. Press the **SPACEBAR** to initiate playback.
4. In the Eleven Free plug-in window, lower the **GAIN** setting on the left side of the DC Vintage amp head to reduce the distortion. (Try a setting between 2 and 3.)

Figure 11.24 Adjusting the Gain control (left side) for the DC Vintage amp

5. Increase the MASTER setting on the right side of the amp head to increase the output level and make up for the reduced gain. (Try a setting between 7 and 8.)
6. Adjust the tone controls for the amp to add more character. Try the following settings:
   - BASS: 5
   - MIDDLE: 7.5
   - TREBLE: 8
   - PRESENCE: 8
7. Unsolo the Lead Vox and RadioVox tracks to hear the effect in context. When finished, press the SPACEBAR to stop playback.
8. Close the Eleven Free plug-in window to reduce on-screen clutter.

Add Reverb

Next, you will add some reverb to the background vocal tracks to help them blend into the mix. This project already includes an Aux Input track that was previously set up with the Reverb Bus routed to its input and the AIR Reverb plug-in configured on Insert A.

Additionally, Send A on the BGV 1 and BGV 2 tracks has been assigned to the Reverb Bus. Therefore, all you will need to do is increase the level of the send on the two tracks to add reverb to the mix.

Increase the Send A level on the background vocal tracks:

1. Click on WAITED TOO LONG in the Memory Locations window to select an appropriate area for auditioning.
2. Click on SEND ASSIGNMENT A on the BGV 1 track. The Send A window will appear. (See Figure 11.25.)
3. Click the SOLO (S) button at the bottom of the Send A window to solo the BGV 1 track.
4. Press the SPACEBAR to begin playback.

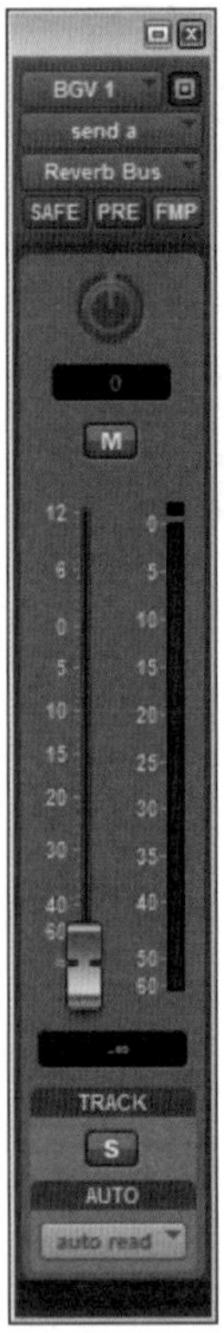

Figure 11.25 The Send A window

5. While listening to the track, raise the level on the Send Fader to introduce reverb. (Try between –9 and –5 dB.)

   The reverb will play back while the BGV track is soloed because the Reverb track is set to Solo Safe mode. Solo Safe mode is commonly used on Aux Input tracks to prevent them from being muted when another track is soloed.

You can place a track in Solo Safe mode by or COMMAND-CLICKING (Mac) or CTRL-CLICKING (Windows) on the Solo button in the Edit or Mix window.

More information on Solo Safe mode can be found in the Pro Tools 110 course.

6. When you are satisfied with the results, press the SPACEBAR to stop playback.
7. Press the SOLO (S) button to take the track out of Solo mode and then close the Send A window.
8. Repeat Steps 2 through 7 for the BGV 2 track. Stop playback when finished.

Save Work in Progress

Before continuing with work on your session mix, you should take this opportunity to save your work.

Save your work:

- Choose FILE > SAVE to save your progress up to this point.

Mix the Project

The project is now ready for mixing to blend all of the tracks together. You will use the Volume Faders and Pan knobs to create an effective stereo mix. The focus of your mixing changes will be the vocal tracks and the piano track.

Getting Started

To get started, you will listen carefully to the entire session to determine the contribution of each of the main tracks (vocals and piano) to the overall mix.

Listen to the main tracks:

1. Click the RETURN TO ZERO button in the Transport window to place the insertion point at the beginning of the Timeline.

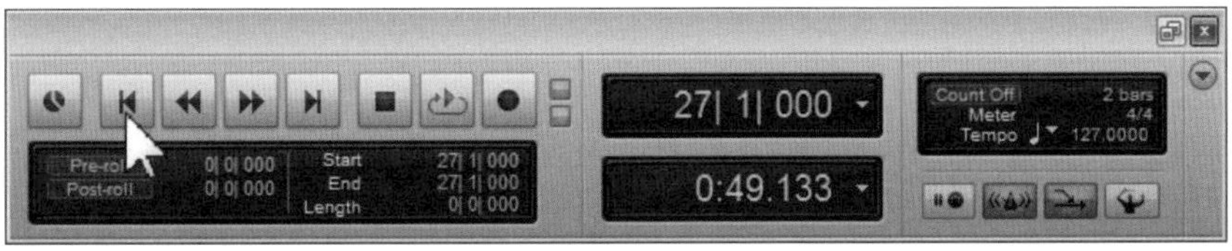

Figure 11.26 Transport window

2. Press the SPACEBAR to begin playback.
3. Listen critically to the session, focusing on the lead vocal level (Lead Vox track), the piano level (Piano track), and the blend of the various other vocal tracks (Vox Dub, BGV 1, BGV 2, Harmony, and RadioVox).
   - Consider how each track contributes to the overall mix and what level adjustments are needed for each track.
   - Consider the stereo balance and what panning changes might improve the stereo image or provide unique placement for individual voices on mono tracks. (Notice that the Lead Vox track has existing pan automation, so its stereo placement cannot be modified during playback.)
   - As you listen, select certain areas of the song to focus on, such as each of the choruses and the section containing the clip on the RadioVox track. (Use the Memory Locations window to move between sections of the session.)
   - Solo individual tracks or groups of vocal tracks to help identify the contribution of each track.

Adjusting the Mix

Complete this portion of the project using your discretion, experimenting with volume and pan settings on the piano and vocal tracks until you are happy with the results.

Mix the main tracks:

1. In the Mix window, use the Volume Faders and Pan knobs (mono tracks only) to give some stereo separation to your mix. Offset panning to the left or right to help distinguish each track in the mix.

   Here are some suggested settings that you can use as a baseline. Feel free to alter these settings using your discretion.

   - **Piano** — Fader: -6.5, Pan: NA (stereo)
   - **Lead Vox** — Fader: +3.0, Pan: NA (automated)
   - **Vox Dub** — Fader: +2.0, Pan: 45 >

- **BGV 1** — Fader: 0.0, Pan: < 50
- **BGV 2** — Fader: 0.0, Pan: 50 >
- **Harmony** — Fader: 0.0, Pan: NA (stereo)
- **RadioVox** — Fader: +2.5, Pan: 40 >

2. When you are finished, press the SPACEBAR again to stop playback.
3. Close the Memory Locations window to reduce onscreen clutter.

Save Work in Progress

You have now created a complete mix for your project. You should take this opportunity to save your work.

Save your work:

- Choose FILE > SAVE to save your progress up to this point.

Finishing Your Work

For this part of the project, you will use the Score Editor to print a score for the Piano and SynthBass tracks. You will then create a stereo bounce of your session mix. Lastly, you will archive your work. This process will allow you to create a backup of your work without consuming excess disk space with unnecessary files.

Print the Score

It is often useful to create a score of a finished session. This might be used as a reference for live performance of the song. It could also be sent for copyright submission or to a publisher for licensing.

Open the Score Editor and modify the score setup:

1. Press RETURN (Mac) or ENTER (Windows) to ensure that the insertion point is located at the beginning of the Timeline.
2. Choose WINDOW > SCORE EDITOR to open the Score Editor window. It may take a moment for the window to open.

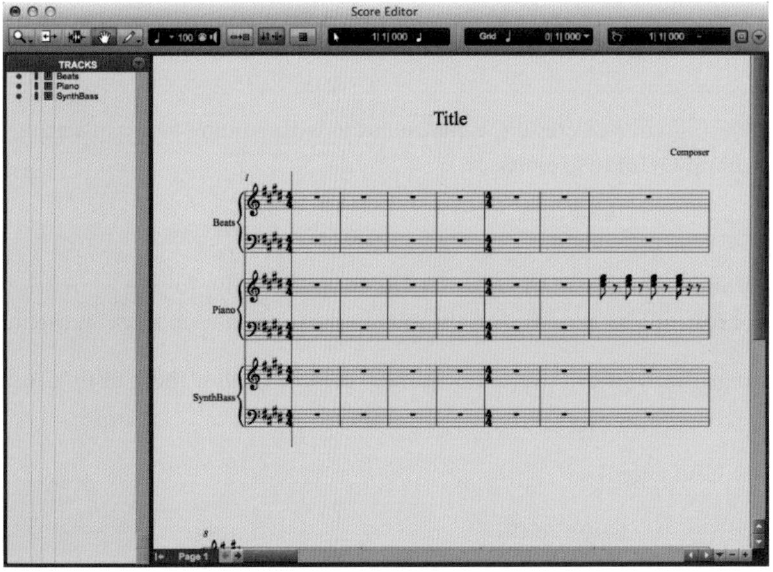

Figure 11.27 Score Editor window

3. Resize or maximize the window, as desired.

4. Right-click in the Score Editor and select **SCORE SETUP** or choose **FILE > SCORE SETUP** to open the Score Setup window.

5. In the Score Setup window, enter a title for the composition in the Title field and enter your name in the Composer field.

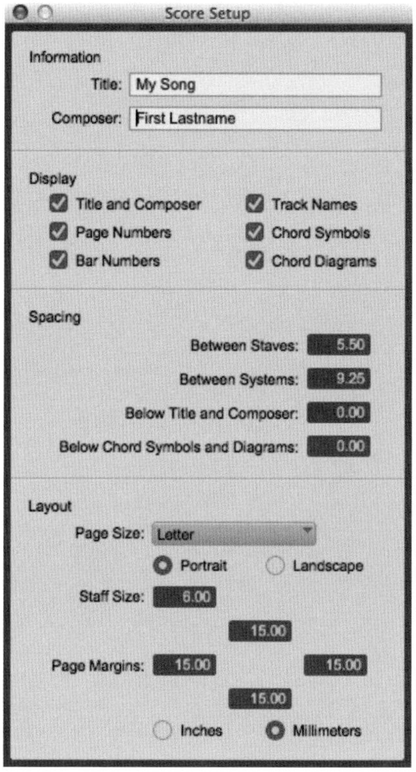

Figure 11.28 Score Setup window

6. Close the Score Setup window when finished.

Determine which tracks will be included in the score:

1. If it is not already visible, display the Track List by clicking the Show/Hide Track List button at the bottom left of the Score Editor.

2. Show or hide tracks as desired by clicking on the **TRACK SHOW/HIDE** icon to the left of each track name in the Track List. The icon will turn light gray to indicate a hidden track. (See Figure 11.29.)

   For this project, hide the Beats track so that only the Piano and SynthBass tracks are shown in the Score Editor.

Figure 11.29 Track List after hiding the Beats track

Configure the staff and print the score:

1. Right-click in the Score Editor and select NOTATION DISPLAY TRACK SETTINGS from the pop-up menu or double-click on a CLEF symbol on the SynthBass track. The Notation Display Track Settings dialog box will open.
2. With the track set to SynthBass, click on the CLEF pop-up menu and change it from Grand Staff to Bass Clef.

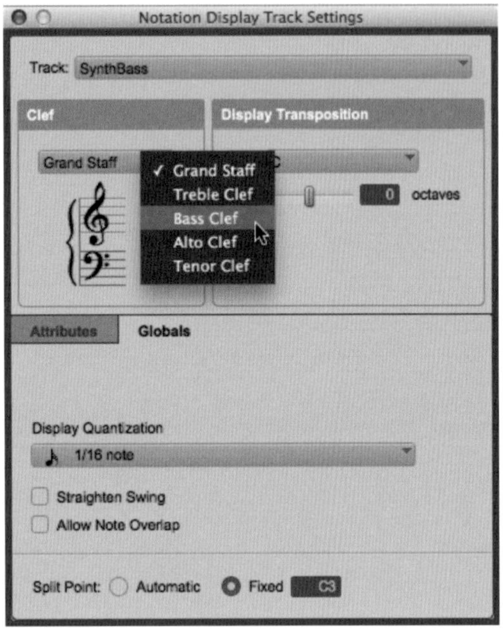

Figure 11.30 Setting the clef for the SynthBass track

3. Close the dialog box.
4. Right-click in the Score Editor again and choose PRINT SCORE or choose FILE > PRINT SCORE. The Print dialog box will open.
5. Configure the Print dialog settings as desired and click PRINT to print the score.
6. When you are finished, close the Score Editor window.

Add Maxim

Next, you will add a Maxim plug-in to the Master Fader. Maxim is a type of plug-in commonly referred to as an *ultra-maximizer*. The purpose of this type of plug-in is to maximize the overall level of the mix, while simultaneously limiting peaks to prevent clipping. The end result is a mix that sounds louder while preserving the overall quality of the mix.

Maxim performs "look-ahead" analysis, anticipating peaks in audio material and preserving attack transients during reduction. This makes Maxim more transparent and maintains the character of the original audio signal without clipping or distortion.

Insert the Maxim plug-in on the Master Fader:

1. In the Mix window, click on INSERT SELECTOR A of the Master 1 track and choose MULTICHANNEL PLUG-IN > DYNAMICS > MAXIM (STEREO). The Maxim plug-in window will appear. (See Figure 11.31.)

2. In the Maxim plug-in window, be sure that the Dither **ON** button is disabled (unlit). (You will insert a separate dither plug-in later.)

Figure 11.31 The Maxim plug-in window

Adjust the Maxim settings to make the mix louder:

1. Open the Memory Locations window (**WINDOW > MEMORY LOCATIONS**) and click on **CHORUS 1** to place the insertion point at the beginning of the chorus.
2. Press the **SPACEBAR** to initiate playback.
3. In the Maxim plug-in window, set the **CEILING** slider to –0.1 dB. This sets the maximum allowable level for the limiting function of Maxim.
4. While listening to the mix, adjust the **THRESHOLD** slider to achieve the desired volume. Adjusting the slider down increases the volume. A good starting point for this mix is around –3.5 dB.

Be careful not to lower the Threshold slider too far, as this can introduce distortion. Use the histogram on the left side of the plug-in window to gauge the input signal level and existing dynamic range.

5. When you're happy with the overall level of the mix, press the **SPACEBAR** to stop playback.
6. Close the Maxim window and the Memory Locations window to reduce on-screen clutter.

Add Dither

Next, you will make an external bounce of the finished project. The purpose of the bounce is to produce a CD-quality stereo audio file that you can burn to an audio CD using iTunes. For this, you will need to create a 16-bit audio file from your 24-bit session. To do so, you will need to add dither to the Master Fader. Dithering helps preserve the quality of audio during bit reduction, preventing quantization errors and LSB clipping.

As a rule of thumb, you should always add dither when bouncing to a lower bit depth.

Add dither to the Master Fader:

1. In the Mix window, click on INSERT SELECTOR B of the Master 1 track and choose MULTICHANNEL PLUG-IN > DITHER > POW-R DITHER (STEREO). The POW-r Dither plug-in window will open.

2. Choose the following settings in the POW-r Dither plug-in window:

   - 16 bit
   - Noise Shaping Type 3

Figure 11.32 The POW-r Dither plug-in

3. Close the POW-r Dither plug-in window.

Dither will now be added to your mix during playback.

Bounce the Song

For this part of the project, you will use the Bounce to Disk command to make a stereo file from your session and add it to your iTunes library.

Make a 16-bit stereo bounce of your session:

1. Press COMMAND+= (Mac) or CTRL+= (Windows) to toggle to the Edit window.

2. With the SELECTOR tool, click anywhere in the session.

3. Press RETURN (Mac) or ENTER (Windows) to place the insertion point at the start of the session.

4. Press OPTION+SHIFT+RETURN (Mac) or CTRL+SHIFT+ENTER (Windows) to make a selection extending to the end of the session.

5. Choose FILE > BOUNCE TO > DISK. The Bounce dialog box will appear on screen.

6. Select the following settings in the Bounce dialog box:

   - FILE TYPE: WAV
   - FORMAT: Interleaved
   - RESOLUTION: 16 bit
   - SAMPLE RATE: 44.1 kHz
   - ADD TO ITUNES LIBRARY: Checked (if you do not have iTunes installed, this option will do nothing)
   - FILE NAME: Music Project-Your Initials
   - OFFLINE: Checked

   Leave all other settings at their default or as specified by your instructor.

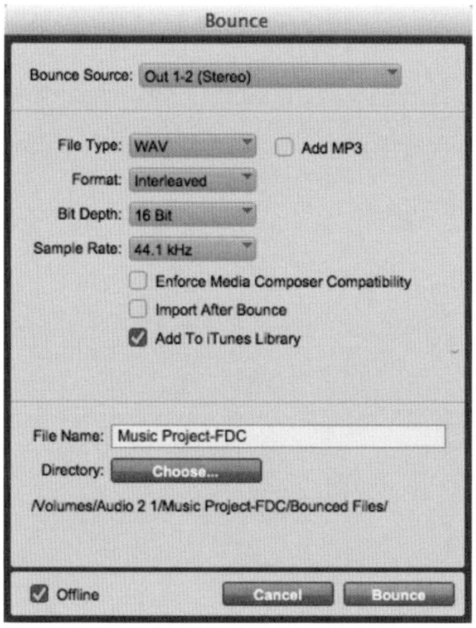

Figure 11.33 Settings for the Bounce dialog box

7. Click **BOUNCE**. A progress bar for the bounce will appear on screen.

   When the bounce completes, iTunes will launch and import the bounced file to the iTunes music library. A copy of the bounced file will also be available in the Bounced Files folder within your session folder.

Archive Your Work

Now that your project is complete, you have the option to back it up for storage. On a real-world project, you might also need to deliver the session to the client. If you are completing this project in an academic classroom environment, you may be required to submit your work to your instructor for grading.

Because many files are associated with a session, something could get lost if the archival process isn't completed properly. In this section, you will use the Save Copy In command to collect all of your session's media files into a new location. This will ensure that your archive includes all of the files you need for the session.

To save a copy of your session and all associated files, do the following:

1. Choose **FILE > SAVE COPY IN**. The Save Copy In dialog box will appear on screen.
2. In the **ITEMS TO COPY** area, place a check next to **AUDIO FILES**.
3. Click the **OK** button. A Save dialog box will appear.
4. Choose a directory to store the session archive and name the archive copy. If possible, it is best to choose a directory on a drive other than the one used for the current session.
5. Click the **SAVE** button. Pro Tools will begin processing the save, copying the session file along with all of the audio files into the directory you chose.
6. Choose **FILE > CLOSE SESSION** to close the original session. If you are prompted to save, choose **OK** or **SAVE** to save your changes in the original session.

This concludes the Music Hands-On Project. If you are completing this work in an academic environment, please check with your instructor for submittal requirements; be sure to include the bounced audio file from your original session folder with your session archive, as appropriate.

Project 2: Post Session

In this lesson, you will work with a 45-second commercial spot consisting of 20 tracks in rough form. To complete the session, you will import video footage as a QuickTime movie, import additional music and sound effects files, make various improvements and enhancements to the audio, and add effects processing to polish the mix.

Duration: 90 Minutes

The media files for this project are provided courtesy of Robert Campbell at One Union Recording:

- **Chief Creative Officer:** Lisa Bennett
- **Director of Production:** Frank Brooks
- **Creative Director:** Mike Andrews
- **Copywriter:** Brett Landry
- **Art Director:** Dave Cuccinello
- **Producer:** Bryan Holt
- **Client:** Glad Trash Bags

The audio and video files provided for this project are to be used only to complete the exercises contained herein. No rights are granted to use the files or any portion thereof in any commercial or non-commercial production or video.

Project Media Files

To complete this project, you will need to have access to the Download Media folder for this course. If needed, you can download the media files by pointing your browser to http://alpp.us/PT101-128.

*Note: The above URL is **case sensitive**.*

Powering Up

To get started on this project, you will need to power up your system. It is important to power up properly to avoid problems that could possibly damage your equipment.

When using audio equipment, you should power up components in the order that the audio signal will flow through them. The general process for powering up a Pro Tools 12 system is as follows (see your system documentation for powering up a system with HD Native or HDX hardware):

1. Power up external hard drives, if used.
2. Verify connections and power up any audio and/or MIDI interfaces.
3. Start the computer.
4. Launch Pro Tools.
5. Power up your monitoring system, if applicable.

Refer to Lesson 2 for more details on powering up your system.

Opening the Post Project

In this section of the lesson, you will open the session and prepare the files for the work you will be doing.

The session you will use for this project has been saved in a *session template*. When you open the session template, Pro Tools will create a new session based on the template, leaving the original template file unchanged. All existing tracks and media files used in the template file will be duplicated in your new session.

Locate and Open the Session Template

Pro Tools provides a number of ways to open a session or session template. You can navigate to the session folder in your computer's Explorer or Finder window and double-click on the session or template file to open it. You can also locate and open the session or template file from the Workspace browser.

Locate and open the Post session template:

1. Do one of the following:
   - Navigate to your copy of the session template from the Dashboard or desktop and open it. The template file is located in the PT101 Download Media (v12.8) > 04. Hands-On Projects > Project 2 – Post Session folder and is named *Post Project-Starter.ptxt.*

   - Or -

   - Locate the session template using the Workspace browser inside of Pro Tools:
     a. If the Dashboard is displayed, click the CANCEL button to dismiss it.
     b. Choose WINDOW > NEW WORKSPACE > DEFAULT.
     c. Click the ADVANCED SEARCH button (magnifying glass with a plus sign) to display the advanced search settings.
     d. Type "Post Project-Starter" in the text field (including the quotes) and click the ADD ROW button (plus sign) to add a second search filter.

e. Specify **[KIND] [IS] [SESSION FILE TEMPLATE]** using the pop-up menus in the second row.

After a few moments the session template will display in the Workspace browser.

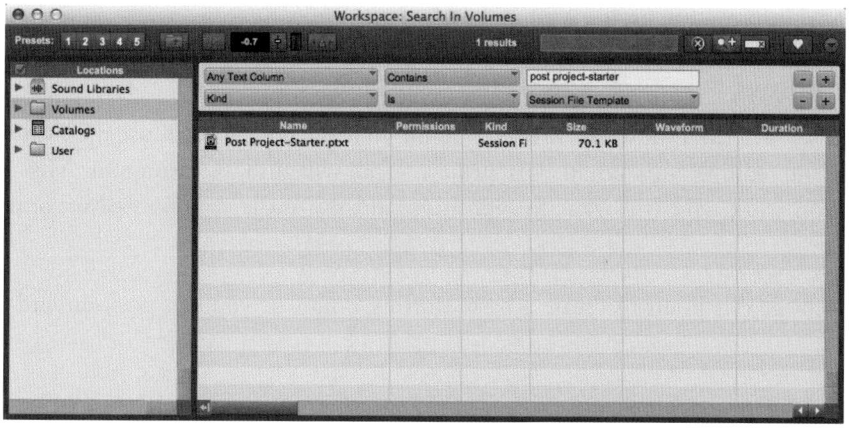

Figure 12.1 Session template displayed in the Workspace browser

f. Double-click on the template file to open it.

A dialog box will open, displaying default parameters based on the template.

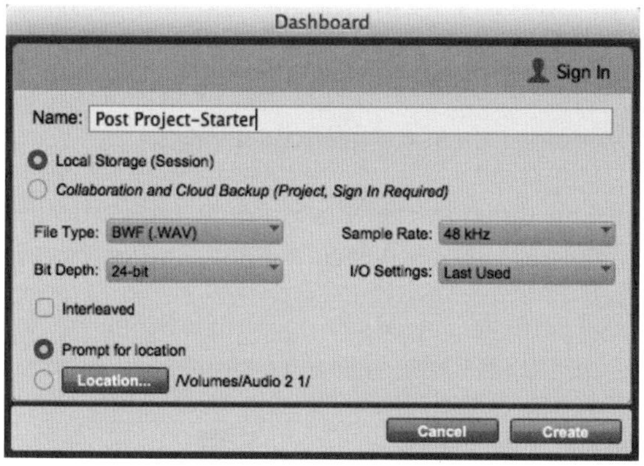

Figure 12.2 Parameters dialog box for the Post project

2. Name the session Post Project-XXX, replacing the Xs with your initials.
3. Click **CREATE** to accept the settings. A second dialog box will open, prompting you for a save location.

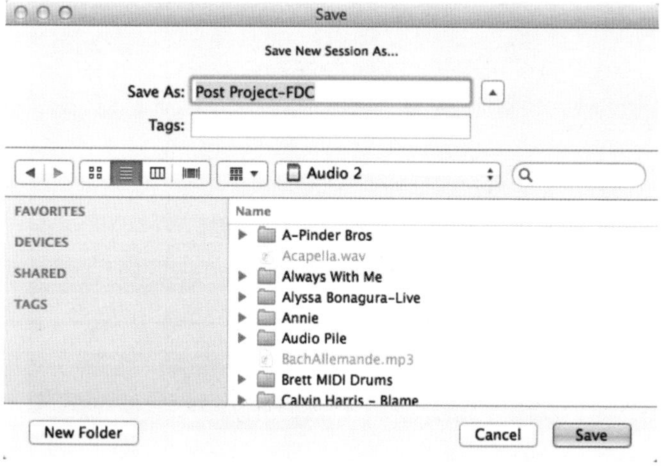

Figure 12.3 Save dialog box for the Post project

4. Navigate to an appropriate location and click **SAVE**. The session will open with the Edit window displayed.

Refer to Lesson 4 for additional information on locating and opening sessions.

Orient the Session Windows

When the session opens, you will see the Edit window displayed on your screen. You will use the Edit window for much of the recording and editing you do in this project. You will also be using the Mix window throughout the project. As you work, you will want to reposition and resize the windows to maximize your efficiency.

You can use the following steps at this point to create a basic starting point, or you can position and size the windows as you go.

Set a starting position and size for the windows:

1. If you used the Workspace browser to open the session, close it by choosing **WINDOW > WORKSPACES > CLOSE ALL WORKSPACES**.
2. Choose **WINDOW > MIX** to open the Mix window.
3. Press **COMMAND+=** (Mac) or **CTRL+=** (Windows) to toggle to the Edit window and bring it to the front.
4. Choose **WINDOW > ARRANGE > CASCADE** to arrange the Mix and Edit windows in a cascading fashion.

   (Alternatively, you can maximize each window as you open them for full-screen views.)

The 20 tracks in the session are displayed horizontally (left to right) in the Mix window and vertically (top to bottom) in the Edit window. From time to time, you might need to scroll each window and/or reposition the Transport window to view and work with a particular track.

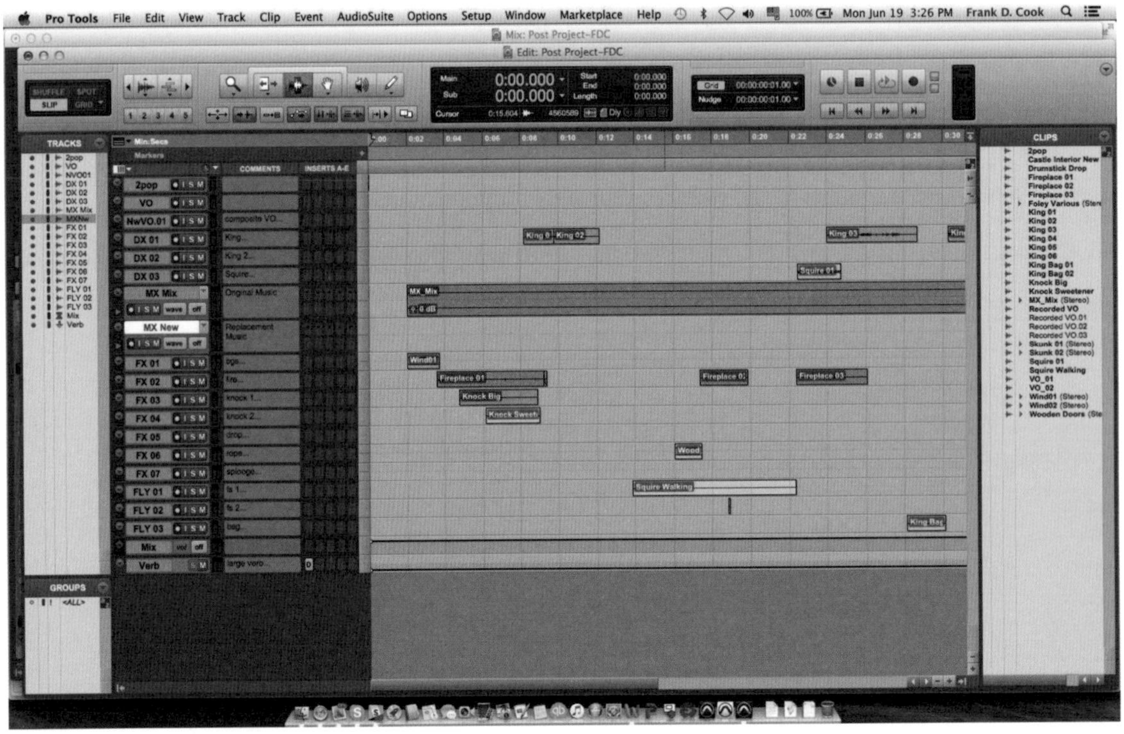

Figure 12.4 Session windows oriented for the start of the project

Set the Preferences

For this project, you will need to configure certain Preference settings that affect the placement of the insertion point/selection during operation. Before continuing, make sure the following Preferences are set accordingly.

Some Preference settings may vary on older systems.

Check Preferences settings:

1. Choose **SETUP > PREFERENCES**. The Preferences window will open.
2. Click on the **OPERATION** tab and verify that **EDIT INSERTION FOLLOWS SCRUB/SHUTTLE** is checked in the top left.

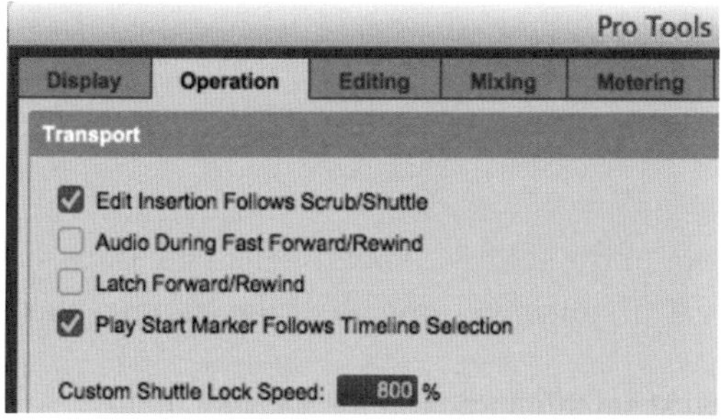

Figure 12.5 Preference settings under the Operation tab

3. Click on the **EDITING** tab and verify that **EDIT SELECTION FOLLOWS CLIP LIST SELECTION** is checked in the Clips section at the top left.
4. Select the following settings in the Zoom Toggle section toward the bottom right:
   - Set **TRACK HEIGHT** to Jumbo.
   - Set **TRACK VIEW** to Waveform / Notes.

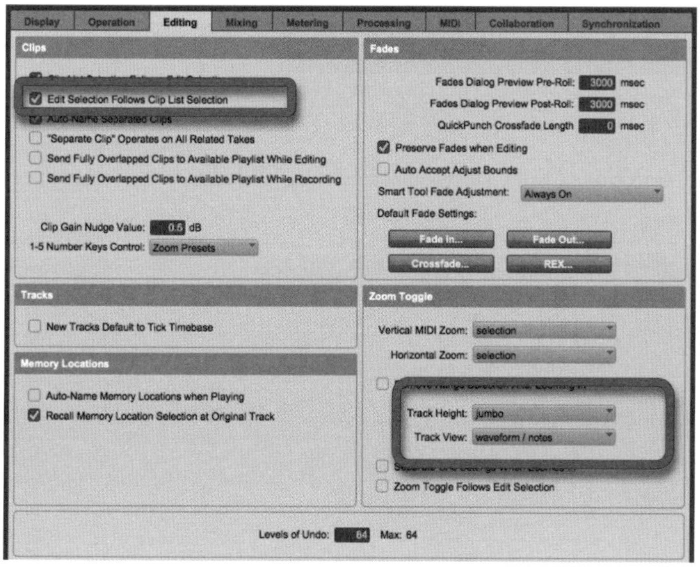

Figure 12.6 Preference settings under the Editing tab

5. Click **OK** to close the Preferences dialog box.

Connect Monitoring Devices

If you have a monitoring system connected to the left and right outputs of your audio interface, you will use that to listen to the session playback. If you do not have a monitoring system, you can listen to the session playback using headphones on a compatible interface or on your computer (if using onboard sound output). Plug in your headphones to an available headphone jack and test the output and playback level.

Creating New Tracks

In this section of the project, you will create a new track needed for the session. Additional details on the commands and processes used in this section can be found in Lesson 4.

Create and Name a Track

For this project, you will need to create one new track that you will use to edit a sound effect. When creating tracks, you should always select the track type and format based on how the tracks will be used. In this case, you will need to edit a stereo sound effect, so a stereo Audio track will be appropriate.

Create a stereo Audio track:

1. Click on the FX 07 track nameplate toward the bottom of the Edit window to select the track. This will ensure that the new track appears directly below the FX 07 track, keeping all of the FX tracks together.

Pro Tools always places new tracks below the lowest selected track in the session. If no tracks are selected, Pro Tools places the new track(s) at the bottom of the session.

2. Choose TRACK > NEW. The New Tracks dialog box will open, displaying Mono, Audio Track, and Samples as default selections from left to right.
3. Click on the TRACK FORMAT selector and choose Stereo from the pop-up menu.

Figure 12.7 Clicking the Track Format selector to create a stereo track

4. Click CREATE in the New Tracks dialog box. A new stereo track will be added to the session, beneath the FX 07 track.
5. Double-click on the track name (Audio 1) to open the Track Name dialog box.
6. Type FX 08 in the Track Name field and add comments to help identify the track function, such as "Skunk FX." (See Figure 12.8.)
7. Click OK. The track will display with its new name.

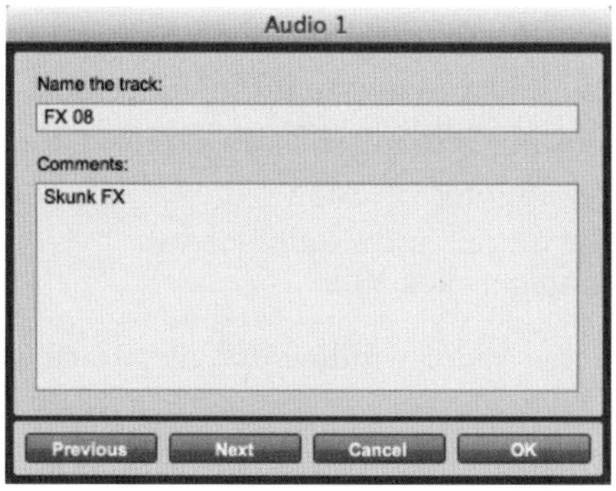

Figure 12.8 Renaming the Audio 1 track

Save Your Session

After making any significant changes to a session, it is a good idea to save your work. That way, if something should disrupt your progress (such as a power outage), you will not have to redo any of your work.

Save your work:

- Choose FILE > SAVE to save your progress up to this point.

Importing Media

Pro Tools provides many ways to import media into your session. For this project, you will import a movie and background music using the Import command, and you will import sound effects using a Workspace browser window.

Import a Movie

In this section, you will import a QuickTime movie and enhance it with music and sound effects.

Import GiftBasket.mov into your session:

1. Choose FILE > IMPORT > VIDEO. A dialog box will open on screen, allowing you to select a video file.
2. Navigate to the VIDEO FILES folder within the Project 2 - Post Session folder from your download media: PT101 Download Media > 04. Hands-On Projects > Project 2–Post Session > Video Files.

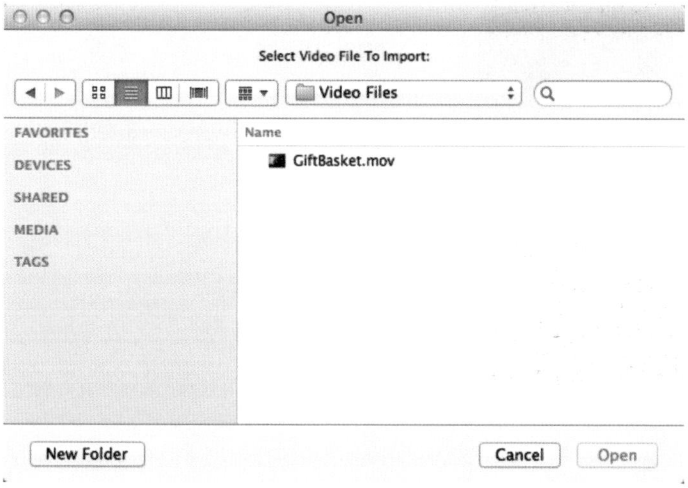

Figure 12.9 Dialog box for importing a video file

3. Select **GiftBasket.mov** and click **Open**. The Video Import Options dialog box will appear.
4. Uncheck the **Import Audio from File** option in the dialog box, if it is selected.
5. Select **Session Start** in the Location menu and click **OK**.
6. If a dialog box appears asking whether to enable the Video Engine, click **Yes**.

   The movie will be imported into your session and will open in a Video window. A Video track will also display at the top of the Edit window.

Figure 12.10 The Video window as displayed after importing GiftBasket.mov (start of the session shown)

If you need to resize the Video window, click and drag near any window edge or border.

View the movie clip (optional):

1. Press **Return** (Mac) or **Enter** (Windows) to move the insertion point to the beginning of the Timeline.
2. Press the **spacebar** to begin playback. The movie clip will play along with the audio in the session.

Figure 12.11 The Video window during playback

3. When the clip ends, press the **spacebar** again to stop playback. The insertion point will return to the beginning of the Timeline.

Import Files to the Clip List

Next, you will need to import some additional music files into your session and place them in the Clip List for later use.

Import music audio files to the Clip List:

1. Choose FILE > IMPORT > AUDIO.
2. In the Import Audio dialog box, navigate to the New Music folder within the Project 2–Post Session folder from your download media.
3. Select the four New Music files (click on the first and then Shift-click on the last to select them all) and click the ADD button (or ADD FILES button on Windows). The files will be added to the Clips to Import area of the dialog box.

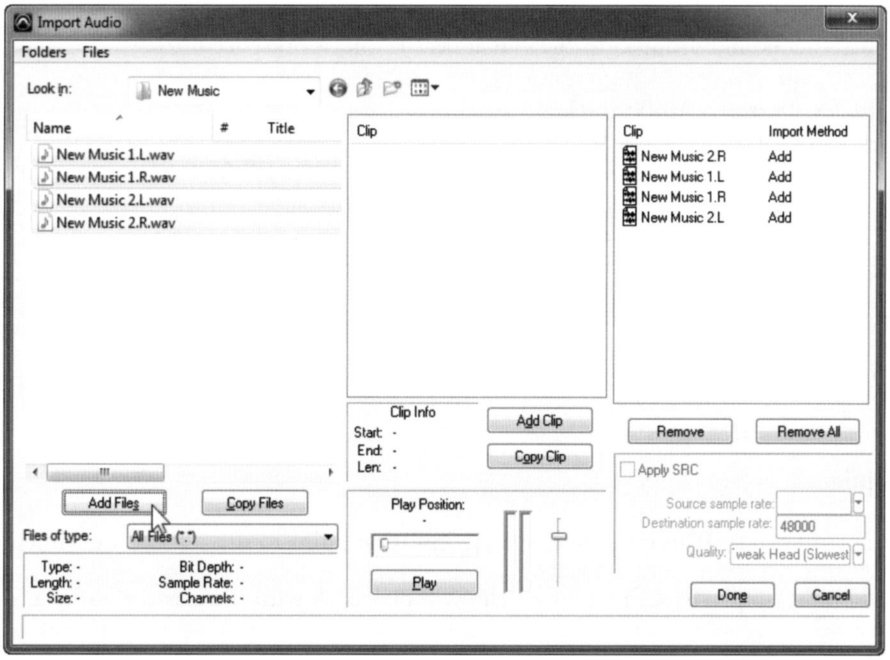

Figure 12.12 The Import Audio dialog box as it appears after clicking Add Files (Windows version shown)

4. Click DONE. The Audio Import Options dialog box will appear.
5. In the dialog box, select CLIP LIST for the destination and click OK. The clips New Music 1 (Stereo) and New Music 2 (Stereo) will be imported and will display in your Clip List.

Import Files from the Workspace Browser

For this part of the project, you will use the Workspace browser to import a clip group containing sound effects. A clip group is a collection of individual clips grouped together to look and act as a single, larger clip.

Clip groups are covered in detail in the Pro Tools 110 course.

All of the sound effects have already been edited outside of the current session and grouped together as a single clip group. You will need to drag the clip group from the Workspace browser onto a stereo Audio track; the clip group will automatically be imported into your session.

Locate the clip group file called "Skunk Group" using a Workspace browser:

1. Choose WINDOW > NEW WORKSPACE > DEFAULT to open a Workspace browser. Reposition/resize the windows as necessary so that the Workspace browser is not obscured by the Video window.

You can also press ALT+I (Windows) or OPTION+I (Mac) to open a new Workspace browser window.

2. Click the ADVANCED SEARCH button (magnifier with a plus sign) to display the advanced search settings.
3. Type Skunk Group in the text field and click the ADD ROW button (plus sign) to add a second search filter.
4. Specify [KIND] [IS] [CLIP GROUP FILE] using the pop-up menus in the second row.

   After a few moments, the Skunk Group.cgrp file will appear in the Workspace browser.

Drag the clip group to the FX 08 stereo Audio track:

1. Reposition the Workspace browser, if necessary, so you can see both the FX 08 track in the Edit window and the Skunk Group file in the Workspace browser.
2. Drag the Skunk Group.cgrp file onto the FX 08 track in the Edit window.
3. Use the GRABBER tool to drag the Skunk Group to the start of the session.
4. Choose WINDOW > WORKSPACES > CLOSE ALL WORKSPACES browser to dismiss the Workspace browser.

Audition the changes (optional):

1. Press RETURN (Mac) or ENTER (Windows) to move the insertion point to the start of the Timeline.
2. Press the SPACEBAR to begin playback. The movie clip will play back with the existing audio and newly added effects.
3. When the clip ends, press the SPACEBAR again to stop playback. The insertion point will return to the beginning of the Timeline.

Save Work in Progress

Now that you have imported the movie and audio files for the project, you should take the opportunity to save your work.

Save your work:

- Choose FILE > SAVE to save your progress up to this point.

Editing in Pro Tools

Next, you will do some editing on your project. In the following sections, you will use the Zoomer, Trim, and Scrubber tools to modify the project so that it sounds more complete.

Review the Project

Before you begin editing this project, you should familiarize yourself with the progression of the movie. To do so, you can navigate along the Timeline to get a feel for the movie's transitional points.

Using the Selector tool, you can click at different points within the project and use the Video window to view the action based on the location of the playback cursor location.

Experiment with the Selector tool to update the Video window:

- Click on various parts of the Video track with the SELECTOR tool to get a rough idea where the main action and transitions fall on the Timeline. Use the SPACEBAR to control playback.
- Experiment with making selections on the Video track; try to select an entire scene from beginning to end.

The Video window will always reflect the start time of a Timeline selection. When you make a selection based on the Video track, you may find it useful to locate the end point first and select backward to the start.

Add Sound Effects

The session is still missing some sound effects. During this part of the project, you will use various editing techniques to add the missing material.

Add a Wind Effect

The first sound effect that you will add occurs at the point in the movie when the squire walks through the castle. You will need to add the sound of wind to match the action using the Wind02 sound effect in the Clip List.

Place the Wind02 clip onto the FX 01 track and spot it to the proper location:

1. Identify the FX 01 track on screen and make sure it is visible.
2. Select the Wind02 clip in the Clip List (Edit window). If necessary, use the scroll bar to scroll the list until the clip is visible.
3. Drag the Wind02 clip from the Clip List to any open space on the FX 01 track.
4. Click the SPOT button in the upper-left corner of the Edit window to activate Spot mode. (You might have to reposition the Video window first.)
5. With the GRABBER tool, click on the clip that you placed on the FX 01 track. The Spot dialog box will open.

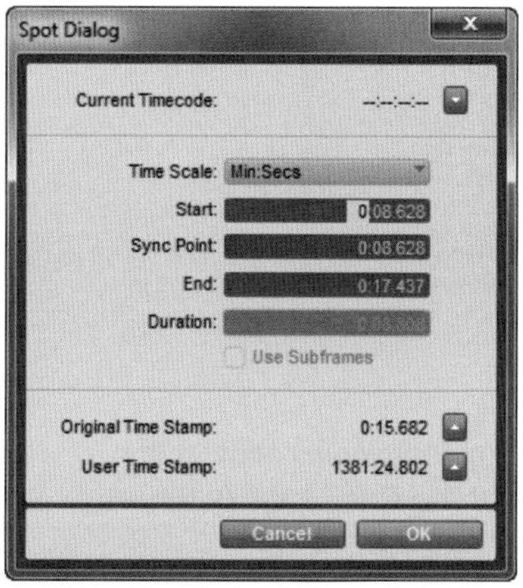

Figure 12.13 The Spot dialog box

6. If needed, set the Time Scale to **MIN:SECS**.
7. In the Start field, type 0:13.680 (Min:Sec) and click **OK**. The clip will move to the start time you typed.
8. Click the **SLIP** button to return to Slip mode.

Audition the sound effect:

1. Activate Loop Playback by choosing **OPTIONS > LOOP PLAYBACK**. The Play button will display a looping arrow to indicate Loop Playback mode.
2. With the clip still selected, press the SPACEBAR to play back the sound effect with the picture. During playback, you can solo the FX 01 track by clicking the **S** button in the track controls.

> **Pro Tools also lets you toggle Solo mode on and off for any track containing the Edit cursor by pressing SHIFT+S on the computer's QWERTY keyboard.**

3. When you are finished, press the SPACEBAR again to stop playback and click the **S** button if necessary to take the track out of Solo mode.

Edit the Wind Effect

The wind you've added is a little longer than the scene to which it corresponds. You will use this extra time before and after the scene to create a fade-in and a fade-out effect.

Create a fade-in and a fade-out on the Wind02 clip:

1. If it is not already selected, click on the **A-Z** button in the Edit window to enable Commands Keyboard Focus mode. The **A-Z** button is located above the tracks display area on the right. When selected, the button becomes highlighted in yellow.

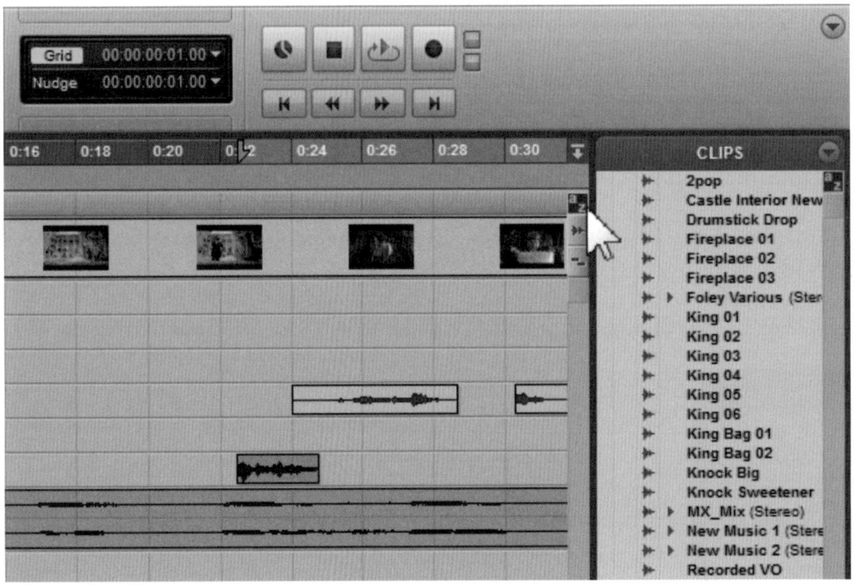

Figure 12.14 Clicking the Commands Keyboard Focus button

> **Commands Keyboard Focus mode gives you access to many Pro Tools commands at the touch of a single keystroke. Focus keys are covered throughout the Avid Learning Series courses and are summarized in the Pro Tools 310M and 310P books.**

2. Using the **Grabber** tool, click the Wind02 clip to select it.
3. Press **E** on your keyboard to activate Zoom Toggle. The selected clip will expand to fill the available space in the Edit window.
4. With the **Scrubber** tool, click and drag near the start of the clip. Gradually move the mouse back and forth while viewing the Video window.
5. Locate a point just after the scene changes to the squire walking. Release the mouse to position the insertion point at this spot.
6. Press **D** on your keyboard to create a fade-in.
7. With the **Scrubber** tool, click and drag near the end of the clip. Gradually move the mouse back and forth while viewing the Video window.
8. Locate a point where the squire is approaching the stairs, just before the scene changes to the king's throne room. Release the mouse to position the insertion point at this spot.
9. Press **G** on your keyboard to create a fade-out.
10. Press **E** on your keyboard to deactivate Zoom Toggle, returning the session to the previous view.

Add the Drumstick Drop Sound Effect

The next sound effect you need to add is the Drumstick Drop. For this sound effect, you will need to sync the impact point of the sound effect to the point in the movie at which the drumstick hits the plate. To do this, you will use a Sync Point.

Place the Drumstick Drop sound effect on the FX 05 track and identify a Sync Point:

1. Identify the FX 05 track on screen and make sure it is visible.
2. Locate the Drumstick Drop clip in the Clip List and drag it onto any open space of the FX 05 track.
3. With the clip selected, press **E** on your keyboard to activate Zoom Toggle and zoom in on the clip.
4. With the **Scrubber** tool, click and drag across the clip until you hear the sound of the drumstick making impact. Release the mouse to position the insertion point as close as possible to the beginning of the impact.
5. Choose **Clip > Identify Sync Point**. A small triangle will appear in the lower part of the clip, under the insertion cursor, signifying a Sync Point at that spot.
6. Press **E** on your keyboard to deactivate Zoom Toggle, returning the session to the previous view.

Having identified a Sync Point in the sound effect clip, you will now need to determine the corresponding point in the movie and spot the sound effect to that point.

Spot the Drumstick Drop sound effect to the movie:

1. With the **Scrubber** tool selected, click and drag on the Video track to locate the point when the drumstick hits the plate. The impact should occur somewhere between 0:13.200 and 0:13.500 (Min:Sec). Take note of the exact time location shown in the Main Counter.
2. Click the **Spot** button in the Edit window to activate Spot mode.
3. With the **Grabber** tool, click on the Drumstick Drop clip on the FX 05 track. The Spot dialog box will appear.

4. In the Sync Point field, type the time that you noted in Step 1. Be sure to use the same Time Scale in this dialog box as displayed in the Main Counter (Min:Sec).
5. Click **OK**. The clip's Sync Point will be spotted to the point where the drumstick hits the plate.
6. Click the **SLIP** button to return to Slip mode.

Audition the sound effect:

1. Using the **SELECTOR** tool, place the insertion point somewhere around 0:12.000.
2. Press the **SPACEBAR** to play back the sound effect with the picture.
3. When finished, press the **SPACEBAR** again to stop playback.
4. Press **RETURN** (Mac) or **ENTER** (Windows) to return to the beginning of the Timeline.

Change the Music

Next you will need to replace the existing music for the project to give the soundtrack a different emotional undertone. To do this, you will select from the music that you previously imported to the Clip List, place the selected music onto the MX New track, and deactivate the old music on the MX Mix track.

Audition the music in the Clip List:

1. Locate the New Music 1 and New Music 2 clips on the Clip List. If necessary, scroll the Clip List until the New Music clips are visible.
2. **OPTION-CLICK** (Mac) or **ALT-CLICK** (Windows) on the New Music 1 clip in the Clip List. The audio clip will play back as long as you hold down the mouse button.
3. Release the mouse button to stop the audition.
4. Repeat Steps 2 and 3, auditioning the New Music 2 clip.
5. After listening to each music clip, select the clip that you feel is more appropriate for the project. (You can use either clip to complete the project.)

Place the selected clip onto the MX New Audio track:

1. Locate the MX Mix track and the MX New track in the Edit window.
2. Using the **GRABBER** tool, click on the MX Mix clip on the MX Mix track. The clip will become highlighted.
3. Hold the **CONTROL** key (Mac) or **START** key (Windows) while dragging your preferred New Music clip from the Clip List onto the MX New track (below the selected clip). The New Music clip will appear on the second track, aligned to the same start time as the MX Mix clip on the track above it.

Holding the CONTROL key (Mac) or START key (Windows) while dragging a clip from the Clip List constrains the placement to begin at the insertion point (or start of a selection).

4. Make the MX Mix track inactive by right-clicking on the track nameplate and selecting **MAKE INACTIVE** from the pop-up menu.
5. Press **RETURN** (Mac) or **ENTER** (Windows) to move the insertion point to the beginning of the Timeline, followed by the **SPACEBAR** to play back the session with the new music track.
6. When finished, press the **SPACEBAR** a second time to stop playback.

Save Work in Progress

You have now completed the editing tasks for your project. You should take this opportunity to save your work.

Save your work:

- Choose **FILE > SAVE** to save your progress up to this point.

Mixing in Pro Tools

Now that all of the editing is complete, you will use some of the mixing features in Pro Tools to add some real-time processing and blend all of the sound elements together.

Remove the Hum

The Squire 01 clip on the DX 03 track contains a low-frequency hum that you will now need to remove. Using some creative EQ, you can eliminate most of the hum. To do so, you will need to locate and zoom in on the clip, insert an EQ plug-in on the track, and selectively adjust the EQ settings.

Locate and zoom in on the Squire 01 clip:

1. Click on the Squire 01 clip in the Clip List to select the clip on the Track Playlist. If necessary, scroll the Clip List until the clip is visible (toward the bottom).

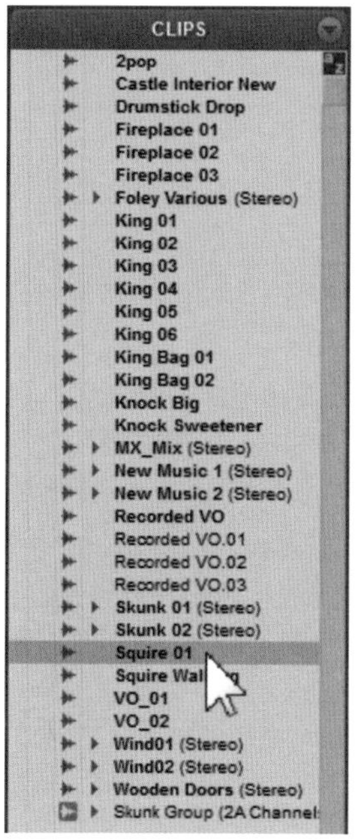

Figure 12.15 Clicking on the clip in the Clip List to select it

2. Press **E** on your keyboard to activate Zoom Toggle. The Squire 01 clip will expand to fill the Edit window.

Insert the EQ III 1-Band on the DX 03 track:

1. Choose **WINDOW > MIX** to activate the Mix window or press **COMMAND+=** (Mac) or **CTRL+=** (Windows).
2. Locate the channel strip for the DX 03 track.
3. Click on **INSERT SELECTOR A** for the track and choose **PLUG-IN > EQ > EQ3 1-BAND (MONO)** from the pop-up menu. The EQ III 1-band plug-in window will appear.

Adjust the EQ settings to reduce the hum:

1. Solo the DX 03 track by clicking on the **S** button just above the Volume Fader in the Mix window.
2. Press the **SPACEBAR** to initiate playback. With Loop Playback enabled, the clip will loop until playback is stopped.
3. In the EQ III 1-Band plug-in window, activate a Notch filter in the **TYPE** section and drag the gray ball in the graphic display to the left until you hear the hum reduced (around 60 Hz).

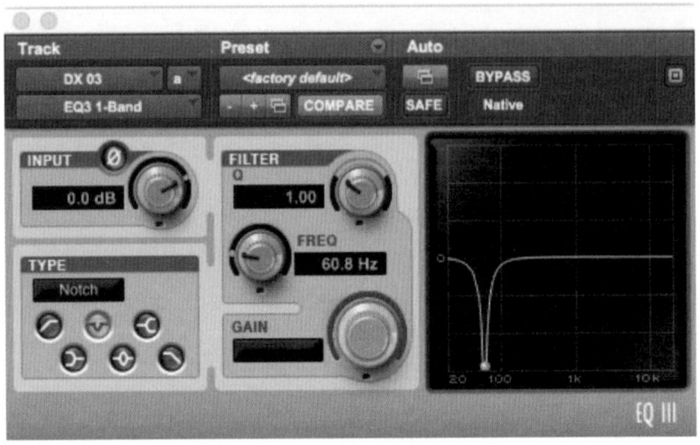

Figure 12.16 Notch filter activated in the EQ III 1-band plug-in window

4. Press the **SPACEBAR** to stop playback.
5. Close the plug-in window and un-solo the track.
6. Press **COMMAND+=** (Mac) or **CTRL+=** (Windows) to toggle to the Edit window, and press **E** on your keyboard to return the session to the previous view.

Add Reverb

Next, you will need to add some reverb to the FX 08 track to help it fit into the rest of the mix.

This project includes an Auxiliary Input track that has already been configured with the D-Verb plug-in assigned and the track input assigned to the Reverb bus.

Assign a reverb send on the FX 08 track:

1. Press **COMMAND+=** (Mac) or **CTRL+=** (Windows) to toggle to the Mix window.
2. Locate the FX 08 channel strip for the Skunk FX.
3. Click on the **SEND SELECTOR A** for the track and choose **BUS > REVERB (STEREO).** The Send A window will appear. (See Figure 12.17.)

Figure 12.17 Selecting a send assignment opens the Send window (foreground)

Increase the Send A level on the FX 08 track:

1. Click the SOLO button near the bottom of the Send A window to solo the FX 08 track.
2. Press COMMAND+= (Mac) or CTRL+= (Windows) to toggle to the Edit window.
3. Using the SELECTOR tool, select the audio near the end of the Skunk Group clip group (starting around 0:31.500 and continuing through the end of the clip).
4. With Loop Playback enabled, press the SPACEBAR to begin playback.
5. While listening to the track, raise the level on the send fader to introduce the reverb.

   The reverb will play back while the FX 08 track is soloed because the Reverb track is set to Solo Safe mode. Solo Safe is commonly used on Aux Input tracks to prevent them muting when another track is soloed.

You can place a track in Solo Safe mode by COMMAND-CLICKING (Mac) or CTRL-CLICKING (Windows) on the Solo button in the Edit or Mix window.

More information on Solo Safe mode can be found in the Pro Tools 110 course.

6. When you are satisfied with the results, press the SPACEBAR to stop playback.
7. Press the SOLO button to take the track out of Solo mode and close the Send A window.

Enhance the Knock

This project includes a knock sweetener effect that sounds a bit dull. You will need to add some delay and EQ to liven up the sound. You will add delay using an AudioSuite plug-in and EQ using a plug-in insert.

A Note about AudioSuite Plug-Ins

You will be using the Mod Delay III AudioSuite plug-in to add a delay sound effect. AudioSuite plug-ins are different from insert plug-ins in that they are not real-time processors. These plug-ins process and modify audio files on disk, rather than adding the plug-in effect in real time.

More information on AudioSuite processing can be found in the Pro Tools 110 course.

Zoom in on the Knock Sweetener clip on the FX 04 track:

1. Select the Knock Sweetener clip in the Clip List; the clip will become selected in the Track Playlist.
2. Press **E** on your keyboard to activate Zoom Toggle. The Knock Sweetener clip will expand to fill the Edit window.

Use the Mod Delay III to process the Knock Sweetener clip:

1. Choose **AUDIOSUITE > DELAY > MOD DELAY III**. The Mod Delay III plug-in window will appear on screen.
2. Verify that **USE IN PLAYLIST** is selected (highlighted in blue).
3. Adjust the parameter settings to create a long echo effect. Try the following settings as a starting point:
   - **MIX** = 25 to 35%
   - **DELAY** = 500 to 600ms
   - **FEEDBACK** = 35 to 45%

Figure 12.18 Mod Delay III AudioSuite plug-in

4. To audition the effect, click the **PREVIEW** button (speaker icon) at the bottom of the window. During Preview, you may continue to adjust the effect parameters, as desired.

5. When you are satisfied with the effect, click **Render** to process the audio clip. A new clip will be generated, combining the source audio with the Delay effect and replacing the selected clip.

6. Close the Delay AudioSuite window to reduce on-screen clutter.

Add the EQ III 7-Band to Insert A on the FX 04 track:

1. Using the Inserts column in the Edit window, click on **Insert Selector A** for the FX 04 track and choose **Plug-in > EQ > EQ3 7-Band (mono)**. The EQ III plug-in window will open.

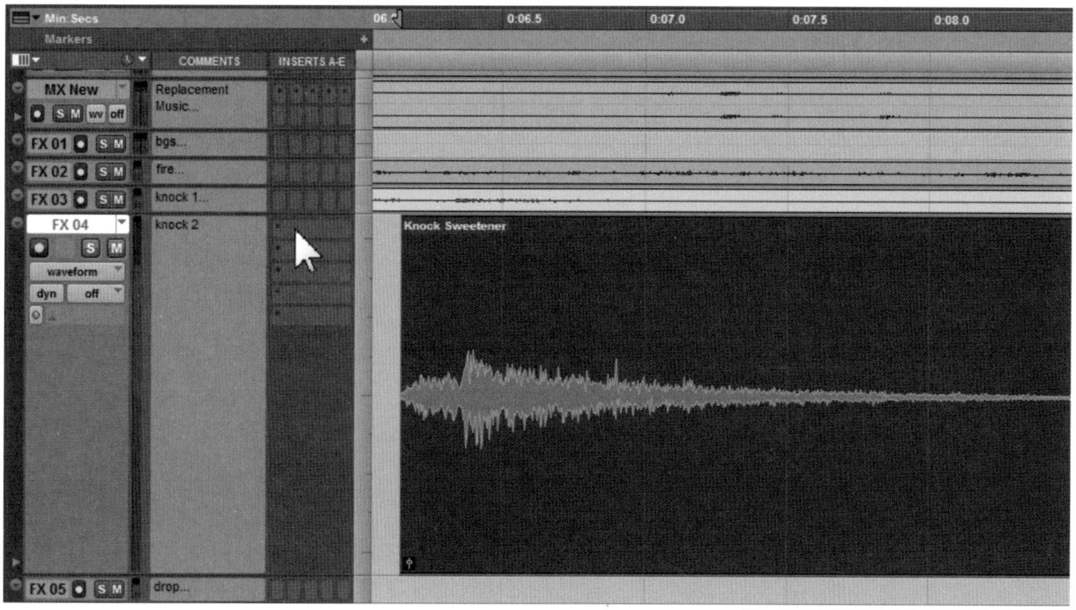

Figure 12.19 Clicking Insert Selector A in the Edit window

2. With Loop Playback still active, press the **Spacebar** to start playback. The Knock Sweetener clip will repeat until playback is stopped.

3. Experiment by raising and lowering the colored balls in the graphic display of the EQ III plug-in window.

   Try adding a low boost at around 250 Hz with the LMF band and high boost at around 4.25 kHz with the HMF band.

4. When you are satisfied with the results, close the plug-in window and press the **Spacebar** to stop playback.

5. Press **E** on your keyboard to return the session to the previous view.

Save Work in Progress

You have now created a complete mix for your project. You should take this opportunity to save your work.

Save your work:

- Choose **File > Save** to save your progress up to this point.

Listen to the Automated Mix

This portion of the project allows you to experience some of the power that automation offers by activating the preset automation included in the session.

Throughout this project, you have completed your work with all of the track automation set to **OFF** mode. Now you will switch the tracks to **READ** mode and play back the session using the previously recorded automation playlists.

Automation features are covered in detail throughout the courses in the Avid Learning Series.

Enable Read automation mode for all tracks:

1. Choose **WINDOW > MIX** or press **COMMAND+=** (Mac) or **CTRL+=** (Windows) to activate the Mix window.
2. **OPTION-CLICK** (Mac) or **ALT-CLICK** (Windows) on the **AUTOMATION MODE SELECTOR** for any track and choose **READ**. All of the tracks in the session will switch to Read automation mode.

Figure 12.20 Selecting Read mode from the Automation Mode selector (Mix window)

3. Choose **VIEW > NARROW MIX** to maximize the number of channel strips being displayed on screen.
4. Press **RETURN** (Mac) or **ENTER** (Windows) to move to the beginning of the Timeline; then press the **SPACEBAR** to play back the session.
5. During playback, notice that the Volume Faders and Pan knobs move automatically to help create a more dynamic mix.
6. When finished, press the **SPACEBAR** a second time to stop playback.

Finishing Your Work

Now that the project is mixed, you will need to create a bounce of the movie to add your version of the soundtrack to the movie file. This will enable the file to be played in a standard video player application with the soundtrack you've created so that you can share your work with others.

Lastly, you will need to archive your work. Through the process of creating a project you generate many files, not all of which are needed for the completed session. By archiving your session, you can preserve your work without taking up excess disk space due to unnecessary files.

Bounce the Video

You will use the Bounce to QuickTime command to add your soundtrack mix to the video file.

Bounce your mix into the video file:

1. Choose **WINDOW > EDIT** or press **COMMAND+=** (Mac) or **CTRL+=** (Windows) to activate the Edit window.
2. With the **GRABBER** tool, click on the GiftBasket clip on the Video track to select it.
3. Choose **FILE > BOUNCE TO > QUICKTIME**. The Bounce dialog box will appear on screen.
4. In the QuickTime Bounce dialog box, configure the following options for your bounce:
   - **IMPORT AFTER BOUNCE:** Deselected (unchecked)
   - **ADD TO ITUNES LIBRARY:** Deselected (unchecked)
   - **INCLUDE VIDEO:** Selected (checked)
   - **SAME AS SOURCE:** Selected (checked)
   - **REPLACE TIMECODE TRACK:** Selected (checked)
   - **FILE NAME:** Post Project-Your Initials
   - **OFFLINE:** Selected (checked)

   Leave all other settings at their default or as specified by your instructor.

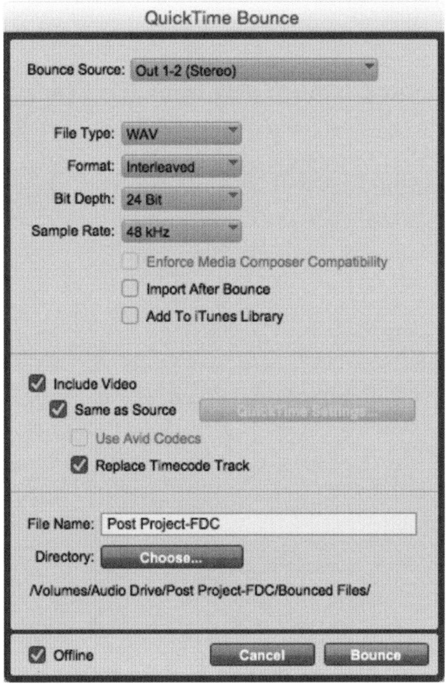

Figure 12.21 Settings for the QuickTime Bounce dialog box

5. Click **BOUNCE**. A progress bar will appear, showing the bounce progress.

When finished, your exported QuickTime movie will be available in the Bounced Files folder within your session folder.

Archive Your Work

Now that your project is complete, you will need to back it up for storage. On a real-world project, you might also need to deliver the session to the client. If you are completing this project in an academic classroom environment, you may be required to submit your work to your instructor for grading.

In this section, you will remove unused audio files that are consuming space on your hard drive. Then you will use the Save Copy In command to collect all of your session's media files into a new location.

Remove Unused Material

To remove unused audio files and clips, complete the following steps:

1. Click on the **Clip List pop-up** menu and choose **Select > Unused**. All of the clips that are not included on a Track Playlist will be selected.

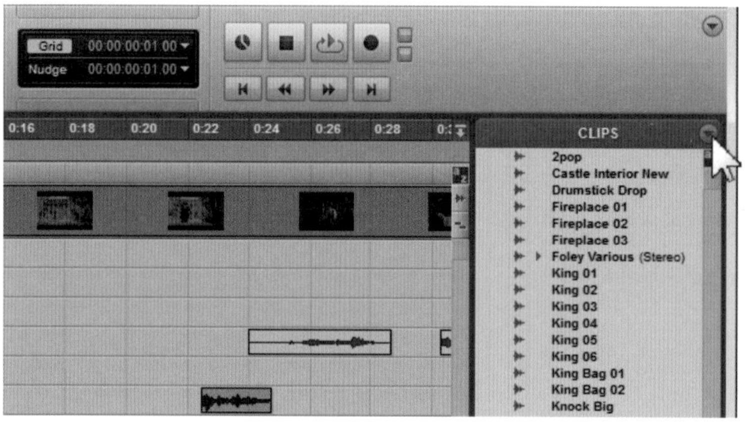

Figure 12.22 Clicking the Clip List pop-up menu to select unused clips

2. Click on the **Clip List pop-up** menu a second time and choose **Clear**. The Clear Clips dialog box will appear on screen.
3. Click **Remove** in the Clear Clips dialog box. The selected audio files will be removed from the session without being deleted from the drive.

Collect Session Files in a New Location

To save a copy of your session and all associated files, do the following:

1. Choose **File > Save Copy In**. The Save Copy In dialog box will appear on screen.
2. In the **Items to Copy** area, select the following:
   - **Audio Files**
   - **Movie/Video Files**
3. Click the **OK** button. A Save dialog box will appear.
4. Choose a directory to store the session archive and name the archive copy. If possible, it is best to choose a directory on a drive other than the one used for the current session.

5. Click the **SAVE** button.

   Pro Tools will begin processing the save, copying the session file along with all of the audio and video files into the directory you chose.

6. Choose **FILE > CLOSE SESSION** to close the original session. If you are prompted to save, choose **SAVE** or **OK** to save your changes in the original session. (It will be saved with the unused material removed.)

This concludes the Post Hands-On Project. If you are completing this work in an academic environment, please check with your instructor for submittal requirements; be sure to include the bounced QuickTime file from your original session folder with your session archive, as appropriate.

APPENDIX A

Course Completion Information

The Pro Tools 101 course is designed to be completed in an instructor-led environment at an official Avid Learning Partner location. When you enroll at an Avid Learning Partner school, you will have the opportunity to work with additional project material, including music sessions and video post-production sessions (such as television advertisements and movie trailers). Upon completing the coursework, you will be eligible to enroll in the Pro Tools 110 course (Pro Tools Production I) or the Pro Tools 130 course (Pro Tools for Game Audio) to continue your Pro Tools training and further your pursuit of Avid Pro Tools certification.

Locating an Avid Learning Partner

The Pro Tools 101 course can be completed at any of the hundreds of Avid Learning Partner facilities located worldwide. Partner locations offering the Pro Tools 101 course include colleges, technical programs, trade schools, high schools, and other institutions. Depending on the school's training format, Pro Tools courses may span days, weeks, or semesters and may be integrated within a broader educational curriculum.

Avid Learning Partner locations have the ability to deliver exams and certification directly, giving students additional enrollment benefits. With locations in countries such as Australia, Canada, China, France, Germany, Ireland, the Netherlands, Spain, Switzerland, the United Kingdom, the United States, and others, official Pro Tools training is available in most major cities worldwide.

A list of available training centers can be found online by visiting the partner locator on Avid's website (go to http://www.avid.com/education/find-an-avid-learning-partner). The web-based partner locator can be used to search for training centers by name or by geographic location.

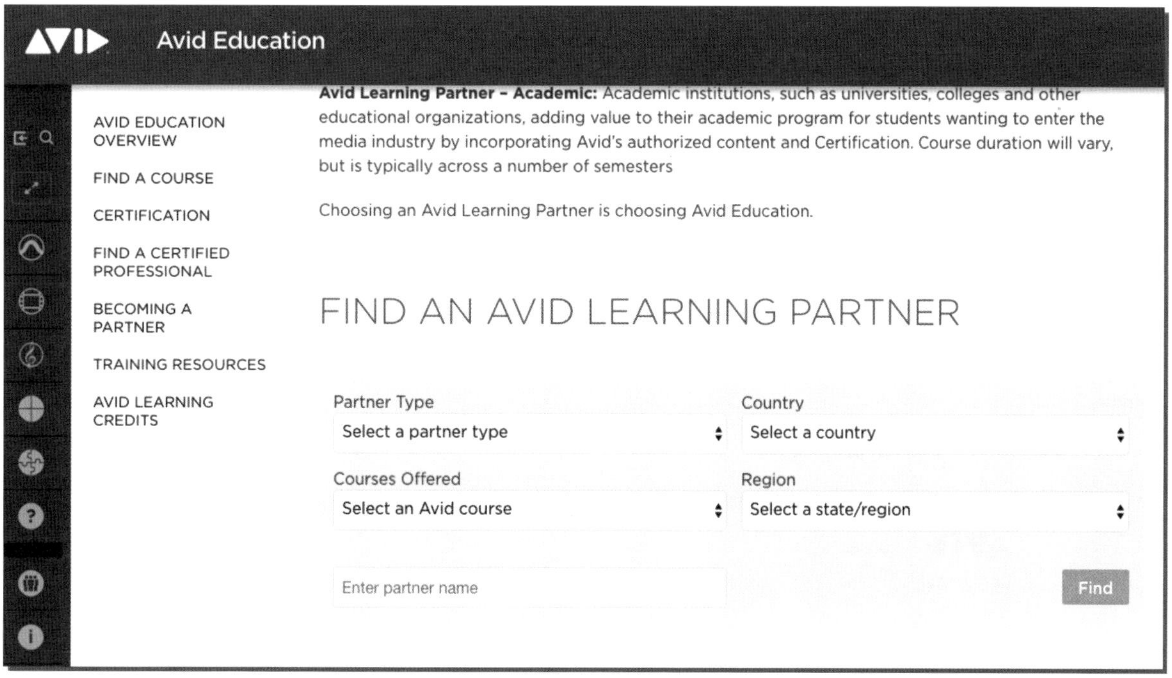

Figure A.1 Training partner lookup page on the Avid website

Course Completion Exam

The Pro Tools 101 exam consists of 50 multiple-choice questions. The exam is conducted at Avid Learning Partner facilities upon course completion. Students have a specified time limit to answer all questions.

Upon successful completion of the coursework and the course exam, you will be fully prepared to enroll in the Pro Tools 110 course and continuing progress toward User, Operator, or Expert Certification.

Pro Tools 110 and Beyond

After completing the Pro Tools 101 course, you may enroll in the next course, Pro Tools 110, at any Avid Learning Partner facility, subject to any school prerequisites. Successful completion of the Pro Tools 110 course readies students for the Pro Tools User Certification exam, which is also administered at Avid Learning Partner facilities.

Certification Options

Additional certification options are available at the 200- and 300-level (Operator and Expert Certification, respectively).

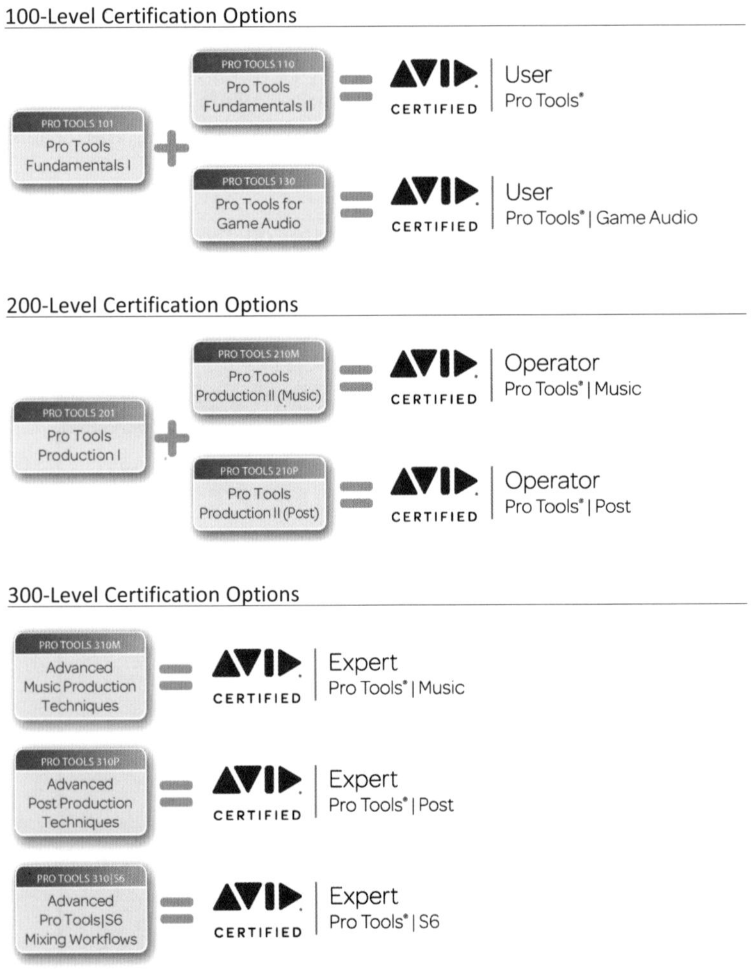

Figure A.2 Avid audio coursework and certification options

Additional Projects

Additional project materials are available at official training partner facilities. As part of your official Avid coursework, you may have the opportunity to work with some of these projects.

- Video post-production sessions from television and film productions:
  - Ugly Duckling. TV commercial ideal for beginning students interested in post-production applications for Pro Tools.
  - Fisker Karma. Car advertisement good for experienced students who want to dig in to additional post-production features in Pro Tools.
  - The Time Machine. Trailer for the 2002 movie featuring video footage along with dialogue, music, and sound effects.
  - NewsRadio. Scene from the U.S. sitcom containing video footage and audio that lends itself to editing and replacing dialogue.
- Music sessions of releases by popular recording artists, including:
  - Arcade Fire, "Rococo"
  - Switchfoot, "Meant to Live"
  - MrNorth, "Everything"
  - Romero/Rich Tozzoli, "La Vida Nueva"
  - Westside Connection, "Gangsta Nation"

Project availability varies by school. Check with the school for available courses and completion requirements.

APPENDIX B

Avid Pro Tools Plug-Ins

The following DSP, Native, and AudioSuite plug-ins are installed with Pro Tools 12:

- **BF-76**. Provides vintage-style compression modeled after the solid-state (transistor) 1176 studio compressor.
- **Channel Strip**. Combines EQ, Dynamics, Filter, and Gain effects processing in a single user interface. The Channel Strip processing algorithms are based on the award-winning Euphonix System 5 console channel strip effects.
- **Click II**. Creates an audio click during session playback to serve as a metronome-type tempo reference when performing and recording.
- **Dither**. Minimizes quantization artifacts when reducing the bit depth of an audio signal.
- **DownMixer**. Provides down-mixing (fold-down) for surround formats (7.1 to stereo, 5.1 to stereo, LCRS to stereo, and LCR to stereo) and stereo-to-mono processing.
- **D-Verb**. Provides studio-quality reverb effects for an audio signal.
- **Dynamics III**. Compressor/Limiter, Expander/Gate, De-Esser. Provides compression/limiting, expansion/gate, and de-esser processing for level control and gain reduction.
- **EQ III**. 7-Band and 1-Band. Provides equalization, allowing you to choose the number of bands you need to properly EQ each track.
- **Lo-Fi**. Provides retro and down-processing effects, including bit-rate reduction, sample-rate reduction, soft clipping distortion and saturation, anti-aliasing filter, and a variable amplitude noise generator.
- **Maxim**. Provides peak-limiting and sound maximizing for critical mastering applications, as well as standard peak-limiting tasks.
- **Mod Delay III**. Provides delay effects of various lengths, including delays synchronized to the session tempo.
- **POW-r Dither**. An advanced type of dither providing optimal bit-depth reduction for critical mixdown and mastering tasks.
- **Recti-Fi**. Provides additive harmonic processing effects through waveform rectification; includes subharmonic synthesizer, full wave rectifier, pre-filter for adjusting effect frequency, and post-filter for smoothing generated waveforms.
- **ReWire**. Provides real-time audio and MIDI streaming between Pro Tools and ReWire client applications, with sample-accurate synchronization and transport control.
- **Sci-Fi**. Provides analog synthesizer-type effects, including ring modulation; frequency modulation; variable-frequency, positive and negative resonator; and modulation control by LFO, envelope follower, sample-and-hold, or trigger-and-hold.
- **Signal Generator**. Produces audio test tones in a variety of frequencies, waveforms, and amplitudes, such as reference signals for calibration.

- **TimeAdjuster.** Provides compensation for delays due to DSP or Native routing; also provides gain compensation (+/– 24 dB) and phase inversion for correcting out-of-phase signals.
- **Trim.** Can be used to attenuate an audio signal from –infinity to +6 dB or +12 dB; a multi-mono Trim plug-in provides muting control over individual channels of a multi-channel track.

The following AudioSuite-only plug-ins are installed with Pro Tools 12:

- **DC Offset Removal.** Removes DC offset (a type of audio artifact) from audio files to prevent pops and clicks in edited material.
- **Duplicate.** Duplicates the selected audio in place, creating a new, continuous audio file.
- **Gain.** Boosts or lowers a selected region's amplitude by a specific amount.
- **Invert.** Reverses the polarity of selected audio.
- **Normalize.** Optimizes the volume level of an audio selection to correct low amplitude signals or inconsistent volume levels.
- **Reverse.** Replaces audio with a reversed version of the selection to create a reverse envelope effect or backwards playback of a selection.
- **Time Shift.** Provides high-quality time compression and expansion (TCE) algorithms and formant-correct pitch shifting.
- **Vari-Fi.** Provides a pitch-change effect similar to a tape deck or record turntable speeding up from or slowing down to a complete stop.

APPENDIX C

AIR Effects and Instrument Plug-Ins

The following AIR effects plug-ins are included with Pro Tools 12 (via the AIR Effects Bundle installer):

- **Chorus.** Applies a short modulated delay to give depth and space to the audio signal.
- **Distortion.** Colors the audio signal with various types and amounts of distortion.
- **Dynamic Delay.** Provides a delay (echo) that can synchronize to the Pro Tools session tempo and be modulated by an Envelope follower.
- **Enhancer.** Enhances the low and high broadband frequencies of the audio signal.
- **Ensemble.** Applies fluid, shimmering modulation effects to the audio signal.
- **Filter Gate.** Adds aggressive or subtle rhythmic filtering effects to audio signals.
- **Flanger.** Applies a short modulating delay to the audio signal; the Rate control can be synchronized to the Pro Tools session tempo in various rhythmic patterns.
- **Frequency Shifter.** Changes the pitch of the audio signal.
- **FuzzWah.** Colors the audio signal with various types and amounts of distortion and wah filtering.
- **Kill-EQ.** Zaps out the Low, Mid, or High broadband frequency range from an audio signal for instantaneous "kill switch"[nd]type EQ effects.
- **Lo-Fi.** Provides bit-crushing, down-sampling, clipping, rectifying, and mangling effects.
- **Multi-Chorus.** Applies a thick, complex Chorus effect to the audio signal, with a user-selectable number of voices (layers).
- **Multi-Tap Delay.** Applies up to six delay lines to the audio signal with selectable rhythmic values, levels, and pan for each.
- **Non-Linear Reverb.** Applies special gated or reversed Reverb effects to the audio signal, creating a synthetic, processed ambience.
- **Phaser.** Applies the classic "whooshy," "squishy" phaser sound to an audio signal; the Rate control can be synchronized to the Pro Tools session tempo in various rhythmic patterns.
- **Reverb.** Applies reverberation to an audio signal to create a sense of room or space.
- **Spring Reverb.** Applies the familiar analog spring reverb sound found in many classic guitar amps and vintage audio gear.
- **Stereo Width.** Creates a wider stereo presence for mono audio signals.
- **Talkbox.** Adds voice-like resonances to audio signals.
- **Vintage Filter.** Applies a modulating, resonant filter to the audio signal.

The following AIR instrument plug-ins are included with Pro Tools 12 (via the AIR Instruments Bundle installer):

- **Boom.** A virtual drum machine featuring a broad range of percussion sounds, paired with a simple, drum-machine-style pattern sequencer.
- **DB-33.** A virtual organ with a focus on re-creating the sounds and controllability of classic tonewheel organs and rotating speaker cabinets.
- **Mini Grand.** A virtual piano instrument with seven different acoustic piano sounds to suit a range of styles.
- **Structure Free.** A sample player that brings the world of Structure-compatible sample libraries to Pro Tools.
- **Vacuum.** A virtual analog synthesizer focused on creating rich timbres with a lot of sonic control and employing a new vacuum-tube synthesis method.

The following additional AIR instrument is included with Pro Tools 12 (via the Xpand II installer):

- **Xpand!2.** A virtual workstation synthesizer featuring multi-sampled instruments, FM synthesis, wavetable synthesis, and virtual analog synthesis.

INDEX

S